The regulation of monopoly

The regulation
of monopoly

ROGER SHERMAN
University of Virginia

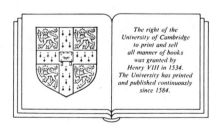

The right of the
University of Cambridge
to print and sell
all manner of books
was granted by
Henry VIII in 1534.
The University has printed
and published continuously
since 1584.

CAMBRIDGE UNIVERSITY PRESS

Cambridge
New York   New Rochelle   Melbourne   Sydney

Published by the Press Syndicate of the University of Cambridge
The Pitt Building, Trumpington Street, Cambridge CB2 1RP
32 East 57th Street, New York, NY 10022, USA
10 Stamford Road, Oakleigh, Melbourne 3166, Australia

First published 1989

Printed in the United States of America

Library of Congress Cataloging-in-Publication Data
Sherman, Roger, 1930–
The regulation of monopoly / Roger Sherman.
p.   cm.
Includes index.
ISBN 0-521-36315-2.   ISBN 0-521-36862-6 (pbk.)
1.Monopolies – Government policy.   2. Welfare economics.
I. Title.
HD2757.2.S48   1989   88–14185
338.8′2 – dc19

British Library Cataloguing in Publication Data
Sherman, Roger
The regulation of monopoly.
1. United States. Telecommunication
services : American Telephone and Telegraph
Company. Monopolies. Regulation
I. Title
338.8′2

ISBN 0 521 36315 2 hard covers
ISBN 0 521 36862 6 paperback

Contents

Contents

Preface

The regulation or control of monopoly is being reconsidered today in economies as different as those of China and Singapore, or the United States and the Soviet Union. Beneath catchwords like *privatization, liberalization, deregulation,* or *perestroika* lies a fuller awareness of the pitfalls in both private and public ownership of monopoly enterprises than ever existed before. Governments seem willing to consider introducing new institutions on the basis of their expected effects rather than their ideological bloodlines alone, and to undertake radical reform. It is a good time to consider the purposes of regulatory institutions and to attend to their design.

There is a vast economics literature on optimal pricing and technological choices. Anyone at all familiar with it must be struck by how it seems to differ from daily experience. One of our aims here is to present a large portion of that admirable normative material, in up-to-date form, and to explain the welfare representations underlying it. But we also want to stress that little has been done to adopt means of pursuing welfare goals in the absence of competition. Our institutions of monopoly regulation were not carefully designed for pursuing economic welfare or efficiency, at least not by today's standards. Experiments with new institutions of monopoly regulation will be valuable in the challenging design task that remains to be accomplished.

This book was begun more than five years ago as a set of notes for a graduate course in regulation at the University of Virginia. Only elementary mathematics, mainly calculus, is employed, frequently in straightforward constrained optimization problems. The important ideas are developed from what undergraduate economics students encounter fairly early in their studies. I have used some of the chapters successfully as class notes with undergraduates who found them understandable, and I think the book should be useful in upper-level undergraduate courses as well as in graduate courses. I also hope that it will serve those concerned with the practice of regulation.

Work on the book has been interrupted often for long periods. This makes me especially grateful to the Rockefeller Foundation Study Center in Bellagio, Italy, the Oxford University Institute of Economics and

Statistics, and the University of Sydney for most hospitable visits that enabled me to complete the book, and to the University of Virginia for making those visits possible. I am grateful also to the publishers for letting me reprint from papers that appeared previously in books and journals, and to the National Science Foundation for support of some of that work. These earlier papers have been modified and abbreviated so they join smoothly with the remainder of the text. Passages from "Congestion Interdependence and Urban Transit Fares," *Econometrica,* May 1971, appear in Chapters 4 and 10. Several pages from "The Rate-of-Return Regulated Public Utility is Schizophrenic," *Applied Economics,* March 1972, Chapman and Hall, publishers, appear in Chapter 8. Chapter 5 contains modified pages from "Second-Best Pricing with Stochastic Demand" (with Michael Visscher), *American Economic Review,* March 1978, and pages from "Second-Best Pricing for the U.S. Postal Service" (with Anthony George), *Southern Economic Journal,* January 1979. Chapter 9 contains material from "Pricing Inefficiency under Profit Regulation," *Southern Economic Journal,* October 1981. In Chapters 4, 5, and 9 are parts of "Rate-of-Return Regulation and Two-Part Tariffs" (with Michael Visscher), February 1982, *Quarterly Journal of Economics,* copyright © John Wiley & Sons, Inc., 1982, by permission John Wiley & Sons, Inc. Chapters 7 and 9 contain passages from "Is Public Utility Regulation Beyond Hope?" reprinted by permission of the publisher, from *Current Issues in Public Utility Regulation,* edited by A. L. Danielsen and D. R. Kamerschen (Lexington, Mass.: Lexington Books, D. C. Heath and Company, copyright 1983, D. C. Heath and Company). And Chapter 10 contains parts from "Pricing Behavior of the Budget-Constrained Public Enterprise," *Journal of Economic Behavior and Organization,* 1983 (Elsevier Science Publishers B.V., P.O. Box 1991, 1000 BZ Amsterdam, copyright 1983, Elsevier Science Publishers).

It is doubtful that anyone ever had more skillful help in turning raw beginnings into a finished book. That task was begun with relish by Esther Cash and Marie Childress. The manuscript was completed (many times over) by Peggy Claytor who, instead of introducing errors, actually made it better than it was originally. Working with copyeditor Vicki Macintyre and others at Cambridge University Press was a pleasure throughout.

Although they bear no blame for remaining flaws, Charlie Holt, Len Mirman, and David Sappington commented very helpfully on parts of the manuscript. For the preciseness he added, readers should be especially grateful to Len Mirman. Many former students also improved the book, including Tony Creane, Cathy Eckel, Jeffrey Eisenach, Eric Engen, Anthony George, Philip Jefferson, Marios Karayannis, Michael Kehoe, Todd

McCallister, John Mullahy, and Zhen-hui Xu. The most help came from a former student who became an especially dear friend, the late Michael Visscher, who coauthored some of the work that is included here. The book is dedicated to our memory of him.

PART I

Introduction

CHAPTER 1

The regulation of monopoly

1.1   Introduction

Market economies face the same problem throughout the world: how to deal with technologies that complicate the smooth functioning of competition. Television, telephone, water, natural gas, electricity, and railroad transportation illustrate large and/or complex technologies, the use of which, for one reason or another, is guided in many countries by administrative institutions rather than competitive markets. Our aim is to examine the circumstances that cause alternative means of regulation to be substituted for competition, and to consider the approaches taken. We shall find that although normative guidelines can be developed for the alternative institutions, incentives to use them are weak or nonexistent. Designing institutions so they will pursue social goals is not a simple matter, and creating real institutions with that aim is even more difficult.

In the United States an unusual solution to the regulatory problem was chosen for many services. The services are still provided by privately owned firms, but those firms are regulated by public agencies. The firms are called *public utilities,* a title traceable to their nineteenth-century origin, and they are seen as providing goods or services in which the general public has a great interest. The public regulatory agencies that oversee them are commonly operated at the state level, as a Public Service Commission, State Corporation Commission, or similarly titled agency. The vast majority of electricity, natural gas, television, and local telephone service, plus large amounts of water, public transportation, and other services are provided by privately owned and governmentally regulated public utilities.

Public rather than private ownership is common in many countries. It may be accomplished through substantial government ownership of an otherwise private firm, through independent wholly state-owned, or public, enterprises, or otherwise through government departments or bureaus. Organized as public enterprises in the United States are the U.S. Postal Service, the Tennessee Valley Authority, and the Corporation for Public Broadcasting, among many others (Walsh 1978). Postal service in the United States was provided by a government department, the Post Office

Department, for many years prior to its reorganization in 1970 as a public enterprise called the U.S. Postal Service.

Here we are concerned with principles that can be used to guide the design and operation of public enterprises and public utility firms. We begin in this chapter by describing the circumstances in which public enterprises or public utilities come to replace competition – circumstances in which competition fails to serve the public well. We then indicate how economic welfare standards might be used for judging when price and output policies are ideal. We also point out that it is difficult to induce an organization to pursue welfare, and we briefly sketch how public enterprises and public utilities are regulated. The two other chapters in Part I examine representations of economic welfare that can serve as goals for regulation and show how difficult it is, in the absence of competition, to induce organizations to pursue those goals.

Parts II and III are devoted to normative principles and to features of existing institutions, respectively. Part II develops ideal pricing for maximizing economic welfare, implicitly assuming that regulation can induce organizations to pursue welfare even if incentives for doing so are not provided. The problems of institutional goals and incentives are taken up in Part III, where two major institutions of regulation – public enterprises and rate-of-return regulated public utilities – are analyzed and evaluated for some of the incentives they engender. They will be found lacking in incentives to pursue general welfare. Indeed, a major purpose of the book is to show that institutions for the regulation of monopoly have not been designed as well as they might be. Part IV briefly discusses possible improvements in regulation. Most of these improvements are expected to come from the application of ideas discussed in Chapter 3.

1.2   Problems for competition

Competition coordinates decentralized economic choices by individuals so they will serve a community well. For such a system to function ideally, each person alone must face the full cost and/or benefit consequences of his or her decisions. This requirement is not met when your neighbor plays a television too loudly and forces you to bear the cost of listening when you would prefer not to. Such spillover effects are called *externalities,* and they cause problems for competition. If a factory spews unhealthy wastes into the air, it imposes costs on others in the form of air pollution. Such externalities are not usually weighed or measured, so they cannot be charged to the factory and recovered in the price of its output. With widespread externalities, costs and benefits are not reflected fully in market prices, whether they are negative ones such as air pollution or positive ones such as planting flowers or keeping the lawn mowed at your house. When costs of such externalities can be estimated, decentralized choices can be modified by taxes or subsidies, however, and then competition may serve effectively to regulate resource use.

In addition, unregulated competitive markets may not function adequately if the *failure of an individual firm* imposes large burdens on consumers. Under competition, we must expect that less efficient firms will fail. Ordinarily, consumers can then turn hopefully to other, more efficient, firms where they will be better served. But what if the consumer depends for service on the continued existence of a particular firm? As an example, consumers carrying life insurance policies with a particular firm can suffer enormous losses if that firm fails. Or if a bank fails, depositors may lose their savings. And neither insurance policyholders nor bank depositors can really be expected to detect financial weaknesses reliably in the firms that serve them. In such cases, mainly of banks and insurance companies, regulation has been imposed in order to prevent failure (Lereah 1983). The regulation may require procedures and practices that ensure protective reserves and encourage conservative decisions. Sometimes insurance such as Federal Deposit Insurance for banks can moderate the effects of firm failure on consumers, but usually other forms of regulation are also employed in an effort to reduce the probability of failure.

Another problem that can affect the functioning of competition is a property of technology called *economies of scale*. Suppose a particular technology that produces a well-defined product or service requires a high fixed cost and a small constant variable cost; when all demand is satisfied at a price equal to marginal cost, the average cost per unit is still falling with output and is above marginal cost. Several firms competing in this situation will drive price equal to marginal costs, so all will lose money. The high fixed cost makes large-scale operation more economical. Indeed, with this technology one producer obviously is the lowest cost form of market organization, but with only one firm there might appear to be no competition. Another property of technology that can raise problems for competition is called *economies of product scope*. When economies of scope exist, one firm can produce several products at lower cost than any combination of several firms could. Since our focus is on monopoly regulation, economies of scale and economies of scope will concern us more than any other source of competitive market failure, because they make monopoly the lowest cost way to organize production. And they arise primarily when fixed costs involve long-term commitments that are durable and cannot easily or quickly be reversed.

The competitive market process is particularly handicapped when the most efficient form of capital input into production is highly durable, inflexible, and costly. The cost of such an input is "sunk," in that it is committed to one use and cannot be changed. With perfect certainty in a static world, no serious problem might arise even from great durability. But when circumstances are changeable, large sunk costs can handicap the competitive process because they discourage entry. Ordinarily, when price rises above average cost in an industry, new entry will be attracted. But when the new entrant knows there can be no exit from the industry for a very long and uncertain time, its response will not be so immediate and price may be quite high without inducing entry.[1]

Of course, capacity may be engineered so that its durability is consistent with the time period over which it will be reliably used, or it may be designed to be flexible and have other uses.[2] But as a result production is likely to be more costly per unit. Then, with stockholders unwilling to bear the high risks and uncertainties associated with investment in very durable equipment, separate competing firms might maintain less durable and more flexible capacity, which is less efficient. Much of the uncertainty that invites this action may be due to lack of knowledge by each firm about others' actions. If that strategic source of risk could be removed, durable and more efficient equipment might be used. By reducing uncertainty and fostering more coherent long-run planning, monopoly organization might permit more efficient production.

This problem of nonoptimal technological choice arises in competition when sunk costs are large. If each of several competing firms had a great proportion of fixed cost and a low proportion of variable cost in the short run, their bad times could be protracted; disequilibrium capacity conditions might cause losses for several years. To avoid being caught in an unprofitable condition over such a long period, each competitor might prefer a less efficient but more flexible, or less long-lived, form of capacity. This could even be a desirable development if it brought forth investment capital more readily, but the result also could be much less efficient than using the technique with the more durable inputs. So regulated monopoly might be considered in place of competition in order to reduce investor risk and thereby allow more efficient technological choice. Building a dam for electricity generation and also water supply (and even recreation) serves as an extreme example. Undertaking large durable investments collectively through a public institution does not avoid the risks inherent in them, but it does spread those risks over so many individuals that each bears only a small amount (Arrow and Lind 1970; McKean and Moore 1972).

---

[1] This argument is set out in Baumol and Willig (1981). See also von Weizsäcker (1980).
[2] Stigler (1939) examined such possible effects of production flexibility. For a more recent treatment, see Mills (1984, 1986) and Mills and Schumann (1985).

The need for coordination of large investments can be overemphasized as a reason for accepting monopoly rather than competitive markets. For example, coordination has been claimed necessary for the connection of telephone callers, which could be complicated if each caller had to determine which (of many) firms served the party being called and then have his or her own company try to arrange the connection. But long-distance telephone service recently was deregulated in the United States, on grounds that contracts for service could foster sufficient coordination for efficiency to be achieved, aided by competition among suppliers. Similarly, digging up streets to lay electricity or communication lines may be claimed to interfere less with street use if one organization plans it rather than many separate ones. But if we charged firms when they dug up city streets, we might be able to create incentives that would help to determine just how valuable coordination is.

Uncertain and unreliable product quality can greatly reduce the effectiveness of a competitive market when information is costly for consumers to obtain. If the product or service involved is one that is important to society, information problems under competitive market organization may not be tolerated, and monopoly may be imposed in its place. Before New York City built magnificent underground tunnels that could bring water from mountain reservoirs, for example, it relied on competitive markets for drinking water. Anyone who owned a pond and a long hose seemed to be in the water business, and there were serious problems of contamination. Quality standards enforced by inspection might have controlled the situation without resort to monopoly, however. If information is not easy to convey, then regulation in the form of quality standards could be effective. Of course, reliability or quality standards must still be decided upon and enforced, for when a monopoly seeks to evade them, consumers may be harmed more than under competition because they have no competing supplier to turn to. If consumers themselves can become well informed about brand quality, competition may even serve them better. Competing firms meeting safety, quality, or reliability standards, as in the airlines, automobile parts, drugs, lawn mowers, and other industries, may then perform better than monopoly by giving consumers a choice.

Thus externalities, the possibility of firm failure, technologies with economies of scale or scope that require great sunk cost, and imperfect information about quality all can cause functional problems for competitive markets. Regulation of economic activity by means other than competition may or may not perform better, and to evaluate outcomes some standard of performance is needed. Such a standard can be found in representations of economic welfare.

1.3   The idea of economic welfare

When we say that competition could regulate economic activity "well" in the right circumstances, we have in mind a notion of what is desirable that goes beyond the process of competition. In asking a monopoly supplier to choose socially desirable prices, we clearly must be able to describe what "desirable" prices are. In the field of welfare economics, a set of precise concepts for thinking about such welfare questions has been developed over many years, and many of these concepts have been related in various ways to observable measures that can have useful application. Even ideas that cannot be applied directly can inform one's thinking about regulatory issues. Since regulation presumably is undertaken to advance economic well-being, it cannot be fully understood without some knowledge of welfare economics.

The most appealing notion of economic welfare is called Pareto optimality.[3] It simply requires that no action remain untaken that, without harming another, could improve one person's situation as that person sees it. The attractive feature of this criterion is its dependence on individuals' own evaluation of their situations, rather than on the value judgments of outside observers. The disadvantage is that there are many Pareto optimal positions, one for every possible distribution of income. Choices *between* Pareto optimal positions, in which some persons gain while others lose, are usually required in public decisions. But the Pareto criterion alone only identifies Pareto positions; it offers no basis for choosing among them. A stronger representation of social welfare can be created in which individual consumers are assigned specific weights, and a unique policy can then maximize the representation. Although this approach requires stronger assumptions in the form of the weights assigned to individuals, it is more generally useful for analyzing regulatory problems. We demonstrate alternative representations for this kind in Chapter 2. In Part II, this approach is applied to a number of pricing problems and related also to income distribution.

Let us summarize how an ideal market economy can achieve Pareto optimality. The Pareto conditions are clearly virtues however they may be attained, and understanding them equips one to think clearly about economic efficiency. The first condition may be called *consumption efficiency;* it is met when every consumer has the same ratio of marginal valuations between two goods, and therefore the same willingness to exchange

---

[3] This condition is named for the man who first described it, the Italian economist and sociologist, Vilfredo Pareto. For a brief summary of his contributions to economics, see Allais (1968).

them, for every pair of goods. This result occurs when no exchange can benefit one person without harming another, for if two persons differ in the values they attach to marginal units of two goods an exchange can benefit them. (Each gives up some of the less valued good for some of the more valued good.) The second condition may be called *production effi- ciency,* when a comparable condition among producers holds for the in- puts they use, namely that every producer has the same ratio of marginal productivities for every pair of inputs. If this condition were not satis- fied between two producers, an exchange of inputs from the low-valued use to the high-valued use could increase output. Achieving efficient pro- duction and efficient consumption separately will not ensure overall *eco- nomic efficiency.* For that, the relative marginal costs of any two goods in production must match the common ratio of marginal valuations of con- sumers. Otherwise the efficiently produced goods are not going to satisfy consumers' strongest needs, and for that reason the result is not ideal. Production of the less valued good should be reduced while production of the more valued good is increased, thereby giving more satisfaction to consumers from the same resources, until consumers' ratios of marginal valuations for all pairs of goods exactly equal the ratios of marginal costs for those same goods.

Notice that beyond a "more-is-preferred-to-less" efficiency maxim, Pa- reto optimality does not make any measure of social welfare explicit. For that, some measure of individual satisfaction must be aggregated into so- cial welfare, as we do in Chapter 2. Economic welfare is represented by a summation of welfare for separate individuals, where the summation requires a weighting of individuals that can be accomplished by specify- ing an income distribution. The Pareto features we have described – of consumption efficiency, production efficiency, and overall economic effi- ciency – can then be shown under reasonable assumptions to yield a unique Pareto optimum, a maximum of such economic welfare for the given dis- tribution of income. Practical measures of welfare, such as consumer sur- plus (which usually can be inferred from demand information) and pro- ducer surplus (which is related to profit), can be derived. They are valuable for evaluating prices and other policies in the absence of competition, and in interpreting a host of regulatory issues.

Representing welfare is discussed in Chapter 2. Although competition can discipline firms and force them to pursue economic welfare, no such mechanism exists under monopoly. Problems inducing the pursuit of wel- fare under monopoly regulation are the topic of Chapter 3. Ideally, the choice of regulatory institution will be influenced by the extent to which it can lead the monopoly to pursue welfare.

1.4   The pursuit of economic welfare

When technology affords economies of scale or economics of scope, the lowest total cost to society can be obtained if production is concentrated in a single firm rather than being shared by many competing firms. It is conceivable that competition for the position of single supplier can force efficient production of desirable output, if capacity costs have alternative uses and so are not "sunk" when committed to this industry. If prices can then be found that sustain the monopoly and prevent inefficient entry, the market is called *contestable*.[4] A new firm can enter to challenge the existing supplier whenever its price rises above the average cost that efficient use of technology allows, so price will be forced to equal average cost. Free entry pressures the incumbent to control costs. Free entry also tends to prevent cross-subsidization and so can avoid the redistribution of income. Indeed, free entry makes an incumbent supplier try to pursue economic welfare.

What if capacity cost is sunk when it is undertaken in the industry? A new entrant will then be reluctant to challenge an established firm because entering will commit excessive resources to the industry and thus almost certainly lead to low prices. In that case the market is not considered contestable, and competition through entry may not yield an efficient result. A statutory monopoly may be created instead, because one firm is thought able to achieve low cost, and is regulated in an effort to prevent it from taking unfair advantage of its position. Professional engineering standards may contribute positively to technical decisions and devoted bureaucrats may attempt faithfully to serve the public, but the incentives in such a monopoly organization do not impel it to maximize economic welfare. Indeed, a welfare goal is even hard to describe in concrete terms, and eliciting its pursuit through some sort of incentive scheme is an ambitious aim.

Without competition in the form of free entry, a single supplier must be expected to follow many understandable tendencies of monopolies. To raise revenues, prices may be adjusted so that markets with less elastic demands will have prices proportionately farther above marginal costs; and more subtle discrimination by price may be attempted, again because it allows more revenue to be raised. Unless quality is clearly defined and easily monitored, it may be altered. Reliability of service may suffer, for

---

[4] This possibility of a "contestable" market is described in Baumol et al. (1977), Baumol and Willig (1981), and Baumol et al. (1982). For criticism, see Shepherd (1984). For discussion of possible competition in electricity see Cohen (1979), Joskow and Schmalensee (1983), Primeaux (1986), Schmalensee and Golub (1984), and Schulz (1980); and in airlines see Levine (1987).

example, when there is no threat from alternative suppliers, and consumers may be forced to wait for service. Costs rise too as managers shirk or avoid difficult decisions. Innovation may not occur either, for the enterprise has no great incentive to make its own ways of doing things obsolete. These tendencies are natural in any organization. Although they can be driven out when competition reigns, they must be reckoned with in some way when competition is forgone.

The incentives that might be created in the monopoly firm will depend in part on whether it is privately or publicly owned. Private ownership of means of production raises many kinds of issues, but most observers agree on one consequence it can have: strong incentives that arise from profit seeking. When disciplined by competition, this profit incentive can induce socially desirable outcomes, but without competition it can bring the socially perverse monopoly behavior we have noted, which is harmful to consumers. Regulation, on the other hand, may destroy the profit incentive, and lead to an inefficient bureaucracy.

Admittedly, less strong, or less narrow, incentives than those in privately owned firms may sometimes be preferable in an institution of public service. When goals or purposes are many and diffuse, a bureaucracy of professional staff may serve better, in part because their self-interest is less apt to interfere with institutional purposes. So service quality may be better maintained, for example. Also, a publicly owned enterprise which is devoted to a well-defined purpose may accomplish desired goals, such as pricing at marginal cost or redistributing income through pricing policies, which a privately owned firm might find difficult to pursue. When aims are clear enough for a public enterprise to be formed, however, ways usually can be designed to accomplish them through private firms. Indeed, mixed public and private ownership may be an effective arrangement that combines the incentives of private ownership with responsibility to the public.

The profit incentive of private ownership originates in the shareholder, who is expected to hire and fire management to enforce pursuit of profit, and extends from there through the organization. Making the shareholder interest salable enhances this profit incentive by making it operate even in a protected monopoly. If the salable monopoly is not yielding as much profit as is possible, it will be worth someone's while to purchase it and make it do so, as long as the cost of carrying out such a large transaction is not too great (Williamson 1975). But will these incentives be preserved if the privately owned and salable monopoly is to be regulated? That question, along with the question of whether antisocial monopoly behavior can be tamed, will determine whether a sound institution of regulation can be designed for a monopoly firm.

Considering the institution of private ownership coldly for its instrumental effectiveness in promoting efficiency, rather than accepting or rejecting it because of its ideological foundation, is quite a new approach. Many nations are seeing debates today about how to organize public services. Planned economies are making growing use of markets, and market economies are taking some steps toward privatization of firms that formerly were publicly owned. Wherever these trends may ultimately settle, the idea of evaluating economic institutions on the basis of their probable effectiveness for specific purposes is bound to be a constructive force.

1.5   Institutions of monopoly regulation

This discussion is concerned primarily with two forms of organization that provide most goods or services under a monopoly market structure: public enterprises and public utilities. A public enterprise is one that is government owned. This type of organization is more common in European countries than in the United States, where it is also quite widely used. Although its history goes back to ancient times, it did not come into wide use until after World War II. Normally created by a legislative body, each public enterprise is a creature with its own distinctive features. The U.S. Postal Service, the Corporation for Public Broadcasting, the Federal Deposit Insurance Corporation, the St. Lawrence Seaway Corporation, and the Tennessee Valley Authority are public enterprises at the federal level, and there are thousands of others at the state and local level (Walsh 1978). These enterprises are overseen in many different ways that are difficult to characterize, but in general some rule limits the profit or loss that each enterprise is allowed to earn (Aharoni 1986).

In West Germany the railway, postal, and telephone services are provided by special public enterprises like government departments, in that employees are civil servants, but with finances separated from the federal budget. Local communities in West Germany typically use public enterprises for electricity distribution, but many other forms of organization exist, including mixtures of public and private ownership. Federal legislation coordinates electricity service through a national grid and imposes some broad requirements for pricing policy and data provision. It also exempts the enterprises from cartel (antitrust) law. France has a renowned public enterprise providing electricity nationally, Electricité de France (EdF), which has led the world in applications of economics to problems of pricing. It was created in 1946 out of many formerly private concerns, much damaged by war, and was extremely successful in developing an admirable national electricity network. Another well-known public enterprise is the Japanese National Railways, which has achieved the fastest train service in the world. At the same time, private firms provide electricity in Japan (Yoshitake 1973), and the Nippon Telegraph and Telephone Corporation (NTT) was sold to the public in 1986 and 1987 at remarkably high prices (with price/earnings ratios above 200, for example). In the United Kingdom "privatization" has proceeded beyond the aerospace, cable and wireless, automobile, and oil industries to gas and telecommunications, and the sale of public electricity and water enterprises is also planned.[5] Modest movement in the same direction has occurred in France, Italy, Spain, and West Germany.

Virtually all countries provide postal service either through a government department or a public enterprise. Sometimes postal and telecommunications services are provided by the same enterprise, as they were in the United Kingdom until telecommunications were separated and sold to private shareholders as British Telecom. A public enterprise ordinarily is responsible for collecting its own revenue, out of which it pays for expenses it decides to incur. In contrast, a government department usually has its expenditures approved through a governmental budgeting process, and often the revenues from its services go into the government's treasury. But the public enterprise may need governmental approval for some of its expenditures, especially on major investments, and because it often has very limited authority to borrow, its spending can be confined to the level of its revenue.

Robson (1960) has identified five distinguishing characteristics of public enterprises. Note, however, that he was focusing primarily on Great Britain at perhaps the height of post–World War II success for public enterprises in Europe. First, they are free from legislative inquiry into management, although subject to it with respect to policy. Second, employees are not part of the civil service. Third, public enterprises are independent financially, separate from the government budget. Fourth, members of their government boards are to be appointed for a fixed term of years and thus are not given the permanent tenure of civil servants nor do they face the threat of sacking that goes with ministerial service. I have saved for last the characteristic of "disinterestedness," which Robson saw as part of such organizations in undertaking a broad but well-defined goal without narrow concern for profit. He quoted with approval the following

---

5 The British spelling, "privatisation," may be appropriate here because Britain started the conversion of nationalized industries to largely private ownership in the last decade, and even in other languages the phenomenon is called "privatisation." For accounts, see Kay and Thompson (1986), Kay, Mayer, and Thompson (1986), Veljanovski (1987), Vickers and Yarrow (1985), and Waterson (1988). Planned economies seeing major change toward greater use of market processes include Bulgaria, China, Czechoslovakia, Hungary (which recently introduced an income tax), Poland, and the Soviet Union. For an account emphasizing problems of change in the Soviet Union, see Goldman (1987).

statement of Lord Morrison (1933), who provided part of the intellectual foundation for Labor Party nationalization of industries in Great Britain after World War II:

> The public corporation must be no mere capitalist business, the be-all and end-all of which is profits and dividends, even though it will, quite properly, be expected to pay its way. It must have a different atmosphere at its board table from that of a shareholders' meeting; its board and its officers must regard themselves as the high custodians of the public interest.

Disinterestedness may have real meaning when one is considering the Royal Mint or the Scottish Development Agency in the United Kingdom, or the National Science Foundation in the United States, because these organizations clearly have goals beyond profit making. But when applied to enterprises in monopoly market positions, including even postal service, the idea may be more wishfully applied, with hope that the organizations will be effective in place of competitive markets. The means of bringing about reliable public service in such circumstances are not self-evident.

Public enterprises usually face some degree of regulation, either by a ministry of government or by a regulatory commission, although the legal foundations are so new in many instances that oversight arrangements are still developing. One advantage of organizing services through public enterprises is that the government as owner can obtain by command the information needed for oversight, although ideal information seldom seems to be available in practice. In addition, for better or worse, the enterprise can be managed to meet governmental objectives. For example, electricity price increases probably have been restrained during inflationary periods in France, and employment in the domestic coal industry appears to have been protected by public enterprise policies on electricity in Germany and the United Kingdom. Incentives to keep costs low and to avoid discriminatory prices are not particularly strong, however.

The public utility is a privately owned corporation serving public purposes. It is widespread in the United States because public services were provided by private firms early in the country's history, and they began to be regulated, as public utilities, little more than a century ago. In 1877 the states won the right to prescribe rates to be charged by private firms in certain circumstances,[6] and that right led gradually to the establishment of state regulatory agencies, which now exist in all states. The guidelines for setting rates grew out of decisions handed down in often controversial court cases. Public utilities or other parties appealed the decisions of regulatory agencies through the regular court system, sometimes all the way

---

[6] See the Supreme Court case of *Munn v. Illinois,* 94 U.S. 113 (1877).

to the Supreme Court. The resulting institution of regulation therefore is not neatly designed for a clear purpose, but rather is a set of procedures and constraints developed piecemeal through court decisions made largely out of past experience.

Rate-of-return regulation is the name given to the practice of determining allowed interest payments and profits to bondholders and private owners of a public utility as a specified rate of return on productive assets. The firm is allowed revenues sufficient to cover its operating expenses plus this return on assets that are employed in service to the public. If revenues are represented by R, expenses by E, assets by A and depreciation by D, then revenues satisfy the equation

$$R = E + s(A - D),$$

where s is the allowed rate of return. When a public utility feels that its prices need to be changed, it will propose changes to the agency that regulates it. A lengthy hearing may result. Often a recent "test period" is chosen as the basis for a factual history, although projections into a future period are sometimes allowed so the result of lengthy deliberations will not be out of date as soon as it is completed. The agency will probe the accounting soundness of reported operating expenses and the appropriateness of included assets, and much effort will go into determining the rate of return to be allowed on the assets. Because asset values are so great in many regulated industries, amounting in dollar terms to two or three times more than the annual sales in electricity, for example, the rate-of-return decision is an important determinant of revenue. It has such a crucial effect on stockholders that top officials of the public utility may devote much of their time to developing arguments for favorable returns at rate hearings.

If its allowed return exceeds its cost of capital, a rate-of-return regulated public utility may want to use more assets than is efficient. Besides serving a productive purpose, the assets in the rate-of-return regulated monopoly justify profit.[7] More important, the firm's own costs are used to determine its revenues, so an inefficient firm may simply be allowed higher prices and more revenues to cover its higher costs. Needless to say, the incentive for efficiency or innovation is weakened in such circumstances. In addition, little attention is devoted to preventing inappropriate price discrimination by regulated firms, yet incentives and means for firms to use it are strong. Thus the rate-of-return regulation that has developed out of legal decisions has serious shortcomings, and a better arrangement should be possible.

---

7 This argument was first set out formally by Averch and Johnson (1962).

Institutions of regulation often begin in circumstances in which some parties already have clear and well-defined interests. The possibility of change through government action causes other parties to defend their interests, and the institutions are shaped in the contentious atmosphere that results. Clear interests of knowledgeable and influential parties receive more attention than smaller and more widely dispersed interests of many consumers. Seeking private advantage and finding compromise are apt to play a larger role in the outcome than the dictates of general economic welfare, which the institution presumably is to serve.

1.6   Summary

Competition provides remarkable guidance in a market economy, but some technologies do not allow it to function well. Then the same measure of economic well-being that competition maximizes can be useful for designing alternative institutions and for determining socially optimal prices. Economic welfare is specified for this purpose in Chapter 2, and problems of inducing its pursuit through regulatory institutions are treated in Chapter 3. Pricing to maximize economic welfare is developed in Part II, although no effort is devoted there to designing institutions that will reliably use such prices. Existing institutions are considered in Part III, and found deficient in their incentives for efficiency. Thus, although much is known about improving welfare, existing institutions are not designed to exploit that knowledge. Part IV contains conclusions and suggestions for reform.

CHAPTER 2

Representing economic welfare

2.1   Introduction

Regulation seeks the same outcome that an ideally functioning market can achieve. However, it usually is undertaken where markets cannot or do not function in the ideal way. The great framework of welfare economics, in which – under ideal conditions – competitive markets reach a Pareto optimal[1] allocation of resources, can be deployed to define an ideal against which regulation can be compared. Welfare economics is not an infallible guide to such policies, for it can require strong assumptions. Not all the important features of a particular market may be captured as a result. Some framework for representing economic welfare is needed before optimal pricing can be defined and described, though, and the logical soundness of welfare economics makes it a good starting point for clear thinking about regulatory problems.

We begin by noting how rigorous analysis of individual welfare can be developed and related to observable demand behavior for a single good or service. The problems of assessing welfare effects in cases involving more than one good or service are treated, and individual preferences or welfare are aggregated to obtain measures of welfare for a group or an entire economy. In aggregating representations of individual well-being we must face the issue of income distribution. We discuss the assumptions typically made about income distribution in welfare measures and illustrate them by application to the choice of socially optimal prices. Since it will be a dominant topic in this book, we examine specifically a situation in which technology prevents competition from achieving an ideal solution. This will show how representations of economic welfare can guide choices between imperfect outcomes. Finally, we discuss imperfect information and risk.

---

[1] Pareto optimality exists when no improvement for one person is possible without harming another. The condition is named for its originator, Vilfredo Pareto, whose work is described by Allais (1968).

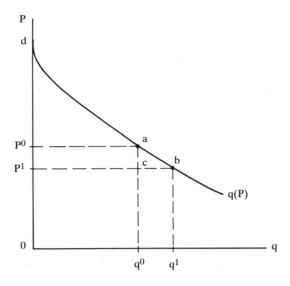

Figure 2.1. Demand and consumer surplus.

2.2   Individual welfare from one service

The most useful representation of individual welfare, *consumer surplus,* can be obtained from an observable demand curve. The measure is not reliably exact, however, and to show why, two alternative measures, the *compensating variation* and *equivalent variation,* are introduced for comparison. Before getting to them it will be helpful to consider the consumer's utility maximization problem and to derive the *indirect utility function,* which allows elegant representation of compensating or equivalent variation. We shall then be well equipped to evaluate the effect of a price change on an individual's welfare.

Consumer surplus

The total net benefit that a consumer enjoys from being able to purchase a good or service is called *consumer's surplus.*[2] It is intended to represent the amount a consumer would be willing to pay for the opportunity to purchase at a certain price.[3] In Figure 2.1 the price (P) that a consumer

---

[2] The first description of consumer surplus was by the French engineer and economist Jules Dupuit (1844), although that label for the idea is due to Alfred Marshall.

[3] This definition is due to Marshall (1920, p. 124).

would be willing to pay for various quantities (q) of a particular service is identified by the demand function, $q(P)$. We assume that the consumer's money income and the prices of all other goods are known and constant. The area P^0ad represents that consumer's benefit from purchasing at price P^0, because it is the difference between what the consumer is willing to pay for each unit and the required payment, P^0. For this reason, P^0ad is the maximum amount the consumer would be willing to pay for the opportunity to purchase q^0 units at price P^0 per unit.

To see the logic behind such a claim, notice that the consumer in Figure 2.1 would have been willing to pay roughly an amount $d0$ for the first unit, a slightly lower amount for the second unit, and so on until paying P^0 for the q^0th unit. The sum of the evaluations that the consumer makes of the separate units, less the amount actually paid for the units, P^0q^0, is the consumer surplus, CS, from consuming q^0 units of the good at price P^0:

$$CS = \int_{P^0}^{q^{-1}(0)} q(P)\, dP. \tag{1}$$

Here $q^{-1}(q)$ is the inverse demand function[4] for the consumer whose money income is constant at y^0, and $q^{-1}(0)$ is the marginal willingness to pay 0 units, or $d0$. Thus, CS in (1) is the area P^0ad, the amount the consumer is willing to pay above the amount that is actually paid.

An alternative expression for CS that is sometimes more convenient, since it carries out the integration over quantities, captures the area representing CS plus the total revenue consumers pay, TR. This measure is

$$TR + CS = \int_0^{q^0} P(q)\, dq, \tag{2}$$

where $P(\cdot) = q^{-1}(\cdot)$ is the inverse demand function. In Figure 2.1 the area represented by (2) is daq^00. This area can be divided into P^0aq^00, which is total revenue, and P^0ad, which is consumer surplus.

The net benefit to the individual from consuming at price P^0 is the area daq^00 less the amount the consumer must give up, the total revenue P^0aq^00; this net benefit, $daq^00 - P^0aq^00$, is of course the consumer surplus, P^0ad. From society's standpoint, welfare is consumer benefit less the value of resources needed to serve the consumer. Since the consumer's total willingness to pay is represented by (2), subtracting cost from it will yield a representation of welfare, $TR + CS - TC$. Note that computing

---

4 A demand function ordinarily represents the quantity of a good consumed given its price, the prices of other goods, and the consumer's income. Quantity consumed is assumed to be decreasing monotonically in price, so there is a unique quantity for any price and vice versa. This means that we can define price as a function of quantity, as a quantity inverse; the resulting function is called the inverse demand function.

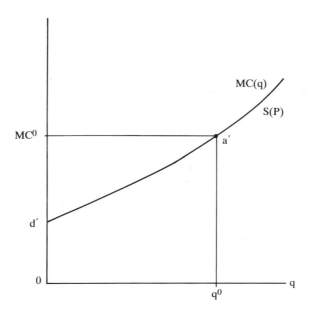

Figure 2.2. Supply and producer surplus.

$TR + CS$ as in (2) may be simpler and more direct when the $TR + CS - TC$ representation of welfare is wanted.

We shall also define *producer surplus* in a manner analogous to consumer surplus. The producer surplus (PS) of a firm operating at marginal cost MC^0 along the supply function of the firm, $S(P)$ in Figure 2.2 will be the area $MC^0a'd'$. Producer surplus can be represented by the integral

$$PS = \int_{MC(0)}^{MC^0} S(P)\, dp, \tag{3}$$

where $MC(q)$ is marginal cost at quantity q. If price equaled MC^0, total revenue would be $MC^0a'q^00$ in Figure 2.2, and total cost would be $d'a'q^00$. Since the difference in those two areas is producer surplus, we see that $PS = TR - TC$.

The supply function in the example of Figure 2.2 assumes that price equals marginal cost, so $P = MC(S(P))$. If we integrate the marginal cost function along the quantity axis, we of course obtain total cost:

$$TC = \int_0^{q^0} MC(q)\, dq. \tag{4}$$

Thus equations (1) and (3) together give consumer surplus plus producer surplus $(CS + PS)$, and equation (2) minus equation (4) yields the same total $(TR + CS - TC = CS + PS)$. The sum of consumer and producer surplus is usually taken as the representation of economic welfare to be maximized, since it represents consumer welfare from a good or service less the cost of providing it.

Several qualifications must be noted for this $CS + PS$ welfare measure. It is possible to argue that maximization of consumer surplus alone is a reasonable goal (with profit limited, for example, to some fair return on assets). Such a position depends on an implicit weighting of consumers, on one hand, and those receiving profit, on the other. We discuss this question of weights for individuals in Section 2.4, but postpone real discussion of income distribution to Chapter 6. For now, we simply note that profit can be as valuable as consumer surplus, and seeking to make their combined sum large is a common normative goal when the present distribution of income is accepted. Indeed, under ideal conditions, a competitive market economy will lead to an equilibrium in which the sum of consumer and producer surplus is maximized. No measure of that sum need be calculated, however, because no issue depends on the value of the surpluses as well-functioning markets adjust and change through individual transactions. Surplus measures become useful when a question must be decided collectively, as in a public decision whether to build a bridge[5] or in setting a price for a public service.

To use consumer surplus (CS) in evaluating a public action it is necessary also to determine resource costs accurately. This is most easily done when any resources needed, to build a bridge or to expand output upon lowering price, can be drawn from many other industries so the price in no one of them is seriously altered. If the necessary resource adjustment was so great that some other market in the economy would no longer exist, for example, then the lost CS from that market would have to be considered in addition to resource cost at market prices. As long as marginal resources can be drawn from many other markets without greatly affecting their market prices, consumer surplus can be estimated in one market as we have indicated. Resources are withdrawn from other markets then at their market prices, which represent the marginal values consumers place on them in the other uses.

What if the demand curve does not meet the vertical axis because the quantity demanded never falls to zero (e.g., presumably one would always demand a positive amount of water)? Although CS is not defined

---

[5] It was in such an example that Dupuit (1844) worked out the role of consumer surplus for evaluating public projects.

then, the *change* in consumer surplus can still be obtained, as the change from P^0 to P^1 in Figure 2.1, by evaluating

$$\Delta CS = \int_{P^1}^{P^0} q(P, y^0)\, dP, \tag{5}$$

where y^0 is included to remind us that it is fixed (as are other prices). The welfare effects of a change in price can thus be obtained even if demand never falls to zero, and the effect of such a change in price is often what is of interest in regulatory situations. The area given by (5) is the area P^0abP^1 in Figure 2.1.

Consumer surplus does not always yield a precise measure of welfare for an individual in the simple way Figure 2.1 suggests. As price changes while the consumer's money income remains constant, the effect on real income may by itself affect consumption of the good and shift the demand curve. For instance, a substantial price reduction would enable a person with the same money income to buy more of everything. Figure 2.1 is not adequate to represent such a possibility. If real income had such an effect, the consumer might evaluate a price reduction, as from P^0 to P^1 in Figure 2.1, differently from a price increase, as from P^1 to P^0. Because an income effect would lead to more consumption for a price decrease and less consumption for a price increase, it cannot be present in Figure 2.1. Does this possibility of income effects mean the area P^0abP^1 is not always a reliable measure of welfare change? Yes, it does. The case shown in Figure 2.1 yields a reliable measure of welfare change only if there is no income effect; in Figure 2.1 the income elasticity of demand for the good is zero.

The representation of individual benefit is examined next by going behind the demand curve and looking at individual choices in detail, to find a more basic representation of individual well-being that does not require zero income elasticity of demand. From there we can return to evaluate how effective consumer surplus will be for representing harm or benefit from a price change. We turn first to the consumer's utility maximization problem, which yields an indirect utility function representing well-being as a function of prices and income. With that we can easily examine two other measures of welfare effect, *compensating variation* and *equivalent variation*, which we shall compare with consumer surplus.

Utility and indirect utility functions

Since we want to consider an economic system in which consumers seek as much satisfaction as possible, given the prices of goods and their incomes, we should examine the problem that leads to an individual consumer's demand curve. We can do this by expressing the individual's well-being, or utility, as a function of goods consumed, and considering the problem of maximizing utility subject to a budget constraint. The ith individual's utility function over n goods or services,

$$u^i = u^i(q_1^i, \ldots, q_n^i), \tag{6}$$

is assumed to be strictly increasing $(du^i/dq_j^i \equiv u_j^i > 0$ for $j = 1, \ldots, n)$ and strictly quasi-concave[6] with continuous first and second derivatives. These assumptions mean that all goods are desired and the rate of substitution between one good and any other will diminish smoothly as the consumer increases consumption of that first good. With these restrictions we assume only that an individual can recognize being better off. We represent being better off with a higher level of utility, but need not assume that the difference in utility can be evaluated with precision. Indeed, we are developing an alternative to consumer surplus so we can assess a consumer's evaluation of a change while holding the consumer at the same utility level. That is the only way we can be precise while adhering to weak assumptions.

Let the budget of the ith consumer be given by

$$y^i - t^i = \sum_{j=1}^{n} P_j q_j^i, \tag{7}$$

where y^i is money income, t^i is any income tax (or transfer to the consumer if negative), and $\sum_{j=1}^{n} P_j q_j$ is the total expenditure that is linear on the assumption that P_j's are parametric and unaltered by the amounts of consumption. Some relations that can be derived from the budget constraint will be useful in a moment. Differentiating the budget constraint (7) with respect to P_j's yields

$$q_j^i + \sum_{k=1}^{n} P_k q_{kj}^i = 0, \quad j = 1, \ldots, n. \tag{8}$$

And differentiating (7) with respect to y_i and t_i yields

$$-1 + \sum_{k=1}^{n} P_k q_{ky^i}^i = 0 \tag{9}$$

and

$$1 + \sum_{k=1}^{n} P_k q_{kt^i}^i = 0. \tag{10}$$

Presuming that the ith consumer maximizes utility (6) subject to the income constraint (7), the consumer's problem is represented by the Lagrangian

$$\max \pounds(q_1^i, \ldots, q_n^i, \eta^i) = u^i(q_1^i, \ldots, q_n^i) + \eta^i(y^i - t^i - \sum_{j=1}^{n} P_j q_j^i), \tag{11}$$

[6] For an illustration of the economic meaning of quasi-concavity, see Chiang (1984, pp. 394–7) and Silberberg (1978, pp. 221–2). In economic terms, it represents a diminishing rate of substitution between commodities without assuming diminishing marginal utility.

where η^i is a Lagrange multiplier. Necessary conditions for a maximum are

$$\pounds_j = u_j^i - \eta^i P_j = 0, \quad j = 1, \ldots, n \tag{12}$$

and

$$\pounds_{\eta^i} = y^i - t^i - \Sigma_{j=1}^n P_j q_j^i = 0. \tag{13}$$

In principle, we can solve these $n+1$ equations for the unknowns, $q_1, \ldots,$ q_n, η^i, in terms of known $P_1, \ldots, P_n$, y^i, and t^i.[7] The results will be the individual's n demand functions

$$q_j = q_j^*(P_1, \ldots, P_n, y^i - t^i), \quad j = 1, \ldots, n, \tag{14}$$

and also

$$\eta^i = \eta^{i*}(P_1, \ldots, P_n, y^i - t^i). \tag{15}$$

The asterisks mark simultaneous solution values for the problem (11), obtained on the assumption that prices and net incomes are constant.

Now if values from the solution in (14) are substituted into (6), we have

$$u^i(q_1^{i*}(P_1, \ldots, P_n, y^i - t^i), \ldots, q_n^{i*}(P_1, \ldots, P_n, y^i - t^i))$$
$$\equiv v^i(P_1, \ldots, P_n, y^i - t^i), \tag{16}$$

a utility function that depends on parameters $P_1, \ldots, P_n$ and $y^i - t^i$, and is called the *indirect utility function*. We use v^i to indicate the indirect utility function. It is often convenient to represent utility in terms of price and income parameters through the indirect utility function, and some basic relationships can be expressed simply and directly through it.

Notice, in particular, that

$$v_{P_j}^i = \Sigma_{k=1}^n u_k^i q_{kj}^{i*}.$$

Substituting for u_k^i's from (12) then yields

$$v_{P_j}^i = \eta^{i*} \Sigma_{k=1}^n P_k q_{kj}^{i*}$$

and using (8) we can obtain

$$v_{P_j}^i = -\eta^{i*} q_j^{i*}. \tag{17}$$

Having considered the solution q_j^{i*}, let us examine η^{i*}. It is obvious from (12) that

---

[7] The sufficient conditions for a solution will be satisfied because of our assumption of constant, parametric prices and of properties that we have assumed for individuals' utility functions; they are strictly increasing in their arguments and strictly quasi-concave with continuous first and second derivatives. See Silberberg (1978, pp. 159–64).

$$\eta^{i*} = \frac{u_j^i}{P_j}, \quad j = 1, \dots, n. \tag{18}$$

The marginal utility from the jth good divided by the cost of that good, P_j, is the marginal utility of good j per dollar spent, which at equilibrium for the consumer must be the same for every good and equal to η^{i*}. That η^{i*} is the marginal utility of income of the ith person can be shown by differentiating the indirect utility function with respect to income to obtain

$$v_{y^i}^i = \sum_{j=1}^n u_j^i \frac{\partial q_j^{i*}}{\partial y^i} = \sum_{j=1}^n u_j^i q_{jy^i}^i. \tag{19}$$

Using (12), this becomes

$$v_{y^i}^i = \eta^{i*} \sum_{j=1}^n P_j q_{jy^i}^i,$$

which, with (9), reduces to

$$v_{y^i}^i = \eta^{i*}. \tag{20}$$

Of course, from the form of the Lagrangian, (11), we know that at the optimum $\pounds_{y^i} = \eta^{i*}$.

The indirect utility function is a convenient measure of well-being, so we should know its properties. In particular, because it defines utility as a function of prices and income, it yields a precise representation for the change in income that will offset a given price change. Precision is achieved by making the evaluation while holding utility constant, and thus avoiding the consequences of an income effect due to the price change.

Compensating variation, equivalent variation, and consumer surplus

Demand curves can be observed in practice, whereas utility functions cannot be, at least not for pricing applications. Whether the observable individual demand curve will give rise to a measure of consumer well-being such as *consumer surplus*[8] that is useful for judging the value to the consumer of a particular change in price can be determined by comparing it with a measure from the indirect utility function. Consider the example illustrated in Figure 2.3a.

Let us start with price P^0 at point a in Figure 2.3a and consider a price decrease to P^1. (We assume that all other prices and all incomes are constant.) Suppose we represent that change by the indirect utility function, suppressing for simplicity other prices since we assume they are constant.

---

[8] We rely here on the analysis by Willig (1976). See also Buchanan (1953), Gabor (1955), Hicks (1943), Mohring (1971), and Ng (1980, pp. 84–110).

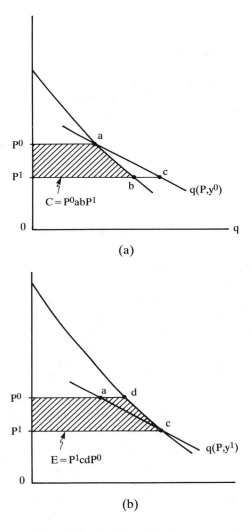

Figure 2.3. Demand with income effects.

We begin with $v(P^0, y^0)$ and define a "compensating variation" change in income, C, that accompanies the price change and has the effect of keeping the individual at precisely the same utility level after the price change as before:

$$v(P^0, y^0) = v(P^1, y^0 - C). \tag{21}$$

This *compensating variation, C*, can be considered the benefit to the consumer of a lowered price.

By definition, the consumer must have exactly the same utility, whether at the point where price and income are P^0 and y^0, or at the new price P^1 with income $y^0 - C$. If we draw a demand curve holding utility constant through point a and through point b, the amount C will be the shaded area $C = P^0abP^1$ in Figure 2.3a, for that area represents the payment that is necessary to make the consumer at point a (with price P^0 and income y^0) as well off as at point b (with price P^1 and income $y^0 - C$). Note that the demand curve in Figure 2.3a that adjusts money income to keep utility constant is not the kind of demand curve we can observe. An observable demand curve, such as that in Figure 2.1, represents responses to price changes as *money income* remains the same, whereas the demand curve through points a and b in Figure 2.3a was constructed keeping utility, or *real income*, the same. A demand with no adjustment in money income to keep utility constant, as in Figure 2.1, is drawn through point a in Figure 2.3a to point c, and is identified as $q(P, y^0)$. This observable demand curve calls for greater consumption of the good at the lower price P^1, by passing through point c rather than point b. The good is assumed to be normal,[9] so with higher money income more of it will be consumed. That means that if we attempt to measure compensating variation, C, using an observable demand curve we shall be in error by the difference, $P^0acP^1 - P^0abP^1$, which is caused by the income effect. We shall interpret this difference in a moment, after we introduce another representation of welfare change.

At this point the reader might wonder whether it is possible to adjust the consumer's initial income rather than final income as in the compensating variation. Adjusting initial income could make utility at the starting point the same as it is *after* the price change. Such an adjustment in income is precisely what is called the "equivalent variation," defined as E in the following:

$$v(P^0, y^0 + E) = v(P^1, y^0).$$
(22)

The *equivalent variation* focuses on the income change (E) that makes initial well-being (or utility) the same as it would be *after* the price change has occurred. Thus it is an adjustment in income *equivalent* to the proposed change. The *compensating variation* focuses on the income change (C) that makes final well-being the same as the starting point, *before* the price change. Compensating variation *compensates* for the price change.

9 A *normal* good is one for which greater income induces more consumption. If an increase in income causes less of a good to be consumed, that good is said to be *inferior*. An example of an inferior good could be margarine, which might be consumed at a lower income but gives way to butter as income increases.

To see that equivalent variation is just the reverse adjustment to that of compensating variation, suppose we had begun in Figure 2.3b at point c, with the consumer having money income y^0 and price at P^1, and then raised price to P^0. The demand curve that would compensate the consumer for any loss in utility due to the price rise is drawn from point c through point d. (Notice that more will be purchased at point d than at point a when price is P^0; the reason is that at point d income has been augmented by an amount equal to E, to keep utility the same despite the price increase from P^1 to P^0.) Now the shaded area identified as E in Figure 2.3b, the area $P^1 cd P^0$, is obtained by adjusting the starting income so the choice at d can allow the same utility as would point c on the ordinary demand curve. Thus the area labeled E in Figure 2.3b then would actually fit the definition of C, compensating variation, if the case had begun at P^1 rather than P^0. These measures of welfare effect depend on whether our analysis isolates an amount that would compensate so the action leaves us at the existing status quo point (C), or adapt in an equivalent way to the final point to be reached after action is taken (E).

We have come to see that two measures of welfare change can be obtained directly from the consumer's utility maximization problem. One makes comparisons at the income level *before* any action is taken and the other makes comparisons *after* the action has been completed. Neither measure is observable from a demand function. Fortunately, these two precise measures straddle the observable value, one being larger and the other smaller. Furthermore, Willig (1976) has shown that in virtually any practical application the area from an observable demand curve will give a good approximation to both C and E. The error tends to vary directly with the size of the observed area and with the income elasticity of demand, and inversely with the income level. Willig has also provided rules for estimating C and E from the observed area when values for the income elasticity of demand for the good at points a and c in Figure 2.3 are known. Of course, if the income elasticity of demand for the good is zero, there will be no error; the areas C and E will coincide exactly and will equal the observed CS area.

Thus there is a potential for error in measuring consumer surplus from an observable demand curve, because of income effects. But the error from the income effect will ordinarily be small. The income effect of a price change will be greater as the income elasticity of demand for the good differs from zero by a greater amount and as the amount spent on the good is larger. In most practical situations, a small fraction of income is spent on the good in question, and estimation of consumer surplus from observable demand curves will yield an adequate measure of consumer benefit.

2.3   Individual welfare from many services

One other issue bears on the effectiveness of consumer surplus as a measure of individual benefit from price changes. When many goods or services, and perhaps many price changes, are involved, the question arises whether a unique consumer surplus measure exists.[10] As an example, consider two substitute goods, butter and margarine, and suppose they both become unavailable. What is the consumer surplus loss for the individual shown in Figure 2.4, whose demands were D_B (for butter in Figure 2.4a) and D_M (for margarine in Figure 2.4b)? The separate consumer surplus areas abP_B and efP_M obviously are inadequate as measures of welfare loss when *both* goods are withdrawn, because when one good is withdrawn the consumer surplus from the other good would increase. When butter is withdrawn, for instance, the consumer surplus from margarine will be hgP_M because margarine demand will shift to D'_M; or if margarine is withdrawn, the consumer surplus from butter will go to dcP_B because butter demand will rise to D'_B. This yields a way to think about both goods being unavailable. The total consumer surplus loss if both are withdrawn would either be $abP_B + hgP_M$, or $efP_M + dcP_B$, which are not necessarily the same in area. Notice that if the two shaded areas, *abcd* in Figure 2.4a and *efgh* in Figure 2.4b, are equal, the total consumer surplus is the same regardless of the order in which goods are withdrawn, meaning that the particular path followed does not affect the results.

With indexes j and k representing two different goods, if for all possible combinations of goods and all sets of prices we always have

$$\frac{\partial q_k}{\partial P_j} = \frac{\partial q_j}{\partial P_k}, \quad \text{all } j, k, \tag{23}$$

there is no ambiguity; the shaded areas in Figure 2.4 are equal then, and consumer surplus will not depend on the sequence of actions or the path followed. If all demands are independent, as an example, (23) would be trivially satisfied because $\partial q_k/\partial P_j = \partial q_j/\partial P_k = 0$; if the goods are neither substitutes nor complements, the shaded areas in Figure 2.4 will be zero.

Each side of condition (23) involves a partial change in quantity demanded due to a change in price, with income and other prices held constant. By the Slutsky equation,[11] the two sides of (23) can be represented as

---

10 This point was first raised by Hotelling (1938). The example that follows is based on the expositions of Ng (1980, pp. 92–6). See also Willig (1979a).

11 The Slutsky equation contains precisely the sort of income compensation discussed in Section 2.2. The quantity response to a price change that will hold utility constant was shown by Slutsky (1915) to be

$$\left.\frac{\partial q_j}{\partial P_k}\right|_u = \frac{\partial q_j}{\partial P_k} + q_k \frac{\partial q_j}{\partial y}.$$

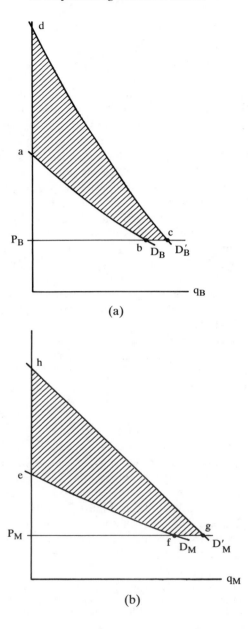

Figure 2.4. Estimating consumer surplus from two interrelated goods or services.

$$\frac{\partial q_k}{\partial P_j} = \frac{\partial q_k}{\partial P_j}\bigg|_{\bar{u}} - q_j \frac{\partial q_k}{\partial y}$$

and

$$\frac{\partial q_j}{\partial P_k} = \frac{\partial q_j}{\partial P_k}\bigg|_{\bar{u}} - q_k \frac{\partial q_j}{\partial y},$$

where $\partial q_k/\partial P_j\,|_{\bar{u}}$ and $\partial q_j/\partial P_k\,|_{\bar{u}}$ are changes in quantities with utility held constant at $\bar{u}$ while $q_j\,\partial q_k/\partial y$ and $q_k\,\partial q_j/y$ are income effects. In each case the left-hand side is the slope of an ordinary demand curve (as the curve through a and c of Figure 2.3a), and the right-hand side is the slope of a constant utility demand curve (as the curve through a and b of Figure 2.3a). The constant utility responses will be denoted as $\partial q_k/\partial P_j\,|_{\bar{u}} = S_{kj}$ and $\partial q_j/\partial P_k\,|_{\bar{u}} = S_{jk}$. We shall encounter them again in later chapters. Properties ordinarily assumed for utility functions, such as differentiability (twice) and strict quasi-concavity imply that

$$S_{kj} = S_{jk}. \tag{24}$$

So what is really required for (23) to hold (i.e., for CS to be exact) is that the income effects must be equal, which will be true if income elasticities of the two goods are equal:

$$\frac{\partial q_k}{\partial y} \cdot \frac{y}{q_k} = \frac{\partial q_j}{\partial y} \cdot \frac{y}{q_j}. \tag{25}$$

Although these income elasticities may not always be equal, their differences will usually be small, especially for small price changes. We shall assume quite often that the difference is not important and (23) can be satisfied.

2.4 From individual welfare to social welfare

Is it possible, or appropriate, to combine the consumer surpluses from different persons into an aggregate social welfare measure? We approach this question by assuming that social welfare can be obtained from individual welfare alone. It might be argued instead that since it takes two to tango, or to play tennis, social welfare depends on something beyond individual satisfaction to reflect collective involvement. But even with collective involvement, individual satisfaction is always a final result. So it is reasonable to use individual satisfaction, even from collective activities, to assess social well-being.

That social welfare can be represented as a function of individuals' welfare is presumed in the mathematical function of the general form

$$W = W(u^1, \ldots, u^I), \tag{26}$$

where $u^1, \ldots, u^I$ are utility levels of I individuals and W is a rule for combining them. Social welfare in (26) is thus some function of the utilities of all I individuals. As long as a change in individual utility always alters W in the same direction, as when compensation is paid to individuals for any harm suffered, the exact form of the W function need not affect qualitative results. Any proposed action that leaves a positive social net benefit should be undertaken, for it allows a Pareto improvement through which all gain. Typically, however, some consumers will benefit from an action and some will be harmed and not compensated. Use of a function such as (26) that weighs consumers' utilities relative to one another then rests on judgments stronger than Pareto optimality. Aggregate consumer surplus is one such measure.[12]

Combining one consumer's surplus with another's by simple addition to obtain a total welfare measure (indicated by relocating the apostrophe from consumer's to consumers' surplus) essentially accepts as legitimate the current distribution of income. To show this connection to income distribution we consider two alternative ways to distribute goods in a society. The familiar way is to have individuals solve allocation problems themselves through market transactions when each has a limited income; another way is to distribute goods according to some explicit weighting of the satisfactions of individuals, deliberately allowing more satisfaction to some than to others. By comparing these two ways of distributing goods we can see how incomes implicitly weight satisfaction in the market process. We can be more concrete with a two-person, two-good example in which there is no interdependence among goods in consumption or production (i.e., there is no external effect of one's decision on another, as with noise, air, or water pollution).

Suppose that two persons have the utility functions u^1 and u^2 defined over quantities of two goods, q_1 and q_2. The two functions are $u^1(q_1^1, q_2^1)$ and $u^2(q_1^2, q_2^2)$ and the consumers each maximize utility subject to their budget constraints $y^1 = p_1 q_1^1 + p_2 q_2^1$ and $y^2 = p_1 q_1^2 + p_2 q_2^2$. With η^1 and η^2 the respective Lagrangian multipliers on these constraints, and with λ the equal marginal cost prices of q_1 and q_2, it is easy to derive the individual constrained utility maximization conditions from the two consumers' problems,

$$u_1^1 = \lambda \eta^1, \qquad u_2^1 = \lambda \eta^1 \tag{27}$$

for person one and

---

[12] For an example of welfare analysis based explicitly on the equivalent variation (E in equation (20)), see Barton and Olsen (1983). Applications of consumer surplus are shown in Currie, Murphy, and Schmitz (1971).

$$u_1^2 = \lambda \eta^2, \qquad u_2^2 = \lambda \eta^2 \qquad (28)$$

for person two.

On the other hand, let us assign weights β^1 and β^2 to the two individuals' utilities in a linear sum and imagine optimally distributing goods to them. We also assume an extremely simple production process which allows conversion of the limited resource, Z, into the goods so they are equally costly, $q_1^1 + q_1^2 + q_2^1 + q_2^2 = Z$. We would then have the social problem of maximizing welfare, $\beta^1 u^1 + \beta^2 u^2$, subject to the production constraint $q_1^1 + q_1^2 + q_2^1 + q_2^2 = Z$. With λ the Lagrangian multiplier on the production relation so it will represent the goods' equal marginal cost, necessary conditions are

$$u_1^1 = \lambda/\beta^1, \qquad u_2^1 = \lambda/\beta^1 \qquad (29)$$

for person one and

$$u_1^2 = \lambda/\beta^2, \qquad u_2^2 = \lambda/\beta^2 \qquad (30)$$

for person two. Now notice, by comparing (27) with (29) and (28) with (30), that when these two ways of distributing output produce *identical* distributions and satisfactions for the two consumers, we shall have $\beta^1 = 1/\eta^1$ and $\beta^2 = 1/\eta^2$. This illustrates that a market outcome, found through conditions (27) and (28), implicitly weights individuals in a social welfare function, and the weights are reciprocals of the marginal utilities of income.[13]

Since the η^i's in the market problem giving rise to (27) and (28) can be interpreted as the consumers' marginal utilities of income, the implicit social welfare weights or β^i's assigned to individuals in (29) and (30) must be the reciprocals of their marginal utilities of income. This means that if an added unit of income can be provided in a society, the effect on social welfare will be the same no matter who receives it. If the income increase is given to any individual i, for example, the unit of income will add to the ith individual's utility by η_i and then be weighted in social welfare by $1/\eta_i$ so, since $(\eta_i)(1/\eta_i) = 1$, the effect on society will always be 1 times the income increase. The weighting of individuals implicit in the social welfare measure at a market outcome clearly depends on their current incomes, through the marginal utilities of income, the η_i's. Moreover, these weights work in a way that makes income distribution unimportant, in that social welfare is the same no matter who benefits (or loses). When we say that an aggregate consumer surplus measure accepts, or is based on, the current distribution of income, we mean exactly this weighting of individuals by the reciprocals of their marginal utilities of income. Because

13 For early derivation of this form for welfare weights, see Negishi (1960).

it renders income distribution unimportant, accepting the current income distribution in this way focuses attention on efficiency.

Efficiency will dominate in determining a maximum of welfare when welfare is aggregate consumer surplus, precisely because the solution is predicated on the existing income and wealth distribution. For clear efficiency improvements, the income distribution may not be crucial and the issue of income distribution may reasonably be ignored. When efficiency questions are dominant, the aggregation of a consumers' surplus measure should not draw objections for being based on the existing distribution of income and wealth. If the existing income distribution is regarded as unsatisfactory, that issue should be attacked directly, and of course a consumer surplus evaluation may not then be appropriate.

Consumer surplus evaluations can be made from the demands estimated for products or services. When profit is affected, it also must be included in assessing welfare effects. A change in public utility price often involves profit as well as consumer surplus changes, for example, so effects on both must be estimated. More generally, an incremental unit of a good or service has a social opportunity cost represented by the willingness of suppliers to produce it under competitive conditions. Any difference between this supply price and actual price is a producer's surplus that is comparable to the consumer's surplus. Each dollar of producer surplus can have the same effect on social welfare no matter who ultimately receives it, just as each dollar of consumer surplus does, if individuals are weighted by the reciprocals of marginal utilities of income in reckoning social welfare so the existing income distribution is implicitly accepted.[14]

2.5   Socially optimal pricing

Let us now present a socially ideal price for a simple problem involving maximization of some representation of consumer welfare. To represent welfare in these examples we use, first, consumer surplus and, second, a socially weighted sum of individual welfare indicated either by indirect or direct utility functions. Prices equal to marginal cost always maximize welfare as defined in these problems. We assume that marginal cost

[14] As to the *feasibility* of adding representations of consumers' well-being, some difficulties may arise if the action being considered would bring an income transfer that is so great that relative prices would be altered by it. For example, the compensating variation determined by holding utility constant in (21), when repeated for several consumers, may be aggregated into a positive value but would call for an allocation of goods that simply cannot be produced (Boadway 1974). Since the compensating variation or any other single theoretical measure is unlikely to be used in practice by itself, however, and since the price ratio change from any income effect is not apt to be large, this problem is probably not a serious one.

is constant and that total cost will equal zero at $q = 0$, so there will be no excess profit or loss to consider at the solution. As a result, the net benefit to producers, producers' surplus, will be zero, allowing emphasis on consumer welfare measures. We call attention to the form of each problem and to the particular weighting of individual utilities that is implicit in the representations of welfare.

First we formulate the social problem as maximizing $CS + PS$ using equations (1) and (3),

$$CS + PS = \int_{P^0}^{q_d^{-1}(0)} q(P)\, dP + \int_{q_c^{-1}(0)}^{P^0} S(P)\, dP. \tag{31}$$

Differentiating with respect to P and setting the result equal to zero, we obtain:

$$P = MC.$$

We could also use consumer surplus as represented in equation (1) and add total revenue less total cost to represent producers' surplus:

$$CS + TR - TC = \int_{P}^{q^{-1}(0)} q(P)\, dP + Pq - C(q). \tag{32}$$

Differentiating with respect to price, the necessary condition is

$$-q + q + P\frac{dq}{dP} - MC\frac{dq}{dP} = 0.$$

Solving for P we obtain

$$P = MC.$$

Alternatively, we might consider the social problem as maximizing total revenue plus consumer surplus as in equation (2), less total cost as in equation (4):

$$CS + TR - TC = \int_0^q P(Q)\, dQ - \int_0^q MC(Q)\, dQ. \tag{33}$$

Differentiating with respect to quantity and solving for P, we again find

$$P = MC.$$

A similar procedure can be followed using a social welfare function. Let us first use indirect utility functions weighted by β^i weights, as in Section 2.4, as a measure of consumer welfare. Because this representation will yield marginal effects due to changes in price, it is like (1), and must be analyzed like consumer surplus, with total revenue less total cost added to define a social welfare measure. The social welfare problem using a weighted sum of indirect utility is thus to maximize

$$\sum_i \beta^i v^i + Pq - C(q). \tag{34}$$

Differentiating with respect to P we have, using (17) (which shows that $\partial v^i/\partial P = -\eta^i q^i$),

$$-\sum_i \beta^i \eta^i q^i + q + P\frac{dq}{dP} - MC\frac{dq}{dP} = 0.$$

Now if we assume $\beta^i = 1/\eta^i$, by accepting the existing income distribution as illustrated in Section 2.4, and noting that $\sum_i q^i = q$, this necessary condition will reduce to

$$P = MC.$$

In Chapter 6 we consider other assumptions regarding income distribution. But for now we simply observe that this assumption yields an outcome the same as the consumer surplus representation of benefit.

If we use a socially weighted sum of individual utility functions that depend on quantity of goods rather than on prices, our analysis would be like that with the total revenue plus consumer surplus representation in (2). This social problem would be to maximize

$$\sum_i \beta^i u^i - C(q). \tag{35}$$

Differentiating with respect to q and using (12) (which shows that $\partial u^i/\partial q = \eta^i P$) yields

$$\sum \beta^i \eta^i P - MC = 0.$$

Once again, if we accept the current distribution of income so $\beta^i = 1/\eta^i$, we have

$$P = MC.$$

All of these optimal pricing problems show that price should equal marginal cost to maximize welfare. The welfare representation that is maximized with respect to prices is consumer surplus alone, without revenue, so revenue must be added and cost subtracted to form producer's surplus. The welfare representation maximized with respect to quantities already includes total revenue plus consumer surplus, and the social problem can be formed accordingly just by subtracting total cost. This difference arises whether consumer welfare is represented by consumer surplus or by a social welfare function made up of individual utility functions. In the latter case the social weights attached to individuals must be explicitly set equal to the reciprocals of the consumers' marginal utilities of income if the solutions are to match those obtained with the consumer surplus representation. Thus the consumer surplus representation implicitly requires the welfare weights of individuals (the β^i's) to equal the reciprocals of marginal utilities of income ($1/\eta^i$'s).

All of these examples of socially optimal pricing have assumed that demand and cost functions are known perfectly and are unchanging. If demand fluctuates randomly, we can still obtain the same solutions, as long as marginal cost is constant, unaffected by level of output, and capacity does not limit output. When the level of output affects marginal cost, demand fluctuations that cause output to vary will affect expected marginal cost, to complicate finding an optimal price. If price could be adjusted perfectly to every change in demand, and if new prices could immediately and costlessly be transmitted to consumers, who could then alter their consumption plans, a perfect solution would be possible. But such communication and consumer response is either terribly costly or infeasible, and instead an attempt usually is made to maintain a single price that is optimal under the circumstances. Complications arise when the level of marginal cost depends on the nature of demand fluctuations, because optimal price then depends on properties of demand, and the complications are greater when capacity limits prevent some consumers from being served, because to evaluate welfare we must know who is served. We shall not explore the general problems of demand uncertainty here, but we shall examine specific cases of uncertain demand in chapters that follow.

2.6 The decreasing average cost problem

When competition fails, representations of economic welfare enable us to evaluate what outcome would be most efficient and socially desirable for a given goal. We cannot claim that regulation should always replace the market, for identifying an efficient price will not necessarily provide a workable way to put it into effect. Although we can set out a price that is ideal in the light of its definition, no institution may be motivated to adopt it and operate efficiently at the same time. Moreover, an ideal price may be difficult to agree on because of conflict over what is ideal. All of these problems must be solved if the regulation of price is to be effective, and we cannot solve them here. Our aim in this section is to sketch briefly some of the main issues that arise when average costs decrease with output, and to indicate the types of results that welfare analysis can provide.

Suppose that a service can be produced at constant marginal cost per unit, b, up to a capacity limit. There is also a cost per unit of capacity that depends on total output, q, according to the function $\beta(q)$ where β is the average capacity cost. We assume β falls with output, or $\partial\beta/\partial q < 0$, so average cost is decreasing with output. Since unit cost is lower at a greater scale of operations, we say there are *economies of scale,* which cause a problem because a price equal to marginal cost will be below average cost and will not yield enough revenue to cover total cost. A problem similar to that caused by economies of scale can arise in the number-of-products dimension of a firm's activity. When one enterprise can produce a set of products at less cost than any collection of separate enterprises, we say that *economies of scope* exist.[15] In this case also the prices that reflect marginal social costs may not yield revenue equal to total cost. Since we only wish to illustrate the pricing problem, we shall not pursue effects of scope economies here, but consider only the effects of scale economies on optimal pricing.

The marginal cost-pricing "solution"

Demand is given by the function $q = q(P)$, where P is market price. We accept consumer surplus as our measure of consumer welfare:

$$CS + TR = \int_0^q P(q)\, dq.$$

Total welfare, W, will be represented by consumer surplus plus producer surplus, or $CS + TR - TC$,[16] where total cost is $(b + \beta(q))q$. The social problem is therefore to maximize

$$W = \int_0^q P(q)\, dq - (b + \beta(q))q. \tag{36}$$

Necessary conditions for a solution to this problem yield the efficient pricing rule,

$$P = b + \beta(q) + q\, \partial\beta/\partial q. \tag{37}$$

Since $b + \beta(q) + q\, \partial\beta/\partial q$ in (37) is long-run marginal cost, we see once again that the efficient price equals long-run marginal cost.

In this case of decreasing average cost, a price equal to marginal cost causes a problem. With $\beta > 0$ and $\partial\beta/\partial q < 0$, marginal cost lies below average cost, so the marginal cost price is below average cost and will result in a net loss for the firm. If the firm is privately owned, it will not survive to reach the social optimum at a marginal cost price that does not cover costs. Indeed, even a community-owned firm might not accept losses from pricing at marginal cost, in part because of objections on equity grounds.

---

[15] See Baumol et al. (1982).

[16] The problem we examine here was set out as equation (32) in Section 2.5 with a more general cost function. For a game theory approach, see Sorenson, Tschirhart, and Whinston (1976).

If nonusers of the service were required to contribute to make up the deficit, that could be deemed unfair. This is the problem that results from pursuing efficiency without paying compensation to those who are made worse off. In specific cases, losers might object so vociferously that no project could win approval through political institutions, although if the gains and losses from many projects were distributed evenly over the population, there would be net gains in efficiency.

Notice that if political institutions become involved in a decision about the pricing of this service, the number of persons who gain and the number who lose could be crucial in any voting outcome. If majority rule is used in the decision, for example, and those benefiting from a price below average cost outnumber those who do not use the service but are forced through taxes to contribute to its support, the price below average cost might be adopted. Indeed, then the price might even be set below marginal cost. This result illustrates how inefficient outcomes might be chosen through political institutions, and how minority interests can suffer as a consequence. Even though political institutions cannot be counted on to balance subtly the equity and efficiency interests in economic problems, they often are regarded as the *legitimate* arbiters, so their role inevitably will be important.

Pricing at marginal cost in the example above will cause a loss, and funds to cover that loss are not easily obtained. Taxes or other means of raising revenue themselves can cause a loss in efficiency, because they push prices away from marginal costs. If *all* means of raising money to meet the deficit cause price distortions, with consequent inefficiencies, then the price in (37) itself cannot be efficient and it should be raised, so it will share with other available means the task of covering the deficit. Thus, as it is posed, the problem in (36) ignores the fact that a deficit will result that may not be covered without introducing inefficiencies. Modifying (36) to require that revenues cover cost can take us to the general problem of second-best pricing, pricing that achieves as great a level of social welfare as possible in the presence of realities that prevent the use of prices equal to marginal costs.

Second-best pricing with decreasing cost

One way to deal with cases in which pricing a service at long-run marginal cost will result in a deficit is to charge a higher price. Lump-sum taxes are generally infeasible, and financing the deficit by other means such as taxation can have income redistribution consequences that are unacceptable. Perhaps those who do not use the service would have to pay taxes to support its deficit, for instance, and that is regarded as unfair. To avoid this result, the community might require that all costs of the service be met by payments from users of the service. A socially optimal price can still be pursued, but subject to the requirement that sufficient revenues be raised to cover total cost. The resulting problem belongs to a general class of problems called *second best,* which are examined in detail in Chapter 5.[17] Solving such a problem yields a result as close as possible to the ideal, or welfare maximizing, solution, but subject to some unavoidable limitation or constraint.

We can illustrate the second-best problem by appending to (36) a constraint that revenues equal cost $(Pq = (b + \beta(q)q)$:

$$L = \int_0^q P(q)\,dq - (b + \beta(q))q - \lambda[Pq - (b + \beta(q))q]. \tag{38}$$

Maximizing L with respect to q we obtain

$$\frac{P - (b + \beta(q) + q\,\partial\beta/\partial q)}{P} = \frac{\lambda}{1 - \lambda}\frac{1}{\xi}, \tag{39}$$

where $\xi = (\partial q/\partial P)(P/q)$ is the elasticity of demand. From the constraint that total revenue must equal total cost, as long as average cost intersects the demand curve from below, we know that price must equal average cost. Notice also that the price in (39) is like a monopoly price except for the $\lambda/(1 - \lambda)$ term, which lowers the markup over long-run marginal cost to the level that will allow the firm merely to break even. That the second-best price is some fraction of a monopoly price holds also in the multiple-product or service case, where "average cost" is not so well defined.

If $i = 1, \ldots, n$ services are to be provided and they are independent of one another, the same procedure followed in solving (38) will yield for the ith service the pricing rule:

$$\frac{P_i - MC_i}{P_i} = \frac{\lambda}{1 - \lambda}\frac{1}{\xi_i}, \quad i = 1, \ldots, n.$$

Such prices are called Ramsey prices after the discoverer of their properties in the form of optimal taxes (Ramsey 1927). With multiple services, average cost per service is not easy to define, but we know the solution value of λ will allow total revenue that covers total cost. Here again the similarity to monopoly pricing is striking. Every ratio of price minus marginal cost over price is modified from the monopoly level by the same constant, $\lambda/(1 - \lambda)$, to yield revenue merely sufficient to cover total cost. It is as if all elasticities are multiplied by the same constant to make them larger. Ramsey prices thus eliminate the deficit while minimizing the loss in welfare that results.

---

[17] For game theory approaches, see Sorenson, Tschirhart, and Whinston (1978).

Nonuniform pricing

Obviously, one reason that we have had difficulty in pricing with economies of scale is that we have presumed a single uniform price must be set. Suppose instead that we use prices that are not uniform over all units consumed. With the decreasing cost technology that we have considered, for example, think of every incremental unit as a separate product. Suppose also that there is only one consumer. Then let us set prices that vary exactly with marginal cost for every unit:

$$P(q) = \beta(q) + b. \tag{40}$$

This is a *quantity-dependent* price schedule, in that the marginal price varies with the quantity that the individual consumes. Every unit is asked to pay the marginal cost of providing it in (40), which is ideal. By applying the marginal cost-pricing solution to every unit in this way, we can avoid a deficit, too, and thereby solve the decreasing cost problem.

A nonuniform price for a single good or service may not persist, of course, when there are many consumers, since exchange would allow consumers to trade until they agreed on a single price. But nonuniform prices can be used where exchange is not possible, or at least where it is not easy, which is often the case with public services. Two consumers cannot exchange electricity easily, for instance, or phone service, so a degree of nonuniform pricing is feasible for those services. Indeed, we are all quite familiar with telephone rates that involve a fixed monthly fee plus a fee for usage, at least for long-distance calls, which makes the average price nonuniform. And electricity rates for marginal units per time period often vary as total units consumed vary.

Difficulties still remain for nonuniform prices. For example, if there are many consumers, which of them may buy at low prices and which must pay high prices? No problem of this sort would exist if there were only one consumer, but it arises when the actions of many must be coordinated and the seller does not know the demand of each. For then, since the same price schedule must be offered to all consumers, some may pay higher marginal prices than others because they prefer smaller quantities, even though the marginal cost of serving them is identical. However, it may be possible to present each with a schedule like that in (40), so all pay higher prices for their earliest consumption units each period and lower prices approaching marginal cost for later units, and because their demands are similar they all choose virtually the same quantity. Then if resale by consumers is infeasible, an ideal solution to the decreasing cost-pricing problem is in principle achievable.

When a nonuniform price can improve welfare, there still may be problems in conveying its details to consumers so that they can choose soundly.

Approximation may be desirable, to achieve some benefit of optimal pricing and yet not overburden consumers with price schedules so complex that they must attend school just to understand them. A crude approximation can be accomplished, for example, by a *two-part price*. Under it the supplier could set a price per marginal unit at b and charge a fixed fee, for consuming even one unit in a given time period, to cover what otherwise would be a deficit. If n consumers each consumed the same quantity, $\hat{q}$, the appropriate fixed fee would be $\beta(n\hat{q})/n$. And if all consumers willingly paid this fee, an ideal approximation would be made to the nonuniform price in (40), as demonstrated effectively by Coase (1946).

Since the fixed fee of our two-part price is merely an approximation of the solution and does not faithfully reflect the cost of consuming a first unit, results under it might be distorted away from the ideal. If consumers differed in their demands, for example, some who intend to consume smaller amounts might find the fixed fee so high that they would decide not to consume at all, even though they might willingly pay more than the true marginal cost of their small consumption. In such a case, if a two-part price is to be used, departures from marginal cost should be made consistently, in order to minimize the welfare loss from resulting distortions, as they were under second-best Ramsey prices. The fixed fee should be lowered, for instance, and the price per unit should be raised above marginal cost of b, to make each of the two prices comply with Ramsey pricing principles. Even where attention must be paid in this way to Ramsey principles, a nonuniform price still offers greater scope for conveying information to consumers about the effects of their decisions on costs.

2.7   Information and welfare

Before leaving our discussion of ways to represent economic welfare, it is useful to illustrate how information can affect it. To do so we shall consider the pricing problem that arises when the seller does not know individual demands. Suppose there is a fixed cost, B, and constant marginal unit cost, b, for any quantity of output; thus total cost is $B + bq$. We already noted that, if consumers are similar in their demands, a two-part price may serve ideally in a situation like this (Coase 1946). But if consumers differ considerably in their demands, so that some intending to consume small quantities find it better to forgo consumption of the good rather than pay the fixed fee asked of them, the outcome may be nonoptimal. Indeed, we shall construct an example in which one consumer decides not to consume, making necessary a rise in the fixed fee for other customers. Of course, if the supplier knew everyone's demand, he could charge marginal cost per unit and a different fixed fee to every consumer,

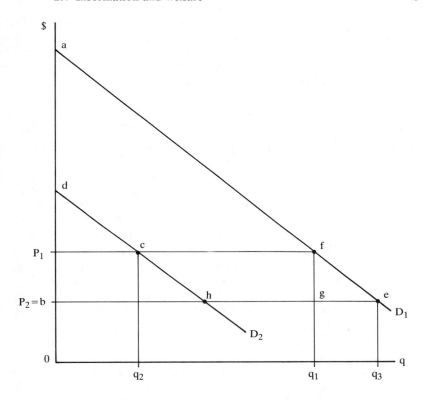

Figure 2.5. An example where a two-part price causes harm.

making the fee always less than consumer surplus. Then as long as total consumer surplus exceeded fixed cost the service could be provided, and with positive benefit in economic welfare.

Thus the problem of pricing in this decreasing cost situation involves not only technology, the source of decreasing cost that can handicap the functioning of a competitive market, but also information. The seller *does not know* consumers' demands, except in the aggregate. Lacking information about individual demands, the seller cannot find the optimal price structure for each one. Some observations are still possible about optimal pricing in this situation, however.

Consider our simple cost situation with marginal cost of b per unit and fixed cost B, as in Figure 2.5. Suppose, first, that every consumer has the same demand at D_1. To be eligible to buy at b, each consumer would also be required to pay a fixed fee. Each consumer would then be willing to pay as fixed fee an amount up to that represented by the area abE in Figure 2.5. If there are n consumers, the fixed fee per consumer that will cover all costs is B/n, and as long as that is less than abE the service can be provided. Indeed, this is an ideal solution if no consumer decides not to use the service because of the fixed fee, since all consumers contribute to fixed costs and are able to consume at marginal cost per unit.

An equal sharing of fixed cost among consumers may cause a problem when consumers differ in their demands and the seller does not know demands, if the fixed fee drives away consumers who use small amounts of service. In Figure 2.5 we illustrate a case with two consumers whose demands for units of a service are shown as D_1 and D_2, assuming zero income elasticity of demand (no income effect). Let us say that the price, P_1, is equal to the average cost of producing quantity $q_1 + q_2$: $P_1 = b + B/(q_1 + q_2)$. Consumer 1 consumes q_1 units at price P_1 while consumer 2 consumes q_2 at that price. Suppose a fixed fee at the level of $F = B/2$ is introduced, a fee equal for both consumers, which entitles customers to consume units at $P_2 = b = $ marginal cost. This new two-part price structure replaces the uniform price P_1, which no longer is available. It is possible that a fixed fee equal to one-half B will exceed the consumer surplus for consumer 2 at marginal price b, the area dbh. Then consumer 2 will decide not to purchase, and will be worse off than at the price of P_1 where consumer surplus of dP_1c was available. With consumer 2 out of the market, consumer 1 will have to pay *all* of the capacity cost and is bound to be worse off than with the uniform price of P_1. Thus the two-part tariff with equal fixed fees has made things worse than they were under the simple price-equals-average-cost-per-unit tariff.

What is needed to make two-part prices effective is information about consumer willingness to pay, so a two-part price can be tailored to the situation of each. Such information is hidden from the seller. Even if they are asked, consumers have incentive to understate their willingness to pay, hoping to mislead the seller in order to obtain a lower fee. But it is possible to give consumers a choice through which they reveal their situation at the same time they face an appropriate rate tariff. The principle involved is called *self-selection,* because under it consumers will select themselves into the appropriate rate category. Using this possibility of choice by consumers among alternative two-part tariffs, a resulting "block" tariff was shown by Willig (1978) to benefit every consumer and also the seller, compared with any uniform price above marginal cost. Willig also proved that the lowest marginal price should be equal to marginal cost. We shall illustrate his argument.

Suppose that, in the Figure 2.5 example, consumers were given a choice for a certain time period of either paying P_1 per unit *or* paying the fixed

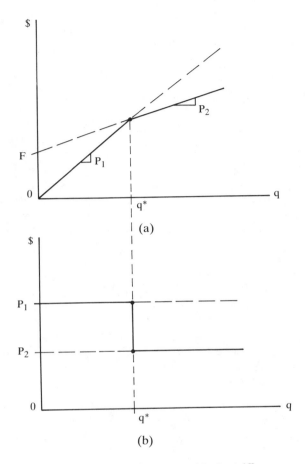

Figure 2.6. An example of a block tariff.

fee and thereafter P_2 per unit. Figure 2.6 illustrates the outlays they have to make for different quantities under the two price structures. Two outlay schedules are shown in Figure 2.6, one at a simple per-unit price of P_1 and the other requiring a fixed payment F after which a price of P_2 per unit is required. Up to quantity q^* the simple P_1 price per unit allows the lowest outlay, and that is what consumer 2 would prefer. At quantities above q^* the two-part price involving F and P_2 allows a lower outlay. Thus, if they are given a choice, we should expect to find consumers along the solid portions of the two outlay schedules in Figure 2.6a rather than the dashed portions. Prices in the solid-line portions dominate dashed-line portions of the outlay schedules. The rates per unit, and the way they switch at q^*, are shown by the solid line in Figure 2.6b. The tariff shown in Figure 2.6 is called a *block tariff*, because a different price applies to different blocks of the quantity range. A block tariff is of course a non-uniform tariff, since price does not remain constant over all quantities consumed.

Giving the consumer a choice among tariffs can improve economic welfare compared with either of the P_1 or F plus P_2 rate structures taken by itself, and such choices can be offered through a block tariff. We already noticed for the two-part tariff in Figures 2.5 and 2.6 that P_1 could have an advantage over F plus P_2 if consumers differed substantially in the amount they would tend to consume and in the consumer surplus benefit they enjoyed. With a choice of rate structures, the consumer who wishes to consume more is bound to be better off by having access to marginal usage at marginal cost. And out of this benefit it should be possible to adjust F and P_1 so that P_1 is lower, in which case the consumer wanting less of the service also will benefit.

To see this effect suppose consumers can *either* purchase at the uniform price of P_1 *or* pay a fixed fee $F = q^*t$ for the right to buy at the lower marginal price of $P_1 - t$. At the quantity q^*, revenue to a seller will be the same whichever choice a consumer makes. A consumer with income y^i who selects the uniform price has indirect utility $v^i(P_1, \ldots, P_n, y^i)$ while one who selects the two-part price has indirect utility $v^i(P_1 - t, P_2, \ldots, P_n, y^i - q^*t)$. A household will therefore prefer the two-part tariff if

$$dv^i(P_1 - t, P_2, \ldots, P_n, y^i - q^*t)/dt > 0, \tag{41}$$

taking the derivative where $t = 0$. From (17) and (20) we know that

$$v^i(P_1, \ldots, P_n, y^i)/P_j = -q_j^i v^i(P_1, \ldots, P_n, y^i)/y^i. \tag{42}$$

Using (42), we can interpret (41) at $t = 0$ as

$$\left.\frac{dv^i}{dt}\right|_{t=0} = -\frac{v^i}{P_1} - \frac{v^i}{y^i}q^* = \frac{v^i}{y^i}(q_1^i - q^*). \tag{43}$$

Since we can be sure that additional income increases utility, or $\partial v^i/\partial y^i > 0$, we know from (43) that

$$\left.\frac{dv^i}{dt}\right|_{t=0} \quad \begin{array}{l} > 0 \text{ if } q_1^i > q^*, \\ \leq 0 \text{ if } q_1^i \leq q^*. \end{array}$$

Thus consumers of quantities above q^* will choose the two-part tariff, whereas those who choose lesser quantities will prefer the uniform price.

To be sure that the benefits of a block tariff, or a choice of tariffs, can be achieved, it must be in the interests of the enterprise to offer it. We need *incentive compatibility,* meaning that incentives of the firm are compatible with its offering the preferred rate structure to consumers. Of the two price structures we considered, a single average cost price of P_1 is preferred by the firm over the two-part price with price per unit P_2 and fixed charge $F = B/2$, which will drive consumer 2 from the market and leave the firm with a loss of $B/2$. If consumers are allowed a choice of tariffs, the same revenue can be obtained from consumer 2 as under the $P_1 = $ average-cost tariff. From Figure 2.5 we can see that a fixed fee of F equal to the value of the reduction in unit price $(P_1 - P_2)q_1$, or the area $P_1 fg P_2$, could be charged to consumer 1 for the right to purchase at unit price P_2, and this would yield the same revenue to the firm. But consumer 1 would be willing to consume q_3 units at the marginal price per unit of P_2, and would enjoy the added benefit represented by the consumer surplus triangle *fge.* The consumer therefore would be willing to pay a fixed fee up to the larger area $P_1 fe P_2$, which means *more* revenue could be raised by the firm. Thus the firm will want to offer the choice between tariffs that will improve welfare, and consumers will want to accept it; the desirable offering is incentive compatible. (A general proof of this result may be found in Willig 1978.)

A tariff involving three blocks is illustrated in Figure 2.7, which shows a total outlay for any quantity represented first by the line *ab* having slope of P_1 for quantities up to q_1. A lower slope or marginal price of P_2 is represented in the total outlay line *cd* for quantities from q_1 to q_2, and a still lower marginal price of P_3 is represented in the total outlay line *ef* for quantities above q_2. The marginal prices are illustrated in Figure 2.7. There it is clear that the marginal price begins at P_1 for the block of consumption quantities up to q_1, then switches to P_2 for quantities up to q_2, and switches to P_3 for quantities above q_2. Notice that to maximize economic welfare the lowest marginal price, P_3, must equal marginal cost, for otherwise an opportunity to bring benefit to the consumer must go unexploited.

When they have large regions where marginal price is constant, it is easier to use block tariffs for market-level analysis, assuming consumers differ in their incomes or tastes and therefore in their demands. A division between groups of consumers will be created through self-selection at each price jump, as illustrated for the change from P_2 to P_3 in Figure 2.7. Consumers with demands to the left of D_1 at price P_2 who demand q_1 and q_1' units will pay P_2. Consumers with demands of the sort represented by D_1 or greater will switch into price block P_3. From paying P_2 at q_1' to paying P_3 at q_2' the consumer shown is indifferent, because the shaded areas are equal; the loss suffered on units from q_1' to q_2, where price exceeds the consumer's willingness to pay, is offset by the gain on units from q_2 to q_2', where consumer willingness to pay exceeds price. If

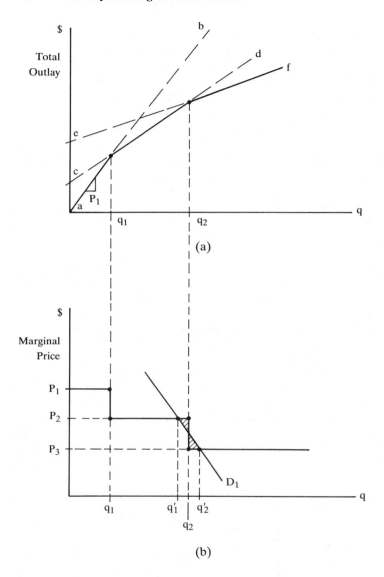

Figure 2.7. The choice between two blocks of a block tariff.

other consumers have similarly sloped demands, no one will consume a quantity between q_1' and q_2'. Demands within each price block are at the same marginal price and can reasonably be aggregated, so market-level analysis is still possible.

2.8   Risk and welfare

Risk obviously can affect regulation, since risk of firm failure and the harm it would bring to innocent parties is what motivates bank and insurance industry regulation. Its role in monopoly regulation is also quite pronounced. We shall consider its detailed analysis only selectively, simply because so many other matters require attention, but general discussion of its influence will quite often be necessary. Here we present a brief sketch of expected utility as a way of representing welfare in the presence of risk, and we also comment on expected consumer surplus as a welfare measure.

Individual utility can be affected by risk. Consider a lottery that offers income y with probability w and income Y with probability $1-w$. The expected value of this lottery is

$$E(\text{value}) = wy + (1-w)Y.$$

The expected utility may differ from expected value, of course, and if we suppress prices – regarding them as unchanging so utility depends only on income – we have

$$E(\text{utility}) = wu(y) + (1-w)u(Y).$$

The effect of risk on utility can be seen as any difference that arises between this expected utility of the lottery and the utility of the expected value of the lottery, or $u(wy + (1-w)Y)$.

An example is shown in Figure 2.8 where $w = 1/2 = (1-w)$. This utility-of-income function indicates that risk is undesirable, since the utility of the expected value $(u(y/2 + Y/2))$ is higher than the expected utility of the lottery $(u(y)/2 + u(Y)/2)$. The individual with the utility-of-income function shown in Figure 2.8 would thus rather have the expected value of the lottery with certainty than accept the lottery and thereby gamble on receiving a value either higher (Y) or lower (y). This tendency toward risk aversion is widespread in the population. Perhaps we learn from experience to avoid risk because it brings pain when we lose. Or perhaps aversion to risk is a trait that has raised the likelihood of survival, so only those of us who have it remain in the population.

The shape of the utility-of-income function in Figure 2.8 is consistent with diminishing utility of income, which was routinely assumed before ordinal utility came into use with its weaker assumptions. Obviously, when marginal utility of income diminishes, the gain on an even money bet will give a smaller increment in utility than the loss will take away, so an even money bet is unattractive and the person with such utility is averse to risk. The opposite curvature would represent increasing marginal utility of income, which is consistent with risk-loving, or gambling, behavior. A

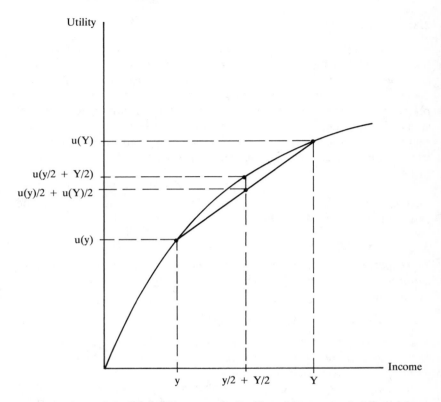

Figure 2.8. Diminishing marginal utility of income and risk aversion.

person with a linear relationship between utility and income would be regarded as risk-neutral.

Indeed, a convenient measure of risk aversion can be formed from the curvature of the utility of income (or, more generally, wealth) function. Since curvature depends on the second derivative, it is natural to use it when representing risk aversion. The Arrow (1970) and Pratt (1964) measure of absolute risk aversion (*ARA*) is thus

$$ARA = -\frac{u''(y)}{u'(y)}.$$

A measure of relative risk aversion (*RRA*) is sometimes useful and may take the form

$$RRA = -\frac{yu''(y)}{u'(y)}.$$

Such representations, and indeed the whole question of how best to represent behavior under risk, are presently the subject of active research (Machina 1987).

We shall use expected utility as a welfare representation on occasion, and also expected consumer surplus. The latter measure essentially assumes risk neutrality, since it merely makes the source of uncertainty take the form of shifts in demand, and the measure is average consumer surplus. It can be quite easy to analyze, however, and the results of using it can easily be compared to analysis under certainty.

2.9   Summary

Our first concern in this chapter was to express precisely individual benefit from a social decision, such as a change in the price of a government-regulated good or service. We find that we cannot claim there is a perfect and unique measure of individual benefit, but a practical measure that is based on observable demand curves – consumer surplus – is reasonably accurate for most uses. We noted also that if more than one price is affected by a social decision, care must be taken in considering also the effects in substitute or complement markets.

We then considered the aggregation of individual measures into social welfare measures, which for consumer surplus can be described as going from *consumer's* surplus to *consumers'* surplus. To make this transition in the simple cases considered here, individuals must be weighted somehow to make up a combined representation of social welfare. One solution to this weighting problem is to weight individuals in society by the reciprocals of their marginal utilities of income. This weighting essentially accepts the present income distribution, and regards any benefit as equally desirable for soceity, no matter who receives it. Applications with several representations of welfare showed that socially optimal prices will equal marginal costs. Where economies of scale cause marginal cost to be below average cost, marginal cost prices may cause losses, and welfare representations then are valuable in analyzing optimal departures of price from marginal cost. Allowing consumers to select a rate structure based on the quantity they consume can lead to improvements in part by conveying information about demands to the seller. Representations of attitude toward risk were discussed briefly, since there are situations to be analyzed where risk plays an important role.

In Part II we develop optimal prices using economic welfare as a goal according to the representations introduced here. Before examining such optimal pricing, however, we consider in Chapter 3 the problem of inducing a monopoly firm to pursue the welfare goal.

Questions

2.1. In the analysis of compensating and equivalent variations in Section 2.2 and Figure 2.3 the good under consideration is normal, since more of it is consumed when real income increases. Carry out the analysis for an inferior good (see n. 9 for a definition of normal and inferior goods), of which less will be consumed when real income increases. How is the result of the analysis affected when the good is inferior rather than normal?

2.2. In Section 2.3 is is argued that conditions on individual utility functions (see equation (24)) make it likely that no serious ambiguity will arise in evaluating consumer surplus for multiple products that are substitutes or complements, because they tend to help satisfy equation (23). But market demand functions could involve not merely aggregation over the same individuals: Some individuals might leave and enter the markets as prices change. Could this tend to make a unique measure of consumer surplus more elusive when multiple products are involved?

2.3. Professor William Vickery (1955) presented an example involving a train that is to be operated from A to B and return, and the question is whether it should also go on to C and return. If there were many trains (divisible service units), and only some continued on to C, then ideal conditions could be satisfied on each part of the trip, but with only one train an either-or decision must be reached. Travel from A to B will be called one leg of the train trip and B to C another, with the returns also called legs. Constant returns to scale prevail and costs are of three kinds: 20 cents per seat per day for capital and similar charges on the equipment, independent of the distance operated; 30 cents per seat for operating expenses for each leg of the trip; 10 cents per passenger for each leg of the trip for wear and tear on the equipment, cleaning, and service to passengers. It is assumed that equipment can be found to make the train up to any desired number of seats at strictly proportional costs. But it is impractical to change the makeup of the train at B, so that if it is to run through to C at all the entire train that traveled from A to B must be run to C. Demand each way for the AB leg is linear, ranging from 2,000 passengers at a price of zero to a maximum price of \$2.00 that the most eager passenger is willing to pay; demand each way for the BC leg is one-fourth as great, ranging up to 500 passengers at a zero price, with the same maximum price of \$2.00.

(a) Calculate the maximum sum of consumer surplus profit that is obtainable through optimal prices and capacity for serving A to B and return, and also for serving A to B to C and return.

(b) "Should" train service be extended to C, on the basis of your results in (a)?

CHAPTER 3

Pursuing economic welfare

3.1 Introduction

Market competition is driven by the pursuit of profit. Through one of the marvels of economic life, when competition can function perfectly this profit-seeking behavior is harnessed to provide a maximum of economic welfare. Economic welfare is seldom profitable to pursue directly, however, and incentives having this purpose are hard to develop, so when competition cannot operate well, alternative institutions may not be any more effective at promoting welfare. We know that economic welfare is a sophisticated conception that can be elusive to measure, and alternative institutions can be expected to have other goals, goals that do not serve the general welfare reliably.

The competitive process must be seen as a regulator of economic activity in evaluating other means of regulation, so we begin with a brief review of competition and how it brings about the pursuit of economic welfare. For one reason or another, competition may not be relied upon, and instead monopoly franchises may be awarded with governmental protection from entry by others. We examine the general difficulty of pursuing economic welfare through political institutions, and also how inimical to welfare their major instrument, the statutory monopoly, may be. We describe information and incentive schemes that are intended to induce desirable behavior in protected monopoly markets. Under certain conditions one aspect of competition, free entry, can force pursuit of welfare even in markets where only one supplier is the lowest cost form of market organization. So we examine free entry in what is called a *contestable* market, which can function if there is no sunk cost and if *sustainable* prices can prevent entry from occurring where it is legally permitted. The properties of sustainable prices are important since they may be forced on an incumbent firm when it wants to prevent entry by others, and also because they possess properties of axiomatic cost-sharing prices that are desirable for their own sake.

3.2   The great regulator: competition

In the United States and in most other market economies, alternative ways of regulating economic activity have been adopted where, for one reason or another, competitive markets do not perform the regulation function adequately. In adopting extramarket forms of regulation, we incur added administrative costs, for competition can function with remarkably low coordinating costs. Moreover, in a well-functioning competitive system, profit-seeking firms act to discipline one another so their combined actions serve to maximize economic welfare. Alternative forms of regulation lack this disciplining function, but are undertaken because of some drawback of competition in the specific circumstances. Because extramarket regulation still occurs within a market economy, knowledge of market processes is needed to apply it soundly, and indeed such knowledge is crucial to the diagnosis and choice of appropriate regulatory action. We present here a brief sketch of the benefits of regulation by competition in a market economy.

One simple observation is at the base of what we think is good, or at least potentially good, about the way resources are allocated to alternative uses in a well-functioning competitive market economy: If two persons trade, we may assume they both benefit. The consequence of this result is embodied in perhaps the weakest of economic value judgments, *Pareto optimality*,[1] which is achieved only when no trade remains that can benefit one person without harming another. Of course, the simple case of two traders involves only exchange, and it takes some analysis to project its benefits to the act of production too. But the case can be made, and regulation in the right circumstances can deliver it.

When technology and other conditions in a market economy combine to allow competition to function, it is a great regulator of economic activity. One of the main reasons is that competition forces the suppliers of goods to keep the cost low and to produce only as long as marginal cost does not exceed market price. Relative productivity must be the same for all pairs of inputs, because suppliers all face the same input prices in competitive markets and must equalize productivity per dollar to be efficient. The sanction applied against firms to bring about production efficiency is the harshest of enforcement mechanisms; in competition with others, enterprises that fail to satisfy consumers with adequate quality in relation to cost do not *survive*. In competitive markets consumers have many suppliers, and so if one does not satisfy them they will turn to others. Entry

---

[1] In honor of the Italian economist and sociologist, Vilfredo Pareto, whose contributions are described in Allais (1968).

is unlimited, too, so a new firm may come into a market and force an inefficient one out of business. Thus, one side effect of competition, whether from within or from outside a market, is that firms fail. But consumers can be well served when the competitive process weeds out less efficient firms and imposes efficiency in those remaining.

Production at lowest possible cost is desirable in itself. But while bringing about that result, competitive markets involve consumers in crucial ways also, so that consumers determine what products actually are produced, for markets also can achieve an outcome that we called consumption efficiency in Chapter 1, in which all consumers place the same relative marginal valuation on every pair of goods. Many consumers being willing to trade in competitive markets will cause this result by forcing a single price to reign for each good. At equilibrium, a single ratio of prices for every possible pair of goods will then be faced by all consumers. If a consumer values one unit of any good relative to a unit of another good differently from those prices, he or she can benefit by trading. But eventually no exchange that offers such benefit will remain, and at that point all consumers have the same marginal relative values for every pair of goods.

Imagine an alternative arrangement, whereby economic activity is organized so that central planners specify what is to be produced. Competing firms supply those goods, and suppose they do it at minimum cost. Even with low-cost production, the ensuing consumer satisfaction might not be as high as possible because the goods and their quantities may not be those that consumers value most; the market-clearing price ratios for every pair of goods may not equal the corresponding ratio of marginal costs. Under competition, the price at which a good or service sells will reflect exactly the cost of marginal inputs needed in its production; prices equal marginal costs. So in competitive markets, where consumers compare relative prices in choosing what to consume, they also face relative marginal costs that represent the true technological opportunities open to them. When they achieve consumption efficiency, where all consumers have the same marginal relative valuation for every pair of goods, those valuations will match exactly relative marginal costs, and no further change, of output mixture or of alternative input uses, can improve one consumer's position without harming another; this is Pareto optimality again. Besides efficient consumption, this point involves efficient production. The relative marginal costs from efficient production match the relative valuations of consumers for the goods, which means the consumers want no change in the mix of goods being produced, given their genuine technological opportunities.

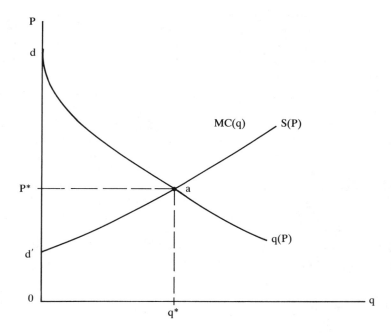

Figure 3.1. Demand, supply, and total surplus.

Having many consumers can prevent exploitation of sellers (as by a single buyer) and can force sales to occur at the single price. As a result, the demand for a product can be well defined for every price, as shown in Figure 3.1 (which is like Figure 2.1). Having many competing producers in a market, and still others who can freely join in when the price rises, will force each one to seek production at a low cost per unit in order to survive. Competition among such producers can force price to equal marginal cost. Supply behavior can then be represented for every price by an industry marginal cost curve; one is presented in Figure 3.1 (the supply curve is from Figure 2.2). Since consumers then face in market prices the true opportunities that resources and technology allow, their demands might be described as enlightened, in that each demand indicates wants for one good from all those genuinely available. Consumers and/or producers will be motivated to take action until all benefits available to both are fully exploited, which will occur at quantity q^* and price P^* in Figure 3.1. Any smaller quantity will lead to a higher price than P^*, which will invite increased output. The reverse is true for any quantity above q^*. Notice that consumer surplus daP^*, plus producer surplus $d'aP^*$, is as great as it can be at P^*, q^*. Under such ideal conditions in the particular market of Figure 3.1, economic welfare in the form of consumer plus producer surplus is maximized. The goods consumers want most will be produced, and their costs will be as low as available resources and technologies allow.

Of course, this brief and abstract description of how a competitive market can deliver an ideal outcome ignores some important questions: whether consumers can ever be well enough informed about products and prices to choose so well, whether competition will be effective enough to force all prices equal to marginal costs so consumers can genuinely see available alternatives, whether technology will even permit competitive organization to survive as allocator of resources in all industries, or whether innovation will be optimally stimulated, and others. But even without these considerations the argument has a limitation: There is no unique result. A different distribution of wealth brings a different equilibrium outcome. Ideally, the market may allocate resources in a desirably efficient way, but the result is only as legitimate as the distribution of income and wealth on which it was based.

In some respects, markets actually help to determine the distribution of income, as more "able" persons become more valuable because the market allocates them to more valuable work. Also, interference with that market-determined rate of pay can reduce market efficiency. Although it is true that market-determined wages may help to allocate labor efforts and thereby improve overall economic productivity (there is room for debate about this when information is not free and perfect), that effectiveness alone does not make the income distribution inherently proper or correct. A society of barbarians could leave a very talented artist unemployed (or perhaps worse), or dishonest dealers might prosper where rules for proper behavior are hard to enforce. The question of income or wealth distribution remains one that deserves debate and can influence outcomes. Yet the question of income or wealth distribution is not amenable to the same kind of efficiency analysis that can be applied to minimizing cost. So economists often try to consider income distribution separately, preferably to devise policies that can affect it in ways that are already socially agreed upon. Methods of pursuing efficiency are less controversial, and economic analysis often is focused on them rather than on income distribution. That is why economists seem to show little interest in hot political questions, which often affect income distribution (Blinder 1982, 1987; Rhoads 1985).

Given the great efficiency benefits of competition compared with other forms of market regulation, the most important question for us is, When can competition among sellers work to ensure their efficient production and cause sound pricing of goods and services? Or when will competition fail? In Chapter 1 we noted that externalities and firm failure could cause difficulties. But we emphasized how technology might allow firms to be efficient only at sizes so large that few suppliers could operate, perhaps only one. Competition would seem to fail if the technology gave each producer such great scale economies in relation to the size of the market that all output demanded could be provided at lowest cost by one producer, particularly if costly and durable investments were necessary. With two producers serving the entire market, the marginal cost for each would be below average cost and if they competed, so that prices equaled marginal costs, both would lose money. In such circumstances a single producer has often been installed, to be called a "natural monopoly," and has been protected from new entry through a government grant of monopoly franchise.

3.3   Government intervention

Other institutions besides markets influence economic activity in Western countries, and the way welfare is expressed and even the extent to which it is pursued can depend on them. Courts become involved when regulatory agencies and firms disagree. Political institutions create regulatory institutions and often are seen as legitimate ultimate arbiters. Constitutional checks and balances in the structure of the U.S. government may be seen as an example (although certainly one too complex to analyze here) of elements, such as entry and competition, that make government more accountable. When there are shared responsibilities among the three branches of government, as in foreign policy, one branch may encroach on and thereby discipline another. Political institutions seldom function as markets do to generate economic welfare, however, and some awareness of their different structure is valuable in considering their role in the process of regulation.

A social consensus, sometimes given the form of legislative statute, may help to settle disputes by favoring one position over another. For instance, lowering a price by eliminating monopoly advantage will harm shareholders of the monopoly while benefiting consumers, but a long tradition of denying monopoly advantage could allow action that simply ignored the harm to stockholders; their monopoly advantage would not be accepted as legitimate. On the other hand, a majority might also impose its will unfairly on a minority when majority voting is used for resolving social issues. This problem of settling disputes about collective action is a problem of social choice.

Table 3.1. *An example of inconsistency in
majority voting*

	Individual preference rankings		
Project	Smith	Jones	Brown
Airport	1	3	2
Bridge	2	1	3
Coliseum	3	2	1

Social choice, or *public choice,* is a field of study concerned specifically
with how collective choices might be well made even between possible Pareto optima.[2] The prevalent institution of social choice in western democ-
racies is that of voting by individuals, rather than market transactions,
and one common voting scheme we are all familiar with is majority voting. As a social choice rule, majority voting is surprisingly different from
individual choice; majority voting easily can lead to intransitive, or inconsistent, choices which a rational individual is assumed never to make.

For example, given three possible expenditures a community might
make, an airport (A), a bridge (B), and a coliseum (C), it is possible for
a majority of the community's citizens to favor A over B, another majority B over C, and still another majority C over A, whereas one individual
would never be expected to fall into such irrationality.[3] The preference
or rankings of A, B, and C by three thoroughly rational individuals are
shown in Table 3.1. A majority (Smith and Brown) prefers A to B, a
majority (Smith and Jones) prefers B to C, and a majority (Jones and
Brown) prefers C to A. The way to avoid such inconsistency is to offer
only two options to the public for a vote, and then an odd number of
voters will assure a social choice by majority rule. Even then, whoever
controls the voting agenda can greatly influence the outcome (Plott and
Levine 1978). Our tendency to array political issues on a greatly simplified scale, from "right" to "left," may actually help to make majority rule
more effective, although it also cedes power to those who set the agenda.

[2] For major social choice analyses, see Arrow (1963), Buchanan and Tullock (1966), Feldman (1980), and Mueller (1980). Applications to regulation may be found in Buchanan
(1968) and in Maloney, McCormick, and Tollison (1984).
[3] This voting problem has been known as Condorcet's problem for over 200 years. For the
original treatment, see Caritat (1785). For a voting analysis of nuclear plant location, see
Wood (1981).

Inconsistency and other difficulties with majority voting were analyzed carefully by Kenneth Arrow (1963), who concluded that any procedure for determining social choice will have some feature that we ordinarily should regard as a flaw. He first showed desirable properties for social choice among at least three possibilities. These properties called for social choice (1) to be consistent, which was not the case in the majority voting example above, (2) to change always in the same direction as any individual's preferences changes, (3) to be based only on individual preferences for relevant alternatives, and (4) not to be imposed by a dictator. He then proved it impossible for a group to choose among the three or more alternative possibilities without violating at least one of the reasonable sounding properties he had described.

Condition (3), which requires independence of irrelevant alternatives, calls for choices to be based only on preferences for leading possibilities. Yet often the entry into an election campaign of a candidate with virtually no hope of winning a majority (and thus an irrelevant alternative) will have a crucial effect on the election. It is difficult to avoid such an effect, and it certainly is one we are accustomed to. Condition (2) may not be satisfied because voting is based essentially on rankings, and makes no allowance for intensity of feeling. In political bodies, intensity of feeling may operate through a process known as "log-rolling," whereby a representative who feels strongly about proposal A but is indifferent between noncompeting proposals B and C may trade away his vote on those issues in exchange for help on A. Thus, within legislatures intensity of feeling may find expression, even though decision by voting does not appear to give it scope.

Political institutions such as majority rule are also capable of generating perverse outcomes, as James Buchanan (1962) has demonstrated. Buchanan argued against replacing market institutions with governmental or political institutions simply because of imperfections or market failure, such as an externality, without plumbing possible imperfections in the alternative institution being embraced. He pointed out how, in the absence of carefully considered restrictions, a majority could bring repeated harm to a minority under seemingly democratic political procedures. So the difficulties of social choice may also lead to unfair outcomes, at least as possibilities.

Realizing the limitations of political mechanisms for social choice can be useful in tracing possible consequences when issues reach political institutions. Their inherent imperfections owe much to the fact that voting is less precise than market transactions as a means for expressing or for serving preferences. Voting, and political institutions in general, often are called upon to deal with difficult economic choices that markets cannot easily handle, so it is not surprising that problems in making the choices persist. Those problems may even invite parties who can exploit the imprecision of public choice to bring forward issues that they can use to their advantage in a political decision process.

Political influences in public utility and public enterprise pricing have been seen to a considerable degree, as a few examples will show. Peltzman (1971) found evidence that customers who were more numerous, and therefore more important politically, benefited relative to a minority of customers in regulated liquor pricing, but not in public utility pricing. Littlechild and Rousseau (1975) found that the rulings of a state regulatory commission favored residents of the state relative to customers who were not residents, and that pattern was obvious in Union Pacific rate setting deliberated in the *Smyth vs. Ames* (1898) decision (Huneke 1983). Waverman (1977) saw public enterprise telephone pricing in Great Britain as favoring richer customers. Jordan (1972) noticed that after regulation greater concentration developed in formerly oligopolistic and competitive industries. Jones (1985) observed lower prices for urban rather than rural customers of public enterprises in developing countries, and saw the political unimportance of rural constituents as one explanation. Kahn (1987) saw long-distance callers and travelers both suffering under rates set through telephone and airline regulation. And Posner (1971) regarded regulatory agencies generally as taxation authorities, able to confer benefits on politically effective customer groups at the expense of unorganized consumers.

An early, "public interest," theory of regulation envisaged a demand from the public at large for correction of inefficient or inequitable market practices, to which politicians responded (Johnson 1984). George Stigler (1971) conceived instead of suppliers (usually businessmen) who would benefit as providing the demand for regulation and politicians, in response, supplying it. His explanation is consistent with the view of Buchanan and Tullock (1966), who represented self-interested parties in the political decision process rather than altruistic actors sometimes postulated in political science. Gabriel Kolko's (1963) interpretation of early railroad regulation would be consistent with this self-interest pattern, as are portraits of other industries that came to be regulated (Anderson 1981 and Brock 1981). Stigler and Friedland (1962) had given empirical support to this view by finding that prices were not lower in states that introduced regulation. But that evidence could go the other way because imposition of a weak standard of significance, such as 10 percent, would find the regulated prices significantly lower. It was also claimed that over time regulators would be "captured" by the industries they were to regulate, and then regulation would favor the regulated firms. This process would be aided if regulators were drawn from the industry being regulated, and frequent movement from industry to regulatory position and return was suspiciously labeled the "revolving door." But work of this kind did not rely on the tools of economics and the presumption of self-interest as powerfully as the Buchanan and Tullock and Stigler approach did.

The mere possibility that governmental authority will grant a monopoly can change the situation fundamentally, as it causes parties to expend their effort to obtain the monopoly position (Posner 1975; Tullock 1967). An effort to obtain monopoly rents, called "rent seeking," can have allocative consequences that alter our assessment of welfare loss from monopoly. Suppose that a profit is expected from a statutory monopoly position that is to be awarded. Then resources equivalent to that expected profit might reasonably be devoted in an effort to attain the monopoly position by those who covet it. If that happens, the monopoly profit that ultimately results will not be a social benefit, as assumed in Chapter 2, because real resources will have been used up – perhaps in lawyers' time, for example – trying to obtain the monopoly profit. To the extent that profit is just a return to efforts made, deregulation that would eliminate it will be more difficult (McCormick, Shughart, and Tollison 1984). This sort of effect was not foreseen when economic regulation was first undertaken.

There can be no doubt that, in the early days of regulation in the United States, in the last quarter of the nineteenth century, markets were not regarded as robust institutions to be relied on extensively, whereas regulation by governmental institutions was seen as reliable and also costless. Professor Stigler has humorously likened the embrace of governmental regulation in view of market problems to a judge awarding a prize between two singers; on hearing the first, the judge immediately awarded the prize to the second. But the history of the twentieth century suggests that regulation frequently has served the regulated parties and indeed often was induced to do so at their urging (Posner 1969, 1974). The cost of political bodies reaching agreement for regulatory purposes is also seen now as being quite high (Ehrlich and Posner 1974), and so well-motivated urging probably was needed to bring it into existence. And yet government regulation of economic activity cannot be regarded as an outcome necessarily preferable to market competition. One reason is that the behavior of a statutory monopoly, created by governmental authority, will not reliably be ideal.

3.4   Behavior of a statutory monopoly

A monopoly franchise often has been awarded to the provider of a public service, with the provider being given statutory protection from entry

(Schmalensee 1979). The resulting monopoly might be a government department, such as the Virginia Alcoholic Beverage Control Department, which operates all liquor stores in that state; a government-owned enterprise such as the U.S. Postal Service; or a privately owned public utility such as Dominion Resources, which provides electricity in much of Virginia and part of North Carolina. Government departments are usually controlled by executive and legislative political institutions whereas more independent government-owned enterprises are often overseen by separate regulatory bodies such as the Postal Rate Commission, which regulates the U.S. Postal Service. All 50 states of the United States have regulatory agencies overseeing privately owned public utilities in their states. Here we examine briefly some questions about management effort, pricing, and service qualities that can arise in such a statutory monopoly.

Management effort

Once entry is forbidden, the engine of competition is derailed. After a monopoly has been awarded a service franchise, consumers typically will have virtually no alternative source of supply, no matter how poor the service or how high the price. The general possibility for anyone from anywhere to try to provide better service is foreclosed. A governmental organization may be created to oversee the monopoly provider of service, but that regulator is not apt to be as motivated as a potential competitor, nor as relentless as hordes of potential competitors would be. So managers will not be motivated to work as hard, and costs may be higher (Leibenstein 1966). There are many possible ways for a monopoly supplier to lower its service quality, too (Besanko, Donnenfeld, and White 1987; White 1972). Even if consumers could detect quality differences and transfer their purchases based on price-quality combinations to other suppliers if they existed, it is difficult for a regulator to follow all aspects of service quality in order to regulate it as fully. The result is a loophole in regulation that managers can exploit.

The monopoly may be privately owned by profit-seeking shareholders, or publicly owned without as intense an interest in profit. This lack of the public enterprise profit motive is sometimes thought to be beneficial, for it allows publicly responsible attention to nonfinancial goals, as is expected of a bureaucracy, and might avoid the distortions caused by monopoly pricing. But the goals of a public enterprise can be so vague that accountability is impossible, and inefficient performance may result against any of the desired goals. Monopolistic profit-seeking actions also may be undertaken simply because they make life easier for managers. Government enterprise is often adopted when goals are clear enough for one organization to pursue them independently, so it may have clearer, or at least narrower, goals than a government department. But the public enterprise has no group of residual profit-claiming shareholders who emphasize fiscal goals and enforce efficient performance by ousting managers.

Private ownership may allow greater reign to the profit motive in principle. But with entry barred and regulation imposed, the force of this motivation will be reduced (Williamson 1967). Salability of the legal right to operate a monopoly no longer induces the same cost-cutting incentive for efficiency when regulation protects the monopoly from entry and limits the profit that it can earn. In competitive markets, the rate of return depends on decisions of marginal entrants, who look at different possibilities and invest where returns are most attractive relative to risks. Although efforts have been made for many years under rate-of-return regulation to substitute regulators' estimates for these market-determined returns, they lack the necessary participation of entrants willing to commit their own funds. For that there simply is no substitute. Even if a rate of return could somehow be obtained as if it had come from potential entrants' judgments, the pressure on incumbents due to entrants' actual behavior would still be missing.

The statutory monopoly also will become the primary source of information about possibilities for the industry in its franchised area, whether ownership is public or private. Although the monopoly has some discretion, it probably will not suffer as a competitive firm would when it is wrong, because regulators either cannot appreciate its errors or will forgive them. Regulators cannot evaluate all decisions, and inefficient technologies might be chosen and used for years, for example, causing substantially higher prices for consumers. Since only slight threat from outsiders exists, there also is no great urge to innovate. It is easier in this protected, franchised, position to use the existing plant until it is worn out.

The price level

Although a statutory monopoly may be weakened, it can still be expected to have some of the urges of an unregulated monopoly, particularly when it comes to raising revenue from consumers. Regulation must contend with those motives because life will always be easier with more revenue, through means available to the monopoly. It is well known, for instance, that if a monopoly sets a uniform price it will want to set the price so that marginal cost is equal to marginal revenue, in order to maximize profit. The same motive arises in market competition, but there marginal revenue is forced by alternative suppliers to equal price ($dp/dq = 0$), and so having it also equal to marginal cost is ideal. A monopoly faces a downward-sloping demand, however. If inverse demand is $p(q)$, then marginal revenue for the monopoly is $p + q\,dp/dq$, where $dp/dq < 0$; so instead of setting price equal to marginal cost for maximizing welfare, the monopoly tendency is to set price above marginal cost, at $p = MC + q(-dp/dq)$. Of course, if management effort is not as great in the monopoly, the level of marginal cost may also be higher.

Coase (1972) raised an interesting question about the monopolist's capacity to charge such a price above marginal cost for an extremely durable product: If the monopolist's product would last forever, to take the case of extreme durability, then once all demand was met at the monopoly price, the seller would want to sell more units at a lower price. Indeed, the seller should continue until the price of the last unit equals marginal cost. In anticipation of this pricing behavior, the buyers may not pay the monopoly price and instead may wait until the price is reduced. If the good is purchased at the monopoly price and then more units are produced, the price of the purchased unit will fall and so the purchaser will take a loss. The argument has been analyzed powerfully (Gul, Sonnenschein, and Wilson 1986; Stokey 1981) and it holds up quite well. Thus, for an extremely durable product, the monopoly pricing incentive may need modification in the direction of competition.

Price discrimination

Classical price discrimination was set out by Pigou (1920), who expected that the power to discriminate would often accompany monopoly power. His analysis of the requirements for price discrimination is still to be recommended, for he discusses the subtleties of the necessary conditions, such as the impossibility of resale. He envisioned three degrees of discrimination, the first involving a different price for every unit purchased by every person, the prices so tellingly set that the monopoly obtained as producer surplus virtually all of the possible consumer surplus. Because marginal decisions are made at marginal cost, this pricing can be efficient, yet it can be opposed on income distribution grounds since the monopolist may benefit so abundantly. Moreover, greater total surplus could result if resources went into a different use, where not as much of the potential consumer surplus went to producers. Second-degree price discrimination involved pricing to groups according to willingness to pay, but not perfectly. All those with a demand price above a certain level would be charged one price, those with a lower demand price would be charged a lower price, and so on. Thus, second-degree price discrimination would be less exacting in its taking of potential consumer surplus but would approximate first-degree price discrimination. Third-degree price discrimination arose when consumers were divided somehow into separate groups, each group then being charged a different monopoly price. Just how this might be applied would depend on possibilities for the seller to identify groups in a particular case, but Pigou regarded third-degree price discrimination as most important from a practical standpoint. Notice that marginal rates of substitution between this good and others will differ for different consumers under third- (or second-) degree price discrimination.

The means of separating consumers into groups will vary with market circumstances. The use of the quantities or qualities of goods consumed is examined in the next two subsections. The difference between buyers of new and replacement parts may be used, such as tires or sparkplugs sold on one hand to auto manufacturers and on the other to individual vehicle owners (Crandall 1968). Customer classes are defined directly by telephone and electricity monopolies, such as residential and commercial customers, who pay different prices (Eckel 1983; Naughton 1986; Primeaux and Nelson 1980). Another means of separating consumers into groups is to require tying (Burstein 1960; Cummings and Ruhter 1979) or bundling (Adams and Yellen 1976), which can sort customers into categories by willingness to pay. If a supply item that is sold with a related good can be monopolized, the related good may even be sold at a loss in order to create more business for the supply item (Mohring 1970). Some product distinctions, perhaps in certain cases automobile brands, for example, might serve in part to separate consumers. When there are uncertainties in demand (or supply) and prices must be established before demand (or supply) is known, special product distinctions may be used to separate consumers (Leland and Meyer 1976; Sherman and Visscher 1982b). Examples here could be various "saver" airfares requiring early booking, or perhaps price distinctions for hotel rooms.

The incentive to discriminate among consumers is illustrated in Figure 3.2a, which is an elaboration of a figure from Sherman and Visscher (1982a). The marginal cost is assumed to be constant so total cost of serving any consumer is represented by the downward-sloping straight line TC, where total cost of supplying any quantity of q is the vertical distance from the starting point y to TC. That starting point is the income of each of three consumers whose indifference curves between q and some composite good c (measured vertically) are represented as U_1, U_2, and U_3. The common point on the vertical axis at y is where all three consumers would spend all their incomes y on good c and buy no q. If the monopoly seller knows U_1, he can create a two-part price schedule that will collect virtually all of consumer 1's surplus; the price per marginal unit will equal marginal cost (notice that p has the same slope as TC) and a fixed fee equal to F_1 will be charged to consumer 1. At this combination,

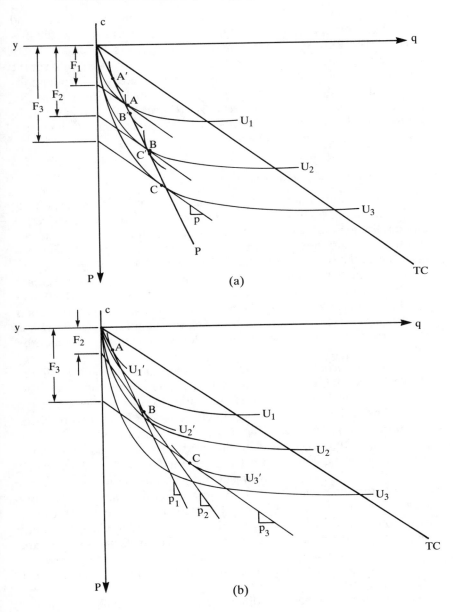

Figure 3.2. Discriminating two-part prices.

person 1 is just about indifferent between buying q and not buying it, and virtually all benefit from its consumption is going as profit to the monopoly seller. Knowing also the interests of consumers 2 and 3, the seller would charge them higher fees F_2 and F_3 for the right to consume at the marginal price p. Profits from each consumer are measured from points A, B, and C to the line TC. For comparison, a single uniform price P is also shown; positions of consumers at A', B', and C' along that price obviously yield less profit to the monopolist. Of course, competition would force price equal to marginal cost for every consumer.

Quantity-dependent pricing

The monopolist may not be able to isolate each consumer as the perfectly discriminating solution (A, B, C) requires in Figure 3.2a, because the monopolist lacks information about consumers' utilities and demands. If consumers cannot be recognized by the seller, for example, all may turn up to buy at the entry price F_1. But if the monopoly can observe the quantities consumed, it can alter its price structure to allow consumers a choice by which they will identify themselves, as analyzed by Spence (1980) and by Maskin and Riley (1984). The procedure is much like that of Section 2.7, where welfare was improved by giving consumers a choice. Here it is used to raise revenue for the monopolist unable to identify consumers by willingness to pay.

The greatest profit can be obtained from consumer 3, and it is still desirable to have marginal price equal marginal cost for that consumer, with a large fixed fee. The trick is to set other prices so they are less attractive to consumer 3 than the set of prices intended for her. Such a set of prices is illustrated in Figure 3.2b. The set of prices shown in Figure 3.2b depends on quantities consumed. Such a price structure is called a "block tariff" when each quantity range has a price and is considered a "block." The whole schedule of prices by quantity ranges must be offered to everyone, since the seller is unable to tell one consumer from another. The first price is a uniform price, p_1 ($F_1 = 0$). The second option involves the fixed fee of F_2 and marginal price p_2, and the third option has fixed fee F_3 and marginal price p_3. By not having p_1 or p_2 equal to marginal cost, they are prevented from dominating consumer 3's decision, and in fact those options are kept less attractive to consumer 3 than a marginal price equal to marginal cost.

Recall that all manner of indifference curve patterns are possible for consumers who differ in their preferences. The pattern we show in Figure 3.2 calls for the consumer who consumes the greatest amount of the good (consumer 3) also to receive the greatest consumer surplus, and therefore to be willing to pay the highest fixed fee for the right to purchase at marginal cost. Had a demander of less quantity of the good, say consumer 1, had the most intense interest in the good (say by an indifference curve in Figure 3.2 that dropped steeply at low quantity and then became almost horizontal), the monopolist's problem of separating consumers to raise the most money from them would be more complicated (Oi 1971). A high fixed fee at small quantities might be hard to implement if it kept others from consuming. We rely on the case more convenient for the monopolist because it illustrates clearly how he might separate consumers without being able to recognize them. It is also plausible as a pattern of demand and a general way to separate consumers.

Quality and price

The lack of information about consumer willingness to pay for quality can also influence the monopoly choice of quality, as illustrated in Figure 3.3, which is based on the example of Mussa and Rosen (1978). Here we assume that product or service quality is recognizable by consumers, so information about quality itself is not a problem. The cost of producing different quality products is represented by curve $TC(g)$ in Figure 3.3, where g indicates the grade or quality of the product. Costs again are measured vertically from y, $TC(g)$ curves now becoming more steep as g is greater because the cost of improving quality is assumed to rise as quality rises. The preferences of consumers are kept extremely simple as linear indifference curves U_1, U_2, and U_3 between quality and price. Consumers are assumed to purchase or not purchase a single unit each period, where the unit can vary in its grade g.

Under a competitive regime, we would expect consumer 1 to be served a quality in keeping with her preferences for quality at A, consumer 2 at B, and consumer 3 at C. A monopoly that could recognize consumers and know their individual demands would rather set different prices for different consumers, so prices and qualities allow them to reach points A', B', and C'. At these points the quality is just right for each consumer, but the required outlay is so high that the consumer is almost indifferent between consuming the good at the quality and price offered and spending money instead on the composite good c. Thus, at this A', B', C' solution each consumer receives the level of quality she is most satisfied with, given the technology for producing quality represented in $TC(g)$, but the monopolist obtains virtually all of the consumer surplus that is available.

Once again, however, if the monopoly cannot recognize consumers, this most profitable solution will not be available to it. Observe that consumer 3 would be better off purchasing the quality offered to consumer 2

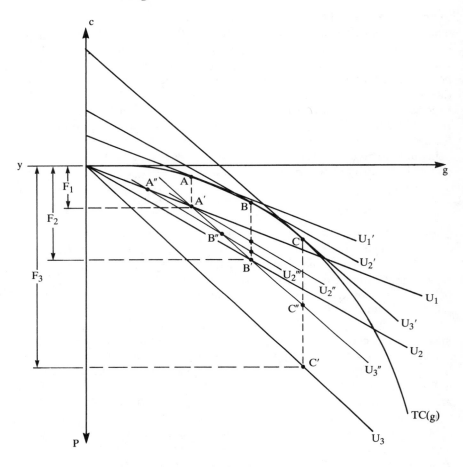

Figure 3.3. Quality and discrimination.

at B' (U_3'' is higher than U_3), and indeed consumer 2 would prefer A' to B' (U_2'' is higher than U_2). The monopolist can allow consumers to select themselves into categories by offering a price schedule dependent on quality much like the quantity-dependent price schedules we just examined. A monopolist who cannot recognize consumers will want to protect its opportunity to profit from the consumer who values quality the most (consumer 3), and can do so by delivering less quality to others. As any consumer's price–quality offering in Figure 3.3 is shifted to the left, it is less attractive to those willing to pay more for quality, and this allows more money to be raised from those who value quality more. If the point A' is moved to the left, for example, say to point A'' along U_1, where consumer

1 will still select it, the opportunity for consumer 2 to satisfy her wishes at consumer 1's price and quality combination grows smaller (U_2'' is lower than U_2'). With consumer 1 at A'', consumer 2 can be charged the price at B'' for the greater quality level she prefers without losing her to the choice of A''. There is more money for the monopoly in this strategic location of prices and qualities as long as the consumer indifference curve slope is steeper than the slope of $TC(g)$ for the consumer concerned. The argument thus holds also for consumer 2, who should be offered a lower quality to the left along U_2''' at B'', in order to allow more profit to be obtained from consumer 3. The chain of adjustments stops with the consumer most interested in quality (the most steeply sloped indifference curve), where the marginal cost of quality should match perfectly the willingness to trade quality for money as at C''. All other consumers will be offered a quality below their marginal willingness to pay for quality.

The tendencies we have displayed here for a profit-seeking enterprise to withhold information and limit effort, to use old methods rather than innovate, to set prices above marginal cost and discriminate in price, or to provide inefficient quantities or qualities, are difficult to control without the benchmark alternative that other suppliers offer through competition. Next we consider efforts that have been made to understand such situations and provide desirable incentives.

3.5   Incentive schemes

Regulation of a statutory monopoly broadly involves two parties, one in the role of a principal (consumers or the regulator)[4] and the other as an agent (the firm) to operate supposedly on the principal's behalf. Generally in such a principal–agent relationship, the agent's action is not observable directly by the principal, and although the agent's action affects the outcome, other influences prevent it from determining the outcome completely. This means that agent action cannot be reliably inferred from observable results. The agency theory that has grown up around this general relationship focuses on the information possessed by the parties (Rees 1985). In the case of a tenant farmer and farm landlord, for example, soil quality, growing weather, and tenant effort will all influence crop yield, but the landlord can observe only that yield (Stiglitz 1974). In the regulatory setting, the firm (agent) may know all the influences affecting measures of cost and quality performance in a given period, including the soundness of past investments, the luck of weather, and other factors influencing demand levels, plus management effort. The regulator (principal) may be able to observe only the cost/quality performance measure.

---

[4] Of course, more generally the regulator is in the role of an agent also, acting for the consumers who are serving as principal.

In such situations of asymmetric information, the regulator seeks an incentive scheme that will induce the firm to pursue the regulator's (or the consumer's) cost/quality goal (Seagraves 1984).

It can be useful to distinguish two forms of agency problems, which Arrow (1985) calls *hidden action* and *hidden information*. Typically, it is the agent's effort that is the hidden action, as in the tenant farmer case, but sometimes the agent will have information that is hidden from the principal. Hidden action creates moral hazard because the actor can take advantage of having action hidden. We just considered a form of hidden information in Section 3.4, when consumers know their demands for service and the firm did not. Hidden information can cause adverse selection, as when consumers with hidden information about their own demands (see Section 3.4) chose options that were not intended for them, and that were less profitable for the seller. In dealing with incentives to lead management to serve welfare, we shall be more concerned with the problem of hidden action, but both problems are often present. We first examine the reference points by which a principal might attempt to judge an agent's performance and then consider essentials of the principal–agent problem.

Reference points

There are several possible ways for the principal in a regulatory situation (the regulator) to gain information useful in overseeing the agent (the regulated firm). First, a process that determines who has the right to be the franchised monopoly might reveal information helpful in controlling it. Second, information about demand may in principle enable the regulator to control the firm. Third, information about other firms' costs might be used to create a performance standard. Finally, data on the firm's costs, outputs, or other factors during the last period might be used in ways that favorably motivate the firm in the next period.

Over a century ago, Chadwick (1859) suggested that competitive bidding, in terms, say, of the price of service offered, was a way to determine who would have the right to *be* the franchised monopoly, and that, if such bidding was successful, it could virtually eliminate the need for a principal–agent relationship. Harold Demsetz (1968) has even questioned the need to regulate in the light of this bidding possibility. Regulators need know neither demand nor cost precisely in order to select a firm on the basis of the service and price combination it offers, the winner presumably providing service at promised terms for a specified period of time. It has recently been proposed that the auctions actually be for an incentive contract, so the winner also is bound to a desirable incentive arrangement (Laffont and Tirole 1987; McAfee and McMillan 1987a, b); Riordan and Sappington 1987).

Suppose that bidding could be among unequals, however, once one firm had the franchise for a period of time with exclusive information about cost and operations, and also control over resources needed to supply the service. Moreover, as Oliver Williamson (1976) showed from an examination of bidding for cable television franchises, the winner often does not fulfill the service contract as promised. From well-publicized cost overruns on government contracts, particularly in military procurement, we know that bidders may win contracts by bidding on terms they cannot meet. The main reason for this result is that the services are complicated, and all eventualities cannot be anticipated fully when contracts are drawn up. Long-term contracts may still offer some possibilities – as Ekelund and Higgins (1982), Goldberg (1976), and Masten and Crocker (1985) have demonstrated – and incentives may be improved through the contract-awarding process. But genuine problems remain for inducing effective pursuit of economic welfare through the competitive awarding of monopoly franchises.

Some advantage can be gained from contemporaneous information on consumer demand for regulating a supplier. Martin Loeb and Wesley Magat (1979) devised a simple incentive scheme to induce welfare maximization within the existing agent firm directly, by paying a franchised monopolist the total consumer surplus resulting from any price it chooses. To estimate consumer surplus for this purpose, however, the regulator must know demand, which also has to be stable so that a structure of payments can be based on it. One desirable feature of this scheme is that regulators do not require cost information, since the firm would benefit by maximizing producer plus consumer surplus directly. The main drawback is the cost of paying a subsidy to the firm as great as all consumer surplus. Loeb and Magat proposed to lessen that burden by charging the firm a fee for the right to hold the monopoly franchise. Since this fee could be determined by a bidding process, the proposal also can have this ingredient. Experimental investigation of the procedure shows it to be promising (Harrison and McKee 1985). But the large sums involved as consumer surplus, together with the need to know demand and have it stable, have no doubt helped to keep the scheme from being used.

Setting prices or evaluating performance by reference to other firms' contemporaneous costs, called "yardstick" competition, was shown in Sherman (1980b) to motivate socially efficient input choices, free of the bias that is possible under rate-of-return regulation when allowed profit is based on the firm's own capital input. That regulating the firm by reference to other firms' input costs would lead to optimal cost reduction effort was proved by Shleifer (1985). An external cost standard will move as competitors' costs would, with changes in input prices or other general influences on costs, so that it forms a reasonable performance standard. The greatest advantage is that the firm will be motivated to operate efficiently when its own costs are not the basis for its prices. Other similarly situated firms have to exist for the method to be applicable, of course, since they are needed to serve as reference for a single regulated firm. An external cost standard would probably require statistical analysis of the costs of other firms in order to predict a benchmark level for the firm being regulated (see Shleifer 1985). In the electrical industry, for instance, consideration would have to be given to the effect on cost of climate (which affects construction costs), locally available fuel, and transmission (which can differ considerably) as opposed to generation (which is often similar) activity.

The source of information used most is last period's results from the firm's own experience. Weitzman (1980) has described the general process of using such information to control performance. It gives rise to the typical relationship between principals and their agents, although the hierarchy may be more complex (Brock and Scheinkman 1985). A surprisingly simple scheme that focuses on dynamic pricing behavior of the regulated firm using prior period information was proposed by Vogelsang and Finsinger (1979). They allow the firm to alter prices in any way it wishes from one period to the next, as long as the new prices, when multiplied by the quantities of the previous period, would add to no more than a certain sum, that sum being the previous period's total cost with perhaps some adjustment.[5] Remarkably, this procedure can induce the profit-seeking firm to adopt Ramsey prices, which are desired because they differ from marginal costs in ways that minimize the resulting welfare loss. However, it is possible that the firm will make only very small adjustments each period and so take a long time to reach the desired set of prices (Sappington 1980). Furthermore, product innovations may not be accommodated readily by the procedure. But it can be adapted to control these weaknesses while inducing desired pricing actions (Finsinger and Vogelsang 1981, 1982). Some modifications that have been introduced are also based on experimental study of the procedure (Cox and Isaac 1987), and they improve the prospect for successful implementation.

The principal–agent problem

When only the performance outcome is observable, the principal–agent setting gives rise to a fundamental incentive problem. The agent may be

---

[5] A similar procedure is set out in Sherman (1980a), and developed further in Finsinger and Vogelsang (1981, 1982).

expected to exert greater effort as compensation is tied more closely to the outcome (the crop yield, or other performance measure), for he will share the benefit more in a good outcome than a bad one. But tying compensation to outcomes also will force the agent to absorb more risk due to factors beyond effort, such as weather in the tenant farmer case, even though the principal, who will often be the wealthier of the two parties, may be in a better position to bear risk. Thus as incentives are able to entice more effort from the agent, risk bearing may be distributed less effectively between agent and principal. For when risk bearing remains with the principal, the agent has little incentive to perform well.

However, in their role as agent, the owners of a public utility are capable of bearing risks, perhaps even better than the consumers for whom the regulator acts as principal, so strong incentives should be feasible. As an illustration, strong agent incentive can be seen in the lawyer (agent) and client (principal) relationship in which a contingent fee arrangement is used. The lawyer might receive a percentage of any settlement or, in more extreme form, the client might be assured a fixed payment while the lawyer receives any settlement less that payment. Where contingency fee arrangements are more common, as in medical malpractice cases, for instance, the client may be more averse to risk and also less wealthy than the lawyer, and hence less willing or able to bear risk. When an agent can bear risk, the conflict between incentive for effort and risk bearing is less serious.

It often is desirable for a principal and agent to share in the results when effort and uncertainty are intermingled. Cross (1970) emphasized the advantages of sharing as a basis for agreement in negotiations because it could strengthen incentives for the firm to control costs; Holt (1979) pointed out the role that sharing can play in bidding incentives when risk attitude is important. Although they present a much more sophisticated framework for analyzing a regulator who has some demand information but does not know a firm's cost, in a special case the system of Baron and Myerson (1982) corresponds to the Loeb and Magat (1979) proposal with sharing. Pareto-optimal arrangements for compensating agents also tend to involve sharing. If the agent is risk neutral,[6] he should be paid the outcome minus a fixed fee to go to the principal, but then of course the agent bears risk. If the agent is risk averse, he should not bear all the risk this way, although the payment should be related in some degree to the outcome (Borch 1962; Shavell 1979). If information about the agent's effort also is available, even only imperfectly, and the agent is risk averse, then the Pareto-optimal fee schedule will pay the agent an amount that depends

---

6 A risk-neutral person has a constant marginal utility of wealth and so cares only about mean, or expected, outcomes. See Section 2.8.

on effort to the extent it is observed (Harris and Raviv 1978; Holmström 1979; Shavell 1979).

The incentive contract illustrated by Cross (1970) offers an early concrete example for a case in which cost performance relative to expectation can be observed. It would make the agent's fee, F, a function of expected and actual cost as follows:

$$F = BC_T + S(C_T - C), \tag{1}$$

where C_T is the initial estimate of cost, C is final realized cost, and B and S are parameters;[7] they may be thought of as bonus (B) and sharing (S) terms. Observe that with $S > 0$, as realized cost is lower relative to the initial estimate of cost, the contractor (agent) will receive a greater fee; but the benefit of lower realized cost is shared with the government (principal) as long as $S < 1$.

Incentives in the principal–agent situation have been further developed (e.g., Baron and Myerson 1982; Myserson 1983), and a simple linear reward structure similar to (1) has been proven optimal (Laffont and Tirole 1986; McAfee and McMillan 1987a). Monopoly regulation based on cost observation was treated in two recent contributions by Baron and Besanko (1984) and by Laffont and Tirole (1986). These authors seek optimal bonus and sharing parameters, in a general framework. Laffont and Tirole represent total cost, TC, as

$$TC = (C - E)q + \psi + K, \tag{2}$$

where ψ is a random term, K is a fixed term such as capital cost, q is output quantity, and $C - E$ is unit cost with C an inherent efficiency parameter and E effort. It is assumed that K is known and all remaining cost is observed by the regulator only in total, as $V = (C - E)q + \psi$. For an ensuing period, the regulator asks the firm to submit an estimate of V, denoted V_T. The regulator defines bonus and sharing terms, $B(V_T)$ and $S(V_T)$, which can also be represented as $B(q)$ and $S(q)$ because q is nonincreasing in a vital determinant of V_T, C. Then the firm's profit under an optimal incentive scheme can be represented as

$$\pi = K + B(q)V_T + S(q)V. \tag{3}$$

Laffont and Tirole show that the optimal S is always less than one and tends normally to decrease with output q; the optimal value for B increases with output but is lower as V_T is higher. Picard (1987) shows that quite simple rules can implement this form of incentive scheme.

---

[7] The supplier would be paid C plus F in contracts Cross was describing, so sharing applied only to the fee F. Cross pointed out that for military procurement, B was often 0.08, because the initially planned fee was 8 percent of expected cost, and S ranged from 0.05 to 0.50, but often was about 0.20. Contracts often had an upper limit also on C plus F.

In the Laffont and Tirole analysis, the regulator for given q has an idea of the range and extreme values for V. If V_T is high, this signals that the firm is less efficient. When B is set relatively low and S relatively high, it will give a greater incentive to reveal efficiency. If V_T is low, on the other hand, high B and low S encourage more effort. As the range of outcomes approaches zero, meaning there is little uncertainty, the optimal B again is high while S is low. The outcome, as one might expect, will not be perfectly efficient, but if bidding for these contracts is introduced (e.g., Laffont and Tirole 1987), the result becomes more efficient as there are more bidders.

All of these schemes share the limitation that as the regulator gains information it may act differently, and this fact affects the regulated agent's behavior, motivating it to behave strategically in that it is acting in part to influence the regulator. Alkan and Sertel (in press) and Koray and Sertel (in press) have demonstrated that consistent action over time can improve outcomes. They allow parties to pretend to have whatever goals they want as long as they adhere to them, in a "pretend-but-perform" mechanism. Baron and Besanko (1987) point out that a regulator who makes a commitment to go through more than one period without changing policies based on new information makes available generally more beneficial contracts. Even stopping short of full commitment by agreeing not to undertake certain *kinds* of policy changes, which Baron and Besanko describe as fairness, can be an improvement. It is difficult for regulators to make commitments, even to fairness in treating the firm as agreed, in part because future governments cannot be bound to agreements made.[8] But agreement on some principles that bind the regulator can improve efficiency by reducing the strategic aspects of the agent firm's behavior. Indeed, as Sappington (1986) has argued, a regulatory bureaucracy provides some of the advantages of such commitments, in the form of predictable procedural limitations.

3.6   Entry and contestable markets

We should not presume that where one firm can offer the lowest cost of production a statutory monopoly always is needed, to be protected from entry and induced by some other regulation to set ideal prices. In the special case where costs are not sunk (sunk costs are discussed in Section 1.2) and entry can be accomplished easily, suppose that a single firm can produce industry output at the lowest possible cost and with prices based on that low cost can prevent entry by others. Then competition via entry can discipline the single firm and prevent it from exploiting its

---

[8] In some states regulatory commissions are elected, so their tenure is uncertain.

position, thus preserving advantages of competition even in markets where large numbers of competing firms would not be efficient. Although entry is barred into many regulated industries in the real world today, while prices are controlled by regulatory agencies, this control over entry recently has been relaxed. In the airline and long-distance telephone markets, for example, competition with entry is now relied on to determine who serves consumers and what prices they can charge. The adjective *contestable* has been used to describe a market with free entry, where even a single firm will face pressure to keep costs low and to price efficiently (Baumol, Panzer, and Willig 1982).

If single-product firms have U-shaped average cost curves and if the minimum average cost point is at a small output relative to total demand, there will be many firms in the market. Their competition plus easy entry by new firms due to the absence of sunk costs, which is the distinguishing feature of a *contestable market,*[9] will force operation at minimum cost and allow no economic profit. Having some portion of the average cost curve flat at its minimum level, where average cost is constant over a range of outputs, will ensure this result; otherwise an integer number of firms times the minimum cost output level for each of them might not equal demand precisely at a zero-profit outcome. Cost studies in many industries have found substantial ranges of constant average cost, so this assumption is reasonable. Therefore the problem of having the sum of exact minimum cost output levels of firms not equal market demand is not apt to arise. Even with economies of scale, if there is no sunk cost so entry and exit are easy, competition through new entry might still yield a better outcome than forms of extramarket regulation. Although the optimum number of producers in this case is only one, as soon as that one attempts to exploit its seemingly monopolistic position, a new entrant can easily displace it. The market in that case is still contestable, in that an outsider can enter to enforce the essentially competitive, no-excess-profit, equilibrium.

When all markets have many firms supplying output at the minimum of U-shaped average cost curves, market price will equal both marginal cost and average cost. We know from our examination of welfare economics that this outcome is ideal. When demand in any market can be served by one firm that is still experiencing economies of scale, however, marginal cost for that firm must lie below average cost. In that case, price obviously cannot equal both marginal cost and average cost. If we require independent firms and rule out nonuniform prices, then the resulting price will have to equal average cost. A firm that charges a lower price

---

[9] See Baumol et al. (1982). For analysis of possible competition among electric utilities, see Joskow and Schmalensee (1983) and Primeaux (1986).

may protect itself from entry for a time, but it cannot survive, since it cannot cover costs. If it attempts to set price higher, the firm will be supplanted by a new entrant willing to set a price that equals average cost. Thus, if free entry is relied upon to discipline producers when economies of scale are so great, price will equal average cost and exceed marginal cost.

A single firm may be able to produce two or more products at lower cost than two or more separate firms, and then efficiency will require production by multiproduct firms. In this situation we say there are *economies of scope,*[10] because economies arise from the scope of products offered. In the multiproduct firm the older idea of economies of scale requires new definition, because scale expansion can now involve more than one product, and the simple idea of average cost is no longer well defined. Axiomatic approaches to defining average cost have been developed for this situation.[11] Using these ideas it is possible to define an average cost for each product in the multiproduct case, and contestable markets can be expected to force prices equal to such average costs. Thus, in principle, the lack of sunk costs will allow the force of entry to discipline even one multiproduct firm in a market that is contestable.

When a market is contestable, all who participate as sellers have to keep costs low, because otherwise they may be replaced by a more efficient supplier. This is true even if there is currently only one supplier. Focusing on effects of entry in this way also has led to clearer definition of what is meant by cross-subsidization among products, for prices involving subsidy may not survive with free entry. Cross-subsidization has been a major problem in regulated markets, and entry has been permitted into some markets in part to end such practices. In the United States, for example, it has been claimed that long-distance flights subsidized short flights under Civil Aeronautics Board regulation of air fares, and business and long-distance callers subsidized residences under state regulation of telephone rates. Deregulation can prevent such pricing practices, but more knowledge is needed to determine when it is likely to succeed.

Coursey, Isaac, and Smith (1984) examined experimental markets in which one seller was the lowest cost form of organization. They found that prices were closer to a competitive level when entry was free and closer to a monopoly level when entry was impossible. More intermediate entry costs were studied by Coursey, Isaac, Luke, and Smith (1984), where entry required a payment and lasted for five market periods. The strongest form of the contestable market hypothesis (price at or below a

---

10 See Panzer and Willig (1977b) for a description of economies of scope.
11 See Mirman and Tauman (1982), Billera and Heath (1982), Bös and Tillman (1983), Mirman et al. (1983), and Mirman et al. (1986) for development of this axiomatic approach.

competitive level, where entry determines the competitive level) was not always supported, and results were not always stable. But the power of entry to discipline an incumbent was still considerable, and the force of the entry threat was certainly important. Further evidence that entry will discipline an experimental market has been provided by Harrison and McKee (1985).

Even when there is no sunk cost, which would allow a market to be contestable in principle, there may be no set of prices that will allow the incumbent firm to prevent inefficient entry and to sustain itself. We can briefly describe an example based on Faulhaber (1975) in which this is true. Suppose that three firms are seeking water supplies in conditions where any one can install a system of supply itself for $250,000 but any two can join and supply themselves together for $300,000. Moreover, all three can join in a larger system costing $500,000. Obviously the lowest cost means of serving all three firms is through the $500,000 system. But two firms have incentive to go together, because by dividing $300,000 two ways they have a lower cost than if they divide $500,000 three ways. However, the third firm suffers if any two provide water jointly. Thus we have to ask what conditions will allow a most efficient firm to set prices that will sustain its position, especially if it is the lowest-cost supplier in natural monopoly circumstances.

3.7   Sustainable prices

When entry is free, the question arises whether a single firm possessing the most efficient production capability could choose prices that would *sustain* it as a monopoly. Sustainable prices leave no incentive for entry by another firm that can use the same technology, yet at the same time allow only a normal profit rate for the monopoly. Faulhaber (1975) showed that a firm might be unable to sustain itself even with efficient prices. In his example, entry could be motivated, yet efficiency would decline as a result. This raises the question of when prices can be found that actually will sustain the monopoly firm so inefficient entry will not be motivated.

If the technology that produces economies of scale and/or economies of scope has convenient properties, a single firm can choose prices that will protect it from entry; its prices will be sustainable. The single firm can be expected to choose such prices, for otherwise it will be subject to competition that may threaten its position. For prices to be sustainable, the cost function must have a property called subadditivity, although this alone is not sufficient. A multiproduct firm's cost function $C(q)$ is *subadditive* if for any output vectors $q_1, \ldots, q_n$ $(n > 1)$ such that $\sum_{i=1}^{n} q_i = q$ and $q_i \neq 0$, we have

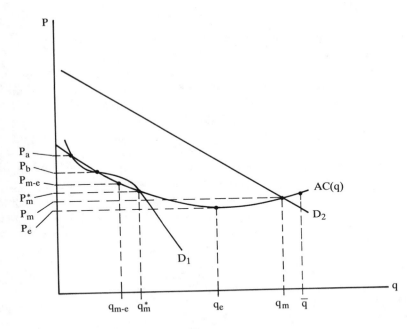

Figure 3.4. Subadditivity and sustainability.

$$\sum_{i=1}^{n} C(q_i) > C\left(\sum_{i=1}^{n} q_i\right). \tag{4}$$

Equation (4) requires that production of a good or service by separate units will cost more than production by one organization. Since this condition implies that one firm can produce output at lowest cost it also is called a "natural monopoly" condition. Figure 3.4 illustrates an average cost function $AC(q)$. Notice that the natural monopoly can satisfy demand D_1 by setting a price equal to average cost of P_m^* while no other firm using the same technology could enter at a lower price and survive. Thus in this case the price P_m^* is sustainable. Price also equals average cost at P_a but is not sustainable because it is higher and would lose to a firm charging P_m^*. The same can be said for price P_b, which also equals average cost. But there the firm should realize that (since demand is above average cost) a lower price will be profitable.

Suppose that the cost function in Figure 3.4 is subadditive up to output level $\bar{q}$. So at the level of output q_m the cost function will still be subadditive (e.g., $C(q_e) + C(q_{m-e}) > C(q_m)$). If demand is at D_2, a price equal to average cost of P_m is not sustainable despite subadditivity of cost there, because a new entrant using the same technology could produce the smaller quantity q_e, sell it at a price P_e slightly below P_m, and make a profit. Thus subadditivity of the cost function is necessary for price to be sustainable, but it is not sufficient.

Figure 3.4 illustrates a distinction that is made between partial quantity entry and full entry. Consider demand D_2 and price P_m. If an entrant is required to meet full market demand at whatever price it charges, it will not be able to produce only q_e and enter the market with a price as low as P_e. In that case P_m will be sustainable, and we can say that it is sustainable against full entry. But P_m is not sustainable against entry when the partial quantity q_e can be offered by an entrant. Of course, prices sustainable against partial entry must be sustainable against full entry. From Figure 3.4 for a single-product firm, it is obvious that decreasing average cost will ensure the existence of a price sustainable against partial entry. Whether at full entry or partial entry, when demand is at D_1 – where average cost is decreasing – no entrant can charge less than P_m^* and make a profit.

Conditions to ensure sustainability are more difficult to identify in the multiproduct case, because the products may be interdependent in both their costs and their demands. Although it is possible for some consumers of a single product to pay more than others, whether one group subsidizes another also is more obviously important in the multiproduct case. Since each product has its own price, some products might be sold below marginal costs and others above, and so some products of a multiproduct firm would effectively be cross-subsidizing others. In order to be sustainable, then, a set of prices must foster no such subsidy, or it must be *subsidy-free*.

Suppose that total revenues over all n products equal total costs,

$$\Sigma_n p_i q_i = C(\Sigma_n q_i),$$

or, in vector notation,

$$\mathbf{p} \cdot \mathbf{q} = C(\mathbf{q}).$$

Denote any subset s of n products by the vector $\mathbf{q}_s$, where $s \leq n$, and suppose their prices are represented by the vector $\mathbf{p}_s$. Then to avoid having consumers of a subset of goods or services be motivated to band together and supply themselves, prices must satisfy

$$\mathbf{p}_s \cdot \mathbf{q}_s \leq C(\mathbf{q}_s), \quad \text{all } s.$$

Together these two conditions also imply that

$$\mathbf{p}_s \cdot \mathbf{q}_s \geq C(\mathbf{q}) - C(\mathbf{q} - \mathbf{q}_s),$$

or prices must at least cover the incremental cost of serving any subset of goods. Prices that satisfy these requirements for all possible product subsets are subsidy-free. Subsidy-free prices thus yield sufficient total revenue to cover the cost of meeting market demands at those prices. In addition, the revenue from *any* subset of the goods produced cannot exceed the cost of producing that subset by itself. This latter requirement, that revenue not exceed cost for any subset of goods produced separately, is called the "stand-alone" test. Were it not satisfied, we should expect the consumers who pay more than the cost of providing the subset of goods involved to go into business for themselves separately, that is, to stand alone. And if prices do not at least cover incremental cost for a subset of goods, the other consumers would find it in their interests to eliminate those goods. Thus prices that are not subsidy-free are not sustainable.

Baumol, Bailey, and Willig (1977) showed that, if a firm's cost function possessed the natural monopoly cost properties of decreasing ray average cost and transray convexity, a form of optimal prices called Ramsey prices (introduced in Section 2.6 and examined further in Chapter 5) would be sustainable. Like optimal taxes, Ramsey prices differ from marginal costs, raising needed revenue while causing the minimum possible loss in welfare. *Decreasing ray average cost* is represented as

$$C(\alpha\mathbf{q}) < \alpha C(\mathbf{q}) \tag{5}$$

for $\alpha > 1$ and the vector $\mathbf{q} > 0$. *Transray convexity* requires of two output vectors on different rays from the origin, $\mathbf{q}_1$ and $\mathbf{q}_2$, that for $0 \leq \gamma \leq 1$:

$$C(\gamma\mathbf{q}_1 + (1-\gamma)\mathbf{q}_2) \leq \gamma C(\mathbf{q}_1) + (1-\gamma)C(\mathbf{q}_2). \tag{6}$$

When satisfied as an inequality, the condition (6) indicates a form of cost complementarity in the production of the firm's outputs. With decreasing ray average costs and these cost complementarities of goods or services in production, a firm could prevent entry by choosing Ramsey prices. Thus, in the absence of sunk cost, the threat of entry by other firms can, in principle, force a multiproduct natural monopoly to choose socially desirable prices in order to prevent entry.

Although having sustainable prices that turn out to be optimal Ramsey prices is an interesting possibility, the requirement that decreasing ray average cost and transray convexity hold everywhere is too strong to be satisfied reliably. Indeed, the two conditions are inconsistent at some points and so cannot be expected to hold generally. More general conditions to ensure sustainability have been set out by Mirman, Tauman, and Zang (1985a), who prove with subadditive costs that, if prices are subsidy-free and in addition marginal profits are nonnegative,[12] those prices are sustainable against full entry in all product markets. Mirman, Tauman, and

---

[12] If the profit for any subset of goods is $\pi^S(p)$, then marginal profits are nonnegative if $\partial\pi^S/\partial p_j \geq 0$ for every j in S.

Zang (1985b) show the sustainable outcome to be a very stable Bertrand–Nash equilibrium among potential producers.

To ensure sustainability against partial entry it is necessary to consider the interdependence of multiple products in their effects on costs and demands.[13] An alternative and more general measure of cost complementarity that may be used if the cost function is twice differentiable is the condition that

$$C_{ij} = \frac{\partial^2 C}{\partial q_i\, \partial q_j} \leq 0. \tag{7}$$

As the output of any product is increased, this condition requires that the marginal cost of any other product will not increase. Condition (7) can be expected to hold for the technologies that are associated with natural monopoly, and it implies subadditivity (condition (4)) of the cost function and also can give rise to decreasing ray average cost (condition (5)). Regarding demand, suppose that the goods produced by the multiproduct firm are not complements, but can instead be classified as weak gross substitutes for satisfying

$$\frac{\partial q_j}{\partial p_i} \geq 0 \quad \text{for } i \neq j. \tag{8}$$

Mirman et al. (1985a) show that if prices are subsidy-free while profits are nonnegative (assuring sustainability against full entry), and in addition cost complementarity (7) and weak gross substitutability (8) are present, then the prices will be sustainable against partial entry. The same sort of result was obtained by Panzar and Willig (1977a), but with decreasing ray average cost (5) in place of cost complementarity (7).

With conditions specified that will reliably ensure sustainable prices, we naturally wonder what the prices will be like. One answer comes from an axiomatic approach to cost-sharing prices, which sets out the desirable properties of prices and then defines prices that satisfy those properties. Billera and Heath (1982), Billera, Heath, and Raanan (1978), Bös and Tillman (1983), Mirman and Tauman (1982), and Mirman, Samet, and Tauman (1983) have constructed prices that satisfy desirable properties and are like average cost prices extended to the multiproduct circumstance. Moreover, these prices have been shown to be sustainable (Mirman, Tauman, and Zang 1986). The desirable properties are specified in the form of axioms. As set out by Mirman, Samet, and Tauman (1983) the

---

[13] A problem of definition was raised by Mirman et al. (1986) when goods are complements. When partial quantities may be supplied, there are many ways in which a firm might lower one price but limit output while raising the price of a complement whose demand is favorably affected, and generalizations about results are difficult to reach. In most regulated industries, firms are required to meet all demand with satisfactory quality, and partial entry might be prevented by similar rules.

axioms begin with *cost sharing,* the idea that costs will be shared among products and services in such a way that when axiomatic prices are used total revenue will equal total cost. A second, *rescaling,* axiom requires simply that prices will change correspondingly if scales of measurement of the goods or services are changed. Four remaining axioms cover details about how prices are influenced by the cost function.

The first of these remaining four axioms imposes a *consistency* requirement on prices, calling for prices to be the same for all members in any subset of outputs whose costs depend only on the sum of their outputs; for example, if costs depend on the total of $q_1 + q_2$, then the price of q_1 should equal the price of q_2. This axiom shows the strong cost basis of the axiomatic prices, for it rules out effects of demand elasticity that might reduce welfare loss when prices differ from marginal costs as Ramsey prices do. Beyond requiring the same price for outputs that have the same effect on costs based on this consistency axiom, a *positivity* axiom requires that if one cost function has higher marginal cost than another it should also have a higher price. Two more axioms concern the allocation of fixed costs, which are common to all outputs since they do not depend on output at all. An *additivity* axiom requires that if production can be separated into stages, each with its own variable cost, then any fixed or common cost can also be assigned to the stages and added to variable cost by stage, and those sums of variable cost plus assigned common cost by stage can be added together to obtain output cost. Another axiom makes the allocations of common cost for any pair of outputs *correlate* with the relative variable costs of those outputs. As a result of these latter two axioms, fixed costs can be incorporated into axiomatic cost-sharing prices.

Prices that satisfy all of these axioms are modifications of Aumann–Shapley (1974) prices, which do not themselves apply when fixed costs are present. Aumann–Shapley prices can be obtained for any output combination by examining all smaller portions of that same output combination and calculating marginal costs of each output at all those smaller portions. Averages of all such marginal costs for each output will then yield Aumann–Shapley prices. Using an axiomatic approach, Mirman et al. (1983) extended this Aumann–Shapley pricing principle to cost functions involving fixed costs. They found that they could satisfy the six axioms above if they multiplied Aumann–Shapley prices, which apply only when all costs are variable, by one plus the ratio of fixed to variable cost. Essentially they would "blow up" Aumann–Shapley prices that are based only on variable cost by a multiple large enough to cover fixed cost. It is the modified Aumann–Shapley prices that Mirman et al. (1986) proved to be sustainable.

The modified Aumann–Shapley prices that are sustainable are not necessarily the most efficient in principle, for we know that they exclude any influence of demand elasticity as found, for example, in Ramsey prices. But if we accept the free-entry mechanism for its practical allocative advantages, that alone may undercut Ramsey prices by making demands infinitely elastic at entry prices, and so the lack of efficiency should not be surprising. Also, the efficiency available in principle from Ramsey prices may never be realized, because if entry is not allowed then no clear incentive urges the firm to keep cost low and to adopt Ramsey prices. Thus, where sustainable prices can be forced into use by allowing free entry, they may be desirable in part for the incentive effects of free entry.

Furthermore, conditions that allow sustainable prices might also allow excess profit to a monopoly firm, profit beyond a normal competitive profit rate. Sunk costs, which tend to intimidate new entrants, can have this effect, of course; and an incumbent firm can have advantages in its relations with customers and even in its being well known, which will make effective challenge from an outsider more difficult. Having a basis for analyzing when an incumbent can sustain itself through prices is important, nevertheless. When sustainable prices are not available, the most efficient policy may require that free entry be abandoned. Then the main alternative is to choose a single supplier as a franchised monopoly and oversee its actions so that welfare can be served.

Cost-axiomatic prices have application beyond the sustainability circumstances in which they serve so effectively, however. Samet and Tauman (1982) have shown that marginal cost prices can be approached effectively by focusing on cost axioms. And Bös and Tillman (1983, 1984) have urged more widespread use of axiomatic costs in regulation. They extend a form of axiomatic costs beyond the break-even condition, to consider regulation of enterprises that are explicitly to show net profits or be subsidized. The regulated enterprise is to develop multiproduct prices through axiomatic cost sharing, and Bös and Tillman show that resulting prices will be compatible with demands. Von Weizsäcker (1985) has argued for greater reliance on such cost-based guidance in regulatory price setting, rather than value-based guidance, in part because it is more immune to politically induced price distortions. Since costs by product are often the subject of regulatory disputes, this orientation toward cost might prove to be very useful.[14]

3.8   Summary

The free entry of competition can put any supplier to a test of efficiency and thereby force behavior that serves economic welfare. In special circumstances in which sunk costs are unimportant, free entry can serve to

---

[14] Fully distributed cost pricing has not always been soundly based (Braeutigam 1979; Cole 1981) but might be applied as cost-axiomatic pricing.

discipline even a single monopoly supplier effectively. And the sustainable prices that will result can serve economic welfare. But often when sunk costs are great and economies of scale or scope handicap competition, free entry is abandoned for other forms of regulation. Usually a single enterprise is franchised to provide service and is supervised by a regulatory agency. Without the force of competition it is difficult for the regulator to induce welfare-maximizing behavior from the monopoly enterprise. Incentive schemes have inherent flaws in this situation, which political institutions are unable to remedy. Much as the economic institution of market competition may stress efficiency and ignore income distribution by accepting the status quo, political institutions tend to focus on income distribution and may choose inefficient economic outcomes. Thus, designing institutions that will reliably pursue economic welfare is a difficult task.

We now examine in more detail optimal pricing, which is the subject of Part II. In Chapter 4 we consider a range of problems involving peak-load pricing, nonuniform pricing, and externality pricing. The models used illustrate alternative representations of social welfare from Chapter 2, and nearly all the problems yield neat, ideal price-equals-marginal-cost solutions, at least in the models used. More awkward problems involve constraints that prevent achievement of such a direct ideal solution. Optimal solutions pursued in the light of such constraints are called second-best solutions; they are taken up in Chapters 5 and 6. In determining optimal prices in Part II we are not concerned with whether an institution will actually pursue welfare. That question is taken up in Part III, where we examine real-world institutions to see whether they can be expected to adopt welfare-maximizing policies.

Questions

3.1. Consider the geometric comparison of a uniform monopoly price with perfect price discrimination via two-part prices in Figure 3.2a. Monopoly profit is lower with a uniform price, but consumer welfare is higher.

(a) Can you determine which of the two pricing schemes yields the greatest total welfare (and why)?

(b) Compared with a uniform monopoly price, would you expect the price structure in Figure 3.2b to allow more or less total welfare (and why)?

3.2. Profit from a business you own in a foreign country depends on weather (good or bad) and on the effort (high or low) of a resident manager, according to the relationship:

		Weather	
		Good	Bad
Effort	High	100	50
	Low	50	−20

You are able to observe neither the weather in the foreign country, nor your manager's effort.

(a) Design an incentive scheme for the manager and briefly explain how it operates.

(b) Describe advantages and disadvantages of your incentive scheme.

3.3. Suppose four neighboring farmers want irrigation and flood control systems for their farms. Each farmer can install his own system for $15,000. If two farmers go together they can build a joint system for $25,000, and three farmers can build one for three farms at a cost of $30,000. If all four farms are provided for in a single system, its cost will be $44,000. Assume that all systems are equally effective.

(a) Which way of providing irrigation and flood control protection has the lowest cost to society?

(b) Can you identify sustainable prices for the lowest-cost system?

3.4. Consider Question 2.3 of Chapter 2.

(a) Is the solution that maximizes consumer surplus in part (a) sustainable?

(b) In part (b) of Question 2.3, if train service is extended to C, entry may have to be prevented. Would this condition influence your recommendation about extending service to C?

PART II

Optimal pricing

CHAPTER 4

Ideal public pricing

4.1   Introduction

Our purpose in this chapter is to gain an understanding of the problems that arise in choosing ideal prices and to see how welfare economics can help solve them. We use both consumer surplus and individual utility measures of welfare, and very simple representations of cost. The cases that we consider here almost always yield an ideal price, in the sense that users pay the marginal costs that follow from their decisions. If for some reason the process of competition is not to be relied on and if cost-minimizing actions can be induced without it, whatever institution replaces competition can find ideal guidance in the solutions of this chapter. Just what institution might play this role, and to what extent it could be induced to pursue welfare, are questions we shall not pursue yet. Our aim here is to identify ideal prices, not to implement them. Even apart from implementation, the welfare-maximizing prices of this chapter ignore realities such as budget constraints that lead to second-best pricing.

Second-best pricing is considered in Chapters 5 and 6. Chapter 5 deals with a problem that frequently arises in public utilities and public enterprises, where – because of technological conditions such as economies of scale or economies of scope – prices equal to marginal costs will not yield enough revenue to cover total cost. Chapter 6 considers effects of pricing on income distribution. Let us briefly explain why technology can prevent the ideal ($P = mc$) solutions of this chapter from serving satisfactorily and can make further study in Chapters 5 and 6 necessary. First, uniform prices equal to marginal costs at all outputs may not be feasible. Since economies of scale or economies of scope cause marginal or incremental costs to lie below average costs, after competition among firms drives uniform prices to marginal costs all firms will incur losses. Consequently, many cannot survive. Even if a monopoly supplier is organized as a governmentally chartered public enterprise, its deficit will still have to be covered. Exacting lump-sum payments from consumers to meet a deficit may not be feasible because lump sums cannot magically be taken from every person. Consequently, any feasible tax to cover the deficit probably would cause prices to differ from marginal costs, which would distort consumers' choices away from welfare-maximizing levels. In addition, the tax might fall on some nonusers of the service or fall unfairly among the users, causing unwanted effects on income distribution. The second-best public enterprise prices we consider in Chapter 5 will not achieve perfection, but they will allocate goods and resources as well as possible in the presence of constraints that prevent losses when there are economies of scale or economies of scope. With the same methods, we can study income distribution issues in Chapter 6.

Here we ignore problems of tax or subsidy, or of altering the income distribution, and instead focus attention on efficiency with simple technology. We employ several of the welfare representations that were introduced in Chapter 2.

4.2   Limitations of marginal cost pricing

When technology interferes with the functioning of a competitive market, an alternative institution, perhaps a regulated statutory monopoly, may be chosen to replace it. Many questions arise when competition is replaced. We know from Chapter 3, for instance, that one such question is, How will the enterprise be motivated to produce efficiently? The question we emphasize here is, What prices should be set for the monopolist's outputs? Even though the pricing outcome of competition is usually a desirable standard to follow wherever possible, circumstances that prevent competition from functioning can make competitive pricing inimitable. With its welfare basis, marginal-cost pricing is better defined as a standard than is "competitive pricing," which obviously is not well defined when competition cannot function. Recall that in Section 2.5 we found welfare-maximizing pricing was marginal cost pricing, unless some limitation or constraint interfered, and this result was independent of market organization. Indeed, the decision to rely on competition or to regulate an economic activity by some other means (such as public utility regulation) will depend in large part on whether competition can achieve and sustain the marginal cost-pricing standard.

Although the principle of pricing at marginal cost may serve desirable efficiency goals, in pure form it is not always workable, even when it yields enough profit that firms can survive.[1] Marginal costs of some goods and services change markedly at different locations and times of day and, even if it were feasible, having prices respond to those changes can be disruptive. Apparently simple taxi service from an airport to a city, for example,

---

[1] See William Vickery (1948, 1955) for a description of difficulties with marginal cost pricing. See also Kahn (1970, 1971). For a different pricing principle see Tschirhart and Jen (1979).

has different short-run marginal costs at different times and places. When many people want rides from the airport into town, marginal cost may be high, because additional passengers can be served only by quickly gathering together drivers, vehicles, fuel, and other scarce resources to serve them. On the other hand, when no one wants a ride from the airport, marginal cost may be low because there are idle taxis and drivers. Of course, taxi fares tend to be the same at all times, often at regulated levels. There is an advantage in such price stability; it enables consumers to control their financial outlays by knowing what the taxi charges will be. The drawback of the constant price is that taxis may be more scarce at peak times, because the price does not rise to attract more resources into service, so consumers have to wait longer for rides and have less control over their time.

Determining marginal cost, especially at precise places and times, can be a difficult accounting problem because often data are not collected over time intervals short enough to pinpoint the marginal costs for different levels of output at different times. Consequently, marginal cost may not even be known. Should this problem of estimating marginal cost be solved, there are still difficulties in using such precise estimates of marginal cost as a basis for price. First, it is not easy to inform consumers about continuously changing marginal cost prices. And even if they can be informed, consumers may not be able to change their plans quickly enough to take advantage of low prices when marginal costs are low. For these reasons, momentary marginal costs are not used as an influence on price. Efforts are made to create more stable pricing arrangements that can be known and understood by consumers and so can effectively guide their decisions.

If there is a regular periodic pattern over the day or the week, as there often is for electricity demand or for telephone usage, preset prices that depend on time of day may reflect changing costs reasonably well (Hausman and Neufeld 1984; Houthakker 1951). Even when demands follow such conveniently predictable patterns, the patterns may be difficult to translate into a rate schedule that is simple enough to be readily understood by consumers. Moreover, some unpredictable departures from the patterns will almost certainly occur. So it may be difficult to achieve the goal of marginal cost pricing, which is to inform consumers all the time of true alternative costs of their available choices while also giving producers information about consumers' preferences.

Regulated industries typically have prices set through quasi-judicial procedures, which are so time-consuming they are seldom undertaken unless their results will last for some time. As a result, prices in regulated industries tend to be more rigid than in competitive industries. Some responses to input price changes can lead automatically by prearranged formula to output price changes, as fuel adjustment clauses tie the price of electricity partly to the prices of fuels used to produce it. And whenever demand patterns are sufficiently predictable, prices can be set in advance at different levels according to the time of day, week, or year. Of course, such contingent pricing schedules cannot ensure that prices reflect marginal costs with subtlety.

The optimality of prices that are equal to marginal costs for a particular good or service also presumes that prices elsewhere in the economy equal marginal costs. When this condition is not satisfied in one part of the economy, it no longer necessarily follows that prices should equal marginal costs in other parts, and so the prescription may not be appropriate (Davis and Whinston 1965). For example, pricing at marginal cost in one industry may result in a deficit that can be made up only through taxes that distort prices away from marginal costs in other industries. Since prices then must depart from marginal costs elsewhere they should differ from marginal cost also in the industry where prices are being set. This raises the general problem of second-best pricing, to be taken up in Chapter 5.

Despite the difficulties in applying marginal cost pricing, its soundness often can repay the effort many times over. We consider next an especially important opportunity to have prices reflect marginal costs, that of peak-load pricing. When the regularities in demand patterns are great enough that certain periods predictably will have the highest demand, price schedules can vary by time of day, day of week, month of year, and so forth, as needed to reflect the high costs in those periods. Such prices are common for many goods and services, such as seasonal resort accommodation, time-of-day electricity rates, or long-distance telephone service.

4.3   Peak-load pricing

A special opportunity for marginal cost pricing arises when demand follows a periodic cycle, demand predictably being high at some times and low at others. Since marginal cost typically rises with output, having price vary with time will allow it to reflect that higher cost. Prices that vary with time can moderate the magnitude of the demand cycle and therefore allow more effective use of capacity. Electricity use follows a daily cycle, as needs for factories, cooking, lighting, and so forth pass through a daily routine, and it also follows a yearly cycle due largely to climatic change. Then higher prices during periods of peak demand might discourage use and thus save costly capacity, and, when demands are low, lower prices might encourage use of otherwise idle capacity. We are concerned here with the form of this pricing problem and the nature of an optimal solution.

Single technology

We shall first make the problem especially sharp by assuming that only a single, very simple, technology is available. Let capacity cost per unit of output be B, and let capacity be divisible so any number of units of capacity may be chosen.[2] Operating cost per unit of output is b. No unit can be produced unless capacity for it exists, so the presence of $\bar{q}$ units of capacity at cost $B\bar{q}$ would allow production of any output $q \le \bar{q}$, at operating cost bq. This technology and cost implies a cost function that is perfectly flat (at the level of b) up to capacity $\bar{q}$, where it essentially rises vertically, since no further output beyond $\bar{q}$ is possible.

For simplicity, we use consumer surplus to represent welfare. This will be a perfectly accurate measure, of course, only if the good we analyze has zero income elasticity of demand, or at least the income effects are very small. And we accept the current income distribution. We assume there is one uniform demand during the peak period, and another in the off-peak period, represented by the inverse demand functions $P_1(q_1)$ and $P_2(q_2)$. At the same price for both periods we can expect $q_2 < q_1$.

The simplest peak-load pricing situation is one in which peak-period users determine completely the level of capacity to be provided. Suppose that demand D_1 occurs at the peak and demand D_2 at the off-peak, with each defined for equal 12-hour periods, as is operating cost per unit, b. The cost per unit of capacity, B, is defined for the entire demand cycle as the cost to maintain one unit of capacity for one 24-hour day. In that case, peak users may reasonably pay capacity plus operating cost ($P_1 = b + B$), while off-peak users pay only the operating cost ($P_2 = b$). This situation is illustrated in Figure 4.1, where the capacity level $\bar{q}$ is just enough to serve the peak demand D_1 when price is $b + B$, which represents the long-run marginal cost of providing the service. Because off-peak demanders represented by D_2 never use the service at a rate that presses upon the available capacity, the marginal cost per unit of serving them is only b, and that also is the optimal off-peak price. One can see that if D_2 were shifted to the right, so that at the price level b it would fall on the right side of point f, the off-peak demanders willing to pay $P_2 = b$ could not be accommodated by the available capacity, $\bar{q}$. We should then have a case in which the cost of capacity should be shared by peak and off-peak users.

---

2 This classic treatment is due to Boiteux (1960). Indivisibility of capacity is considered by Williamson (1966) and indivisibility with differences in cost is treated by Crew (1968).

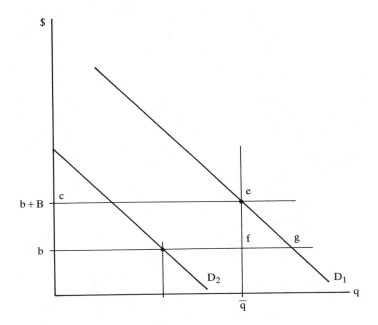

Figure 4.1. Separate peak and off-peak demands.

Some care is required in combining demand, operating cost, and capacity cost in order that sharing in the capacity cost may be correctly analyzed. The key question is: How much are peak and off-peak users, together, willing to pay toward the cost of a marginal capacity unit? In one of the early analyses of this problem, Peter Steiner (1957) used an intuitively appealing approach in which operating cost was zero, so sharing capacity cost could be the main issue. Peak and off-peak demands were for periods of equal length, too. With demands defined for equal-length periods, one can simply add, for every level of capacity, the amount that marginal peak and off-peak users are willing to pay for it. That combined consumer valuation of a unit of capacity can then be compared with cost to determine the optimal capacity level and then, in turn, the optimal peak and off-peak prices.

Figure 4.2 shows peak and off-peak demands for capacity. They are determined by deducting operating cost, b, which we assume to be zero here for simplicity. At each possible level of capacity, the willingness of peak and off-peak users to pay for a marginal capacity unit are added together, to form a total value of capacity curve, the line labeled $\sum D$ in

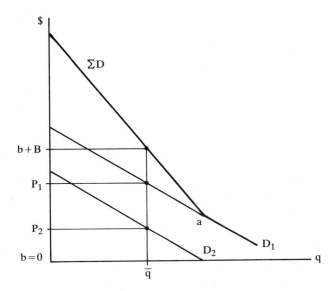

Figure 4.2. Adding two demands defined for separate pricing periods.

Figure 4.2. Where that line intersects capacity cost B, the combined marginal valuation of capacity just equals its cost, so that is the optimal capacity level $\bar{q}$. Prices that will cause peak and off-peak users to demand just that capacity are P_1 and P_2 in Figure 4.2, where $P_1 + P_2 = B$. Notice that with constant operating cost $b > 0$, the same analysis could be carried out with b subtracted away from price. We should then find $(P_1 - b) + (P_2 - b) = B$ at the optimum. The case above, where peak users paid all capacity cost, could also be analyzed in this way (this sort of solution would result in Figure 4.2 if capacity cost was lower, so it intersected peak demand D_1 to the right of point a).

Simple addition of peak and off-peak users' willingness to pay for capacity can be carried out only for time periods of equal length, and so this analysis would not apply if, say, the peak period was 8 hours long and the off-peak period was 16 hours long. Oliver Williamson (1966) introduced a modification to escape this restriction; he used the entire cycle as the time period for which to define consumer demand and operating cost, as well as capacity cost, B. Then each demand function and operating cost function was weighted by the portion of the demand cycle for which it was relevant. The result of this formulation is presented in Figure 4.3, where for comparability with Figure 4.2 it is still assumed that

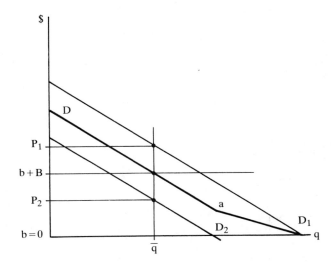

Figure 4.3. Weighting two demands when each is defined for an entire cycle.

peak and off-peak periods are each 12 hours long. With terms defined this way, the combined demand-for-capacity curve is a weighted average, D, of the peak and off-peak curves D_1 and D_2, rather than a simple sum. Notice that curve D has a kink at point a. Beyond that point the price b, rather than willingness to pay D_2, is weighted with D_1 to form D, because D_2 is below b and no price below b can ever be relevant since marginal cost is always at least b. This region of D is comparable to the region of $\sum D$ to the right of point a in Figure 4.2, when only peak users contribute to capacity. Optimal capacity is now determined where the demand for capacity curve D intersects the cost, $b+B$, at $\bar{q}$. This solution is exactly the same as the solution in Figure 4.2, but any weights could have been used here (such as $\frac{1}{3}$ and $\frac{2}{3}$ for 8 hours and 16 hours per day) so the analysis in Figure 4.3 is potentially more general.

Let us work through a problem analytically to see the role of a welfare goal and the advantages of these more general weights. We shall take as a welfare measure consumer surplus plus profit, where profit is total revenue less total cost:

$$W = CS + TR - TC. \tag{1}$$

To represent $CS + TR$, we shall use the area under a demand curve, such as $\int_0^q P(Q)\,dQ$. The peak and off-peak demands are each defined for the full cycle and labeled $P_1(Q)$ and $P_2(Q)$. Then in $CS+TR$ we weight period 1 and period 2 demands by their relative lengths out of the cycle, denoted w_1 and w_2 for peak and off-peak, where $w_1+w_2=1$. Thus we have

$$CS+TR = w_1 \int_0^{q_1} P_1(Q)\,dQ + w_2 \int_0^{q_2} P_2(Q)\,dQ. \tag{2}$$

In total cost we shall weight b, which also is now defined for the full cycle, by the portion of the cycle for which it is relevant. Thus,

$$TC = w_1 b q_1 + w_2 b q_2 + B\bar{q}. \tag{3}$$

This serves for any division of the cycle into two fractions, w_1 and w_2, as long as $w_1+w_2=1$.

We must recognize that there are two possible types of solution to this problem, one in which peak users determine capacity and one in which capacity is shared. In the latter case, $q_1 = q_2 = \bar{q}$. If we substitute (2) and (3) into (1) and differentiate with respect to q on this assumption, and then set the result equal to zero, we obtain

$$w_1 P_1 + w_2 P_2 = b(w_1 + w_2) + B.$$

This is equivalent to

$$w_1(P_1 - b) + w_2(P_2 - b) = B,$$

or

$$w_1 P_1 + w_2 P_2 = b + B. \tag{4}$$

The solution in (4) expresses the weighted average contributions to capacity cost shown in Figure 4.3 for $w_1 = w_2 = \frac{1}{2}$. Without the weights, and with operating cost and demand defined over two periods of equal length (one-half as long as that for which B is defined), the solution also corresponds to that shown in Figure 4.2. The solution in (4) is more general than the Figure 4.2 solution, however, because it can be analyzed for pricing periods of any length.

If we do not have $q_1 = q_2 = \bar{q}$, we must maximize W with respect to both q_1 and q_2, to obtain

$$w_1 P_1 = w_1 b + B$$

and

$$w_2 P_2 = w_2 b.$$

These conditions can be rearranged to obtain solution prices

$$P_1 = b + B/w_1 \tag{5}$$

and

$$P_2 = b. \tag{6}$$

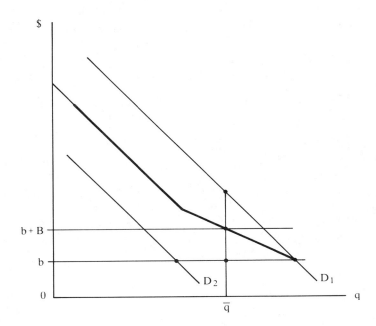

Figure 4.4. Weighting peak and off-peak demands defined for the cycle.

Here, because at the solution $q_1 > q_2$, peak users pay all the cost of capacity in addition to operating cost, whereas off-peak users pay only operating cost. These are the prices obtained in Figure 4.1, except that demand and operating cost there were defined for half the demand cycle. Here demand and operating cost are defined for the full cycle and weighted for the portions where they apply. The solution given in (5) and (6) is illustrated in Figure 4.4, and it corresponds to the companion case of shared capacity cost in Figure 4.3, just as Figure 4.1 corresponds to Figure 4.2.

It should be evident that this approach to the problem of peak-load pricing could easily be modified to deal with more periods and more demands for those periods. Demands and operating costs would still be defined for the full cycle and weighted by the fraction of the period when they would be relevant. There could then be a mixture of the two possible cases we have shown. In some periods users might share capacity costs. In other periods price would cover only operating costs because capacity was not fully used.

Since an example by Faulhaber and Levinson (1981) fits this case, we digress briefly to show by modifying their example whether the prices in (5) and (6) are subsidy-free as defined in Section 3.5, considering peak and off-peak services as two goods. For prices to be subsidy-free, consumers of each good must pay no more than stand-alone costs:

$$w_1 P_1 q_1 \leq C(q_1, 0) = (w_1 b + B) q_1,$$

$$w_2 P_2 q_2 \leq C(0, q_2) = (w_2 b + B) q_2.$$

Total revenue also must equal total cost:

$$w_1 P_1 q_1 + w_2 P_2 q_2 = B q_1 + b(w_1 q_1 + w_2 q_2) = C(q_1, q_2).$$

Combining this requirement with the inequalities above, we find that the incremental cost test requires

$$w_1 P_1 q_1 \geq C(q_1, q_2) - C(0, q_2)$$
$$\geq (w_1 b + B) q_1 - B q_2,$$

$$w_2 P_2 q_2 \geq C(q_1, q_2) - C(q_1, 0)$$
$$\geq w_2 b q_2.$$

Thus, to be subsidy-free, P_1 and P_2 must satisfy

$$b + (1 - q_2/q_1) B/w_1 \leq P_1 \leq b + B/w_1,$$

and

$$b \leq P_2 \leq b + B/w_2.$$

Clearly, the prices in (5) and (6) are subsidy-free, for they satisfy all the requirements, but there exist other prices that meet the above constraints and would also allow the firm to break even. So (5) and (6) are not unique subsidy-free prices.

There was only one simple production method in the problem we have considered. In many instances in which peak-load problems arise there are different techniques of production available. For example, electricity might be produced either with large capacity costs and relatively low operating costs, as by nuclear reactor, or with low capacity costs and high operating cost, as by internal combustion engine. Naturally, the technology with large capacity cost can be attractive only if the capacity can be utilized much of the time, for with capacity idle its large cost will be wasted. The technology with lower capacity cost might be more attractive if utilization of capacity is low. We now examine how the solution should be modified for such diverse technology.

Diverse technology

Let us now assume that two techniques are available for electricity production, one with capacity cost B_1 and operating cost b_1, the other with capacity cost B_2 and operating cost b_2. We also assume that $B_2 > B_1$ and

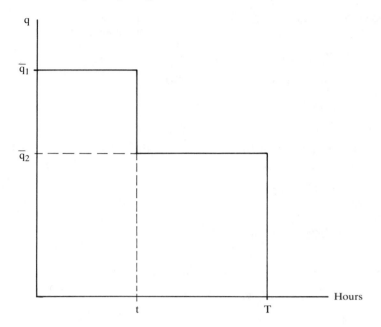

Figure 4.5. Simplified cumulative load duration curve.

$b_2 < b_1$, and that $B_2 + b_2 < B_1 + b_1$. These assumptions make B_2, b_2 the lower cost technique if it can be fully utilized, but since its capacity cost is high it may not be economical at low rates of utilization.[3] In Figure 4.5 we present a cumulative load duration curve, which shows that part of the total cycle of length T hours (horizontally) when any given load on the system (vertically) will be equaled or exceeded. Figure 4.5 presumes that certain prices have already been set, and as presented it has one load or quantity of service, $\bar{q}_2$, being provided over the entire cycle of T hours, and another quantity, $\bar{q}_1 - \bar{q}_2$, being provided only t hours, or for the fraction t/T of the total cycle. At the optimal division of generation between the two techniques, their marginal costs should be exactly the same (Turvey 1968, pp. 28–31). We can express equal marginal cost of the two techniques at that point as

$$B_1 + (t/T)b_1 = B_2 + (t/T)b_2.$$

[3] John Wenders (1976) reported rough Tucson Gas and Electric Company estimates of per-kilowatt values for B for three techniques: coal steam, $100; oil steam, $40; and internal combustion, $20. The corresponding values for b were coal steam, $20.81; oil steam, $175.20; and internal combusion, $240.90.

Equal marginal cost thus implies

$$\frac{t}{T} = = \frac{B_2 - B_1}{b_1 - b_2}. \tag{7}$$

Let us suppose that technique 2, with costs B_2, b_2, operates over the whole cycle and technique 1, with costs B_1, b_1, operates at the peak, just t/T of the cycle. Operating costs are

$$C_0 = b_2 \bar{q}_2 + (t/T) b_1 (\bar{q}_1 - \bar{q}_2) \tag{8}$$

and capital costs are

$$C_K = B_2 \bar{q}_2 + B_1 (\bar{q}_1 - \bar{q}_2). \tag{9}$$

We shall also assume as before that demands for peak (q_1) and off-peak (q_2) periods can be defined for the entire cycle. Now the weights correspond to the demand pattern of Figure 4.5 so the welfare measure is

$$CS + TR = \frac{t}{T} \int_0^{q_1} P_1(Q)\, dQ + \left(1 - \frac{t}{T}\right) \int_0^{q_2} P_2(Q)\, dQ. \tag{10}$$

We seek optimal levels of q_1 and q_2, which will yield optimal prices implicitly. Necessary conditions for a maximum of welfare, $W = CS + TR - TC$, where $TC = C_0 + C_K$, are

$$\frac{\partial W}{\partial q_1} = \frac{t}{T} P_1 - \frac{t}{T} b_1 - B_1 = 0$$

and

$$\frac{\partial W}{\partial q_2} = \left(1 - \frac{t}{T}\right) P_2 - b_2 + \frac{t}{T} b_1 - B_2 + B_1 = 0.$$

These conditions yield the optimal prices

$$P_1 = b_1 + B_1/(t/T) \tag{11}$$

and

$$P_2 = (b_2 - (t/T) b_1 + B_2 - B_1)/(1 - t/T). \tag{12}$$

After rearranging (12) and substituting for t/T from (7), it simplifies to

$$P_2 = b_2. \tag{12'}$$

The optimal peak-load price in (11), P_1, is the price we should have expected as ideal if the capacity for technique 1 were needed only to serve peak users, which is indeed the case. Those who use the service at the peak-demand time are required to pay for having capacity stand idle the rest of the demand cycle, as they should because such capacity must be installed to serve them. Since part of the peak demand actually is met by

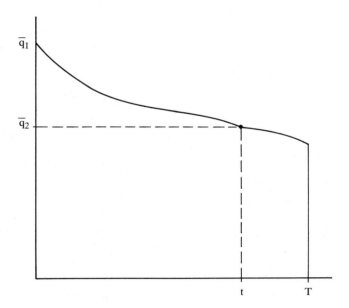

Figure 4.6. Cumulative load duration curve.

capacity of technique 2, which has lower cost, a savings is made that allows off-peak users to pay only operating costs b_2 for technique 2. The true marginal cost of off-peak service in (12′) reflects the benefit of having technique 2 available at peak times, which is translated to P_2 through (7).

The solution represented in equations (11) and (12′) actually presumes that technique 1 should be used at the peak and technique 2 should be used at the off-peak time. It is possible, for given costs and time periods, that technique 2 actually offers lower cost at both times and technique 1 should not be used at all. We should realize this if, with the given parameters, we found

$$b_2 + B_2/(t/T) < P_1 = b_1 + B_1/(t/T),$$

for that would mean that technique 2 could yield a lower cost even at peak times. We also assumed demand was uniform through each of two periods that just equaled t and $T - t$ in length. In practice, demand might follow a pattern more like that shown in Figure 4.6, reaching a range of values within each time period. The optimal time periods could still be guided then by knowledge of costs, following (7) to divide the use of technologies efficiently, with prices like (11) and (12′) then applied in those periods. Of course capacity utilization would be lower than presumed in the case of uniform demand within periods analyzed above (see Turvey 1968, pp. 51–4).

There are likely to be more than two production techniques. Sometimes there are more techniques available than feasible pricing periods. If the price schedule is too complex for consumers to understand or remember, then compromise is in order, and only the most important features of cost are singled out to present to consumers. As a result, the optimal division among techniques may not match exactly the division among pricing periods that is most convenient.[4] Then weights on demands in (10) will differ from the t/T weights on technologies used, and (7) may no longer yield simple off-peak prices as in (12'). As long as the cumulative load curve is continuous, (7) can yield a simple weighting of operating costs (Joskow 1976). Generally, if an off-peak period is served by more than one technique, the optimal off-peak price will include a contribution to capacity cost (Wenders 1976). And if demand is stochastic, the optimal price will equal an expected operating cost that can include capacity costs (Crew and Kleindorfer 1976). Despite complications, when prices and technologies are to be chosen simultaneously, the aim is still the same: to confront consumers as fully as possible with the cost consequences of their decisions.

4.4 Peak-load pricing under uncertainty

When demand fluctuates, we know that consumers cannot immediately be informed of all changes in marginal cost without an enormous expenditure on communications. Nor could consumers easily respond to each resulting little change in price even if they could be informed. When marginal cost tends to change because demand changes systematically with time, it is desirable to have price vary with time, as we saw in Section 4.3, because a time-dependent price schedule can be communicated to consumers who will be able to respond accordingly. The typical level of demand will then be anticipated by suppliers, and their expected costs can be communicated to consumers.

Of course, a predictable periodicity of demand, which allows price to vary by time of day (or week or year), may capture only crudely the fluctuation in demand and leave within each time period substantial fluctuation that is essentially random because it cannot be predicted. We shall treat such uncertainty in demand here for the simple case of a single technology. Uncertainty takes the form of an error term added to demand, so

---

4 Wenders (1976) provides a revealing analysis of such a problem. For a more general treatment, see Crew and Kleindorfer (1976, 1979b, 1986).

an analysis in terms of expected values will be possible. In addition to the assumptions usually required for analysis involving consumer surplus, we add risk-neutrality of all participants when we carry out the analysis in terms of expected values. The best way to deal with the average outcome is then taken to be the optimal solution for the peak, off-peak, or other time period.

We consider two periods, identified by $t = 1, 2$. Suppose that demand in period t is $q_t(P_t) + u_t$, where u_t is a random error term with a mean of zero. Mean demand q_t is downward sloping ($\partial q_t/\partial P_t < 0$) and the inverse q_t^{-1} exists. We assume that demands in the two periods are independent, and error terms u_1, u_2 also are independent. Operating cost again will be b up to capacity, $\bar{q}$, and capacity cost is B per unit. We assume that the rate of output for a service is strictly limited by capacity. Then at the established price P_t in period t, sales, S_t, will equal the minimum of demand or capacity:

$$S_t(P_t, \bar{q}, u_t) = \text{Min}[q_t(P_t) + u_t, \bar{q}]. \tag{13}$$

We shall first modify the consumer surplus measure in the simplest possible way to take uncertainty into account. In doing so we follow the approach of Brown and Johnson (1969), as interpreted by Crew and Kleindorfer (1978). Define a welfare measure for given P, $\bar{q}$, and u as

$$W(P, \bar{q}, u) = \sum_{t=1}^{2} \int_{-\infty}^{\infty} \int_{0}^{S_t(P_t, \bar{q}, u_t)} [q_t^{-1}(q - u_t) - P_t] \, dq \, du$$

$$+ \sum_{t=1}^{2} \int_{-\infty}^{\infty} (P_t - b)(S_t(P_t, \bar{q}, u_t) \, du - B\bar{q}. \tag{14}$$

The last two terms in equation (14) represent $TR - TC$. The first term elaborates consumer surplus in each period by calculating it for all possible values of u_t, and it becomes the expected CS term in an expected value representation of $W = TR + CS - TC$. We now assume consumers are risk-neutral and maximize the expected value of (14) over positive values of prices and capacities. Necessary conditions are

$$(P_t - b)F_t[\bar{q} - q_t(P_t)] \, dq_t/dP_t = 0, \quad t = 1, 2, \tag{15}$$

$$\sum_{t=1}^{2} \int_{\bar{q}-q_t(P_t)}^{\infty} [q_t^{-1}(\bar{q} - u_t) - b] f_t(u_t) \, du_t = \beta, \tag{16}$$

where F_t is the cumulative distribution function of u_t and f_t is the density function.

The term $F_t[\bar{q} - q_t(P_t)]$ is the probability that demand is less than capacity, and is called "reliability." As long as reliability is positive, (15) calls for $P_t = b$, or that price equals short-run marginal cost. Referring to

Figure 4.1, suppose that demands fluctuate randomly about D_1 and D_2. The off-peak demand might be seen as a case in which $F_t[\bar{q} - q_t(P_t)] = 1.0$ if demand fluctuations are not great, so optimal off-peak price is b. Suppose, however, that at the peak demand, $F_t[\bar{q} - q_t(P_t)] = 0$; in that case an optimal price is not clear from (15), because any P_t can then satisfy the condition. Crew and Kleindorfer (1978, p. 32) interpret the capacity condition (16) as calling for $\bar{q}$ to be "just large enough so that the marginal expected losses due to unmet demand are equal to marginal capacity B." If the variance of u_t is low, or if B is large, they point out that at a peak-load price of b the optimal capacity might be small enough to make $F_t[\bar{q} - q_t(P_t)] = 0$. So a peak-load price above b is probably in order.

Robert Meyer (1975), in maximizing profit rather than welfare, constrained reliability to a specified level. We cannot use this method in seeking a welfare maximum, however, for the simple consumer surplus measure in (14) is not correct with uncertainty because the price may not be market clearing. In Section 4.3, where Figure 4.1 was discussed, if price had not been market clearing, or (more specifically) if demand had exceeded available capacity at the going price, there could be no assurance that consumers who value the service most would be served. With the price set at b in Figure 4.1, for example, demands represented in consumer surplus area egf would seek to obtain the service, yet they would not value the service as much as its cost, $b + B$. Since they could not be recognized and denied service, they might displace some of the consumers who would experience greater consumer surplus, with the result that total welfare would be reduced (Visscher 1973). A price of $b + B$ is preferred because it ensures that those who value the service most actually will receive it. Indeed, $P = b + B$ is a "market clearing" price.

Two possibilities are illustrated in Figure 4.7. In Figure 4.7a, even though price $\bar{P}$ is below the market-clearing level at capacity $\bar{q}$, those who value the service *most* are served and consumer surplus is represented by the shaded area $ab\bar{q}0$. This is the result assumed in (14). In Figure 4.7b, those who value the service *least* are the ones who actually receive it, and consumer surplus then is the smaller shaded area $bcde$. The reason $P = b$ turns up in (15) is that (by the assumption that matches Figure 4.7a) price does not have to serve a market-clearing function. But it is unreasonable to assume that scarce capacity will serve the right consumers that way. Crew and Kleindorfer (1976, 1978) imposed a cost for rationing the service to the consumers who value it *most,* and because rationing is more necessary at the peak they found a higher price to be optimal then. Michael Visscher (1973) assumed that those who valued the service *least* would receive it if price were not available to ration service to the right consumers. His assumption thus matched the situation shown in Figure 4.7b. The

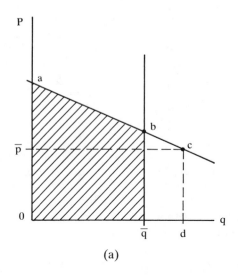

(a)

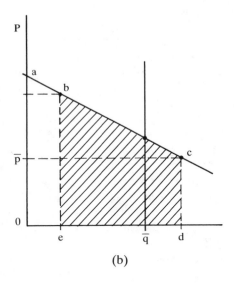

(b)

Figure 4.7. Who is served when demand exceeds capacity?

representation of consumer surplus for the situation in Figure 4.7b is more complex and will not be developed here. It is presented clearly by Visscher (1973). With respect to the assumption that those who value the service least will be served when demand exceeds capacity, he finds that the opti-

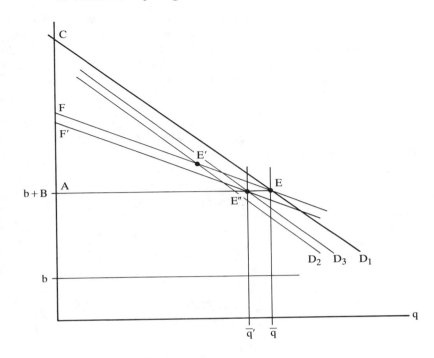

Figure 4.8. Nonuniform prices.

mal peak price then is $b + B$. Optimal capacity may be larger or smaller than $q(b + B)$, depending on demand elasticity and the cost function.

With uncertain demand it is thus possible to determine optimal peak-load price and capacity along the lines developed in Section 4.3, but prices will not be market clearing and capacity will not be fully utilized. Some assumption is needed then about who receives service, or about the cost of nonprice means of rationing service to those who value it the most. If consumers are risk-neutral, so that expected values can be relied upon, optimal peak and off-peak prices can be determined.

4.5   Nonuniform pricing

A uniform price is at the same level over all quantities. In commenting on the Steiner (1957) analysis of peak-load pricing, Buchanan (1966) pointed out that many nonuniform pricing schedules could be created as alternatives to the uniform price solution. Consider a single technology with operating cost b and capacity cost B, as shown in Figure 4.8. The uniform peak-load price is represented by the line AE at the constant uniform price of $b + B$. A nonuniform price is represented by the price schedule FE, which has a higher price than $b + B$ at quantities below capacity and a lower price at quantities above the capacity level. Notice that every unit is available at a lower price than the previous one, but the nonuniform schedule has exactly the same marginal price at capacity output as the uniform price schedule if demand remains the same at D_1.

For the nonuniform price schedule in Figure 4.8, marginal price per unit declines continuously as total units consumed per time period increase. The marginal price decline might be put into effect by having every consumer face a quantity-dependent declining price schedule, with the market outcome then representing an aggregation of consumer behavior. Unless every consumer is the same, however, a nonuniform schedule such as that shown as FE in Figure 4.8 could result in different marginal prices for different consumers, depending on where their individual demands met the price schedule, so aggregation into a market demand could be complicated. To avoid this problem here, let us assume for the moment that all consumers are the same, and that all select the same quantity and reach equilibrium at the same marginal price. Figure 4.8 then simply "blows up" to aggregate quantities the choice situation of each individual.

A nonuniform price structure such as that represented by FE in Figure 4.8 can affect the equilibrium outcome if there are income effects. Early inframarginal purchases made by the consumer occur at higher prices (or, with other conceivable nonuniform price schedules, lower prices), which will alter incomes from the levels obtained at the equilibrium under the uniform price $b + B$. To continue with the Figure 4.8 example, suppose that the income effect in going from uniform price schedule AE to nonuniform schedule FE shifts demand from D_1 to D_2, rather than persisting in the same demand at D_1. Such a downward shift in demand could be expected for a normal good since the higher prices charged for earlier units under the nonuniform price schedule would reduce income remaining for the consumer. Then the nonuniform price schedule would yield a different equilibrium, at E', than the uniform schedule would at E. Marginal price exceeds long-run marginal cost of $b + B$ at E'; so the price schedule can be lowered to $F'E''$, causing demand to shift again to D_3. The new solution is at E'', with smaller capacity $\bar{q}'$. The solution at E'' will yield greater revenue, because of the higher price for earlier units, but less consumer surplus by the same amount. From the information we have, it is not possible to say that one equilibrium is better than the other, for they both satisfy necessary conditions for a maximum of welfare.

A nonuniform tariff can be useful for raising revenue without great loss of welfare wherever a uniform price per unit equal to marginal cost would result in a deficit. The two-part tariff is the simplest nonuniform price, with a fixed fee per customer per time period plus a price per unit. The fixed fee can be used to cover any deficit from pricing marginal usage at marginal cost.[5] Indeed, when all consumers share equally in a fixed cost through fixed fees, and pay a price per unit equal to marginal cost, the result can be ideal (Coase 1946). But if the fixed fee exceeds any cost of serving a customer and one customer decides not to use the service because of that fee, the result cannot be ideal. We examine first a simple case in which the two parts of a two-part tariff equal marginal costs traceable to the two pricing dimensions. We then consider more general price schedules that have price depend on quantity consumed, as in a block tariff that contains different uniform prices for different blocks of quantities. But with the goal of ideal welfare maximization such price schedules are not appropriate, as price should simply be set equal to marginal cost.

Cost and price dimensions

Here we emphasize two-part pricing to cover costs that arise in two dimensions of service.[6] For example, telephone service may involve a fixed charge, just to cover the costs of maintaining a telephone and a connection for a customer to the telephone network, plus a charge for the use of the network based on the duration and the distance of calls made. Connection and usage are then two causes that warrant separate charges. We shall use a combination of direct and indirect utility functions to represent the well-being of consumers.

We assume that consumers may be ordered by type according to an index, θ, for clear and well-defined modeling of their demand behavior. We further assume that a person with a higher θ will consistently benefit either more or less from the service, everything else being equal. If higher θ indicates more benefit, we expect $\partial q/\partial\theta > 0$, whereas if higher θ indicates less benefit, then $\partial q/\partial\theta < 0$. Without loss of generality we assume $0 \le \theta \le 1$. The distribution of θ is given by the density function, $f(\theta)$. A consumer with index θ has the utility function $u = u(g, q, \theta)$, where q is the good of interest and g is a composite good representing everything else. The price of the composite good, g, should be in all demand functions, but since it will be assumed constant at $P_g = 1$, we suppress it. We seek optimal pricing for the good, q, when it is provided by a monopolist whose costs may vary not only with the amount of q produced, but also with the number of consumers served. We assume constant costs in order to avoid the

---

[5] More generally, income distribution goals may be pursued through multipart pricing. See Feldstein (1972b).
[6] A classic illustration of a two-part price problem almost this simple is presented by Coase (1946).

problem of dealing with a deficit or disposing of profit. We assume the monopolist has a constant cost of serving customers, C_n, such as the cost of connecting a residence to receive electricity, and a constant cost of producing units of service, C_q.

The differences among individuals who have different θ may be regarded as differences in tastes for the good. It could also be due to income differences but we assume it is not, for we prefer to assume there is no income effect in order that we may use consumer surplus to represent consumer welfare. Whenever consumers have a choice among two-part tariffs, or whether to consume or not according to a two-part tariff, possible results can be extremely complex.[7] Having consumers differ only by their taste for the good ensures that one consumer's demand will be above or below another's at any price, and that allows well defined separation of consumer groups. The real world may not be as convenient and well defined, but we can obtain general patterns while avoiding inconvenient cases on this assumption, and the pattern should be descriptive of what can be expected to occur in the world.

By assuming that consumers have diminishing marginal rates of substitution between q and the composite good (g) we can obtain a market demand function, $Q = Q(P_n, P_q)$, where P_n is a fixed fee per consumer and P_q is the price per unit of q. There is also a patronage function, $n = n(P_n, P_q)$, which determines the number of consumers. To simplify the analysis we assume both of these functions are continuous (so we can apply calculus). The demand for an individual of type θ will be $q = q(P_n, P_q, \theta)$. Individuals with values of θ below some level $\hat{\theta}$ will not pay the fee P_n and so will not be able to consume q at price P_q; for them $q = 0$.[8] These persons will spend all income y on g, and since g has a price of 1, utility will be $u(y,0)$. The level of θ that identifies the marginal consumer, $\hat{\theta}$, will depend on P_n and P_q. We ignore possible lack of uniqueness here (Auerbach and Pellechio 1978; Ng and Weisser 1974) and we assume $0 < \hat{\theta} < 1$. Then patronage and demand functions can be calculated as

$$n(P_n, P_q) = \int_{\hat{\theta}(P_n, P_q)}^{1} f(\theta)\, d\theta \tag{17}$$

and

$$Q(P_n, P_q) = \int_{\hat{\theta}(P_n, P_q)}^{1} q(P_n, P_q, \theta) f(\theta)\, d\theta. \tag{18}$$

---

[7] Oi (1971) demonstrates the complexity that this problem can take on as he develops a monopoly solution.

[8] The borderline value of $\hat{\theta}$ is defined below in equation (24). Auerbach and Pellechio (1978) used this sort of representation for voluntary affiliation at a fixed fee. See also Ng and Weisser (1974), Schmalensee (1981a), and Sherman and Visscher (1982a).

The demand functions have properties we would expect: $q_\theta > 0$, $q_{P_q} < 0$, $Q_{P_n} < 0$, $Q_{P_q} < 0$, $n_{P_n} < 0$, $n_{P_q} < 0$.

Consumer welfare can now be represented as

$$C = \int_0^{\hat{\theta}(P_n, P_q)} w(y) u(y, 0, \theta) f(\theta)\, d\theta$$

$$+ \int_{\hat{\theta}(P_n, P_q)}^1 w(y) v(P_q, y - P_n, \theta) f(\theta)\, d\theta, \tag{19}$$

where $w(y)$ is the social weight accorded an individual of income y. For indexes up to $\hat{\theta}$, utility is $u(y, 0, \theta)$ since q is not consumed, whereas at higher values of θ, where the good is consumed, utility is represented by the indirect utility function, $v(P_q, y - P_n, \theta)$. Profit is $TR - TC$ or

$$\pi = TR - TC = (P_n - C_n) n(P_n, P_q) + (P_q - C_q) Q(P_n, P_q). \tag{20}$$

The welfare function we seek to maximize is

$$W = C + TR - TC. \tag{21}$$

Substituting (1) and (20) into (21) and differentiating with respect to P_n and P_q, then setting the results equal to zero, yields

$$\int_{\hat{\theta}}^1 w(y) \frac{\partial v}{\partial P_n} f(\theta)\, d\theta + [u(y, 0, \hat{\theta}) - v(P_q, y, \hat{\theta})] w(y) \frac{\partial \hat{\theta}}{\partial P_n}$$

$$+ (P_n - C_n) \frac{\partial n}{\partial P_n} + n + (P_q - C_q) \frac{\partial Q}{\partial P_n} = 0 \tag{22}$$

and

$$\int_{\hat{\theta}}^1 w(y) \frac{\partial v}{\partial P_q} f(\theta)\, d\theta + [u(y, 0, \hat{\theta})) - v(P_q, y - P_n, \hat{\theta})] w(y) \frac{\partial \hat{\theta}}{\partial P_q}$$

$$+ (P_n - C_n) \frac{\partial n}{\partial P_q} + (P_q - C_q) \frac{\partial Q}{\partial P_q} + Q = 0. \tag{23}$$

We note first that by the definition of $\hat{\theta}$,

$$u(y, 0, \hat{\theta}) = v(P_q, y - P_n, \hat{\theta}), \tag{24}$$

which will cause one term in (22) and a similar term in (23) to vanish. Indeed, this shows that we need not consider the welfare of consumers with $\theta < \hat{\theta}$, as allowed for in (19), since they vanish from the necessary conditions. And the relevant benefit for those who consume is $v(P_q, y - P_n, \theta) - u(y, 0, \hat{\theta})$, or the equivalent value that will be recognized as consumer surplus, $v(P_q, y - P_n, \theta) - v(\infty, y, \hat{\theta})$.

From the properties of indirect utility functions (Chapter 2, equations (17) and (20)), if we consider $\partial v / \partial P_n = -\partial v / \partial y$ for a person consuming q (a rise in P_n is like a fall in income), we have

$$\frac{\partial v}{\partial P_n} = -\eta(y), \tag{25}$$

$$\frac{\partial v}{\partial P_q} = -\eta(y)q, \tag{26}$$

where $\eta(y)$ is the marginal utility of income for a person who has income y. Let us accept the current distribution of income and make the assumption about welfare weights that is implicit in the consumer surplus representation of welfare,

$$w(y) = 1/\eta(y). \tag{27}$$

If we now substitute (24), (25), (26), and (27) into (22) and (23), those expressions simplify to

$$(P_n - C_n)\frac{\partial n}{\partial P_n} + (P_q - C_q)\frac{\partial Q}{\partial P_n} = 0$$

and

$$(P_n - C_n)\frac{\partial n}{\partial P_q} + (P_q - C_q)\frac{\partial Q}{\partial P_q} = 0,$$

which yield the simple solution

$$P_n = C_n \tag{28}$$

and

$$P_q = C_q. \tag{29}$$

Thus our elaborate construction yields the extremely simple result that price in each dimension should equal marginal cost. Our care in formulating the problem is nevertheless warranted because the two-part price creates a complicated situation. Consumption of q can occur *only* if the payment P_n is made, and some consumers may drop out of the market by choosing not to consume q at all. To simplify the analysis, we assumed constant costs, so pricing at marginal cost would not create a deficit.

To allow systematic analysis of two-part tariffs we assumed that consumers differed in their taste for the good, represented by θ. For telephone service, consumers might be families of different sizes, where θ could be family size; for gas heating fuel, θ might be size of home. We assume the firm cannot observe θ, for if it could it might discriminate in price. It is necessary that a consumer with a higher value of θ consistently demand greater (or as an alternative, consistently less) quantity than a consumer with a lower value of θ, at any possible price level. This will ensure that clear distinctions can always be made between groups (as demonstrated, for example, in Figure 2.7b). What is crucial to consistent analysis is that demands do not cross, as when person 1 buys a greater quantity than person 2 at price P_1 while person 2 buys the greater quantity at price P_2.

Quantity-dependent nonuniform pricing

Setting a different price for every unit produced can yield an ideal outcome and cover total cost when unit costs vary with output, and can also offer improvement over a uniform price above marginal cost, as noted in Chapter 2. Think of the price schedule as determining a total payment R, which depends on the amount consumed q, $R = R(q)$, where the marginal price per unit is $P(q) = R'(q)$. Of course, such quantity-dependent pricing will survive only if consumers are unable to resell units, or even to exchange units with each other, for we know that exchange leads to a single price, uniform over all units. And if our goal is to find ideal prices, without regard for profit constraints or income distribution, having prices differ with quantities consumed will usually be undesirable unless costs vary with those quantities.

If there were only one consumer of a service, it would be possible to have a welfare-maximizing nonuniform price schedule in which price per unit would vary with quantity to reflect decreasing (or increasing) costs of production. Then the consumer could know the cost consequences of consumption and choose accordingly. When there are many consumers, this approach may be changed considerably. If the seller cannot know the preferences of individual consumers, the price schedule will have to be oriented to individual consumption quantities, so that each consumer can face the same schedule. The seller then avoids having to decide who may consume at the lower prices, which would be difficult when it cannot observe any differences in consumers. If all consumers are the same in their demands, the result can still be ideal, too, just as it was with only one consumer, for all will choose the same quantity. If consumers differ, however, the quantity-dependent price schedule may allow different marginal prices for different consumers. Nevertheless, a quantity-dependent, nonuniform price schedule can separate consumers in ways that allow them to contribute most appropriately toward the total costs of production.

The virtue of nonuniform, quantity-dependent, pricing over uniform pricing above marginal cost has been nicely demonstrated by Willig (1978). The logic of his argument was developed in Section 2.7, where a choice among two-part tariffs led to block tariffs. Spence (1980) developed similar schedules in a welfare context and showed that without some extra condition, such as a budget constraint that creates a second-best problem, the price should simply equal marginal cost. Optimal continuous quantity-dependent prices were set out by Goldman, Leland, and Sibley (1984), and again without second-best complications price equal to marginal cost would be optimal. They did show, however, that ideal prices may differ from marginal cost when income effects are present. We postpone consideration of second-best problems to Chapter 5.

4.6   Externality pricing

When individual decisions create costs (or benefits) felt beyond the individual decision maker, we have negative (positive) externalities. Externalities are effects external to a decision that for one reason or another cannot be priced, and so they usually lead to nonoptimal allocation of resources. Wherever possible, the best remedy is to find a way to set a price for the externality and then to confront the decision maker with that price, thereby effectively internalizing all the consequences of the decision. We examine here an externality that we have all experienced, highway traffic congestion.[9]

In analyzing this problem, we use a welfare function which is a weighted sum of individual utility functions. Individuals have arbitrary weights in the welfare function, and when we maximize with respect to incomes, the result is essentially to compensate consumers for the effects of any changes imposed. This will lead to compensated demand curves, of the type illustrated through points a and c in Figure 2.3 and discussed in Sections 2.2 and 2.3. In analyzing this problem, we shall depart in one other way from the primary method used thus far: Instead of maximizing consumer plus producer surplus, we maximize consumer welfare subject to certain constraints that limit welfare, such as the physical production possibilities that exist. We thus employ the Lagrange multiplier method of analysis, which was introduced in very simple form in Section 2.2.[10] Through a constraint, we can introduce with this method the way we each decide auto use – at its social average cost rather than its social marginal cost.

Suppose the ith individual in a population of I individuals derives satisfaction from miles of auto travel, t, and a composite good, g, so that utility is

$$u^i = u^i(t^i, g^i), \quad i = 1, \ldots, I. \tag{30}$$

As auto travel increases on a given road network, at some point it requires greater average fuel and other resources per mile, f; so $f = f(t)$ where

---

[9] The model that we consider here is a simplified version of one examined in Sherman (1971, 1972a). For more general treatment of externality, see Buchanan and Stubblebine (1962), Coase (1960), and Knight (1924).

[10] Many mathematics textbooks explain the method of Lagrange multipliers. A simple exposition is contained in Chiang (1984), and one stressing applications can be found in Hadley (1964).

$\partial f/\partial t > 0$ (f is a continuous and twice differentiable function of t). The price of f in terms of g will be denoted by π. Let g be numeraire, with $P_g = 1$, and the effective price of auto travel is P_t per mile. If y^i is the ith individual's income, the budget constraint is

$$g^i + P_t t^i = y^i, \quad i = 1, \ldots, I. \tag{31}$$

Maximization of (30) subject to (31) yields

$$\partial u^i/\partial g^i = \eta^i, \quad i = 1, \ldots, I, \tag{32}$$

$$\partial u^i/\partial t^i = \eta^i P_t, \quad i = 1, \ldots, I. \tag{33}$$

The Lagrange multiplier, η^i, represents marginal utility of income for person i. These conditions along with the budget constraint yield demand functions

$$g^i = g^i(P_t, y^i), \quad i = 1, \ldots, I, \tag{34}$$

$$t^i = t^i(P_t, y^i), \quad i = 1, \ldots, I. \tag{35}$$

Let us represent social welfare with a combination of utility functions,

$$W = W(u^1, \ldots, u^I). \tag{36}$$

Suppose that average input per mile traveled, f, times amount of travel in miles, t, equals total resources devoted to travel, r; that is, $tf = r$. The resource r may be transformed into composite good g according to the convex (continuous and twice differentiable) transformation surface $h(g, r) = 0$. We shall say the price of input f is π, which in competitive markets should equal the marginal rate of transformation, $\pi = -dg/dr$. Now we could maximize (36) subject to the two technological relations,

$$tf = r, \tag{37}$$

$$h(g, r) = 0. \tag{38}$$

For completeness we add identities that relate market aggregates, t and g, to individuals' chosen quantities, t^i's and g^i's,

$$\sum_i t^i \equiv t, \tag{39}$$

$$\sum_i g^i \equiv g. \tag{40}$$

We thus can form the Lagrangian,

$$G(P_t, t, g, r, y^i) = W(u^i, \ldots, u^I) - \mu(tf - r) - \phi(h(g, r))$$
$$- \tau(\sum t^i - t) - \gamma(\sum g^i - g). \tag{41}$$

Maximizing with respect to P_t, t, g, r, and the y^i's, we have, in addition to the constraints, the necessary conditions

$$\Sigma_i \, W_i \left(\frac{\partial u^i}{\partial t^i} \frac{\partial t^i}{\partial P_t} + \frac{\partial u^i}{\partial g^i} \frac{\partial g^i}{\partial P_t} \right) - \tau \Sigma_i \frac{\partial t^i}{\partial P_t} - \gamma \Sigma_i \frac{\partial g^i}{\partial P_t} = 0, \qquad (42)$$

$$-\mu \left(f + t \frac{\partial f}{\partial t} \right) + \tau = 0, \qquad (43)$$

$$-\phi \frac{\partial h}{\partial g} + \gamma = 0, \qquad (44)$$

$$\mu - \phi \frac{\partial h}{\partial r} = 0, \qquad (45)$$

$$W_i \left(\frac{\partial u^i}{\partial t^i} \frac{\partial t^i}{\partial y^i} + \frac{\partial u^i}{\partial g^i} \frac{\partial g^i}{\partial y^i} \right) - \tau \Sigma_i \frac{\partial t^i}{\partial y^i}$$
$$- \gamma \Sigma_i \frac{\partial g^i}{\partial y^i} = 0, \quad i = 1, \dots, I. \qquad (46)$$

From these conditions we can obtain the welfare-maximizing price of highway travel. Using (32) and (33), the first term in (42) can be reduced to $\Sigma_i \, W_i \eta^i (P_t \, \partial t^i / \partial P_t + \partial g^i / \partial P_t)$. From differentiating the individual's budget constraint, (31), we know $P_t \, \partial t^i / \partial P_t + \partial g^i / \partial P_t = -t^i$. Thus (42) becomes

$$-\Sigma_i \, W_i \eta^i t^i - \tau \Sigma_i \frac{\partial t^i}{\partial P_t} - \gamma \Sigma_i \frac{\partial g^i}{\partial P_t} = 0. \qquad (47)$$

Recognizing that $(\partial u^i / \partial t^i)(\partial t^i / \partial y^i) + (\partial u^i / \partial g^i)(\partial g^i / \partial y^i) = \eta^i$, and substituting for $W_i \eta^i$'s in (47) the terms obtained from (46), we have

$$\tau \left[\Sigma_i \left(\frac{\partial t^i}{\partial P_t} + t^i \frac{\partial t^i}{\partial y^i} \right) \right] + \gamma \left[\Sigma_i \left(\frac{\partial g^i}{\partial P_t} + t^i \frac{\partial g^i}{\partial y^i} \right) \right] = 0. \qquad (48)$$

The terms in brackets are Slutsky compensated demand effects of a change in the auto mile price, P_t, which we denote as S_{tP} and S_{gP} (Slutsky terms were introduced in Section 2.3). One property of the Slutsky terms is $P_t S_{tP} + S_{gP} = 0$.[11] Replacing S_{gP} by $-P_t S_{tP}$ after inserting Slutsky terms, (48) becomes

$$\tau S_{tP} = \gamma P_t S_{tP},$$

and hence

$$P_t = \tau/\gamma. \qquad (49)$$

To interpret (49), note from (44) and (45) that $-\partial g / \partial r = \pi = \mu/\gamma$, and from (43) that $\tau/\mu = f + t \, \partial f/\partial t$. Substituting into (49) then yields

$$P_t = (f + t \, \partial f/\partial t)\pi. \qquad (50)$$

[11] See, e.g., Samuelson (1947), p. 105, n. 11.

This is clearly the optimal price of an auto mile, for $f + t\,\partial f/\partial t$ is the marginal input requirement for an auto mile, and $\pi\ (= -\partial g/\partial r)$ is the input cost.* The solution obtained here relies on compensated demand functions, which were brought about by maximization of (41) with respect to incomes as well as other variables. If income effects are small, these functions will not differ importantly from observable ordinary demand functions. But it should be remembered that this solution was obtained by optimally adjusting incomes, and that possibility does not exist in the real world. Of course, as we saw in Section 2.3, ordinary demands are just like compensated demands if income elasticities of demand equal zero.

In the real world, each of us actually faces average rather than marginal congestion cost. Whereas the marginal auto mile cost is $(f + t\,\partial f/\partial t)\pi$, as shown in (50), each vehicle is free to join highway traffic and thereby experience only the *average* cost, $f\pi$. To reflect this fact, we can construct a nonoptimal but realistic outcome by imposing a constraint that requires auto travel to be priced at its average cost, $f\pi = P_t$. The constraint imposes the nonoptimal effective price for highway travel that our free choice behavior causes. With a constraint requiring that $P_t = f\pi$, the Lagrangian becomes

$$H(P_t, t, g, r, y^i) = W(u^1, \dots, u^I) - \mu(tf - r) - \phi(h(g, r))$$
$$- \tau(\textstyle\sum_i t^i) - \gamma(\textstyle\sum_i g^i - g) - \lambda(f\pi - P_t). \qquad (51)$$

There is no need to solve this problem as it stands. From the constraint alone we know that we must have $P_t = f\pi$, which is not the optimal price given by (50).

In principle, we can correct this nonoptimal highway price by imposing a tax on the inputs used to produce auto miles. Consider altering π by imposing a tax on f rather than letting its price be determined by competition at $\pi = -\partial g/\partial r$. If we maximize the Lagrangian in (51) not only with respect to P_t, g, r, y^i, and Lagrange multipliers, but also with respect to π, we obtain the conditions

$$\textstyle\sum_i W_i\left(\frac{\partial u^i}{\partial t^i}\frac{\partial t^i}{\partial P_t} + \frac{\partial u^i}{\partial g^i}\frac{\partial g^i}{\partial P_t}\right) - \tau\sum_i \frac{\partial t^i}{\partial P_t} - \gamma\sum_i \frac{\partial g^i}{\partial P_t} + \lambda = 0, \qquad (52)$$

$$-\mu\left(f + t\frac{\partial f}{\partial t}\right) + \tau - \lambda\pi\frac{\partial f}{\partial t} = 0, \qquad (53)$$

$$-\phi\frac{\partial h}{\partial g} + \gamma = 0, \qquad (54)$$

$$\mu - \phi\frac{\partial h}{\partial r} = 0, \qquad (55)$$

$$W_i \eta^i - \tau \Sigma_i \frac{\partial t^i}{\partial y^i} - \gamma \Sigma_i \frac{\partial g^i}{\partial y^i} = 0, \quad i = 1, \ldots, I, \tag{56}$$

$$\lambda f = 0. \tag{57}$$

Using (32) and (33) and the derivatives of the individuals' budget constraints, we can substitute from (56) and reduce (52) to the expression

$$\tau S_{tP} - \gamma P_t S_{tP} = \lambda. \tag{58}$$

With $\lambda = 0$ from (57), which follows from maximizing with respect to π, condition (53) is simply

$$\frac{\tau}{\mu} = \left(f + t \frac{\partial f}{\partial t} \right), \tag{59}$$

and (58) with $\lambda = 0$ yields

$$\frac{\tau}{\gamma} = P_t. \tag{60}$$

From (54) and (55) we know that $\mu = (-\partial g / \partial r)\gamma$, and if we substitute that into (59) and the result into (60), we find that the condition for optimal pricing is

$$P_t = \left(f + t \frac{\partial f}{\partial t} \right) \left(-\frac{\partial g}{\partial r} \right). \tag{61}$$

From the constraint, $f\pi = P_t$, we know that

$$\pi = \left(1 + \frac{t}{f} \frac{\partial f}{\partial t} \right) \left(-\frac{\partial g}{\partial r} \right). \tag{62}$$

The inputs tax needed for optimality, to be added to the competitive input price $-\partial g / \partial r$, is seen in (62) to be $(t/f)(\partial f / \partial t)(-\partial g / \partial r)$. This is the elasticity of unit travel cost to miles traveled.

In practice, of course, inputs taxes are not entirely effective for controlling traffic congestion. The inputs need not be purchased exactly at the time they are used; so an inputs tax that is appropriate for rush-hour traffic would have to be in effect also at other times; and a fuel tax might apply to all uses of fuel, for example, in farm tractors that do not contribute to highway congestion. Also, one of the most significant inputs into highway congestion cost is the travel time of passengers, which cannot easily be taxed. Several devices, including electronic curbside signals that would activate meters in vehicles, have been developed to deal with this problem of correctly pricing road use, but no genuine solution actually has been adopted.[12]

[12] Optimal road pricing requires time value estimates such as those in Mohring, Schroeter, and Wiboonchutikula (1987). For a description of proposals for pricing the use of streets

This congestion problem may be moderated by subsidizing competing travel modes and thereby reducing highway congestion (see Sherman 1971, 1972a). Altering another price away from marginal cost in this way is an example of what is called second-best pricing. Because some nonoptimal condition cannot be remedied, it is simply accepted, and in its presence quasi-optimal prices are determined for substitute and complementary goods. In such cases, quasi-optimal (second-best) prices often depart from marginal cost, but a best possible departure that minimizes ensuing welfare loss can be determined. That is the subject of Chapter 5.

4.7   Summary

We have called attention here to some of the problems of setting prices equal to marginal cost. First, it may be difficult to identify changes in marginal costs over short time intervals, and even if that can be done it may not be possible to notify consumers of new prices and then in addition find them able to change their plans in response to the price changes. Second, the problems of calculating prices equal to marginal cost when demand fluctuates over a cycle may be complex, especially if appropriate production techniques also must be chosen. Sometimes costs arise in more than one dimension, as when each house to be served electricity may add to the cost of an electric utility, apart from the cost of generating kilo-watt-hours of electricity. Ideally, two-part prices are determined for such cases, with each part equaling marginal cost, but fixed fees usefully raise revenue when pricing usage at marginal cost alone could cause a deficit. A choice between two-part tariffs yields a block tariff, which allows improvement in welfare and will have at least one unit price in the largest quantity block equal to marginal cost. Another example of a pricing problem is an externality, which is an unpriced side effect of one person's decision that is felt by another or others. We examined highway congestion, which exists in cities at above optimal levels because each of us can join a traffic flow at average cost rather than marginal cost. We showed how, in principle, a gasoline tax might alleviate this problem.

Several different approaches have been taken in modeling the various problems discussed here. At points, discussions were more lengthy than the problems themselves warranted, in order that the different approaches could be illustrated in relatively simple situations. Consumer surplus represented welfare in our analysis of all the peak-load problems. Indirect

in London, see Ministry of Transport (1964). The proposals could improve the efficiency of road use, but they were unpopular politically. The difference between economists, who tend to favor efficiency goals in this case and in others, and politicians and the public, who focus more on equity, is interestingly described by Blinder (1982, 1987). For more on the economist's frame of reference see Rhoads (1985).

utility functions were used in the multipart pricing problem because they can represent conveniently the more complex individual choice involved when a consumer pays two prices to receive a service and may decide not to consume it at all. Graphic representations of consumer surplus were used in considering block tariffs. Utility functions represented consumer welfare in our analysis of the externality; modeling in this way can be especially useful if one person's consumption affects another directly through the utility functions, as often happens with externalities. In the externality case, income adjustments also were made, and income-compensated (Slutsky) demand functions resulted. The externality problem also took a different form in which welfare was maximized subject to explicit constraints, using the method of Lagrange multipliers.

These examples focused primarily on efficiency, and solutions often were found that served efficiency simply and perfectly. In Chapter 5 we deal with limitations that can prevent such ideal solutions. Income distribution aims of pricing are considered in Chapter 6.

Questions

4.1.   One way to define a peak-load problem is to orient the costs and demands to the separate periods of the demand cycle. Suppose, for example, that each 24 hours is divided into two 12-hour-long pricing periods for electricity demand. We can call them day and night. In the day, kilowatt-hour demand is at the level $P_1 = 20 - 0.01Q$, and in the night, demand is $P_2 = 10 - 0.01Q_2$. Let operating cost be zero and capacity for two units per day, or one unit each period, costs 20. What is the optimal capacity and what are the optimal peak and off-peak prices? Use graphic as well as arithmetic methods to demonstrate a solution.

4.2.   As an alternative to the definitions in Question 4.1, suppose that we orient costs and demands for electricity to the entire demand cycle. For example, let daytime demand for kilowatt-hours, if it lasted 24 hours, be $P_1 = 20 - 0.01Q_1$ and nighttime demand on the same basis be $P_2 = 10 - 0.01Q_2$. The cost of a unit of capacity to turn out a kilowatt of electricity is 10, and operating cost is zero. Then if there are two equal-length day and night periods, demand for capacity can be represented as $(1/2)(20 - 0.01Q_1) + (1/2)(10 - 0.01Q_2)$, with the condition that neither of these terms can be less than zero.

(a)   What is the optimal capacity and what are the optimal peak and off-peak prices? Use graphic as well as arithmetic methods to demonstrate a solution.

(b)   Now assume that the peak demand lasts only 8 hours rather than 12, and that the off-peak demand is in effect 16 hours, while all other facts are the same. Find the optimal capacity and peak and off-peak prices. Explain why the solution differs from that in part (a).

4.3.   Consider the problem of a telegraph service between two cities that faces demands for two periods of equal length over the daily cycle, represented as

$$P_1 = 15 - 0.025Q_1 \quad \text{and} \quad P_2 = 10 - 0.025Q_2,$$

where P_1 and P_2 are prices of messages in the two periods and Q_1 and Q_2 are quantities. The service has capacity to produce 400 telegraph messages per day. Operating cost is $1 per message per day and capacity to connect the two cities costs $2 per day. It is impossible to transmit more than the rated message capacity in the time guaranteed, and so additional customers must be turned away.

(a) At the *given* capacity level, what are welfare-maximizing peak and off-peak prices?

(b) What is the socially optimal capacity level?

(c) What are the optimal peak and off-peak prices at the socially optimal capacity level?

(d) Does the solution in (c) use capacity as efficiently as the solution in (a)? If not, how can the solution in (c) be preferable to that in (a)?

4.4. Consider a telephone service facing demands per call over two equal-length (12-hour-long) periods of the day represented by

$$P_1 = 9 - 0.02Q_1 \quad \text{and} \quad P_2 = 8 - 0.02Q_2,$$

where P_1 and P_2 are prices per call in the two periods and Q_1 and Q_2 are the number of calls. Operating cost for phone service is $1 per call and capacity for one call costs $5 per day. Demand for calls in excess of the capacity cannot be served.

(a) What is the socially optimal capacity level?

(b) What are the optimal peak and off-peak prices per call at the socially optimal capacity level?

(c) Calculate consumer surplus at the solution obtained in (a) and (b).

4.5. Suppose that two techniques of producing electricity have costs per kilowatt and kilowatt-hour corresponding to $B_1 = \$20$, $b_1 = \$220$ (for internal combustion) and $B_2 = \$100$, $b_2 = \$20$ (for coal steam).

(a) Determine the optimal period of the demand cycle for peak and off-peak pricing, indicating which technique(s) should be used in each period of the cycle.

(b) Specify optimal kilowatt-hour prices for peak and off-peak periods, assuming that if a technique is used in a period it is operated 100 percent of the time in that period.

4.6. Suppose that three techniques of producing electricity have costs per kilowatt and kilowatt-hour corresponding to $B_1 = \$20$, $b_1 = \$240$ (for internal combustion); $B_2 = \$40$, $b_2 = \$180$ (for oil steam); and $B_3 = \$100$, $b_3 = \$20$ (for coal steam).

(a) Determine optimal pricing periods and indicate which technique(s) should be used in each period.

(b) Determine optimal kilowatt-hour prices for the periods, assuming that if a technique is used in a period it is operated 100 percent of the time in that period.

CHAPTER 5

Second-best public pricing

5.1 Introduction

Pricing by a public enterprise is labeled "second-best" when the enterprise must depart from ideal marginal cost prices for some accepted reason, such as to avoid too great a financial loss, and does so in a way that minimizes the consequent loss in economic welfare. The traditional "natural monopoly" faced precisely this problem. Since further economies of scale could be realized even after all demand was met, marginal cost would lie below average cost, and pricing at marginal cost would result in a deficit. For two main reasons such a deficit might be regarded as unacceptable even in a welfare-maximizing public enterprise. If price is set at marginal cost and general tax revenue is used to meet the resulting deficit, some nonusers may be forced to contribute to the cost of the service, and that seems unfair. In addition, a general tax probably will introduce price distortions elsewhere in the economy, since only a lump-sum tax would not move prices away from marginal cost levels, and a perfect lump-sum tax is infeasible. So pricing above marginal cost may be proposed for the public enterprise as an alternative way to avoid the deficit.

If more than one good or service is produced by the public enterprise, the question then arises, How are departures from marginal cost prices to be made? Second-best pricing provides one answer, for it defines the most efficient prices that are possible given any specific constraint that must be satisfied, such as a budget constraint requiring total revenue to equal total cost. Second-best multipart prices also can be defined, and effects of uncertainty can be considered. We begin by discussing the taxation principles underlying second-best pricing in this situation.

5.2 The Ramsey optimal taxation principle

One approach we can take to the decreasing cost-pricing problem is to impose a budget constraint on the firm, requiring, for example, that it break even on its operations rather than lose money.[1] By maximizing welfare

---

[1] The problem of pricing under decreasing cost was treated systematically in Section 2.6. Tests to determine whether a natural monopoly exists are set out by Baumol (1977).

124

subject to such a constraint, it is possible to derive second-best pricing rules, rules that are not ideal yet allow as much welfare as possible for a given class of prices while satisfying the constraint. The first to pose the problem this way was the French economist Marcel Boiteux (1956). The budget constraint can be rationalized as a requirement to avoid the unfairness of income transfers that would accompany marginal cost pricing when nonusers of the service had to pay taxes to finance the deficit. Lump-sum taxes, which would magically subtract the right amount of income from everyone without affecting marginal decisions, would of course afford a better way to meet the deficit, but such taxes are going to be ignored here on the ground that they are infeasible. Optimal per unit taxes, which in the public enterprise are like departures from marginal cost prices, were derived by the mathematician Frank Ramsey 60 years ago.

A clear exposition of the Ramsey (1927) optimal taxation principle, as it applies to the public enterprise problem of choosing uniform prices, has been provided by Baumol and Bradford (1970). To present the essence of the problem, they propose a measure of welfare such as consumer surplus, denoted by $W(P_1, \ldots, P_n)$, where $P_1, \ldots, P_n$ are prices of the public enterprise's n goods or services, $q_1, \ldots, q_n$. A profit constraint $\pi(P_1, \ldots, P_n) = M$ is imposed on the enterprise. Maximization of welfare subject to the constraint, with λ the Lagrange multiplier, then yields

$$\frac{\partial W}{\partial P_j} = \lambda \frac{\partial \pi}{\partial P_j}, \quad j = 1, \ldots, n. \tag{1}$$

Baumol and Bradford accept the consumer surplus assumptions that will make $\partial W/\partial P_j = -q_j$, assumptions we examined in Sections 2.4 and 2.5.[2] A concrete form for the welfare function in this case might be the sum of consumer surpluses,

$$W = \sum_{j=1}^{n} \int_{P_j}^{q_j^{-1}(0)} q_j(P_j) \, dP, \tag{2}$$

and the profit or budget constraints, $\pi = M$, could be

$$\pi = \sum_{j=1}^{n} P_j q_j - C_j(q_j) = M,$$

where $C_j(q_j)$ is the total cost for good or service j. Notice that differentiating this welfare function with respect to P_j yields $-q_j$. Differentiating the profit constraint yields $q_j + P_j \, dq_j/dP_j - MC_j \, dq_j/dP_j$, which is equivalent also to $(P_j + q_j \, \partial P_j/\partial q_j) dq_j/dP_j - MC_j \, dq_j/dP_j$, where $P_j + q_j \, \partial P_j/\partial q_j$

---

2 The crucial assumption is that the effect of the ith person's utility on social welfare, W_i, equals the reciprocal of the ith person's marginal utility of income. This assumption accepts the current distribution of income.

equals marginal revenue. Since (1) applies to all j, on substituting $-q_j$ for $\partial W/\partial P_j$ in (1) and solving for $-\lambda$, we have

$$-\lambda = \frac{1}{q_j}\frac{\partial \pi}{\partial P_j} = \frac{1}{q_k}\frac{\partial \pi}{\partial P_k}, \quad \text{all } j \neq k, \tag{3}$$

which indicates that, at the optimum, marginal profit yields will be proportional to outputs. This is the first of four forms in which Baumol and Bradford presented the optimal pricing rule.

Let MR_j, MC_j, and E_{jj} be marginal revenue, marginal cost, and own-price elasticity of demand for the jth good, and for simplicity assume that all cross-elasticities of demand are zero, as in the sum of consumer surpluses welfare function above. Then we can use

$$\partial \pi/\partial P_j = (P_j + q_j\,\partial P_j/\partial q_j - MC_j)dq_j/dP_j,$$

and continuity of $q_j(P_j)$ which permits $dq_j/dP_j = 1/(dP_j/dq_j)$, to rearrange (3) in the form

$$-q_j\,dP_j/dq_j = \lambda(P_j + q_j\,\partial P_j/\partial q_j - MC_j).$$

Adding $P_j + q_j\,\partial P_j/\partial q_j - MC_j$ to both sides then yields

$$\frac{P_j - MC_j}{MR_j - MC_j} = 1 + \lambda = \frac{P_k - MC_k}{MR_k - MC_k}, \quad \text{all } j \neq k, \tag{4}$$

which is a second form of the rule, the ratios of price minus marginal cost to marginal revenue minus marginal cost must be equal for all goods. We can rewrite this equation in the form

$$-\lambda(P_j - MC_j) = (1 + \lambda)q_j\,dP_j/dq_j,$$

which on dividing by P_j and $-\lambda$ yields a third, most common, form of the rule,[3]

$$\frac{P_j - MC_j}{P_j} = \left(\frac{1+\lambda}{\lambda}\right)\left(\frac{1}{-E_{jj}}\right), \quad j = 1, \dots, n, \tag{5}$$

where $E_{jj} = (dq_j/dP_j)(P_j/q_j)$. This is the so-called inverse elasticity rule, indicating that the differences between price and marginal cost, as a fraction of price, should be inversely related to demand elasticities.

One can see from the form of the rule in (5) a similarity to the well-known monopoly pricing rule, which in this case would take the form,

$$\frac{P_j - MC_j}{P_j} = \frac{1}{-E_{jj}}. \tag{6}$$

---

[3] Notice from above that $\lambda = -q_j/(q_j + (P_j - MC_j)\partial q_j/\partial P_j)$. With $\partial q_j/\partial P_j < 0$, it is reasonable to expect $0 < q_j + (P_j - MC_j)\partial q_j/\partial P_j < q_j$, which implies $\lambda < -1$. This means in turn that $(1+\lambda)/\lambda < 1$, so $(P_j - MC_j)/P_j$ must be some fraction of $1/(-E_{jj})$.

The monopoly is very efficient at raising revenue, and when raising revenue is socially desirable it should not be surprising that a rule like (6) is applied, but only fractionally, as indicated in (5) (see n. 3). Thus one interpretation of the Ramsey pricing rule is that it uses monopoly pricing principles just enough to meet the budget constraint that is imposed on it.

Finally, consider the difference between price and marginal cost as $P_j - MC_j = \Delta P_j$. Then (5) can be arranged in the form

$$\frac{dq_j}{dP_j} \Delta P_j = \frac{1+\lambda}{\lambda} q_j.$$

If we interpret the left-hand side of this expression as the change, Δq_j, that would result if we changed price from MC_j to P_j, we can obtain

$$\frac{\Delta q_j}{q_j} = \frac{1+\lambda}{\lambda}, \quad \text{all } j, \tag{7}$$

which calls for all quantities to depart from their marginal cost price levels in the same uniform proportion. This is the fourth form of the rule, and it holds quite generally.

The relation in (7) will hold even after nonzero cross-elasticities of demand are taken into account, or at least it will hold approximately; optimal prices will cause quantities to change by a uniform percentage. This reminds us that optimal resource allocation ultimately is defined in terms of quantities rather than prices. We say the rule is approximate because it holds exactly only if income elasticities of demand among the taxed goods are equal (Sandmo 1976). To derive (7) from a more general model that allows nonzero cross-elasticities of demand, we need $\partial q_k/\partial P_j = \partial q_j/\partial P_k$, and although this holds for compensated demands ($S_{kj} = S_{jk}$) it will hold for ordinary demands only if income elasticities of demand are equal (see Section 2.3).

Several interesting questions are raised by interdependencies in the form of nonzero cross-elasticities of demand among various services. First, we might wonder what happens if there are interactions with private sector services. And in such a complex situation we might also wonder how solution prices actually can be found. We just noted that, when there are interactions due to nonzero cross-elasticities of demand, the question whether quantities are all changed by a uniform proportion in moving to Ramsey prices is more complicated. A related question is when, exactly, will prices move away from marginal costs by the same proportion? To examine these questions we need a more complete model.

5.3 Second-best pricing

We now turn to second-best pricing for a public enterprise in more detail. We assume one price for each service and consider interrelations among demands for different services, not only among the public services but also between public and private services. We postpone discussion of cost conditions such as economies of scale or economies of scope, except to presume here that pricing at marginal cost will not yield enough revenue to cover total cost in the public enterprise. We do not deal with intermediate goods and we ignore any strategic actions between private and public firms, in the event they are few in number, by assuming that the private prices and costs are given. In Section 5.4 we treat uncertainty in demands, but here all is known with certainty.

The framework for second-best analysis first worked out by Frank Ramsey (1927) and formally applied to public enterprise pricing by M. Boiteux (1956) does not rest on the assumption of a totally isolated public sector, where the cross-price elasticities of demand between each of the services of the public enterprise and all other goods are zero. This assumption of zero cross-price elasticity has often been made for convenience, to permit the derivation of easily applied pricing rules or to illustrate a particular case (see Baumol and Bradford 1970; Lerner 1970).[4] And the simple rule is often useful. Of course the cross-price elasticities of demand are not always zero. M. Boiteux's original model (1956) took into account production by private sector firms, but the privately produced goods or services were identical to publicly produced ones and more general cross-elasticity conditions between public and private goods and services were not examined. R. Rees (1968) and H. Mohring (1970) developed models that considered nonzero cross-price elasticities within the public sector, and Rees considered strategic interaction with the private sector. A. Bergson (1972) developed a model that considered all possible cross-price elasticities, with private as well as other public services, but did not allow for a budget constraint. Braeutigam (1979) and Sherman and George (1979) examined the problem faced by the budget-constrained public enterprise when its prices would affect both other public and private demands.[5]

We use the following notation:

q_j^i = the amount of the jth service consumed by the ith individual $(i = 1, \ldots, I; j = 1, \ldots, n)$;

q_0^i = the amount of labor supplied by the ith individual (treated as negative in sign);

$Q_j = \sum_{i=1}^{I} q_j^i$ = the total amount of the jth service;

$Q_1, \ldots, Q_m$ = services of the public enterprise;

---

[4] Indeed, Davis and Whinston (1965) point out that because of low cross-elasticities of demand, second-best circumstances may not have implications as far reaching as Lipsey and Lancaster (1956) had claimed.

[5] The following is based in part on Sherman and George (1979), but is simpler and does not maximize with respect to incomes to obtain Slutsky compensated demands.

$Q_{m+1}, \ldots, Q_n$ = services produced in the private sector;

P_j = prices for labor and the public and private sector services, with $P_0 = 1$ serving as numeraire and $\bar{P}_{m+1}, \ldots, \bar{P}_n$, assumed to be fixed exogenously;

C^m = the total cost of producing the m services of the public enterprise $= C^m(Q_1, \ldots, Q_m; w_1, \ldots, w_l)$ where $w_1, \ldots, w_l$ are input prices (in units of numeraire, Q_0) that are assumed constant and will therefore be suppressed;

C^j = the total cost of producing the jth private service for $j = m+1, \ldots, n$ (in units of the numeraire, Q_0).

Additional subscripts represent differentiation by the subscript variable added.

The ith consumer seeks to maximize the quasi-concave, continuous, and twice differentiable utility function,

$$u^i = u^i(q_0^i, q_1^i, \ldots, q_m^i, q_{m+1}^i, \ldots, q_n^i), \tag{8}$$

subject to the income constraint

$$\sum_{j=0}^{n} P_j q_j^i = 0. \tag{9}$$

Equation (9) is $\sum_{j=1}^{n} P_j q_j^i = q_0^i$ because q_0 is negative and numeraire. With η^i representing the Lagrange multiplier associated with the individual's income constraint, we find from necessary conditions for a solution to the ith consumer's problem

$$-\partial u^i / \partial q_0 = \eta^i, \tag{10}$$

$$\partial u^i / \partial q_j \equiv u_j^i = \eta^i P_j, \quad \text{for } j = 1, \ldots, n, \tag{11}$$

and of course (9) as well. From these conditions we can obtain the (supply and) demand functions

$$q_j^i = q_j^i(1, P_1, \ldots, P_n), \quad \text{for } j = 0, \ldots, n. \tag{12}$$

It will be useful later to have derivatives of the budget constraint (9) with respect to the P_j's $(\partial q_k^i / \partial P_j \equiv q_{kj}^i)$:

$$q_j^i + \sum_{k=0}^{n} P_k q_{kj}^i = 0, \quad \text{for } j = 0, \ldots, n \tag{13}$$

(where q_0^i will be negative). Furthermore, if we aggregate (9) over all i as $\sum_{k=0}^{n} P_k Q_k = 0$ and differentiate with respect to j, we obtain

$$Q_j + \sum_{k=0}^{n} P_k Q_{kj} = 0, \quad \text{for } j = 1, \ldots, m. \tag{14}$$

We take as our social welfare objective a welfare function that combines the utilities of all I individuals,

$$W = W(u^1, \ldots, u^I), \tag{15}$$

subject to two constraints. Since labor is the only input in our very simple economy, total labor incomes must equal total costs:

$$\sum_{i=1}^{I} q_0^i = Q_0 = C^m + \sum_{k=m+1}^{n} C^k. \tag{16}$$

In addition we require that the public sector firm earn only the amount B on all its operations:

$$B = \sum_{k=1}^{m} P_k Q_k - C^m. \tag{17}$$

Equation (17) is the condition that may prevent marginal cost pricing, so it creates a second-best problem.

Maximizing with respect to public sector prices, $P_1, \ldots, P_n$, a Lagrangian function L, comprising the consumer welfare function (15) subject to constraints (16) and (17) (where we have Lagrange multipliers $-\lambda$ for constraints (16) and μ for constraint (17)), we find

$$\frac{\partial L}{\partial P_j} = \sum_{i=1}^{I} W_i \sum_{k=0}^{n} u_k^i q_{kj}^i - \lambda \left[\sum_{k=1}^{m} C_k^m Q_{kj} + \sum_{k=m+1}^{n} C_k^k Q_{kj} - Q_{0j} \right]$$
$$+ \mu \left[Q_j + \sum_{k=1}^{m} (P_k - C_k^m) Q_{kj} \right] = 0 \quad \text{for } j = 1, \ldots, m. \tag{18}$$

We assume $C_j^k = 0$ for all $j = 1, \ldots, m$ and $k = m+1, \ldots, n$; there are no cost interdependencies between public and private sectors.

The necessary conditions (18) can be simplified by making use of information from the individuals' utility-maximizing conditions. Using (10), (11), and (13), the $\sum_{i=1}^{I} W_i \sum_{k=0}^{n} u_k^i q_{kj}^i$ term in (18) can be converted into $-\sum_{i=1}^{I} W_i \eta^i q_j^i$. Accepting the current income distribution by assuming that $W_i = 1/\eta^i$ will reduce this term to $-Q_j$. Next we can use (14) and substitute for Q_{0j} in (18). Then (18) becomes

$$-Q_j + \lambda \left[Q_j + \sum_{k=1}^{m} (P_k - C_k^m) Q_{kj} + \sum_{k=m+1}^{n} (\bar{P}_k - C_k^k) Q_{kj} \right]$$
$$+ \mu \left[Q_j + \sum_{k=1}^{m} (P_k - C_k^m) Q_{kj} \right] = 0, \quad \text{for } j = 1, \ldots, m, \tag{19}$$

where we place bars over the P_k for $k = m+1, \ldots, n$ to remind us that these prices are constant. Let us now assume that income elasticities of demand are equal for all goods. This will make $Q_{kj} = Q_{jk}$ even though we do not have compensated demands (see Section 2.3). Then with $\xi_{kj} = Q_{kj}P_j/Q_k$ representing the uncompensated price elasticity of demand, we can rearrange (19) to obtain

$$\sum_{k=1}^{m} \frac{P_k-c_k}{P_k}(-\xi_{jk}) = \frac{\lambda+\mu-1}{\lambda+\mu} - \left(\frac{\lambda}{\lambda+\mu}\right)\left(\sum_{k=m+1}^{n} \frac{P_k-c_k}{P_k}(-\xi_{jk})\right),$$
$$j=1,...,m. \quad (20)$$

If cross-elasticities of demand are all zero, the public sector price terms other than the jth and the private sector price term on the right-hand side will vanish; the result is the "inverse elasticity" form of the pricing rule, the Ramsey rule as contained in equation (5) of Section 5.2,

$$\frac{P_k-c_k}{P_k} = \left(\frac{\lambda+\mu-1}{\lambda+\mu}\right)\left(\frac{1}{-\xi_{kk}}\right), \quad k=1,...,m. \quad (21)$$

Let us now use the more complicated model we have developed in this section to treat issues that the model of Section 5.2 was unable to shed light on.

Solutions with private goods interaction

In a practical problem, even the simple zero cross-elasticity solutions in equation (21) are not easy to find, because it is usually difficult to solve for values of the Lagrange multipliers. It is sensible then to assume some value for $(\lambda+\mu-1)/(\lambda+\mu)$, say ν where $0<\nu<1$, and find prices using cost and demand elasticity information

$$P'_k = c_k/(1+\nu/E_{kk}), \quad k=1,...,m. \quad (22)$$

With P'_k's thus obtained, Q_k's and C^m also can be found, so it can be determined whether the constraint (17) is satisfied ((16) should always be satisfied because it contains no exogenous value like B in (17)). If more (less) than B is raised by the P'_k's, a lower (higher) value of ν can be chosen and the process repeated. When a set of prices satisfies the budget constraint (17) to a close enough approximation, they are solution prices.

If only two prices are sought $(k=1, 2)$, the knowledge that Ramsey prices require a proportional reduction in quantities from a solution where prices equal marginal costs can be used to determine the relative magnitudes of q_1 and q_2. Since relative quantities will then be the same under Ramsey price as under marginal cost prices, one of the quantities can be eliminated to obtain an analytical solution (see Question 5.1). But in practice most cases involve more than two goods or services, and trial and error repetition is usually required. It is sometimes useful to draw graphs and estimate contributions to meet the constraint (17) from areas in the graphs.

The same general procedure can be applied to the more complicated equation (20). Suppose the right-hand-side elasticities are known and not zero. The price-cost margins are also assumed to be known, and they affect optimal public sector prices only if $P_k \neq C_k^k$ for some private service. If we let $(\lambda + \mu - 1)/(\lambda + \mu) = \alpha$, the coefficient of the second right-hand-side term including private price-cost margins is $(1 - \alpha)\lambda$. We know that $\lambda > 0$ and $\mu > 0$, and $0 < \alpha < 1$. As the budget constraint is more burdensome (B is greater) μ and hence α will be larger, and as α is larger, the influence of private sector price-cost margins will tend to grow smaller. Without knowing values of the Lagrange multipliers it is difficult to weight the right-hand-side terms. However, if prices are not very far away from marginal costs then it is reasonable to expect $\lambda \approx 1$, because if more resources were available they could be translated almost fully into welfare gains. If $\lambda = 1$ is assumed, equations (20) can be solved using matrix methods. For various values of α, specific prices can then be found and tested until they satisfy the budget constraint in (17). In the typical case, prices will equal marginal costs for the private sector firms, and interactions with the private sector can be ignored (Braeutigam 1979; Sherman and George 1979). Without any assumption about λ, α can then be varied until the constraint (17) is satisfied. Modern computers make this method of successive approximation feasible even for large problems.

Although our discussion has been in terms of demand elasticities, it is possible to derive an equation like (20) in terms of demand curve slopes instead. This would follow from rearranging (19) and interpreting Q_{kj}'s as the slopes of linear demand curves.[6] The trial-and-error process can then be employed until convergence is obtained.

Uniform proportional quantity change

Let us now play down the private sector interdependence, by assuming that private sector prices equal marginal costs, so that prices in services $m + 1, \ldots, n$ may be ignored. On that assumption, (19) can be represented as

$$\sum_{k=1}^{m} (P_k - C_k^m)Q_{kj} = \frac{1 - \lambda - \mu}{\lambda + \mu} Q_j, \quad j = 1, \ldots, m. \qquad (23)$$

---

[6] Slopes would usually be available from estimates of linear demand curves, whereas elasticities would be available if log-linear functions were estimated. Recall that, when demand functions that reflect no compensation are used, the outcome requires the assumption described in Section 2.5, that each individual has a social weight equal to the reciprocal of his or her marginal utility of income. See Drèze (1964, pp. 31-3) and Mohring (1970, Appendix II) for interpretation of such a case.

Now if we interpret the departure of price from marginal cost, $P_k - C_k^m$, as ΔP_k, and if $Q_{kj} = Q_{jk}$, (23) can be rearranged as

$$\sum_{k=1}^{m} \Delta P_k \frac{Q_{jk}}{Q_j} = \frac{1 - \lambda - \mu}{\lambda + \mu}, \quad j = 1, \ldots, m. \tag{24}$$

With $\sum_{k=1}^{m} \Delta P_k \, \partial Q_j / \partial P_k = \Delta Q_j$, the left-hand side of (24) is the proportional change in Q_j due to prices that depart from marginal costs, and, since the right-hand side is constant, we have

$$\Delta Q_j / Q_j = \Delta Q_k / Q_k, \quad \text{all } j, k. \tag{25}$$

The result in (25) was demonstrated in (7), but here, with nonzero cross-elasticities explicitly represented, we can see that it holds only if $Q_{kj} = Q_{jk}$ (Sandmo 1976). Having this symmetry in cross-derivatives requires equal income elasticities of demand (shown in Section 2.3). To see how nicely this condition would be satisfied with compensated demands, recall that by definition $Q_{kj} = S_{kj} - Q_j \, \partial Q_k / \partial y$, where y is income leading to an income effect of the price change, $-Q_j \, \partial Q_k / \partial y$, and S_{kj} is the substitution effect. We can then substitute for Q_{kj} in (24) and obtain

$$\sum_{k=1}^{m} \Delta P_k S_{kj} = \frac{-\alpha}{(1-\alpha)} Q_j + Q_j \sum_{k=1}^{m} \Delta P_k \frac{\partial Q_k}{\partial y}, \quad j = 1, \ldots, m. \tag{26}$$

With $S_{kj} = S_{jk}$, we have

$$\frac{\Delta Q_j}{Q_j} = \frac{-\alpha}{(1-\alpha)} + \sum_{k=1}^{m} \Delta P_k \frac{\partial Q_k}{\partial y}, \quad j = 1, \ldots, m, \tag{27}$$

and since the right-hand side is the same for every j (j does not appear), we have (25).

If we do not have compensated demands, which is usually the case, and there is reason to belive that $Q_{kj} \neq Q_{jk}$, we can follow Sandmo (1976) to determine consequences by noting

$$Q_{kj} = Q_{jk} + Q_k \, \partial Q_j / \partial y - Q_j \, \partial Q_k / \partial y.$$

Then our progression from (23) to (24) with $Q_{jk} \neq Q_{kj}$ would lead to

$$\sum_{k=1}^{m} \Delta P_k \frac{Q_{jk}}{Q_j} = \frac{-\alpha}{(1-\alpha)} - \sum_{k=1}^{m} \left(\Delta P_k \frac{Q_k}{y} \right) (E_{jy} - E_{ky}), \quad j = 1, \ldots, m. \tag{28}$$

We now see on the right-hand side that if the income elasticity of demand for service j is higher than the average for all services, using contributions to profit as a fraction of total income as weights, there should be a greater-than-average reduction in the quantity of service j. Of course, when income elasticities are equal, the term on the right in (28) will be zero and the condition in (25) will be satisfied; the proportional quantity changes will be uniform.

Uniform ratio of price to marginal cost

Whether all commodity tax rates should be the same is an old issue in the subject of optimal taxation, and it arises here in the question of whether departures from marginal costs, as fractions of public enterprise prices, should be uniform. If all goods and services, including leisure, can be taxed, we know that all tax rates should be the same to avoid inefficiencies. For a tax on leisure would be equivalent in its marginal effect to a subsidy to labor, and a rate of subsidy to labor that is matched exactly by a tax on all commodities of the same rate will be nondistortionary. Higher effective commodity prices are offset perfectly by greater incomes through the subsidy to labor. But as Baumol and Bradford (1970) emphasized, such a nondistortionary scheme also is not very useful; tax proceeds go entirely to pay the labor subsidy, so the system generates no net revenue.

If labor supply, and therefore leisure demand, is perfectly inelastic, we can show that uniform tax rates, or uniform proportionate departures from marginal cost for public enterprise prices, are in order. If uniform tax rates are optimal when all things are taxed, the same rates might be expected when an item that cannot be taxed has inelastic demand. We shall illustrate this result in a more manageable case than we have considered thus far. We assume that there are only two services, and that both are produced by a public enterprise using labor. This revealing example is based in Corlett and Hague (1953–4) and Sandmo (1976). It is revealing because it shows implications for optimal prices (or optimal commodity taxes) when leisure cannot be taxed.

Utility functions for the simple case of labor and two services are

$$u^i = u^i(q_0^i, q_1^i, q_2^i), \quad i = 1, \ldots, I, \tag{29}$$

and the individual budget constraint is the same as in (9), but the services now are indexed 1 and 2, and labor is q_0^i, so

$$\sum_{j=0}^{2} P_j q_j^i = 0. \tag{9}$$

Welfare is again a function of individual utilities as in (15),

$$W = W(u^1, \ldots, u^I). \tag{15}$$

Because the public enterprise produces all goods, we need only the budget constraint on its operations,

$$B = \sum_{k=1}^{2} P_k Q_k - C^m. \tag{30}$$

Maximizing with respect to P_1 and P_2 the objective function (15), subject to the constraint (30), yields

$$\sum_{i=1}^{I} W_i \sum_{k=0}^{n} u_k^i q_{kj}^i + \mu \left[Q_j + \sum_{k=1}^{n} (P_k - C_k^m) Q_{kj} \right] = 0, \quad j = 1, 2. \tag{31}$$

By using the necessary conditions of individual utility maximization as before (conditions like (10), (11), and (13), plus $W_i = 1/\eta^i$), (31) yields

$$\sum_{k=1}^{n} (P_k - C_k^m) Q_{kj} = \frac{1-\mu}{\mu} Q_j, \quad j = 1, 2,$$

which can be expressed in terms of price-cost margins and price elasticities of demand,

$$\sum_{k=1}^{n} \frac{P_k - C_k^m}{P_k} \xi_{jk} = \frac{1-\mu}{\mu}, \quad j = 1, 2. \tag{32}$$

To obtain (32) we must assume $Q_{jk} = Q_{kj}$ (so that $\xi_{jk} = \xi_{kj} P_k Q_k / P_j Q_j$), and so we must assume equal income elasticities of demand. In view of the small number of services involved, (32) can easily be stated in full:

$$\frac{P_1 - C_1^m}{P_1} \xi_{11} + \frac{P_2 - C_2^m}{P_2} \xi_{12} = \frac{1-\mu}{\mu},$$

$$\frac{P_1 - C_1^m}{P_1} \xi_{21} + \frac{P_2 - C_2^m}{P_2} \xi_{22} = \frac{1-\mu}{\mu}.$$

These two equations can be solved for the two price-cost margins,

$$\frac{P_1 - C_1^m}{P_1} = \left(\frac{1-\mu}{\mu} \right) \frac{\xi_{22} - \xi_{12}}{\xi_{11}\xi_{22} - \xi_{12}\xi_{21}},$$

$$\frac{P_2 - C_2^m}{P_2} = \left(\frac{1-\mu}{\mu} \right) \frac{\xi_{11} - \xi_{21}}{\xi_{11}\xi_{22} - \xi_{12}\xi_{21}}. \tag{33}$$

It remains now to interpret (33). To do this, we first state for our simple example the condition (14):

$$Q_j + P_1 Q_{1j} + P_2 Q_{2j} + P_0 Q_{0j} = 0, \quad j = 1, 2.$$

With the assumption that $Q_{jk} = Q_{kj}$, this can be expressed as

$$\xi_{j1} + \xi_{j2} + \xi_{j0} = -1, \quad j = 1, 2. \tag{34}$$

Using (34) to substitute for ξ_{12} and ξ_{21} in (33), we obtain

$$\frac{P_1 - C_1^m}{P_1} = \left(\frac{1-\mu}{\mu} \right) \frac{1 + \xi_{11} + \xi_{22} + \xi_{10}}{\xi_{11}\xi_{22} - \xi_{12}\xi_{21}},$$

$$\frac{P_2 - C_2^m}{P_2} = \left(\frac{1-\mu}{\mu} \right) \frac{1 + \xi_{11} + \xi_{22} + \xi_{20}}{\xi_{11}\xi_{22} - \xi_{12}\xi_{21}}. \tag{35}$$

Now if labor is perfectly inelastic in supply, we know $\xi_{10} = \xi_{20} = 0$, and then the two right-hand sides in (35) will be identical. That means for P_1

and P_2 that the price-cost margins, or the markups above marginal cost, will be identical if labor supply is perfectly inelastic; the ratios of price to marginal cost will be uniform.

With labor inelastic in supply, the demand for leisure must also be inelastic. Our inability to tax leisure then does not affect its quantity, so the uniform rate, which would be appropriate if leisure could be taxed, is desirable. The Ramsey rule relies on demand elasticity only when labor is not inelastically supplied, and then the rule is an indirect effort to tax leisure. After all, a higher tax on a good with less elastic demand will take more income from individuals and thereby force them to abandon more leisure. This interpretation is confirmed in a different way in (35). Suppose $\xi_{10} > \xi_{20}$, meaning that Q_1 is more complementary with labor than is Q_2. Because $(1-\mu)/\mu < 0$ and $\xi_{11}\xi_{22} - \xi_{12}\xi_{21} > 0$, (35) implies that in that case $(P_1 - C_1^m)/P_1 < (P_2 - C_2^m)/P_2$. The optimal markup, or tax rate, is lower (higher) on the stronger (weaker) complement to labor because taxing that good or service will force a greater (lesser) reduction in labor. The optimal markup is then higher on the complement to leisure, so it forces individuals to abandon more leisure.

Thus, although the statement of optimal price-cost margins with all interactions as in (20) is complex, the effects of the interactions can be interpreted nicely. We see the logic of the second-best that lies behind Ramsey pricing, not only in the budget constraint that may prevent pricing at marginal cost, but also in the achievement of some effects of a tax on leisure, when that is impossible. We also can see that, despite its complexity, a set of equations like (20) can be solved for optimal prices.

5.4   Second-best pricing under uncertainty

When we considered peak-load pricing under uncertainty in Section 4.4, we discovered that uncertainty can prevent prices from always clearing markets. If demand exceeds capacity at the prevailing price, we need to know something about the value of the service to those who actually receive it in order to estimate consumer surplus. This same problem about the efficiency of nonprice rationing without market-clearing prices arises when we consider second-best pricing under uncertainty, because the similarity between Ramsey prices and monopoly prices in equations (5) and (6) persists, but only if nonprice rationing is perfectly efficient even when prices cannot clear markets. If rationing is not perfect when prices cannot clear markets, then prices should be higher and capacity should be greater. Higher prices ration the service to those most willing to pay and can thus assure more benefit, because the service will go to those who value it most. Capacity can also be increased with higher prices, while still satisfying the budget constraint, so service can be provided to more consumers. The particular trade-off to be struck between price and reliability of service will depend on the budget constraint and the efficiency of the nonprice rationing that occurs.

A monopoly solution

We begin by obtaining for later comparison the prices and capacity that would be chosen by an unregulated profit-maximizing monopolist. In turning to welfare-maximizing solutions, we first assume (as did Brown-Johnson 1969; for another representation, see Marchand 1973) that persons who value service most will receive it even when demand exceeds capacity at the unchanging price; that is, markets always are cleared efficiently despite the absence of a genuine market-clearing price. In this case, optimal prices turn out to be equal to short-run marginal costs and generally do not produce sufficient revenue to cover costs. So, by imposing a break-even constraint, we can see how risk will influence optimal second-best prices. We find that both expected profit-maximizing and constrained expected welfare-maximizing solutions must now contain stochastic elements. However, the solutions are related to one another in a simple manner, analogous to the relation exhibited between profit-maximizing and constrained welfare-maximizing solutions when demand is certain.

Consider a peak-load pricing problem involving n services such as units of transportation consumed in n different time periods. The quantity per time period can never exceed the rate determined by capacity z, which has a cost of β for each unit of service that it is capable of producing over the demand cycle. Each unit actually produced also requires an operating cost of b. In the jth period, demand is $Q_j(P_j) + u_j$, where P_j is price, $Q_j(P_j)$ is expected quantity demanded at price P_j, and u_j is a random variable with mean zero.[7] The function $F_j(\bar{u}_j)$ is a cumulative distribution and $f_j(u_j)$ is a density function such that $F_j(\bar{u}_j) = \int_{-\infty}^{\bar{u}_i} f_j(u_j)\,du_j$. The ith period lasts a fraction α_i of the total time interval for the demand cycle under consideration (for example, day, month, year), and n periods account for the total time interval so $\sum_{j=1}^{n} \alpha_j = 1$. We assume that these demands and distributions for different periods are independent of each other, and we consider a horizon of only one time interval.

Now suppose that there is one monopolistic producer whose object is to choose capacity z^* as well as n prices P_j^*, where $j = 1, \dots, n$ time periods

---

[7] As Carlton (1977) has neatly shown, in the special case of random rationing of available supply, whenever excess demand appears, the unconstrained welfare maximum is a break-even solution if the demand uncertainty is multiplicative. In that case there is no need for a second-best, zero-profit constrained analysis.

over the demand cycle, to maximize expected profit. The starred variables represent the producer's chosen values, to distinguish them from other values. The expected profit of this monopoly firm can be represented as

$$E(\pi) = \sum_{j=1}^{n} \alpha_j (P_j^* - b) \left\{ Q_j(P_j^*) - \int_{z^* - Q_j(P_j^*)}^{\infty} [Q_j(P_j^*) + u_j - z^*] f_j(u_j) \, du_j \right\}$$
$$- \beta z^*. \tag{36}$$

Expected profit without any capacity cost or capacity limit is simply the sum of contributions to profits from all periods, $\sum_j \alpha_j (P_j^* - b) Q_j(P_j^*)$. But since quantity is limited by costly capacity, we must also take into account forgone profit when demand cannot be satisfied because $Q_j(P_j^*) + u_j$ exceeds z^*. Moreover, we must subtract the cost of capacity βz^*. To ensure that quantity demanded is never negative, we require that the error term u_j never take a value so negative that $-u_j$ exceeds $Q_j(P_j^*)$. Thus we assume that $Q_j(P_j^*) + u_j \geq 0$. As a practical matter, such a requirement is certainly plausible, because at a given price the fluctuations in quantity that we ordinarily can expect are small in proportion to average quantity.

Taking derivatives of (36) with respect to capacity and the n prices and setting them equal to zero, we obtain

$$\frac{\partial E(\pi)}{\partial P_j^*} = \alpha_j \left\{ Q_j(P_j^*) - \int_{z^* - Q_j(P^*)}^{\infty} [Q_j(P_j^*) + u_j - z^*] f_j(u_j) \, du_j \right.$$
$$\left. + (P_j^* - b) \left[Q_j'(P_j^*) - \int_{z^* - Q_j(P_j^*)}^{\infty} Q_j'(P_j^*) f_j(u_j) \, du_j \right] \right\} = 0,$$
$$j = 1, \ldots, n, \tag{37}$$

$$\frac{\partial E(\pi)}{\partial z^*} = \sum_{j=1}^{n} \alpha_j (P_j^* - b) \int_{z^* - Q_j(P_j^*)}^{\infty} f_j(u_j) \, du_j - \beta = 0. \tag{38}$$

Letting demand elasticities in all periods be represented as

$$\xi_j = \frac{-P_j Q_j'(P_j)}{Q_j(P_j)}, \quad j = 1, 2, \ldots, n, \tag{39}$$

we obtain from (37) the implicit pricing rule,

$$\frac{(P_j^* - b) F_j(z - Q_j(P_j^*))}{P_j^*} = \frac{1}{\xi_j} \left[1 - \frac{E(ed_j)}{Q_j(P_j^*)} \right], \quad i = 1, 2, \ldots, n, \tag{40}$$

where

$$E(ed_j) = \int_{z^* - Q_j(P_j^*)}^{\infty} [Q_j(P_j^*) + u_j - z^*] f_j(u_j) \, du_j \tag{41}$$

is expected excess demand. Notice that, if we place the price-cost margin, $(P_j^* - b)/P_j^*$, on the left side of (40), we shall then have on the right side

$$\frac{Q_j(P_j) - E(ed_j)}{-P_j Q_j'(P_j) F[z - Q_j(P_j)]} = \frac{1}{E(\xi_j)} \tag{42}$$

from the definition of expected elasticity, $E(\xi_j)$, due to Tschirhart (1978). Since $Q_j'(P_j)$ only applies when demand is reliably met, the derivative will on average be $Q_j'(P_j) F[z - Q_j(P_j)]$, and $Q_j(P_j) - E(ed_j)$ is expected quantity sold; so this definition of expected elasticity is appealing. Using it in (40), we have

$$\frac{P_j^* - b}{P_j^*} = \frac{1}{E(\xi_j)}, \tag{43}$$

which shows a great similarity to the familiar monopoly pricing rule under certainty given in (6) above.

Setting $\partial E(\pi)/\partial z^* = 0$ in (38) yields the capacity condition

$$\sum_{i=1}^{n} \alpha_j (P_j^* - b)[1 - F_j(z^* - Q_j(P_j^*))] = \beta. \tag{44}$$

The term $1 - F(z^* - Q_j(P_j^*))$ in the capacity condition represents the probability of excess demand; thus equation (44) clearly states that at expected profit-maximizing z^*, the marginal expected contribution to net revenue (from increasing capacity and allowing an additional unit to be sold at prices P_j^*, $i = 1, \ldots, n$ when excess demand occurs) is just equal to the marginal cost of extra capacity.

Efficient nonprice rationing

Now let us seek criteria for maximizing expected welfare while requiring the firm to break even on its operations. As in the monopoly case, we pose the problem in a partial equilibrium setting, and assume that Pareto conditions are always satisfied elsewhere in the economy. We also ignore income effects and assume risk-neutrality so that expected consumer's surplus can serve as an indicator of welfare.

The objective is to choose prices P_j^* for $i = 1, 2, \ldots, n$, and capacity z^*, to maximize a welfare function equal to the expected consumer's surplus plus revenue (i.e., willingness to pay) less expected cost (i.e., variable cost plus capacity cost), subject to the constraint that total revenue will just equal total cost. Here we also assume that a service is always distributed efficiently, in the sense that consumers who value it most are the ones who receive the service whether or not money price is high enough to ensure that result.

Assume that, as in the expected profit-maximizing model, demand in period j is given by the function $Q_j(P_j) + u_j$, where u_j is distributed with density function $f_j(u_j)$ and mean zero. Again, period j lasts a fraction

α_j of the demand cycle, and z^* and the P_j^*'s are unchanging values to be chosen and held at the same levels regardless of what actual values of u_j occur. Total expected consumer's surplus and revenue is

$$\sum_{j=1}^{n} \alpha_j \left\{ \int_{-\infty}^{\infty} f_j(u_j) \int_{P_j^*}^{Q_j^{-1}(-u_j)} [Q_j(P_j)+u_j]\, dP_j\, du_j + P_j^* Q_j(P_j^*) \right\}$$

less the expected loss in both consumer's surplus and revenue because some consumers are not served (in this case those who value service least) when quantity demanded exceeds capacity:

$$\sum_{j=1}^{n} \alpha_j \left\{ \int_{z^*-Q_j(P_j^*)}^{\infty} f_j(u_j) \int_{P_j^*}^{Q_j^{-1}(z^*-u_j)} [Q_j(P_j)+u_j-z^*]\, dP_j\, du_j \right.$$
$$\left. + P_j^* \int_{z^*-Q_j(P_j^*)}^{\infty} f_j(u_j)[Q_j(P_j^*)+u_j-z^*]\, du_j \right\}.$$

Variable costs are

$$\sum_{j=1}^{n} \alpha_j b \left\{ Q_j(P_j^*) - \int_{z^*-Q_j(P_j^*)}^{\infty} f_j(u_j)[Q_j(P_j^*)+u_j-z^*]\, du_j \right\}$$

and capacity cost is βz. The balanced budget constraint requires that

$$\sum_{j=1}^{n} \alpha_j (P_j^*-b) \left\{ Q_j(P_j^*) - \int_{z^*-Q_j(P_j^*)}^{\infty} f_j(u_j)[Q_j(P_j^*)+u_j-z^*]\, du_j \right\} = \beta z^*.$$

We can thus construct a second-best problem, maximizing expected consumer's surplus plus revenue less variable and capacity costs subject to the break-even constraint, by forming the Lagrangian

$$L_{ER}(P_j^*, z^*, \lambda)$$
$$= \sum_{j=1}^{n} \alpha_j \left\{ \int_{-\infty}^{\infty} f_j(u_j) \int_{P_j^*}^{Q_j^{-1}(-u_i)} [Q_j(P_j)+u_j]\, dP_j\, du_j + P_j^* Q_j(P_j^*) \right.$$
$$- \int_{z^*-Q_j(P_j^*)}^{\infty} f_j(u_j) \int_{P_j^*}^{Q_j^{-1}(z^*-u_j)} [Q_j(P_j)+u_j-z^*]\, dP_j\, du_j$$
$$- P_j^* \int_{z^*-Q_j(P_j^*)}^{\infty} f_j(u_j)[Q_j(P_j^*)+u_j-z^*]\, du_j$$
$$\left. - b\left[Q_j(P_j^*) - \int_{z^*-Q_j(P_j^*)}^{\infty} f_j(u_j)[Q_j(P_j^*)+u_j-z^*]\, du_j \right] - \beta z^* \right\}$$
$$+ \lambda \left\{ \sum_{j=1}^{n} \alpha_j (P_j^*-b) \left[Q_j(P_j^*) - \int_{z^*-Q_j(P_j^*)}^{\infty} f_j(u_j)[Q_j(P_j^*)+u_j-z^*]\, du_j \right] \right.$$
$$\left. - \beta z^* \right\}. \tag{45}$$

Differentiating the Lagrangian with respect to each P_j^* and z^*, and setting results equal to zero, we have

$$\frac{\partial L_{ER}}{\partial P_j^*} = \alpha_j \left\{ \lambda Q_j(P_j^*) - \lambda \int_{z^* - Q_j(P_j^*)}^{\infty} f_j(u_j)[Q_j(P_j^*) + u_j - z^*] \, du_j \right.$$

$$\left. + (1+\lambda)(P_j^* - b)Q_j'(P_j^*)F(z^* - Q_j(P_j^*)) \right\} = 0,$$

$$j = 1, \dots, n, \quad (46)$$

$$\frac{\partial L_{ER}}{\partial z^*} = \sum_{j=1}^{n} \alpha_j \left\{ \int_{z^* - Q_j(P_j^*)}^{\infty} f_j(u_j)[Q_j^{-1}(z^* - u_j) - P_j^*] \, du_j \right.$$

$$\left. + (P_j^* - b) \int_{z^* - Q_j(P_j^*)}^{\infty} f_j(u_j) \, du_j \right\} - \beta$$

$$+ \lambda \left\{ \sum_{j=1}^{n} \alpha_j (P_j^* - b) \int_{z^* - Q_j(P_j^*)}^{\infty} f_j(u_j) \, du_j - \beta \right\} = 0. \quad (47)$$

Remembering from (42) above our definition of expected demand elasticities, we can obtain from (46) optimum pricing rules in the form

$$\frac{(P_j^* - b)}{P_j^*} = \left(\frac{\lambda}{1+\lambda} \right) \frac{1}{E(\xi_j)}, \quad j = 1, \dots, n. \quad (48)$$

Condition (48) is a constrained expected welfare-maximizing counterpart to the expected profit-maximizing implicit pricing rule in equation (43). Comparison of equation (48) with equation (43) shows that the only difference in form between the second-best expected welfare-maximizing profit margin $(P_j^* - b)/P_j^*$ and the expected profit-maximizing profit margin is the constant term $\lambda/(1+\lambda) < 1$ at the right-hand side of (48). The relation between the pricing rules for monopoly (43) and for welfare (48) goals involves only a constant on the right-hand side, as in the relation without risk illustrated in equations (6) and (5) above.

This similarity is not surprising when one realizes that short-run marginal cost b is the first best price here if nonprice rationing is assumed to be efficient. Prices are not used to ensure that service is allotted to those with the highest willingness to pay; some nonprice mechanism accomplishes that by assumption. Prices alone turn away only those unwilling to pay marginal operating costs. Thus prices serve the same function in this case for both the monopoly profit maximizer and the unconstrained welfare maximizer, and that purpose is to raise revenue while turning away as few customers as possible.

From (47) we can obtain the requirement for optimum capacity:

$$\sum_{j=1}^{n} \alpha_j \left\{ \frac{\lambda}{1+\lambda} \int_{z^* - Q_j(P_j^*)}^{\infty} f_j(u_j)[Q_j^{-1}(z^* - u_j) - b] \, du_j \right.$$

$$\left. + \left(\frac{\lambda}{1+\lambda} \right)(P_j^* - b)(1 - F[z^* - Q_j(P_j^*)]) \right\} = \beta. \quad (49)$$

Optimum capacity choice under stochastic demand is analogous to that under nonstochastic demand. When demand is certain, it is known whether excess demand will exist in period j at given P_j^*, z^* choices; if demand is stochastic, excess demand will exist only with some probability. Additional capacity yields benefits in either case only if excess demand exists. The marginal benefit from extra capacity would be known exactly if demand were nonstochastic, but since demand is stochastic here, the left-hand side of (49) represents expected marginal benefit. The benefit appears as added consumer's surplus and added net revenues that contribute to welfare directly and further help to satisfy the break-even constraint. If demand were certain, the break-even constraint would not be binding ($\lambda = 0$) as long as the P_j^* and z^* were optimally chosen for the stochastic case because, given our cost function, total revenue would equal total cost. However, the break-even constraint is binding ($\lambda > 0$) when P_j^*, z^* are chosen optimally in the stochastic demand model, for without the constraint the firm would lose money, as Brown and Johnson (1969) have shown.

Under stochastic demand, the welfare-maximizing capacity rule in (49) can be related to the profit-maximizing rule in (44). Notice that, as the amount of net operating revenue needed to break even increases, the shadow price on the budget constraint λ increases. Marginal net revenue then becomes the important concern for the welfare maximizer when deciding whether to alter capacity size, just as it is for the profit maximizer; as λ becomes larger, equation (49) (the second-best capacity solution) becomes more like equation (44) (the profit-maximizing capacity solution). And (49) also yields implicitly a reliability of service that is optimal given the break-even constraint.

Inefficient nonprice rationing

Sherman and Visscher (1978) proved that when nonprice rationing was not perfectly efficient, the second-best prices would be higher and the capacity larger than under the efficient rationing assumption just examined. The key to their proof was the observation that an iso-expected consumer surplus contour in the P_j, z space would be affected by the efficiency of nonprice rationing, whereas an iso-expected profit contour would not be. After all, the profit-seeking firm is unconcerned about which consumers are served when there is excess demand, because profit is unaffected (Harris and Raviv 1981; Meyer 1975; Mills 1959), whereas consumer surplus depends on who is served. We shall sketch the idea of the proof and then derive the second-best pricing rule for a nonprice rationing case.

In Figure 5.1 a zero-expected profit contour and an iso-expected consumer surplus contour are illustrated for z and a single P_j on the assump-

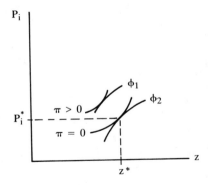

Figure 5.1. Zero expected profit and constant expected consumer surplus.

tion of efficient nonprice rationing. The consumer surplus contour will change when the efficiency of nonprice rationing changes, but the profit contour will not. We shall consider the case of extremely inefficient rationing, in which those consumers willing to pay the lowest price offered will be served first. When we derive the slope of the iso-expected consumer surplus contour for such inefficient rationing at the efficient rationing solution, that is at the point P_j^*, z^*, we find that it is *steeper* than the efficient nonprice-rationing contour. Since the zero-expected profit contour does not change, this can only mean that the solution under inefficient rationing is above and to the right of P_j^*, z^* in Figure 5.1, at a higher P_j and larger z.

It remains to derive second-best pricing and capacity rules when nonprice rationing is inefficient. We can form a new Lagrangian from (45) by substituting the expression for consumer's surplus under the least efficient rationing assumption as set out in Sherman and Visscher (1978). Differentiating this new Lagrangian yields, in place of (46) and (47),

$$\left(\frac{P_j^*-b}{P_j^*}\right) = \frac{\lambda}{1+\lambda}\frac{1}{E(\xi_j)} + \left(\frac{1}{1+\lambda}\right)$$
$$\cdot\left(\frac{Q_j^{-1}[Q_j(P_j^*)-z^*]-P_j^*}{P_j^*}\right)\cdot(1-F[z^*-Q_j(P_j^*)]),$$
$$j=1,\dots,n, \quad (50)$$

$$\sum_{j=1}^{n}\alpha_j\left\{\left(\frac{1}{1+\lambda}\right)\int_{z^*-Q_j(P_j^*)}^{\infty} f_j(u_j)(Q_j^{-1}[Q_j(P_j^*)-z^*]-b)\,du_j\right.$$
$$\left. +\left(\frac{\lambda}{1+\lambda}\right)(P_j^*-b)(1-F_j[z^*-Q_j(P_j^*)])\right\}=\beta. \quad (51)$$

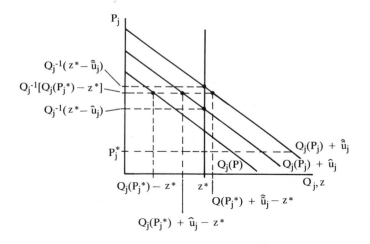

Figure 5.2. Rationing by price.

When rationing was efficient, the second-best welfare-maximizing pricing rule differed from the expected profit-maximizing rule only by a constant term. But that is no longer the only difference if rationing in the presence of excess demand first serves claimants with the least willingness to pay. There is now a positive second term in the right-hand side of (50) that reflects the impact of rationing inefficiency on the pricing rule.

The manner in which the extra term in (50) influences the optimum price can be seen straightforwardly. The term $Q_j^{-1}[Q_j(P_j^*)-z^*]-P_j^*$ is the gain in consumer's surplus if price is raised slightly. When excess demand occurs and capacity is rationed to claimants with the least willingness to pay, this term represents the consumer's surplus lost by the last person turned away. Thus the second term on the right-hand side of (50) is equal to some positive multiple $1/(1+\lambda)$ of the ratio of the net marginal gain in consumer's surplus from a higher price (if there is excess demand) to the value of the price chosen, all multiplied by the probability of excess demand occurring at P_j^*, z^* (the probability $1-F[z^*-Q_j(P_j^*)]$).

As expected, the ideal price is now higher than would be optimal for the same z^* under the efficient nonprice rationing assumption in (48), since the new second term itself will raise the right-hand side of (50). $Q_j^{-1}[Q_j(P_j)-z^*]$ is illustrated in Figure 5.2, and is clearly going to be greater than P^* to make the new term positive. Here price must serve a rationing function not required of it when nonprice rationing was efficient. After all, when price is the only means of assuring that service goes to claimants with the highest willingness to pay, it should be nearer to the market-clearing level than when rationing always is efficient merely by assumption.

Turning to the rules for optimal capacity, note that equation (51) is the inefficient rationing counterpart to equation (49) for efficient nonprice rationing. The only difference between them is in the marginal benefit from a unit of capacity, which depends on the $Q_j^{-1}(z^* - u_j)$ term in (49) and the $Q_j^{-1}(Q_j(P_j^*) - z^*)$ term in (51). We ordinarily expect the expression in (51) to be the larger, inviting larger capacity, because we expect $Q_j(P_j^*) - z^* < z^* - u_j$; that is, uncertainty is not so great that a large random component can make demand twice as great as capacity.

Thus it is possible to derive second-best pricing rules under uncertainty. But when prices must be announced before demand is known, as we have assumed, they will not always clear markets. Then if strict capacity limits exist, so that some consumers will not be served when excess demand arises, it matters who is served. If service is rationed to those who value it most, even when price is not available to ration, then the solution is remarkably like the certainty case. This is also the result when high demand brings general quality deterioration rather than lack of service, as Marchand (1973) has shown. But if some consumers who are not served are those claimants willing to pay the highest prices, a more complicated second-best price is in order. This generally high price helps to ration the service so it goes to those who value it the most.

5.5 Second-best nonuniform pricing

We shall emphasize two forms of nonuniform pricing. First, there is two-part pricing, where a fixed charge or entry fee is required to consume the good at a uniform price and the first unit is therefore more expensive to a consumer than other units. The two prices affect not only the amount a consumer purchases, but whether the consumer purchases the good at all (Ng and Weisser 1974) and thus determine the number of consumers of the good as well as the amounts they consume. Second, there is quantity-dependent pricing, where the price varies more generally with quantities consumed (Spence 1977, 1980; Roberts 1979; Katz 1983, 1984). The latter case may force consumers to have different marginal rates of substitution between the good we are examining and other goods, to the extent that marginal prices are unequal. For such prices to persist, it must be impossible for consumers to resell the good or service, of course, since trade among consumers would eliminate the unequal marginal rates of substitution.

Two-part pricing

When costs depend on the number of consumers as well as the number of units consumed, it is possible to derive two-part prices that reflect those costs but are also second best, and the Ramsey principle will apply to each part. We begin as we did in Section 4.5, where a welfare-maximizing price turned out to equal marginal cost for each part. Suppose that consumers differ in their taste for the good or service of interest according to the index θ, where $0 \leq \theta \leq 1$. Other goods, assumed constant in prices, will be suppressed along with incomes because we assume no income effect. The index θ is distributed according to the density function $f(\theta)$. The demand for an individual having index θ will be $q = q(p_n, p_q, \theta)$. Individuals whose index is below some level, $\hat{\theta}$, will not pay the fee p_n to consume q at price p_q, and for them $q = 0$. The "cutoff" index $\hat{\theta}$, belongs to the marginal consumer, and $\hat{\theta}$ obviously depends on p_n and p_q. Because it represents the most interesting case, we assume that $0 < \hat{\theta} < 1$ (and $\hat{\theta} = 0$ or $\hat{\theta} = 1$ are simple cases). Under these conditions, the total patronage and market demand functions can be calculated as

$$n(p_n, p_q) = \int_{\hat{\theta}(p_n, p_q)}^{1} f(\theta) \, d\theta, \tag{52}$$

and

$$Q(p_n, p_q) = \int_{\hat{\theta}(p_n, p_q)}^{1} q(p_n, p_q, \theta) f(\theta) \, d\theta. \tag{53}$$

These demand and patronage functions will be assumed continuous with $Q_{p_n} < 0$, $Q_{p_q} < 0$, $n_{p_n} < 0$, $n_{p_q} < 0$. With $C(n, Q)$ total cost, the profit for the firm $(TR - TC)$ is

$$\pi = p_n n(p_n, p_q) + p_q Q(p_n, p_q) - C(n, Q). \tag{54}$$

To represent welfare for those who consume q, we again use the indirect utility function, $V(p_q, y - p_n, \theta)$ (see Section 2.2), but we subtract away the utility of not consuming the good at all, $V(\infty, y, \theta)$. This forms a measure of individual consumer surplus,

$$S(p_n, p_q, y, \theta) = w(y)[V(p_q, y - p_n, \theta) - V(\infty, y, \theta)], \tag{55}$$

where $w(y)$ is the social weight given an individual having income y, or the social marginal utility of income for that individual. We assume that the welfare weights equal the reciprocals of the marginal utilities of income, or $w = 1/\mu$, and then from $\partial V/\partial p_n = -\mu$, $w(y)\partial V/\partial p_n$ equals -1, and from $\partial V/\partial p_q = -\mu q$, $w(y)\partial V/\partial p_q$ equals $-q$. As a result, $S_{p_n} = -1$ and $S_{p_q} = -q$. We shall suppress y in $S(p_n, p_q, \theta)$ because its main role is to give welfare weights to yield these derivatives, there being no income effect on consumption. Recall that welfare weights are reciprocals of private marginal utilities of income implicitly when the current income distribution is accepted. Then added income is valued the same by society, whomever receives it. Consumer welfare is thus represented as

$$\int_{\hat{\theta}(p_n,p_q)}^{1} S(p_n,p_q,\theta)f(\theta)\,d\theta, \tag{56}$$

where we assume $\partial S/\partial\theta = S_\theta > 0$.

Now consider the objective of maximizing social welfare subject to the constraint that profit equal some fixed amount B. With increasing returns to scale, this objective would allow pricing for maximum efficiency subject to the constraint, say, that there be no deficit ($B=0$). Even with constant returns to scale in both n and Q but (some) fixed cost, or if a positive profit is required from the enterprise with no fixed cost, there can be a second-best problem. The Lagrangian formed to maximize welfare subject to a profit constraint is

$$L(p_n,p_Q,\lambda) = C + \pi + \lambda(\pi - B). \tag{57}$$

Substituting (54) and (56) into (57) and differentiating yields

$$-\int_{\hat{\theta}}^{1} f(\theta)\,d\theta + (1+\lambda)\left[(p_n-c_n)\frac{\partial n}{\partial p_n} + n + (p_q-c_q)\frac{\partial Q}{\partial p_n}\right] = 0 \tag{58}$$

and

$$-\int_{\hat{\theta}}^{1} qf(\theta)\,d\theta + (1+\lambda)\left[(p_n-c_n)\frac{\partial n}{\partial p_q} + (p_q-c_q)\frac{\partial q}{\partial p_q} + Q\right] = 0, \tag{59}$$

where c_n and c_q are marginal costs of serving customers and producing units. On simplifying (58) and (59), we obtain

$$\left(\frac{p_n-c_n}{p_n}\right)\xi_{nn} + \left(\frac{p_q-c_q}{p_q}\right)\xi_{nq} = \frac{-\lambda}{1+\lambda}$$

and

$$\left(\frac{p_n-c_n}{p_n}\right)\xi_{qn} + \left(\frac{p_q-c_q}{p_q}\right)\xi_{qq} = \frac{-\lambda}{1+\lambda},$$

where $\xi_{nq} = (\partial n/\partial p_q)p_q/n$ (with other elasticities defined similarly) and $\xi_{nq} = \xi_{qn}(p_q Q/p_n N)$. Simultaneously solving these conditions yields the price-cost margins,

$$\frac{p_n-c_n}{p_n} = \left(\frac{-\lambda}{1+\lambda}\right)\frac{\xi_{qq}-\xi_{nq}}{\xi_{nn}\xi_{qq}-\xi_{qn}\xi_{nq}} \tag{60}$$

and

$$\frac{p_q-c_q}{p_q} = \left(\frac{-\lambda}{1+\lambda}\right)\frac{\xi_{nn}-\xi_{qn}}{\xi_{nn}\xi_{qq}-\xi_{qn}\xi_{nq}}. \tag{61}$$

Equations (60) and (61) have the same form as the pair of equations (33) for two services in Section 5.3, but here we really have two parts of the price of one service. Each part of the two-part price is adjusted as if it were a Ramsey price for a separate service. The elasticities in the case of a two-part price may have special properties, owing to the relation between the fixed fee for any use and the price per quantity of use of a particular service. In the case of electricity, for example, we expect the demand for some service, that is the demand for n, to be quite inelastic in most Western countries, because virtually everyone wants to use *some* electricity, but the demand for usage, or for q, may be elastic. For given elasticities, however, the Ramsey principle is applied to each price in the same way as before for separate services.

The special structure of demand in the case of a two-part price for one good or service yields considerably more interpretation, and the conditions that allow it were drawn together usefully by Schmalensee (1981). Notice first that for the marginal consumer with $\theta = \hat{\theta}$, $S(p_n, p_q, \hat{\theta}) = 0$. Totally differentiating this condition with respect to p_n and p_q, remembering that $\hat{\theta} = \hat{\theta}(p_n, p_q)$, we obtain

$$\hat{\theta}_{p_n} = 1/(S_{\hat{\theta}}(p_n, p_q, \hat{\theta}) \tag{62}$$

and

$$\hat{\theta}_{p_q} = q(p_n, p_q, \hat{\theta})/S_{\hat{\theta}}(p_n, p_q, \hat{\theta}) = \hat{q}\hat{\theta}_{p_n}. \tag{63}$$

Since a change in $\hat{\theta}$ implies a change in n, (63) means that

$$n_{p_q} = \hat{q}n_{p_n}. \tag{64}$$

With no income effect, the only way p_n can change Q is through changes in n, so we also have

$$\hat{q}n_{p_n} = Q_{p_n}. \tag{65}$$

We can define the compensated derivative

$$\bar{Q}_{p_q} = Q_{p_q} - \frac{n_{p_q}}{n_{p_n}} Q_{p_n},$$

where p_n is changed in order to hold n constant, and use it to define the compensated demand elasticity,

$$E_{qq} = \bar{Q}_{p_q} p_q/Q = \left[Q_{p_q} - \frac{n_{p_q}}{n_{p_n}} Q_{p_n} \right] p_q \bigg/ Q. \tag{66}$$

Similarly, we can obtain a quantity-constant derivative of n with respect to p_n (denoted $\bar{n}_{p_n}$) and use it to define the compensated elasticity,

$$E_{nn} = \bar{n}_{p_n} p_n/n = \left[n_{p_n} - \frac{Q_{p_n}}{Q_{p_q}} n_{p_q} \right] p_n \bigg/ n. \tag{67}$$

We should also point out that the derivative of quantity with respect to price can be divided into two parts in the case of no-income effect,

$$Q_{p_q} = \hat{q} n_{p_q} + \sigma, \tag{68}$$

where

$$\sigma = \int_{\hat{\theta}}^{1} q_{p_q} f(\theta) \, d\theta. \tag{69}$$

After rearrangement using (64), (65), (67), and (68), the pricing rule in (60) becomes

$$\frac{p_n - c_n}{p_n} = \frac{\lambda}{1+\lambda} \left(\frac{1}{E_{nn}} \right) \frac{[(\bar{q} - \hat{q})Q_{p_n} - \sigma]}{Q_{p_q}}, \tag{70}$$

where $\bar{q} = Q/N$, average quantity consumed. With $\lambda > 0$, $E_{nn} < 0$ and $Q_{p_q} < 0$, we know that $p_n - c_n$ will have the same sign as $(\bar{q} - \hat{q})Q_{p_n} - \sigma$. Since $\sigma < 0$, $p_n - c_n$ must be positive if $\bar{q} = \hat{q}$, which is expected when buyers are identical (Oi 1971). If $\hat{q} > \bar{q}$, which means that consumption of marginal consumers is greater than consumption of average consumers, then (since $Q_{p_n} < 0$) $p_n - c_n$ must again be positive. If $\hat{q} < \bar{q}$, the sign of $p_n - c_n$ depends on the magnitudes of $(\bar{q} - \hat{q})Q_{p_n}$ and σ.

It is also possible to rearrange (61), using (64) and (66) to convert the pricing rule into the form

$$\frac{p_q - c_q}{p_q} = \frac{\lambda}{1+\lambda} \left(\frac{1}{-E_{qq}} \right) \left(\frac{\bar{q} - \hat{q}}{\bar{q}} \right). \tag{71}$$

Notice that $p_q - c_q$ must have the same sign as $\bar{q} - \hat{q}$, since $E_{qq} < 0$ and $\lambda > 0$. If $\bar{q} = \hat{q}$, then price per unit should equal marginal cost, or $p_q = c_q$ (while $p_n > c_n$, as observed above). If $\hat{q} > \bar{q}$, then $p_q < c_q$, and the implication of (70) that $p_n > c_n$ is needed to make up the loss resulting from $p_q < c_q$. If $\hat{q} < \bar{q}$, then $p_q > c_q$ and the sign of $p_n - c_n$ may be positive or negative.

To see the logic behind the Ramsey rule in (71), suppose that the marginal consumer consumes virtually nothing, which could happen if p_n were very small. Think of $\hat{q}$ as being zero then, and note that (71) reduces to the simplest form of Ramsey rule. In (71) the proportionate change in quantity is being calculated from the starting point at $\hat{q}$, when that is not zero, since any change in quantity will have its effect over the range $\bar{q} - \hat{q}$. Indeed, one could redefine elasticity with quantity oriented to the minimum level as $E'_{qq} = \bar{Q}_{p_q} p_q / (\bar{q} - \hat{q})n$, and then interpret (71) as

$$\frac{(p_q - c_q)}{p_q} = \left(\frac{\lambda}{1+\lambda} \right) \left(\frac{1}{-E'_{qq}} \right). \tag{72}$$

Where $q_\theta < 0$ (so $\bar{q} < \hat{q}$), the marginal consumer consumes more than the average consumer. Then $(-E'_{qq})$ becomes negative, requiring $p_q < c_q$.

Having $p_q < c_q$ means that to meet the budget constraint will require that $p_n > c_n$. Ng and Weisser (1974) proved $p_n \geq 0$ in a similar model (but where $c_n = 0$), using this argument. For a good where $q_\theta > 0$, they argued that, if $p_n < c_n$, this subsidy for joining would cause everyone to join up for the service, since with $c_n = 0$, $p_n < c_n$ implies $p_n < 0$. But that ensures the elasticity of customers with respect to p_n, ξ_{nn}, or E_{nn} will be so low that a price yielding nonnegative proceeds (i.e., $p_n \geq c_n$) should be in order instead. If we relax our requirement that $q_\theta > 0$ (or the alternative requirement that $q_\theta > 0$), a greater range of p_n and p_q combinations becomes feasible, because many different demand patterns are then possible. Another influence on optimal p_n and c_n was demonstrated by Phillips and Battalio (1983) to arise from substitutability between admissions and consumption per admission where that is possible, as in Oi's (1971) amusement park example. If people could substitute perfectly between admissions to an amusement park and rides per admission, for example, the admission fee would be forced equal to marginal cost and there would be only a single uniform price. (This may explain why we are not charged for admission to grocery stores.)

Quantity-dependent pricing

We know that if (1) a good cannot readily be exchanged, (2) consumers use different amounts of it, and (3) the seller can monitor usage by each consumer, then a price schedule can make a consumer's outlay vary in a nonuniform way with his or her consumption. Rather than vary in direct proportion, as it does with uniform prices, the outlay may vary in some other way specified in the continuous function $R(q)$, where marginal price per unit $p(q) = R'(q)$. If quantity discounts allow lower marginal prices for greater quantities, exchange must not be possible, or else purchases would be made through one consumer and distributed thereafter through exchanges. If quantity premia are attempted, which would make the marginal price rise with quantity, it must not be possible for consumers to make more frequent but smaller purchases, for their doing so would subvert the pricing scheme. Of course, monitoring of consumption by the seller is necessary to effect quantity-dependent prices. The seller is not able to recognize consumers except by the quantities they consume, however, or to identify their willingness to pay, and so the same outlay schedule, $R(q)$, must be offered to every consumer.

It is difficult to conduct a general analysis of quantity-dependent pricing, because a particular population of consumers may be influenced by many different features. Our brief discussion of quantity-dependent pricing by a monopolist in Chapter 3 (Section 3.4 and Figure 3.2) required that greater utility was obtained by those who chose greater quantities, for example, and such a relation again is needed here if there is to be any benefit in having the prices that consumers pay depend in a nonuniform way on the quantities they consume. But we know from Willig's (1978) analysis (Section 2.7) that, when quantity-dependent prices are applicable, they can benefit consumers and also the seller, compared with a price above marginal cost. Since a second-best uniform price or the uniform per unit part of a second-best two-part price may be above marginal cost, a quantity-dependent price may serve welfare better.

Spence (1980) examined quantity-dependent prices under profit constraints using a simple model in which there were k distinctive consumer types. The utility that a consumer of type i received from consuming the quantity q_i was represented as $u_i(q_i)$, and for that quantity the consumer paid p_i. Consumers maximize utility in selecting among offered price-quantity combinations, (p_i, q_i). The inverse demand of a type i person is given by the derivative, $u_i'(q_i)$. If there are n_i consumers of type i and all consumers are weighted equally, a simple measure of total consumer surplus is

$$C = \sum_i n_i (u_i(q_i) - p_i). \tag{73}$$

With total cost represented by $c(\cdot)$, total profit is

$$\pi = \sum_i n_i p_i - c(\sum_i n_i q_i). \tag{74}$$

Maximizing $C + \pi$ subject to $\pi \geq 0$ is then equivalent to maximizing

$$L = \lambda C + \pi. \tag{75}$$

Spence adopted the convention that larger values of i were associated with consumer types who valued the good more, which implied that for all $j > 0$

$$q_{i+j} \geq q_i \quad \text{and} \quad p_{i+j} \geq p_i.$$

This meant that binding constraints would be of the form

$$u_i(q_i) - p_i \geq u_i(q_{i-1}) - p_{i-1}.$$

These constraints essentially alter the opportunities of consumers of smaller amounts so they interfere less with the profit to be made and the benefit to be created by serving those who consume more. Spence gathered together constraints on prices, assuming quantities were given, as

$$
\begin{aligned}
p_1 &= u_1(q_1) \\
p_2 &= u_2(q_2) - u_2(q_1) + p_1 \\
\vdots \quad &\quad \vdots \qquad \vdots \qquad \vdots \\
p_k &= u_k(q_k) - u_k(q_{k-1}) + p_{k-1},
\end{aligned}
\tag{76}
$$

into the sum for each i,

$$p_i = \sum_{j=1}^{i} [u_j(q_j) - u_j(q_{j-1})], \tag{77}$$

where $q_0 = 0$ and $u_i(0) = 0$. With these relations he eliminated prices from (73) and (74), and so (75) could then be solved for the optimal quantities that had been assumed. (In solving for q_i's, it was assumed that $q_{i+1} \geq q_i$, and if that is not true, some small modifications are necessary in what follows.)

Substituting (73), (74), and (77) into (75) and maximizing with respect to q_i's yields

$$u_i'(q_i) = \frac{n_i}{n_i + (1-\lambda)m_{i+1}} c'(q_i) + \frac{(1-\lambda)m_{i+1}}{n_i + (1-\lambda)m_{i+1}} u_{i+1}'(q_i),$$

$$i = 1, \ldots, n, \tag{78}$$

where $m_i = \sum_{j=i}^{k} n_j$ and $m_{k+1} = 0$. Notice first that $u_k'(q_k) = c'(q_k)$ so that the highest value users obtain the optimal amount, the amount they would select at marginal cost pricing. With $\lambda = 1$ we would have the simple welfare problem of maximizing consumer plus producer surplus in (75), $C + \pi$, and from (78) we see that, since $u_i'(q_i) = c_i$ for all i, price should then equal marginal cost for every i. With $\lambda = 0$, we have the profit-maximizing problem whose solution $u_i'(q_i)$ in (78) will be a weighted average of $c'(q_i)$ and $u_{i+1}'(q_i)$, the willingness to pay of higher value users for the quantity q_i. The profit-constrained problem relies on profit maximizing more as λ approaches 0. It will tend to make all users consume less than the ideal amount, since for them $u_i'(q_i) > c'(q_i)$.

The solution in (78) thus reveals the general pattern of quantity-dependent prices, which were also shown by Spence to allow Pareto improvements over a uniform price above marginal cost. But notice that the solution depends on properties of the population of consumers, who are combined for us here in convenient types; so, for application, more information about consumers is needed than in other instances. Some progress has been made using continuous models of consumer populations, and considering a price schedule that can change continuously.

An optimal continuous nonuniform price schedule can be obtained using optimal control theory. We do not explain the use of this technique here, but we report briefly properties of the optimal price schedule that it determines. An excellent development of the method may be found in Kamien and Schwartz (1981), and the optimal nonuniform price is derived by Goldman, Leland, and Sibley (1984). Excellent instruction for constructing nonuniform price schedules is available in Brown and Sibley (1986). Extension to the multiproduct situation is provided by Mirman and Sibley (1980).

For analytical convenience, it is again necessary that some sort of measure order the consumers by their demands, always in the same way regardless of price level. Assuming that consumers differ by the index θ, distributed according to $f(\theta)$, will accomplish this. A number of properties of the functional relation between θ and q are established by Goldman, Leland, and Sibley (1984), who have the consumer maximize, through choice of quantity, the accumulated willingness to pay, $W(q, \theta)$ minus the outlay, $R(q)$. Setting aside possible discontinuities in $P(q(\theta))$, the optimal q for a consumer with index θ, q^* is such that $W(q^*(\theta), \theta) = P(q^*(\theta))$. The simplest case has no income effect and involves a price schedule that will never cross any demand curve more than once (if marginal price is below willingness to pay for a given quantity, it will be below willingness to pay for every lesser quantity). The welfare-maximizing problem is set out as

$$\text{Max} \int_0^\infty \int_{\hat{\theta}}^{\bar{\theta}} [\gamma(W(q, \theta) - P(q)) + (1 - \gamma)(P(q) - c_q)] \, d\theta \, dq, \tag{79}$$

which involves welfare multiplied by γ on the left and profit multiplied by $(1 - \gamma)$ on the right. Setting $\gamma = \frac{1}{2}$ will result in an ordinary welfare-maximizing problem, where welfare is consumer surplus plus producer surplus. Setting $\gamma = 0$ will result in a profit-maximizing problem.

Goldman, Leland, and Sibley point out that every increment of output, Δq, can be seen as a market, and all such markets are independent of one another. The reason for this independence is that consumers either consume or not at every increment, unaffected by decisions at other increments because of no income effect. At quantity q, for instance, demand is $1 - \hat{\theta}(q_0)$, where $\hat{\theta}$ is the lowest index of any consumer who consumes q_0 or more. Since there is no income effect, consumption is the same at q_0 regardless of what happened at any smaller quantity. They go on to show that demand elasticity may be represented as

$$\eta = \frac{P(q)}{[1 - F(\hat{\theta}(q))] \partial W / \partial \theta}, \tag{80}$$

where $P(q) = W(q, \hat{\theta}(q))$; and necessary conditions for a maximum of (79) are shown to yield the pricing rule

$$\frac{P(q) - c}{P(q)} = \left(\frac{1 - 2\gamma}{1 - \gamma}\right) \frac{(1 - \hat{\theta}(q)) \partial W / \partial \theta}{P(q)},$$

or, since $\hat{\theta}(q)$ is $F(\hat{\theta}(q))$,

$$\frac{P(q) - c_q}{P_q} = \left(\frac{1 - 2\gamma}{1 - \gamma}\right) \frac{1}{\eta}. \tag{81}$$

The rule for optimal price at output q in (81) is obviously of the Ramsey type. If $\gamma = 0$ we would have a profit-maximizing problem and (81) reduces to a monopoly pricing rule, where price minus marginal cost over price equals $1/\eta$. If $\gamma = \frac{1}{2}$ we would have a welfare-maximizing problem and the solution is $P(q) = c_q$. If $0 < \gamma < \frac{1}{2}$, say, because some contribution to profit is needed to meet fixed costs, then (81) would give the Ramsey rule to follow in order to determine the optimal nonuniform price schedule. Goldman, Leland, and Sibley examine second-order conditions carefully and show that the optimal price schedule is apt to have discontinuities, with bunches of consumers served at certain points. One condition that is crucially important in this analysis is whether a consistent value is observed for $\partial q / \partial \theta$, as we assumed above; without it the schedule becomes more complex. With income effects present, the pricing rule becomes more like the one shown for a monopoly in Chapter 3. The price for the consumer wanting the largest quantity will still equal marginal cost.

5.6   Summary

Economies of scale or economies of scope can cause difficulties for marginal cost pricing by preventing the revenues from such prices to cover total cost. Optimal taxation principles due originally to Frank Ramsey (1927) provide a basis for making prices depart from marginal cost in a way that causes the least welfare loss from doing so. The resulting so-called second-best pricing principles are used just enough to meet the budget constraint that is imposed on the enterprise. Underlying this result is an inability to tax leisure, which invites higher prices on complements to leisure, goods with less elastic demands. Second-best pricing rules were elaborated here to take into account uncertainty in demands, which influence prices more when some consumers are denied service through nonprice rationing. Second-best nonuniform prices also were presented, as two-part prices and as more general quantity-dependent prices, all of which possessed the Ramsey form. Where they can be used, quantity-dependent prices allow Pareto improvements over uniform second-best prices that exceed marginal cost. On the pattern of demands assumed for the population, the marginal price equals marginal cost for the highest demander and involves greater departures from marginal cost for smaller demanders.

Questions

5.1. Suppose that the U.S. Postal Service offers only two mail services, First Class (at price P_1 and quantity Q_1) and Second Class (at price P_2 and quantity Q_2), with demands and costs as follows:

First-Class Demand

$P_1 = 20 - 0.0100Q_1$

Second-Class Demand

$P_2 = 15 - 0.005Q_2$

Total Cost (TC)

$TC = 2400 + 10Q_1 + 10Q_2$.

(a) What prices will maximize consumer surplus plus profit, subject to the constraint that total revenue must equal total cost? (Hint: The fact that Q_1/Q_2 must be the same at the solution as at marginal cost prices can be used to simplify the problem; see equations (6) and (7).)

(b) Suppose that rather than the goal in (a), the Postal Service attempted to maximize total revenue $(P_1Q_1 + P_2Q_2)$, subject to the constraint that total revenue must equal total cost. Determine P_1 and P_2, and interpret any changes from those prices given in (a) above (give reasons for any specific changes).

(c) What is the value of consumer surplus at the solutions in part (a) and part (b)?

(d) If free entry is allowed into both main services, is the solution in part (a) sustainable? Is the solution in part (b) sustainable?

5.2. A U.S. railroad serves freight and passenger markets with the following demand functions (price and quantity in tons of freight are p_F and Q_F; of passengers, p_p and Q_p):

Freight

$p_F = 81 - 0.8Q_F$

Passengers

$p_p = 4 - 0.06Q_p$.

Costs of the railroad are:

$TC_R = 100 + 1Q_F + 1Q_p$.

(a) Suppose that the Interstate Commerce Commission (ICC) requires that rates for freight and passenger traffic reflect "fully distributed costs." More specifically, the total fixed cost that is shared by the two rail services is to be divided between them so that the fixed cost borne by one ton of freight equals the fixed cost borne by one passenger. Find rates that will allow the railroad to break even (have total revenue equal total cost) while meeting this ICC requirement.

(b) Assuming that the railroad must break even, determine Ramsey prices for the two services of the railroad.

(c) Do the Ramsey prices in part (b) yield more consumer surplus than the fully distributed cost rates obtained in part (a)? (If there is a difference, show its magnitude.)

5.3. Consider Question 5.2.

(a) Suppose a truckline can carry freight according to the cost function

$TC_T = 80 + 1Q_F$

and buses can operate under the cost function

$$TC_B = 30 + 1Q_p.$$

Then will the Ramsey prices obtained in part (b) of Question 5.2 be sustainable?

(b) Given the alternative costs of trucks and buses in (a) above, are the fully distributed cost prices obtained in part (a) of Question 5.2 sustainable?

Appendix to Chapter 5

Another derivation of second-best two-part prices may be obtained by interpreting the distribution function. Suppose that we represent benefit when units of the service are consumed by the indirect utility from those units, $V(p_q, y)$, ignoring the fixed payment that must be made. Aggregate consumer welfare can be represented through this measure, appropriately weighted, if the necessary outlay p_n is subtracted away, so we have

$$C = N \int_{y_m}^{\bar{y}} (V(p_q, y)/\mu - p_n) f(y) \, dy. \tag{A1}$$

We can then express the budget constraint as

$$\pi = N \int_{y_m}^{\bar{y}} [p_q q(p_q, y) + p_n - C(n, q)] f(y) \, dy = B, \tag{A2}$$

and form a Lagrangian problem as in (57) but with ϕ now the Lagrange multiplier. In addition to (A2), maximizing with respect to p_q, p_n, and ϕ yields

$$\phi N \int_{y_m}^{\bar{y}} f(y) \, dy - (1+\phi)[(p_q - c_q)q(p_q, y_m) + p_n - c_n] f(y_m) \partial y_m / \partial p_n = 0, \tag{A3}$$

and

$$\phi N \int_{y_m}^{\bar{y}} q(p_q, y) f(y) \, dy - (1+\phi)$$

$$\times \left[(p_q - c_q) N \int_{y_m}^{\bar{y}} (\partial q / \partial p_q) \right] f(y) \, dy - [(p_q - c_q)q(p_q, y_m) + p_n - c_n]$$

$$\times f(y_m) \partial y_m / \partial p_c = 0. \tag{A4}$$

Condition (A3) can be reduced to

$$\frac{(p_q - c_q)q(p_q, y_m) + p_n - c_n}{p_n} = \frac{\phi}{1+\phi} \frac{1}{\eta_n}, \tag{A5}$$

where $\eta_n = (\partial y_m / \partial p_n) p_n [1 - F(y_m)] / f(y_m)$. The left-hand side of (A5) represents a ratio of revenue minus cost in relation to revenue, where the revenue in the numerator includes any difference between cost and revenue per unit times the number of units a marginal consumer purchases, in addition to the difference between the fixed entry fee and cost per customer, $p_n - c_n$. The right-hand side takes a

Ramsey price form, where η_n is the elasticity for marginal consumers to become consumers in response to a reduction in p_n. The change in consumption in response to a change in p_n will occur by a change in y_m. We can think of this proportionate change in quantity as being $f(y_m)dy_m/[1-F(y_m)]$. Then η_n is the natural form for elasticity of consumers joining in response to a change in p_n.

To interpret the requirement for an optimal p_q, condition (A4) can be rearranged as

$$\phi N \int_{y_m}^{\bar{y}} q(p_q, y) f(y)\, dy + (1+\phi)$$

$$\times \left[(p_q - c_q) \frac{\partial \phi}{\partial p_q} - [(p_q - c_q)q(p_q, y_m) + p_n - c_n]f(y_m) \frac{\partial y_m}{\partial p_q} \right] = 0. \quad \text{(A6)}$$

We know that for the marginal consumer $V(p_q, y_m) = p_n$, which defines implicitly the function $y_m = y_m(p_q, p_n)$ such that

$$w(y_m) \frac{\partial V}{\partial y_m} \cdot \frac{\partial y_m}{\partial p_n} = 1 \quad \text{and} \quad w(y_m) \frac{\partial V}{\partial p_q} = \frac{\partial V}{\partial y_m} \cdot \frac{\partial y_m}{\partial p_q},$$

which yield (with $w(y_m)\partial V/\partial p_q = q(p_q, y_m)$)

$$\frac{\partial y_m}{\partial p_q} = q(p_q, y_m) \frac{\partial y_m}{\partial p_n}. \quad \text{(A7)}$$

Now substituting (A7) and (A5) into (A6) yields, after some rearrangement,

$$\frac{p_q - c_q}{p_q} = \left(\frac{\phi}{1+\phi} \right) \frac{1}{\eta_q} \left[\frac{Q - Q_m}{Q} \right], \quad \text{(A8)}$$

where

$$\eta_q = \frac{-(\partial Q/\partial p_q)p_q}{Q}, \qquad Q = \int_{y_m}^{\bar{y}} q(p_q, y) f(y)\, dy,$$

and

$$Q_m = \int_{y_m}^{\bar{y}} q(p_q, y_m) f(y)\, dy.$$

The quantity consumed by the marginal consumer is Q_m and the quantity consumed by the average consumer is Q.

Here again in (A8) we have a pricing rule somewhat like the Ramsey rule in form, except that the difference between marginal and average consumption now plays a role in the optimal price. If marginal and average consumption are the same, price per unit should equal marginal cost and any necessary added revenue would be raised through the fixed fee. With a normal good, we can expect $Q > Q_m$, and the Ramsey price per unit is to be relied on more as a source of revenue, as $(Q - Q_m)/Q$ is larger.

CHAPTER 6

Equity in public pricing

6.1 Introduction

Thus far we have emphasized an efficiency goal while accepting the current distribution of income as satisfactory. When entry is freely allowed into a market, the cross-subsidization that is necessary if income is to be redistributed through prices cannot be sustained. Yet it is sometimes reasonable to affect the distribution of income through public pricing decisions, particularly if income redistribution goals are widely agreed upon and other means of affecting income distribution are not available.[1] Even if income distribution is not being sought as a goal, it may be useful to understand how it is affected by prices. Considering how individual welfare weights can affect prices shows more clearly why the assumptions underlying consumer surplus do not call for income redistribution.

We first examine the idea of anonymous equity. It is consistent with free entry, and if its conditions are met, cross-subsidization among consumers is impossible. We next consider the pricing implications of welfare weights that differ from those in consumer surplus based on the current distribution of income. We show how alternative weights affect optimal prices and can even rationalize cross-subsidization, which means they require entry barriers to be effective. The effect of welfare weights is extended to the case in which consumption of certain "beneficial" goods creates positive external effects and so is to be encouraged. Discussion is initially confined to uniform prices, prices that are proportional to quantity consumed for all consumers. Nonuniform price schedules are also shown to have implications for equity as well as efficiency.

6.2 Anonymous equity

When a market is contestable, entry or the threat of entry can prevent cross-subsidy across goods or services, with obvious implications for equity. Redistributing income to achieve a generally desired outcome, which

---

[1] Political institutions often pursue income distribution goals. Causes of such activity are interestingly discussed by Blinder (1982). The tendency of economists to resist considering income redistribution is treated by Rhoads (1985). See also Buchanan (1968).

is one aim in this chapter, is impossible once cross-subsidization is ruled out. Of course, if consumers of one good or service cannot subsidize consumers of another good or service, they also cannot be put at a disadvantage, and in certain circumstances that is a virtue to be attained. Anonymous equity is a condition on prices that is stronger than the notion that prices should be subsidy-free by good or service, and it requires that no consumer subsidize another.

Consider the cost or producing one good or service, $C(q_i)$, or of a subset s of goods and services, $C(q_s)$, the "stand-alone" cost of that individual good or service or subset. *Subsidy-free* prices were defined in Chapter 3 as prices at which total revenue exactly covered total cost while the revenue from each good or service or any subset of goods or services was no greater than the stand-alone cost of providing that good or service or subset. An alternative form of the requirement is that revenue from any subset of goods be no less than the incremental cost of the subset.[2] However, subsidy-free prices do not necessarily ensure that no consumer will subsidize another. The stronger result that no consumer can possibly subsidize another is known as *anonymous equity*. It was introduced by Willig (1979b) and developed by Faulhaber and Levinson (1981). An excellent comparison of these ideas on subsidy-free prices and anonymous equity, together with sustainability, may be found in Mirman, Tauman, and Zang (1985a).

Anonymous equity is defined in terms of consumers rather than goods, so that interest in it turns on how different consumers' demands are. If all demands always are perfectly proportional to one another, for example, then no consumer will subsidize another under any set of uniform prices, even if the prices are not subsidy-free. But if consumers instead prefer different goods and if nonsubsidy-free prices persist, some consumers can subsidize others. Since we are unlikely to know the details of these patterns in consumer demands, we consider every possible consumer demand vector that is less than or equal to observed demand. If prices are to be anonymously equitable, they must first enable total revenues to equal total cost. In addition, revenue from every possible vector of consumer demands cannot exceed the cost of serving that vector. That is, in addition to total revenue equaling total cost, or

$$pq = C(q),$$

for every conceivable vector of consumer demands $q' \le q$, anonymously equitable prices must be such that

$$pq' \ge C(q'), \quad \text{all } q' \le q.$$

2 See Faulhaber (1975) and Faulhaber and Levinson (1981).

These requirements together imply that

$$\mathbf{pq}' \geq C(\mathbf{q}) - C(\mathbf{q} - \mathbf{q}'), \quad \text{all } \mathbf{q}' \leq \mathbf{q}.$$

Faulhaber and Levinson (1981) proved that an anonymously equitable price vector would also be subsidy-free, but that a subsidy-free price vector need not be anonymously equitable. Their revealing peak-load pricing example will demonstrate the latter point.

Assume that demand for a homogeneous good (such as electricity) is at a high level Q_1 during 12 peak hours of the day and at a low level Q_2 for 12 off-peak hours, and that these demands by time of day are independent. The firm employs a single technology to meet these demands, with constant operating cost b and constant capacity cost β. The firm is regulated so that it can earn no profit. We found in Section 4.3 that to be subsidy-free, prices P_1 and P_2 must satisfy (here in Steiner (1957) form)

$$b + \beta(1 - Q_2/Q_1) \leq P_1 \leq b + \beta,$$

and

$$b \leq P_2 \leq b + \beta.$$

These constraints were derived by imposing the stand-alone test

$$P_1 Q_1 \leq C(Q_1, 0) = (b + \beta)Q_1,$$

$$P_2 Q_2 \leq C(0, Q_2) = (b + \beta)Q_2,$$

and, with revenue equaling cost, the implied incremental cost test,

$$P_1 Q_1 \geq C(Q_1, Q_2) - C(0, Q_2) = (b + \beta)Q_1 - \beta Q_2,$$

$$P_2 Q_2 \geq C(Q_1, Q_2) - C(Q_1, 0) = b Q_2.$$

The set of subsidy-free prices is shown in Figure 6.1 by the curved line ad. Point a identifies the lowest value of P_1 and the highest value of P_2 that could be subsidy-free, while d represents the lowest value of P_2 and the highest value of P_1 that could be subsidy-free. Point d is the ordinary solution to this peak-load pricing problem, $P_1 = b + \beta$ and $P_2 = b$, but many other price combinations along ad also would be subsidy-free.

To see whether prices are anonymously equitable, we must examine demands not just by good or service, but for every possible vector of consumer demands. Let us represent an arbitrary set of consumers by K, and its complement, the remaining consumers, by M. If demands of K were eliminated, total revenue would fall by $\sum_{k \in K}(P_1 Q_1^k + P_2 Q_2^k)$ and total cost would fall by an amount up to $\sum_{k \in K}(b + \beta)Q_1^k + b Q_2^k$. If the peak period remains the same after elimination of K demands, the full amount

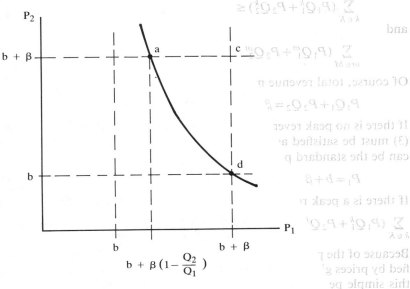

Figure 6.1. Subsidy-free prices.

of the costs indicated would be saved. But it is possible that, when K demands are removed, Q_2 will become the peak period, and then not all the indicated costs would be saved. If we apply the stand-alone test to both sets of consumers, K and M, we must have

$$\sum_{k \in K} (P_1 Q_1^k + P_2 Q_2^k) \leq C\left(\sum_{k \in K} Q_1^k, \sum_{k \in K} Q_2^k\right) \qquad (1)$$

and

$$\sum_{m \in M} (P_1 Q_1^m + P_2 Q_2^m) \leq C\left(\sum_{m \in M} Q_1^m, \sum_{m \in M} Q_2^m\right). \qquad (2)$$

Assuming first that the peak does not shift, these requirements are

$$\sum_{k \in K} (P_1 Q_1^k + P_2 Q_2^k) \leq \sum_{k \in K} [(b+\beta)Q_1^k + bQ_2^k] \qquad (3)$$

and

$$\sum_{m \in M} (P_1 Q_1^m + P_2 Q_2^m) \leq \sum_{m \in M} [(b+\beta)Q_1^m + bQ_2^m]. \qquad (4)$$

If after K demands are removed Q_2 becomes the peak period, the requirements are

$$\sum_{k \in K} (P_1 Q_1^k + P_2 Q_2^k) \le \sum_{k \in K} [(b+\beta)Q_1^k + bQ_2^k] \tag{5}$$

and

$$\sum_{m \in M} (P_1 Q_1^m + P_2 Q_2^m) \le \sum_{m \in M} [bQ_1^m + (b+\beta)Q_2^m]. \tag{6}$$

Of course, total revenue must also equal total cost

$$P_1 Q_1 + P_2 Q_2 = \beta Q_1 + b(Q_1 + Q_2). \tag{7}$$

If there is no peak reversal then we find, on subtracting (4) from (7), that (3) must be satisfied as an equality, which means that the only solution can be the standard peak-load prices,

$$P_1 = b + \beta \quad \text{and} \quad P_2 = b. \tag{8}$$

If there is a peak reversal, we subtract (6) from (7) and find

$$\sum_{k \in K} (P_1 Q_1^k + P_2 Q_2^k) \ge \sum_{k \in K} [(b+\beta)Q_1^k + bQ_2^k] + \sum_{m \in M} \beta(Q_1^m - Q_2^m). \tag{9}$$

Because of the peak reversal, we know $Q_2^m > Q_1^m$, so (9) also can be satisfied by prices given in (8). This means that the standard solution to (8) to this simple peak-load pricing problem is the only price solution that is anonymously equitable. Not surprisingly, anonymous equity is more demanding of prices than the property of being subsidy-free.

By now it should be clear that anonymous equity is very different in conception from income redistribution concerns, which will occupy us for much of this chapter. In tracing anonymous equity, our aim has been to find prices that make *any* redistributive action literally impossible. Anonymously equitable prices guarantee that, whoever might be assigned to any consumer position, each individual will not subsidize in any way another consumer. This view arises out of concerns about the efficacy of free entry. Since free entry will not allow any form of cross-subsidization to persist, it is worth identifying the finest possibility for it. That smallest possibility is what anonymous equity assures against. Thus anonymous equity is equitable only in this sense, that it guarantees no form of redistribution will occur. Equity concerns often lead to explicit redistribution, which is possible through pricing only if attention is given also to entry policy. In the remainder of this chapter, we normally assume that entry is forbidden, since that is necessary for the feasibility of the income redistribution that we discuss.

6.3   Pricing and distributional equity

We begin our discussion of pricing for distributional equity by reconsidering the weighting of individuals in a social welfare function. Recall that, in the pricing rules for externality in Section 4.6, transfers were made to or from individuals so the distribution of income could be adjusted. Because the welfare weights for individuals in the social welfare function remained constant, the transfers t_i served to compensate individuals for any changes imposed, which is why demand elasticities turned out to be compensated (Slutsky) demand elasticities. Of course, in practice such transfer payments are impossible, and yet effects on income distribution that cannot be compensated may be important. For example, certain income distribution goals might be pursued directly through pricing decisions, or income distribution effects might influence the political support behind alternative policies. We shall therefore reexamine the solutions to a second-best pricing problem, to emphasize their income distribution effects when incomes *cannot* be optimally adjusted. Throughout this discussion we must remember that entry limitations may be needed if cross-subsidization is to be sustained.

If maximization with respect to incomes is impossible, and it really is not possible in practice, the question arises whether a pricing rule can be obtained. We know from maximizing only with respect to price, as in equation (18) of Section 5.3, that a term remains from the welfare function, $-\sum_{i=1}^{I} w_i \eta^i q_j^i$, where w_i is the ith individual's weight in social welfare, η^i is that person's marginal utility of income, and q_j^i is his or her consumption of good j. Mohring (1970) emphasized that if the ith person's effect on social welfare, or the value of w_i, is $1/\eta^i$, then $-\sum_{i=1}^{I} w_i \eta^i q_j^i = -\sum_{i=1}^{I} q_j^i = -Q_j$ (see also Negishi 1960). Having made that assumption about individual's weights in social welfare, it is possible to derive optimal pricing rules based on ordinary (i.e., compensated) demand functions, as in equation (20) of Section 5.3.

As pointed out in Section 2.4, using the reciprocal of the ith person's marginal utility of income, $1/\eta^i$, as the ith individual's social weight, w_i, accepts the current income distribution so that a benefit felt by anyone will be of the same value to society. We can create a marginal social utility of income for individual i that is $w_i' = w_i \eta^i$. Observe that a dollar given to any one individual will cause that person to gain the marginal utility of one dollar, η^i, and if that gain is weighted at $w = 1/\eta^i$ by society, the product ($\eta^i \times 1/\eta^i$) will be 1, no matter who receives the dollar, so w_i' will always equal 1. Although this weighting of individuals can suppress the question of income distribution, it by no means solves it. However, it does allow a solution to be reached that is efficient given the existing income distribution.

Martin Feldstein (1972a) has illustrated how preferences regarding income distribution, agreed upon in a society, might be taken into account in setting public prices. This concern for income distribution in pricing has been called "distributional weights" pricing (Harberger 1984). To emphasize the income distribution question, let us consider a case in which there are I consumers who differ *only* with respect to income; utility functions are identical. In Section 4.5 we introduced a measure θ by which consumers differed, and analyzed consumers entering or leaving a market. Here we use a similar representation for income to examine income distribution. Suppose that incomes are distributed according to the density function $f(y)$, so $\underline{y}$ is the lowest income and $\bar{y}$ is the highest. Let $q_j(P_1, \ldots, P_n, y)$ be the demand curve that a person with income y has for the jth good, so the market demand for that good will be

$$Q_j = I \int_{\underline{y}}^{\bar{y}} q_j(P_1, \ldots, P_n, y) f(y) \, dy. \tag{10}$$

The term under the integral in (10) can be considered the average individual demand, and when that is multiplied by the number of consumers, I, total market demand results.

To represent welfare, we take the consumers' indirect utility functions $v(P_1, \ldots, P_n, y)$ and weight them by welfare weights $w(y)$, which vary by income. Here $\eta(y)$ is the marginal utility of income for an individual with income y. As an example, one possibility for these weights is the case just discussed, with $w(y) = 1/\eta(y)$. Then welfare can be represented as

$$W = I \int_{\underline{y}}^{\bar{y}} v(P_1, \ldots, P_n, y) w(y) \, df(y). \tag{11}$$

A simple problem for a budget-constrained public enterprise can be stated as the Lagrangian

$$H = W + \lambda \left[\sum_{j=1}^{n} P_j Q_j - C(Q_1, \ldots, Q_n) - B \right], \tag{12}$$

where B is necessary profit (which may be negative) for the enterprise.

For the problem of this general type, Feldstein (1972a) introduced for each good – say, the jth – a "distributional characteristic," which in modified form is

$$R_j = \frac{I}{Q_j} \int_{\underline{y}}^{\bar{y}} q_j(y) \eta(y) w(y) \, df(y). \tag{13}$$

This distributional characteristic of the good is a weighted average of the marginal social utilities of consumers, $w'(y)$, which equal the products $\eta(y)w(y)$, where the weights depend also on the quantities of the good consumed. In the special case of $w(y) = 1/\eta(y)$, R_j would of course equal one, because the marginal social utilities $w'(y)$ would always be one. Suppose, however, that $w'(y) = \eta(y)w(y)$ is larger for low values of y, meaning that society prefers to favor consumption by those who have lower incomes. If the good has income elasticity of zero, it will be consumed uniformly by all, and again $R_j = 1$. But if the good has a high income elasticity of demand, more of it will be consumed by the rich and the greater weight in R_j for their lower $w'(y) = \eta(y)w(y)$ terms will cause $R_j < 1$. If the good has a low income elasticity of demand, greater consumption by the poor will give greater weight to their higher $w(y)\eta(y)$ values; so then we may expect $R_j > 1$.

To see how R_j can be used, consider the necessary condition for welfare-maximizing pricing through a maximum of the Lagrangian function (3):

$$\frac{\partial H}{\partial P_j} = I \int_{\underline{y}}^{\bar{y}} v_j w(y) f(y)\, dy + \lambda \left[Q_j + \sum_{k=1}^{n} (P_k - C_k) Q_{kj} \right] = 0,$$

$$j = 1, \dots, n. \quad (14)$$

Recalling from Section 2.2 that $\partial v/\partial P_j = v_j = -q_j(y)\eta(y)$, and using also the definition (13) and the $\xi_{jk} = \xi_{kj} P_k Q_k / P_j Q_j$ relation (assuming $Q_{kj} = Q_{jk}$), conditions (14) can be restated as

$$R_j = \lambda \left[1 + \sum_{k=1}^{n} \xi_{jk} \left(\frac{P_k - C_k}{P_k} \right) \right], \quad (15)$$

or as

$$\sum_{k=1}^{n} \frac{P_k - C_k}{P_k} (-\xi_{jk}) = \frac{\lambda - R_j}{\lambda}. \quad (16)$$

In the simple case where cross-elasticities of demand are zero, the jth price would be

$$\frac{P_j - C_j}{P_j} = \left(\frac{\lambda - R_j}{\lambda} \right) \frac{1}{-\xi_{jj}}. \quad (17)$$

From (15) we see that we might have $\lambda > R_j$ or $\lambda < R_j$. If $R_j = 1$ for all j, this would yield the simple inverse elasticity rule, implying Ramsey prices with $0 < (\lambda - 1)/\lambda < 1$ and $\xi_{jj} < 0$. But if $R_j > 1$, the price P_j would be lower. Thus the effect of a preference for consumption by those with lower incomes can be carried through explicitly to pricing policy. Of course, with this objective of favoring those with lower incomes, goods with $R_j < 1$ would have higher prices than would result if income distribution were ignored.

Distributing goods by means other than a price system may also be considered. Weitzman (1977) has emphasized the effectiveness of the allocation of a good of limited supply under a price system versus rationing. Holding income constant, he considered individuals as differing in their tastes for a good, and also in their incomes. Tastes were seen as socially desirable to satisfy. Using simplifications, including a convenient linear form for demand and a quadratic loss function, he found that the effectiveness of a price system could be represented as

$$\text{Effectiveness} = \text{Var}(\phi) - \text{Var}(q(\bar{p})),$$

where $\text{Var}(\phi)$ is the variance in consumers' tastes for the good with no income differences and $\text{Var}(q(\bar{p}))$ is the variance in demands (q's) for the good at market-clearing price $\bar{p}$. If tastes for a good vary by much more than effective demands, the price system will be seen as especially effective. In the Feldstein analysis just considered, $\text{Var}(\phi)$ is zero, since consumers differ only by income, and in that special case Weitzman's analysis would imply that rationing could be better than modifying the price system as (16) and (17) do.

Nichols, Smolensky, and Tideman (1971) treated the problem of getting a merit good, which is desirable to have consumed, to poorer people at low out-of-pocket or money cost by use of a queue. Richer citizens would avoid the queue by paying a higher price, say, in a market, whereas supplies for the poor would be subsidized in order to be offered at a low price that induces the queue. Time value, used in the decision whether to queue, was assumed to be directly related to income. As long as everyone would want to consume the good or service (perhaps an inoculation that is either consumed or not, for instance), so that consumption would be greater in relation to income among the poor, this system is feasible. If the good were a luxury, the rich might conceivably be willing to wait in line for it, especially if availability in the market were limited, and then the desired form of discrimination would not result (Barzel 1974; Holt and Sherman 1982).

6.4   Pricing for beneficial goods

Consumption of certain goods by one person can convey benefits to others.[3] Examples might be education, medical care, housing, or food. In the case of medical care, one person's consumption might benefit others by reducing the spread of disease and pestilence. On the other hand, one's consumption of goods such as cigarettes might harm others. Ideal prices should of course reflect such externality relations where they exist, but it is difficult to determine individuals' valuations of the externality. Optimal pricing needs to be tied to properties of a good and its effects, rather than to properties of the people who consume it, as in distributional weights

---

[3] Such goods have been called "basic needs" goods (Harberger 1984). They are also called "merit" goods, although merit is more vague than what we consider. We call the goods beneficial goods and assume that they provide explicit positive externalities to others. Government action is not the only means of income redistribution; there is a substantial voluntary element (see Steinberg 1987).

pricing. We shall examine second-best pricing for positive consumption externality here, on the general assumption that all goods may have external effects.

Suppose that consumption of some among the $j = 1, \ldots, n$ goods in an economy is socially more beneficial because the goods confer benefits to others through positive external effects. Call these goods beneficial goods and number them $1, \ldots, m$, where $m \leq n$. Subsidizing consumption of such goods then could induce Ramsey pricing. In the simple case where cross-elasticities of demand are zero, we can readily portray the Ramsey price for the jth good as

$$\frac{P_j - c_j}{P_j}(-E_{jj}) = K - G_j, \tag{18}$$

where P_j is consumer price, c_j is marginal cost, E_{jj} is price elasticity of demand, K is a constant, and G_j is some meritoriousness measure we should like to interpret and estimate. In the case of medical care, more consumption by others may reduce the spread of disease and thereby benefit one person in much the same way that the person's own expenditures provide benefit. Another's spending on education might benefit one person somewhat as that person's own spending on education does; and so on for other beneficial goods. Using the individuals' own valuations of the goods to estimate the external benefit will yield a very simple interpretation of G_j. We first present the ingredients in G_j, and then provide the interpretation.

Assume that the external effect of a good depends on its aggregate consumption level, so that every unit contributes equally to the externality. Individual utility for the ith person in a community of I consumers is then

$$u^i = u^i(q_0^i, \ldots, q_n^i; q_1, \ldots, q_m), \quad i = 1, \ldots, I, \tag{19}$$

where q_0^i is labor supplied by the ith person, q_j^i is the ith person's consumption of the jth good, and $q_j = \Sigma_i q_j^i$ is aggregate consumption of the jth ($j = 1, \ldots, m < n$) good. We assume that u^i is quasi-concave. The ith individual's budget constraint will be

$$\sum_{j=0}^{n} P_j q_j^i = 0, \tag{20}$$

where q_0^i is labor, the numeraire good measured negatively, and the consumer price P_j is relative to the (unit) price of q_0^i. The consumer will maximize utility (19) subject to the income constraint (20).

Although each consumer may benefit from others' consumption of beneficial goods, we presume that no one takes others' welfare into account when making consumption decisions; and one individual is unable to determine the consumption of others. Also, since there are many consumers, we assume that each individual ignores the tiny effect of his own consumption of a beneficial good on aggregate consumption of the good. Then the effect of others' consumption will cause no apparent change in the *form* of the necessary conditions for individual utility maximization. Thus with η^i as the Lagrange multiplier for the income constraint, in addition to (20) the necessary conditions for a solution to the ith consumer's problem are

$$\partial u^i / \partial q_j^i \equiv u_j^{ii} = \eta^i P_j, \quad j = 0, \ldots, n, \tag{21}$$

where η^i is i's marginal utility of income.

The demand function of individual i derived from (20) and (21) is denoted by

$$q_j^i = Q_j^i(P_1, \ldots, P_n; q_1, \ldots, q_n), \quad j = 0, \ldots, n,$$

and the aggregate demand function is $\Sigma_i Q_j^i = Q_j$. We shall assume that these $n+1$ equations,

$$q_j = Q_j(P_1, \ldots, P_n; q_1, \ldots, q_n), \quad j = 0, \ldots, n, \tag{22}$$

can be solved simultaneously for nonnegative values as a function of prices only,[4]

$$\bar{Q}_j = \bar{Q}_j(P_1, \ldots, P_n), \quad j = 0, \ldots, n. \tag{23}$$

The demands $\bar{Q}_j$ take q_j's as determined implicitly by (22) rather than exogenously, and we have

$$\bar{Q}_j(P_1, \ldots, P_n) \equiv Q_j(P_1, \ldots, P_n; \bar{Q}_1, \ldots, \bar{Q}_n), \quad j = 0, \ldots, n.$$

We thus can define for each i

$$\bar{Q}_j^i(P_1, \ldots, P_n) = Q_j^i(P_1, \ldots, P_n; \bar{Q}_1, \ldots, \bar{Q}_n), \quad j = 0, \ldots, n.$$

Consider a welfare-maximizing public enterprise pricing problem for the beneficial goods.[5] Since utilities are not explicitly interdependent, individual happiness and utility are maximized at the same point, so an individualistic welfare function comprising utility functions in (19) can serve effectively as a welfare measure:

$$W = W(u^1, \ldots, u^I). \tag{24}$$

We ignore incentive problems within the public enterprise that produces the goods, so we can derive socially optimal prices directly. We impose on the public enterprise the budget constraint,

---

[4] Of course, if the consumption externalities are separable, so $\partial^2 u^i / \partial x_j^i \, \partial x_k = 0$ for $j, k = 1, \ldots, m$, (23) would result directly. This treatment of nonseparable externalities follows Diamond (1973) and Sadka (1978).

[5] For a review of the principles involved in this pricing problem, see Section 5.2. Harberger (1984) discusses optimal pricing of goods that satisfy basic needs, and he also considers pricing for income distribution goals.

$$\sum_{j=1}^{m} (P_j - c_j)\bar{Q}_j = D, \tag{25}$$

where c_j is the constant producer price and marginal cost of good j,[6] and D is a constant. If D is negative, that will call for subsidization of public sector goods; $D = 0$ calls for breaking even, and a positive D requires profit of the public enterprise.

Assume that prices of goods $m+1$ to n are constant, and that changes in the prices of beneficial goods affect only demands for those goods. Differentiating with respect to prices the Lagrangian comprising objective (24) and constraint (25), we obtain

$$\sum_{i} W_i \sum_{k=0}^{n} u_k^{ii} \bar{Q}_{kj}^{i} + \sum_{i} W_i \sum_{k=0}^{m} u_k^{ie} \bar{Q}_{kj} + \mu \left[\bar{Q}_j + \sum_{k=1}^{m} (P_k - c_k)\bar{Q}_{kj} \right] = 0,$$
$$j = 1, \ldots, m, \tag{26}$$

where $u_k^{ii} = \partial u^i / \partial q_k^i$ and $u_k^{ie} = \partial u^i / \partial q_k$, the latter being the externality effect, and $\bar{Q}_{kj}^{i} = \partial \bar{Q}_k^i / \partial P_j$, while $Q_{kj} = \sum_i \bar{Q}_{kj}^i$. From differentiation of (20) with respect to P_j, we must have

$$\bar{Q}_j^i + \sum_{k=0}^{n} P_k \bar{Q}_{kj}^i = 0, \quad j = 1, \ldots, m, \tag{27}$$

and by aggregation over i,

$$\bar{Q}_j + \sum_{k=0}^{n} P_k \bar{Q}_{kj} = 0, \quad j = 1, \ldots, m. \tag{28}$$

Using (27) and (28), together with (20), the first term in (26) reduces to $-\sum_i W_i \eta^i \bar{Q}_j^i$, and (26) can then be rearranged in the equation system

$$\sum_{k=1}^{m} (P_k - c_k)\bar{Q}_{kj} = -Q_j + \frac{1}{\mu} \sum_{i} W_i \eta^i \bar{Q}_j^i - \frac{1}{\mu} \sum_{k=0}^{m} \bar{Q}_{kj} \sum_{i} W_i \eta^i \frac{u_k^{ie}}{\eta^i},$$
$$j = 1, \ldots, m. \tag{29}$$

Note that u_k^{ie}/η_k^i is the ith consumer's marginal rate of subsitution between aggregate consumption of good k and income. If we further assume that $\bar{Q}_{kj} = \bar{Q}_{jk}$, so $E_{jk} = E_{kj} P_k \bar{Q}_k / P_j \bar{Q}_j$, where $E_{kj} = \bar{Q}_{kj} P_j / \bar{Q}_k$, and accept the current income distribution so that $W_i = 1/\eta^i$, (29) can be rearranged as

$$\sum_{k=1}^{m} \frac{(P_k - c_k)}{P_k} (-E_{jk}) = \frac{\mu - 1}{\mu} - \frac{1}{\mu \bar{Q}_j} \sum_{k=0}^{m} (-\bar{Q}_{kj}) \sum_{i} \frac{u_k^{ie}}{\eta^i},$$
$$j = 1, \ldots, m. \tag{30}$$

---

6 A more general assumption that will yield broadly the same results is that of constant returns to scale.

which will be recognized as the Ramsey rule with an extra (externality) term subtracted away on the right-hand side. This externality term is G_j in (18), the term for which we seek a simple estimate.

Since others' consumption of a beneficial good benefits person i, who also consumes the good, we propose to use i's own evaluation to estimate the value of this external effect of others' consumption. We want a value for u_j^{ie}, the effect on person i of total consumption, or of consumption by others.[7] To evaluate the effect on i of others' consumption of Q_j in terms of η^i, consider as an estimate of u_j^{ie}

$$\hat{u}_j^{ie} = M_j^i \eta^i P_j, \tag{31}$$

where M_j^i is a constant that modifies i's measure of marginal satisfaction from q_j^i, which equals $\eta^i P_j$ from (11). Thus (31) proposes as an estimate of the marginal effect on i of consumption of good j by others some constant times the marginal effect on i of *own* consumption of good j, or $\hat{u}_j^{ie} = M_j^i u_j^{ii}$. For a merit good, $M_j^i > 0$, because consumption of good j by others has a positive benefit to i. We might ordinarily expect $M_j^i < 1$, which holds if person i marginally prefers own consumption of the good to consumption by others. To impute to person i a valuation for consumption by others that is some fraction, M_j^i, of i's own marginal evaluation simply assumes that person i values others' consumption proportionally to own consumption. One who purchases immunization from contagious disease, for example, is assumed to value immunization by others as proportional to the value placed on one's own immunization. Although it might not be compelling in every case, this assumption is appealing for many beneficial goods that are widely consumed.

To allow a simple characterization of the effect of the externality when cross-effects among the goods are significant, we have to impose the same value of M_j^i for all changes in others' consumption of beneficial goods resulting from a change in P_j. Why this is needed will be obvious in a moment, but it means that we should define

$$\hat{u}_{kj}^{ie} \equiv M_j^i \eta^i P_k, \tag{32}$$

where k indicates any merit good whose demand is affected by a change in P_j (including $k = j$). The most important effect of a change in P_j will of course be the effect on Q_j, which would be captured by (31).

If we replace u_k^{ie} in (30) with our proposed estimate, $\hat{u}_{kj}^{ie}$ in (32), we have

$$\sum_{k=1}^{m} \frac{(P_k - c_k)}{P_k}(-E_{jk}) = \frac{\mu - 1}{\mu} - \frac{\sum_{k=0}^{m}(-\bar{Q}_{kj})\sum_{i=0}^{n} M_j^i P_k}{\mu \bar{Q}_j},$$
$$j = 1, \dots, m. \tag{33}$$

[7] We do not distinguish between Q_j and $Q_j - Q_j^i$, assuming they are close in magnitude. This is consistent with person i not considering the effect of own consumption on the total.

Since the price of a merit good is assumed to affect only merit goods, (28) can be used to reduce $\Sigma_k P_k \bar{Q}_{kj}$ to $-\bar{Q}_j$. It is to make possible this simple result of substitution from (28) that we use the same M_j^i for all consumption effects of a change in P_j, as called for in (32). With the assumption that $W_i = 1/\eta^i$, while letting $\Sigma_i M_j^i = M_j$, the right-hand-side term in (33) finally becomes $-M_j/\mu$ and (33) can be arranged in the equation system

$$\sum_k \frac{P_k - c_k}{P_k} (-E_{jk}) = \frac{\mu - 1 - M_j}{\mu}, \quad j = 1, \dots, m, \tag{34}$$

which can be solved for optimal price marginal cost ratios to express Ramsey prices implicitly. In the special case of zero cross-elasticities of demand, when the weaker condition (31) can serve in place of (32) for estimating the value of the externality because no aggregation of cross-effects is necessary,[8] the price marginal cost ratios are simply

$$\frac{P_j - c_j}{P_j} = \left(\frac{\mu - 1 - M_j}{\mu} \right) \left(\frac{1}{-E_{jj}} \right), \quad j = 1, \dots, m. \tag{35}$$

Thus the G_j term we introduced at the beginning is seen to be simply M_j/μ. The presence of M_j in (35) has the effect of lowering P_j more as M_j is larger ($\partial P_j/\partial M_j < 0$). Attending to the effect of the M_j's therefore can be expected to make the budget constraint a greater burden, so μ will be larger than if the cases of $M_j > 0$ were ignored. For relatively small values of M_j, the resulting solution P_j may be higher than if M_j's were not considered, because of the larger μ ($\partial P_j/\partial \mu > 0$). But where values of M_j are large, we should expect lower P_j, possibly to the point where $P_j < c_j$ for some P_j because $M_j + 1 > \mu$, even if the public enterprise earns a profit overall because $D > 0$.[9]

The pricing rules in (34) and (35) give workable form to the pricing of beneficial goods. The rules reflect the favoritism to be expected, and in the absence of lump-sum transfers they also moderate consequent economic distortions through the influence of demand elasticities that typify Ramsey (1927) prices. Most important, these are simple pricing rules that differ from Ramsey rules only by the estimates M_j of how individuls together value the total consumption of others relative to their own. For these rules to be applied, the M_j would still have to be approximated for a population. For medical care, as an example, a value might be estimated from empirical knowledge of the effects of others' consumption on one's health. For some goods, the fractional M_j^i will depend more on subjective

---

8 Note that if beneficial good demands depend only on their own prices and there are no cross-effects, we must have $E_{jj} = -1$.

9 If the public enterprise does not break even, or indeed if other parts of the public sector do not, the question of the social marginal cost of public funds needs to be treated. See Browning (1987).

judgments of individuals, but considering consumption externality effects as proportional to own marginal utility through M_j^i still may advance the estimation conceptually. Even if estimates of M_j's are crude, ordinal relations might be obtained, so a set of M_j's could at least reflect an order of merit among the beneficial goods.

Applying pricing rules such as (34) and (35) will allow public enterprise pricing to reflect positive consumption externalities. Although avowedly intended to improve income distribution and welfare generally, public enterprise pricing in developing countries has been criticized for perversely affecting income distribution (Jones 1985). By applying representations here and in Section 6.3, pricing goals could be translated explicitly into operational form, which might make the goals more achievable.

6.5   Combining distributional equity with beneficial goods

We shall now modify the distributional characteristic of a good introduced in Section 6.3 (equation (13)) to make it consistent with the discrete model we used in Section 6.4. Recall that person 1 has the lowest income and person I has the highest income. Modified to be consistent with the model we have employed, the distributional characteristic R_j of good j is

$$R_j = \Sigma_i W_i \eta^i q_j^i / Q_j. \tag{36}$$

Notice that again $R_j = 1$ when $W_i = 1/\eta^i$. For the good j, R_j can be viewed as a weighted average of the marginal social utilities of consumers, the products $W_i \eta^i$, where the weights depend on the relative quantities of the good consumed, q_j^i / Q_j. If the social goal is to benefit those with lower incomes, $W_i \eta^i > 1$ for low values of i (low incomes) and $W_i \eta^i < 1$ for high values of i. Goods with low income elasticities of demand (necessities) will then have higher values of R_j, whereas goods with high income elasticities (luxuries) will have lower values of R_j.

Using the distributional characteristic of a good, we can consider income distribution goals in socially optimal pricing, rather than assume $W_i = 1/\eta^i$ and ignore income distribution. The social problem still is to maximize the objective (24), subject to the constraint (25), with ψ now the Lagrange multiplier. Using our estimate of $\hat{u}_{kj}^{ie}$, necessary conditions for a solution are

$$\sum_i W_i \left[\sum_k u_k^{ii} q_{kj}^i + \sum_{k=1}^{m} \hat{u}_{kj}^{ie} Q_{kj} \right] + \psi \left[Q_j + \sum_{k=1}^{m} (P_k - c_k) Q_{kj} \right] = 0,$$
$$j = 1, \ldots, m, \quad (37)$$

plus the constraint. Now if we use (21), (27), (28), and (32), we find for the first part of (37) that

$$\sum_i W_i \left[\sum_k u_k^{ii} q_{kj}^i + \sum_{k=1}^m \hat{u}_{kj}^{ie} Q_{kj} \right] = -\sum_i W_i \eta^i q_j^i - \sum_i W_i \eta^i M_j^i Q_j,$$

$$j = 1, \dots, n. \quad (38)$$

The first part of the right-hand side of (38) contains the social utility terms weighted by quantities, which will be related to R_j in a moment using (36). The second part contains social utility terms weighted by the estimated magnitude of the benefits derived from consumption by others, the M_j^i.

Let us define a benefit characteristic for the jth good, B_j, as

$$B_j = \sum_i W_i \eta^i M_j^i. \quad (39)$$

Suppose that the rich feel more benefit from consumption by the poor than vice versa, so M_j^i tend to be larger for higher-index i persons who have greater incomes. If income is to be distributed more to the poor, so $W_i \eta^i > 1$ for low values of i (low incomes) and $W_i \eta^i < 1$ for high values of i, B_j will then tend to be smaller than the unweighted $M_j = \sum_i M_j^i$. Of course, it is conceivable, perhaps for education as an example, that the poor place greater importance on consumption by the rich than vice versa, in which case B_j could be greater than M_j. In any case, an interaction develops between merit-good pricing and distributional-equity pricing that can alter the effect of the M_j. In what seems the most plausible case, the interaction will lower the effect of the unweighted M_j, but it conceivably can increase it.

Using (36), (38), and (39), conditions (37) can be simplified to

$$-(R_j + B_j - \psi)Q_j + \psi \sum_{k=1}^m (P_k - c_k)Q_{kj} = 0, \quad j = 1, \dots, n. \quad (40)$$

Applying the Slutsky relation, we can arrange (40) in the form

$$\sum_k \frac{(P_k - c_k)}{P_k}(-E_{jk}) = \frac{\psi - R_j - B_j}{\psi}, \quad j = 1, \dots, n. \quad (41)$$

If we interpret the pricing formulas as before, their form indicates that the effects of R_j and B_j are essentially the same; larger values of R_j or B_j will lower the optimal price P_j. There is an important difference between the two terms, however. The term B_j derives from the property of a good – that it yields consumption externality – plus the distributional-equity policy, which can modify M_j in forming B_j. Knowing that a good yields positive externality, we can in principle adjust its price optimally. The term R_j depends on the given consumption patterns of a population, however, and cannot be adjusted so conveniently. It is possible, for example, that every good is consumed more by the rich than by the poor, so that every $R_j < 1$ even after W_i for high-income individuals have been reduced. Then taxation will be the primary means, and it may be a limited one, for altering the distribution of income.

6.6   Nonuniform pricing and equity

Nonuniform prices offer greater possibilities for redistributing income, but of course if the prices are to achieve that aim the good must be one that cannot be resold; and effectiveness can require quite a bit of information about the pattern of demands. We shall emphasize a convenient situation for two-part prices to yield an intuitively understandable result.

Two-part pricing

Earlier we treated the case in which costs could be traced to two dimensions of consumer service, a cost per customer due perhaps to connection requirements (as in the case of electricity or telephone) and a cost per unit of service. A two-part tariff was shown to be perfectly efficient in the simple case of constant costs in Section 4.5, with a charge per customer and a charge per unit each equal to the corresponding marginal cost. Second-best two-part tariffs were found to reflect Ramsey principles in Section 5.5, allowing maximum welfare while accepting the existing income distribution. A two-part tariff can also be used even if no clear costs are traceable to one of the pricing dimensions, as noted in Section 2.6, to raise enough money from fixed (customer) and per-unit (quantity) charges to cover what might otherwise be a deficit while setting marginal prices equal to marginal costs. Indeed, Wicksell saw the fixed part of a two-part price as an ideal tax to support fixed costs of a public utility while pricing marginal usage at marginal cost (Buchanan 1951); and Henderson (1947) showed how the fixed portion of a two-part price could be interpreted as a (regressive) head tax.

Because of its simplicity, we describe the Feldstein (1972b) model for redistributing income through two-part prices. This model requires that every household consumes the good, which is not unreasonable for many public sector goods. Auerbach and Pellechio (1978) showed that allowing for some not to consume the good – to disconnect from an electricity network, for example – tends not to have a very large effect on results in reasonable circumstances. Incomes are distributed according to the relative density function, $f(y)$, with the lowest income $\underline{y}$ and the highest $\bar{y}$. The marginal social utility of income for an individual of income y is taken to be $w'(y)$, a value that is assumed independent of marginal price or fixed fee. When the marginal price per unit is p_q, the total quantity purchased will be

$$Q = I \int_{\underline{y}}^{\bar{y}} q(p_q, y) f(y) \, dy, \qquad (42)$$

where I is the total number of consumers and $q(p_q, y)$ is the amount consumed by a household with income y at price p_q.

Let us now pose a second-best problem by requiring that the enterprise break even, using a fixed fee as a means of making up any deficit from the marginal price level. Like the marginal price, the fixed fee must be the same for all consumers because the seller is assumed unable to identify consumers individually. (If it could do so, the seller would try to discriminate perfectly through the choices of different fixed fees.) There is no cost of connecting a customer. With $C(Q)$ representing total cost, to break even the fixed charge per time period, p_n, must be

$$p_n = [C(Q) - p_q Q]/I. \qquad (43)$$

A consumer with an income of y will experience a net consumer surplus of $V(p_q, y)/\mu(y) - p_n$, where μ is marginal utility of income. Substituting from (43) directly, welfare to be maximized can be expressed as

$$W = I \int_{\underline{y}}^{\bar{y}} w'(y) \left\{ \frac{V(p_q, y)}{\mu} - \frac{C(Q) - p_q Q}{I} \right\} f(y) \, dy. \qquad (44)$$

Maximizing (44) with respect to p_q yields, after some rearrangement,

$$\frac{(p_q - c_q)\eta}{p_q}$$
$$= \frac{\int_{\underline{y}}^{\bar{y}} q(p_q, y) f(y) \, dy \int_{\underline{y}}^{\bar{y}} w'(y) f(y) \, dy - \int_{\underline{y}}^{\bar{y}} w'(y) q(p_q, y) f(y) \, dy}{\int_{\underline{y}}^{\bar{y}} q(p_q, y) f(y) \, dy \int_{\underline{y}}^{\bar{y}} w'(y) f(y) \, dy}, \qquad (45)$$

where $c_q = dC(Q)/dQ$ and $\eta = -p_q \, \partial Q/\partial p_q Q$. This result can be expressed in Ramsey form as

$$\frac{p_q - c_q}{p_q} = \frac{1}{\eta} \left(\frac{-\text{Cov}(w', q)}{E(w')E(q)} \right), \qquad (46)$$

where $\text{Cov}(w', q)$ is the covariance of marginal social utilities of income, the $w'(y)$'s, with quantities consumed.

For a normal good, we can expect higher-income consumers to purchase greater quantities, but they will also have smaller social welfare weights if the general aim is one that we ordinarily would expect, namely to benefit the poorer members of society. Then $\text{Cov}(w', q)$ will be negative, and so at the optimum $p_q > c_q$. Since the richer members of society purchase more units, at the higher price they contribute more to making p_n smaller, which aids the consumers of smaller amounts. If w' is a constant, as it has been implicitly in earlier chapters, then $\text{Cov}(w', q) = 0$ and $p_q = c_q$ is optimal.

The generalization of Auerbach and Pellechio (1978) allows consumers to disconnect from the system if their net surplus is negative. Thus a marginal consumer may have income y_m such that $\underline{y} \leq y_m \leq \bar{y}$. When $\underline{y} < y_m$ an extra term is subtracted from the right-hand side of (46), reflecting the surplus of marginal consumers who join or disconnect in response to a change in p_q, divided by total quantity. An alternative model that permits consumers to disconnect is presented in the Appendix to Chapter 6.

Quantity-dependent pricing

A continuous nonuniform price was shown in Section 5.5 to take a Ramsey form for every market increment, Δq, to be considered. We might expect the resulting prices to be affected if new welfare weights were assigned individuals, and the effect would depend on who was consuming in each market increment. Spence (1977) has examined this problem using representations like Weitzman's (1977), where consumers have tastes for the goods that differ even if incomes are the same, and marginal utilities of income also differ. If tastes for the good and marginal utilities are negatively related, it is desirable to make price higher for large consumers and price lower for smaller consumers. But it is difficult to give exact form to this general modification in the optimal nonuniform price without having explicit knowledge of tastes and marginal utilities.

6.7   Governmental decisions and equity

The kind of situation that typically comes to political institutions for decision will improve the well-being of some individuals while harming others. Examples include proposals to build airports, bridges, or football stadiums. Even in the case of a public utility, a higher price may help stockholders while harming consumers, or an adjustment in the relative prices of two services may leave the stockholders' position unchanged but create a gain for one set of consumers and a loss for others. In these cases, will a gain in the sum of consumer surplus and producer surplus due to a proposed action adequately serve as a criterion warranting adoption of that action?

Much debate has focused on this question. In principle, the Pareto optimality idea offers a way to settle it. If those who benefit from a change can compensate those who lose, and at least one party ends up better off, then the change should be made; it will be Pareto optimal to do so. A slight elaboration of Pareto optimality yields such a rule for action: *Any action that benefits some person(s) and harms none is an improvement.* This rule is appealing but often impossible to apply, because compensation cannot be carried out. When electricity rates for industrial customers are lowered and those for residential customers are raised, for example, what possible form of compensation can be worked out for the residential consumers?

It is not easy to settle the question of whether an action should be taken if compensation cannot actually be paid. In an effort to justify adoption of social actions that seem potentially desirable, at least on technical efficiency grounds, the British economist Nicholas Kaldor (1939) relaxed the compensation requirement of Pareto optimality and proposed a new rule: *Any action that allows gainers to compensate losers and still be better off is an improvement, whether or not compensation is actually paid.* Sir John Hicks (1939, 1940, 1941) added an alternative but similar rule: *Any action that the losers cannot profitably bribe the gainers to oppose must be an improvement.*

The reason for weakening the Pareto criterion for social decisions as Kaldor and Hicks wanted to do should be clear, once it is realized that the Pareto rule requires virtual unanimity before collective action can be taken. If anyone loses, he or she can block action under the Pareto rule. For one thing, this could give rise to all sorts of strategic behavior. An individual might feign opposition to a proposal, for example, in an effort to be "bought off." In practice, making compensation to harmed parties is virtually impossible. How can reliable estimates of harm be obtained when the person to be compensated is the main source of estimated harm? In relaxing the compensation requirement, Kaldor and Hicks sought a rule that public agencies could follow without endless wrangling.

Using the Kaldor–Hicks rule should improve efficiency, and if projects are so various that one group benefits in one case and a different group benefits in another, on average all may benefit. The present-day application of benefit–cost analysis, which deals in aggregations of benefits and costs, relies on the same principle.[10] Our examples in Section 2.5 actually could satisfy the Pareto rule because users who benefit from the service always pay all the costs that follow from their decision to use the service. (Question 2.3 raised the Kaldor–Hicks kind of issue and illustrated its possible usefulness. See also Question 3.4.)

However, Scitovsky (1941) showed an inconsistency for the Kaldor–Hicks approach. A project might be approved according to the Kaldor rule, but then a proposal to return to the initial position could also pass the rule! Such inconsistency can arise because of changes in relative prices and in income distribution that accompany the action. Those changes can alter valuations and thus change the outcome under the rule. A more apparent objection can be seen if the same kind of project is repeatedly

---

10 A treatment of the Kaldor–Hicks criterion in terms of individuals' compensating variations is provided by Crew and Kleindorfer (1979a, pp. 9–13).

adopted. For example, suppose that projects adopted are golf courses, yachting facilities, landing strips, and other benefits for the rich. Every one of these projects makes the rich who benefit able to place a still higher value on the next project, measured perhaps by consumer surplus, since the rich keep getting richer. When compensation is not actually carried out, blindly following the rule could thus lead to a result many would consider perverse. If instead the benefits and costs fall on different people in different cases, efficiency improvements will tend to dominate. Use of the weaker Kaldor–Hicks rule then could be socially productive, and that is why the rule is followed in benefit–cost analysis of public projects.

We noted in Chapter 3 that majority rule can bring perverse outcomes (Buchanan 1962). In the context of income redistribution policies, a majority might exploit a minority most directly, so the possibility needs to be considered. Under regulation it is likely that some consumers will benefit more than others, due to monopolistic tendencies of the supplier, political preferences of the regulators, or both. There can be no doubt that in their years under regulation the U.S. franchised monopolies (such as telephone companies) and other regulated industries where entry was controlled (such as airlines) have had prices that favored some consumers relative to others. Telephone rates under regulation favored residences (who vote in large numbers) relative to business firms and local calls relative to long distance; and airline fares favored short flights and service to out-of-the-way communities relative to long-distance flights between major cities. Indeed, part of the impetus for deregulation came from a desire to end cross-subsidization and to have prices based on efficiency considerations alone, as anonymous equity would require. Thus, although government decisions can pursue equity aims that many people share, monopoly power and political favoritism may lead instead to results that are inefficient and difficult to sustain. Then government influence may be rejected and market forces accepted in its place.

6.8   Summary

We first introduced a benchmark condition on prices called anonymous equity, which guarantees that no income redistribution can occur. This condition is related to, but stronger than, that implied by subsidy-free prices, and can be a requirement of sustainable prices under free entry. We then showed in subsequent subsections that, to the extent that information can be obtained about the incomes of those who consume particular goods, the prices of those goods can be adjusted to pursue the purpose of redistributing income. With entry limited, it is possible to represent income distribution aims through welfare weights and then to modify Ramsey prices to affect income redistribution, as shown in Section 6.3. Where goods cause positive external effects, their prices can be adjusted to improve welfare, and information about individual consumption can be used to help estimate the value of benefits from the good, as shown in Section 6.4. Externality effects and redistributional effects are combined in Section 6.5. Nonuniform pricing can be used to affect income distribution, as described in Section 6.6. Free entry can prevent income redistribution by preventing consumers of one good from supporting others or being supported by them, so entry policy is involved in all of these possible means of implementing income redistribution policy. Criteria for collective choices through governmental institutions were briefly discussed in Section 6.7.

Questions

6.1. Consider Question 2.3 of Chapter 2. If those with lower incomes traveled A to B and return, while those with higher incomes traveled B to C and return, and the aim was to benefit those with lower incomes, how could the solution be affected?

6.2. Consider a telephone service facing demands per call over two equal-length (12-hour-long) periods of the day represented by

$$P_1 = 0.10Y_1 - 0.02Q_1$$

and

$$P_2 = 0.10Y_2 - 0.02Q_2,$$

where P_1 and P_2 are prices per call in the two periods, Y_1 and Y_2 are the average incomes per day of consumers in the two periods, and Q_1 and Q_2 are the number of calls. Daily incomes and consumers in period 1 average \$90, and incomes of consumers in period 2 average \$80. Operating cost for phone service is \$1 per call and capacity for one call costs \$5 per day. Demand for calls in excess of the capacity cannot be served.

(a) Find a socially optimal level of capacity, plus the accompanying period-1 and period-2 prices.

(b) Calculate the consumer surplus at your solution in part (a). Compare it with the consumer surplus obtained for a similar situation in Question 4.4 of Chapter 4.

6.3. The cost of production implicit in budget constraint (43) has no cost of adding a consumer to the system. Suppose there is a constant cost per consumer, c_n. How do you think optimal pricing rules (43) and (46) would be affected?

6.4. In answering part (b) of Question 2.3, about whether train service should extend to C, is there any possible set of facts that would allow application of the Pareto rule? Relate your considerations to anonymous equity. If such facts do not exist or do not apply, what concern would you have about applying the Kaldor–Hicks criterion?

Appendix to Chapter 6

It is possible to modify the analysis of second-best two-part prices in the appendix to Chapter 5 by introducing social welfare weights. Aggregate consumer welfare becomes

$$C = N \int_{y_m}^{\bar{y}} (V(p_q, y)/\mu - p_n) w'(y) f(y) \, dy \tag{A1}$$

rather than as given by equation (A1) in the appendix to Chapter 5 without the welfare weights, $w'(y)$. Maximizing the Lagrangian formed by this objective, subject to the budget constraint,

$$N \int_{y_m}^{\bar{y}} [p_q q(p_q, y) + p_n - C(Q)] f(y) \, dy = B, \tag{A2}$$

yields

$$\frac{(p_q - c_q) q(p_q, y_m) + p_n}{p_n} = \left(\frac{\lambda}{1+\lambda}\right) \frac{1}{\eta_n} + \frac{\int_{y_m}^{\bar{y}} [1 - w'(y)] f(y) \, dy}{(1+\lambda) f(y_m) p_n \, \partial y_m / \partial p_n} \tag{A3}$$

and

$$\frac{p_q - c_q}{p_q} = \left(\frac{\lambda}{1+\lambda}\right) \frac{1}{\eta_q} \left[\frac{Q - Q_m}{Q}\right] + \frac{\int_{y_m}^{\bar{y}} [q(p_q, y) - q(p_q, y_m)][1 - w'(y)] f(y) \, dy}{(1+\lambda) Q}. \tag{A4}$$

If $w'(y) = 1$, these pricing rules reduce immediately to those in equations (A5) and (A8) in the appendix to Chapter 5. But if the poor are to be benefited, so welfare weights $w'(y)$ are smaller than 1 for consumers with greater incomes y, it appears from (A4) that p_q should be raised, provided the good is normal. What happens to p_n is more complicated, for the rise in p_q might affect both sides of (A3), and we cannot be absolutely certain about how that might affect p_n. However, if the rise in p_q contributes more to profit, as we should expect, the budget constraint will require a reduction in p_n.

PART III

Institutions of monopoly regulation

CHAPTER 7

Rate-of-return regulation

7.1 Introduction

We now turn our attention to the major institution of monopoly regulation in the United States, rate-of-return regulation. That institution was not designed specifically to achieve economic efficiency. It grew slowly out of a history of conflict, which was gradually resolved by the U.S. judicial system. The right of states to prescribe rates was affirmed little more than a century ago by the Supreme Court in the case of *Munn v. Illinois,*[1] and the guidance that has come to be called rate-of-return regulation was essentially worked out over the half-century between *Smyth v. Ames*[2] in 1898 and *Hope Natural Gas Company*[3] in 1944. This history reminds us that once parties have had scope to entertain quite different positions, they may have difficulty bringing their dispute to an efficient outcome. Although legal issues have been settled, in the wake of their settlement economic issues today have become very complex, as observation of any modern rate case will confirm. Economic issues are complex in part because rate-of-return regulation evolved before some economic principles that might have affected its design were fully known. These principles would have made untenable some of the legal positions that partisans in past adversary proceedings created.

Our aim in this chapter is to show how rate-of-return regulation came into being and to describe its operational shortcomings. Its consequences for input inefficiency, output inefficiency, and incentives within the firm are explored in subsequent chapters. The shortcomings of the *Hope Natural Gas Company* decision, which embodies major guidelines of present-day rate-of-return regulation, can be seen and understood best if its achievement is first appreciated. So we begin with a brief review of the question it was intended to settle: What profit should investors receive? That question was originally perceived largely as a matter of fairness. But fairness

This chapter draws on Sherman (1983a).
[1] *Munn v. Illinos,* 94 U.S. 113 (1877).
[2] *Smyth v. Ames,* 169 U.S. 466 (1898).
[3] *FPC v. Hope Natural Gas Co.,* 320 U.S. 591 (1944).

183

required some ground for investor expectation, some basis for anticipating economic value, which is the very thing persistent legal debate denied. That is why the instrumental value of the *Hope* decision lay in its endorsement of a single (compromise) way to answer the profit question, not that this answer was necessarily sound. Indeed, there are inconsistencies in the *Hope* procedure that still complicate its application. What is more, from an economic efficiency standpoint the question of profit for investors should not have been addressed so directly, for doing so entirely ignored the established role of profit as efficiency incentive within a business organization.

7.2   The origins of rate-of-return regulation

American institutions for the regulation of monopoly were built during the past century, which has been one of spectacular economic expansion and change. The groundwork for them was laid after the Civil War, when a steady decline in price level made farmers feel they were suffering unfairly (along with small merchants, and investors in railroad stocks) and brought the great midwestern farm belt to life politically. The Illinois legislature claimed regulatory power in saying, as it regulated prices for grist mills, "For protection against abuses by legislatures the people must resort to the polls, not to the courts."[4] The Supreme Court let this position stand, but subsequent regulatory decisions drew the courts into regulation.[5] Public utilities came to be franchised monopolies, protected from new entry. Regardless of where regulatory power was lodged, the substantive question for regulation became, *How much profit should be allowed a publicly regulated monopoly firm?*[6] Whether it was an appropriate economic question to pose or not, it was the question the *Hope* case was to answer in 1944.

By then it was common practice to grant statutory monopoly franchises to public utilities for providing public services such as electricity and then to regulate the prices charged. The task of regulating prices had been delegated to regulatory commissions in the vast majority of states, and as they wrestled with the question of what profit to allow, these commissions

---

[4] *Munn v. Illinois,* 94 U.S. at 134.

[5] See especially *Chicago v. Minnesota,* 134 U.S. 419 (1889), where the Court reserved power to declare illegal a rate fixed by state legislature or commission, and *Reagan v. Farmers' Loan and Trust Co.,* 154 U.S. 362 (1893), where it exercised such power.

[6] Allowed profit was added to a firm's actual operating costs, depreciation, and taxes to determine the total revenue that rates, once fixed, would be allowed to generate. The way low rates would then benefit consumers or high rates would benefit investors was articulated in *Covington and Lexington Tpk. Rd. Co. v. Sanford,* 164 U.S. 578 (1896).

were guided by judicial review. However, court guidance grew out of extreme cases involving confiscation of investors' property on the one hand and unreasonable burdens for ratepayers on the other, cases that did not immediately reveal the underlying economic process any more than the rules of a game can easily be inferred by consulting records of extreme performances in the *Guiness Book of World Records*. Principles were set out mainly as boundary circumstances, which left much scope for commission discretion. Some of the principles might even have been inconsistent, especially when there were changes in the economic conditions on which they had been based. That is one reason early decisions created conflicts for the *Hope* decision to resolve.

The grounds on which the allowed profit question was settled in *Hope* go back to the late nineteenth century, when the generally declining price level made it all the more puzzling. Falling prices raised the issue of whether profit should be allowed on the amount investors originally invested in assets years earlier or on the lower current asset value that resulted after the price level fell. Basing profit on original investment seemed fair, and the actual outlay had the added advantage of being precisely known. But using the current value appeared to reflect more faithfully the competitive market circumstances, and so relying on it appeared more consistent with the market system on which the rest of the economy turned.

This issue of asset valuation was important in *Smyth v. Ames*,[7] a dispute arising out of Nebraska's effort not merely to regulate railroad rates but, as the Court concluded, to set rates on intrastate traffic sometimes below costs. In defense of its 1893 rate-setting statute, the State of Nebraska could argue that investors had made poor investments because their values fell with the general price level, and that investors rather than the public should suffer as a result. The Court apparently was prepared to use almost any basis for valuing assets, even the low current value urged by Nebraska, because however returns were calculated the Court found them inadequate under the disputed rates. The Court held that "fair value" of property used by a corporation for the convenience of the public should be the basis for rates, and that fair value would consider, inter alia, "the original cost of construction, the amount and market value of its bonds and stock, the present as compared with the original cost of construction."[8] This short passage contains three possible bases of fair value, which rest on very different principles of valuation, and we shall note later how mixing them carelessly can cause serious implementation

---

[7] 169 U.S. 466 (1898). The *Smyth v. Ames* decision and its effects are carefully analyzed by Huneke (1983).

[8] 169 U.S. 466 (1898), at 546–7.

problems. Other potential inconsistencies in *Smyth v. Ames* need not detain us, for they were well analyzed long ago.[9]

The price level finally began to rise after 1898.[10] Then the Court's previous willingness to entertain current estimates of the value of property was seized upon by the utilities, because such values were growing larger so that their use as a basis for profit might benefit rather than harm investors. Whether current value *should* be used as a basis for rates, and how to measure current value – as physical replacement cost or as the market value of bonds and stocks – were still unclear, however. On this valuation point the confusion under *Smyth v. Ames* is well illustrated by three important Court decisions rendered in 1923, when the price level was twice as high as it had been in 1898.[11] The first of these three decisions, the *Southwestern Bell Telephone Co.*[12] case, ruled that a return had been set too low because the current reproduction cost had not been used for valuing assets. A dissent written by Justice Louis D. Brandeis (although he concurred in the judgment for reversal) called instead for original cost, meaning accounting book value, as a basis of valuation. The second and third cases, *Bluefield Water Works and Improvement Co.*[13] and *Georgia Railway,*[14] were both handed down on the same day three weeks later. In *Bluefield* reproduction cost was supported, but in *Georgia Railway* a commission's use of original cost was endorsed for rate-base valuation.

Ambiguity in the *Smyth v. Ames* "fair-value" guideline was criticized by Justice Brandeis in his opinion (joined by Justice Oliver Wendell Holmes, Jr.) in the *Southwestern Bell Telephone Co.* case. Brandeis saw the investor contributing to the enterprise a sum of capital that was well defined without going into costs and later improvements and current market values of bonds and stocks, or the many other notions of asset value that litigants pursued under *Smyth v. Ames*. An explicit return on that capital also was demonstrably acceptable to the investors. Besides being well defined, these historical investment values and rates of return avoided the extreme variations in allowed profit that could follow if current estimates were used instead for the value of all the firm's assets.[15] The drawback in this sound contractual view is that, as circumstances change, the terms

---

[9] See, e.g., Bauer (1925).

[10] The period from 1898 to 1907 was also a time when commissions were formed in many states to regulate public utilities. For a history that emphasizes the electric utilities' role in this development, see Anderson (1980, 1981). Telecommunications history is provided by Brock (1981).

[11] For price-level data over the period, see Warren and Pearson (1933).

[12] *Southwestern Bell Tel. Co. v. Public Serv. Commission,* 262 U.S. 276 (1923).

[13] *Bluefield Waterworks and Improvement Co. v. Public Serv. Commission,* 262 U.S. 679 (1923).

[14] *Georgia Railway and Power Co. v. Railway Commission,* 262 U.S. 625 (1923).

[15] For an analysis of Justice Brandeis's proposal, see Sherman (1977).

are no longer current, so prices based on them are not ideal signals to consumers of true current costs.

Although the *Bluefield* case was settled on quite a different basis from that urged by Brandeis in his *Southwestern Bell* opinion, it also sought consistency between valuing assets and allowing a rate of return. *Bluefield* valued assets at current reproduction cost and focused on comparable risk[16] as a basis for setting a current rate of return. Rather than merely listing possible factors to consider, as in *Smyth v. Ames,* the Court in *Bluefield* accepted a risk mechanism that presumably determined current returns in unregulated competitive markets and might therefore provide the logic needed for setting returns on current-valued assets in regulated markets. Of course, this basis for allowing profit that mirrored the market process differed sharply from the Brandeis proposal, with its historical orientation. By tying rate of return consistently to rate-base valuation, each method offered coherence that had been missing before. Indeed, the two views are polar extreme ways of dealing with price-level change, the historical Brandeis proposal favoring consumers when the price level increases unexpectedly, since returns need not rise accordingly. By the same token, the current valuation proposal is better for investors when the price level increases more than anticipated.

The *Georgia* decision is noteworthy because in upholding the original cost basis for asset valuation it seems so blatantly contradictory to *Southwestern Bell* and *Bluefield.* But in *Georgia* the Court did not find rates confiscatory, as it had in the other two cases.[17] Rates might have been judged confiscatory in *Southwestern Bell* and *Blufield* whether the rate base was determined by using original or reproduction cost, and in those cases some valuation beyond original cost was urged to set things right, whereas in *Georgia* the Court found rates based on original cost could allow an adequate payment to investors. In stating the majority opinion, Justice Brandeis specifically noted that the commission had considered reproduction cost, and he said it had correctly held that reproduction cost did not have to be used for valuing the rate base. So the question of the proper way to value assets still remained open.

Under the 1938 Natural Gas Act, efforts by the Federal Power Commission (now the Federal Energy Regulatory Commission, or FERC) to determine reasonable rates for natural gas transmitted across state lines led to more exacting treatment of economic issues, and finally to the decision

---

[16] Comparative risk had been introduced in 1909 in *Willcox v. Consol. Gas Co.,* 212 U.S. 19 (1909), the first important case after *Smyth v. Ames.* A commission had found no constitutional basis for allowing a return greater than the rate of interest, but the Court said compensation for risk was appropriate beyond the rate of interest.

[17] See Bauer (1925), pp. 97–103.

that has guided rate-of-return regulation for nearly half a century. The *Hope Natural Gas*[18] decision in 1944 ended confusion that had lasted since *Smyth v. Ames* over whether to value assets at their "going-concern" fair market value, which would give a large role to the market value of stocks. Because of its ultimately circular dependence on the rate of return that was to be allowed, the going-concern market value was sensibly rejected in *Hope*, and an external cost basis for asset value was recommended.

Hope did not specify a uniquely correct basis for valuing assets or calculating allowed profit, but it deemed one method acceptable. That method was a compromise between two external bases for asset valuation: the current reproduction cost benchmark of the *Bluefield* decision and the well-defined, historical benchmark set out in the dissent of Justice Brandeis in *Southwestern Bell*.[19] *Hope* followed the Brandeis position with respect to debt capital, accepting original historical cost as reasonable for valuing the debt portion of the asset rate base and allowing the historically agreed upon interest rate as its rate of return. But *Hope* followed the *Bluefield* decision with respect to equity capital, in calling for a current return there. Any reasonable basis for valuing the equity portion of the asset rate base was allowed as long as it was external to, and thus not dependent on, the commission's decision. The rate of return to equity "should be commensurate with returns on investments in other enterprises having corresponding risks,"[20] and "should be sufficient to assure confidence in the financial integrity of the enterprise, so as to maintain its credit and to attract capital."[21] These two *Hope* guidelines for equity returns are well known as the "comparable earnings" and "capital attraction" standards. After separately determining one historical return for debt and one current return for equity, the two could be weighted together by the respective debt and equity portions of the capital structure of the firm into an overall rate of return on all assets, yielding an implied level of profit for the firm.[22]

The effect of *Hope* is difficult to trace precisely, in part because it encouraged regulatory authorities in all the states to follow their own procedures.[23] But in one way or another every regulatory commission follows

---

[18] *FPC v. Hope Natural Gas Co.*, 320 U.S 591 (1944).

[19] For a review of these influences on the *Hope* decision see Leventhal (1965).

[20] 320 U.S. at 603. Besides applying this earnings guideline to equity rather than to all of the firm's assets, *Hope* did not specify the comparison to earnings of firms in the same region of the country as had the *Bluefield* decision.

[21] Ibid.

[22] Such a division of the firm's assets by source of capital had been suggested in Bauer (1925). A greater reliance on debt capital is proposed by Sherman (1970).

[23] Of course, the *Hope* case helped spawn this variety in practice by emphasizing end results. A record of the creation of many state regulatory commissions is available in G. J. Stigler and C. Friedland (1962). For a review of major early regulatory decisions see Montgomery (1931). A description and criticism of monopoly regulation is available in

the general scheme advised in *Hope:* It defines an asset rate base for each firm under its jurisdiction and then rules on the maximum rate of return the firm may earn on those assets. The value of assets in an electric utility can be two or three times greater than annual sales, so how assets and their returns are handled has an enormous bearing on profit. In valuing the asset rate base, most commissions today use original historical cost, recorded as accounting book value, although others use variations that involve estimates of the current replacement or reproduction cost of assets,[24] a practice that also can comply with the guidelines articulated in *Hope.* Some commissions include facilities under construction as part of the asset rate base, while others create an allowance for construction funds that will warrant higher revenues once the facilities are operational.[25] When it comes to allowing a rate of return on those assets, commissions follow different practices, too, although the embedded interest rate on debt is typically accepted as the allowed return on debt capital.

Difficulties in determining the rate of return to allow on equity capital have caused it to receive the most attention in rate cases, especially when heavy use of capital makes it so important. The *Hope* guidelines separate the determination of a firm's allowed rate of return into two problems: (1) the determination of an allowed rate of return on debt using historical facts, and (2) the determination of an allowed rate of return on equity based on current conditions. Each return is then applied only to that portion of total assets financed by each respective source of capital, debt, and equity. The result is a compromise between two alternative ways of dealing with changes in the general price level, the historical basis put forward by Brandeis in his opinion in *Southwestern Bell,* and the current basis set out in *Bluefield.*

We must be mindful of the fact that other goals were sought through the *Hope* decision, beyond economic efficiency or operational effectiveness. Indeed, since at any one time consumers might argue for one of the two valuation principles adopted in *Hope,* current and historical, while investors would favor the other – their positions shifting with changes in the direction of the price-level trend – the *Hope* compromise obviously balanced effects on the incomes of those groups. It also avoided large fluctuations in equity returns that would arise from allowing a current market return on *all* assets while a constant historical interest rate was actually being paid on the debt portion of capital.[26] Applying a separate return

Posner (1969). Practices are described in Thompson and Thatcher (1973). See also Jackson (1969).

24 For brief descriptions of practices by states, see Petersen (1975b).

25 See Pomerantz and Suelflow (1977).

26 If the current return on all assets fluctuates, while the return paid to debt is constant, great fluctuations may occur in the residual to equity. This compromise avoids fluctuations and capital losses, as Owen and Braeutigam (1978) argued.

to debt and equity portions of the asset rate base, as the *Hope* guidelines suggest, would prevent any such spillover of return fluctuations from debt to equity. In seeking to balance effects on income and to moderate fluctuations in equity returns, however, the Court did not ensure that an operational mechanism would result. It also did not analyze consequences for economic efficiency, although a goal of efficiency was implicit in the comparable earnings guideline. Shortcomings of either kind could undermine the *Hope* objectives, and that is why we explore them.

7.3   Finance under rate-of-return regulation

For operational soundness, the *Hope* guidelines require some basis for estimating a return to equity capital on the basis of current conditions. Yet the *Hope* framework complicates this task enormously, and may even prevent it from being carried out. First, the hybrid mixture of current and historical valuation principles that *Hope* suggests for debt and equity does not match that affecting unregulated firms, which are valued on a current basis, so no true benchmark exists in the unregulated firms to reveal "comparable earnings" for regulated firms. Second, observing returns of other regulated firms will not reveal true investor judgments reliably because they can be affected by regulators' actions. To sketch these points will require a brief discussion of the role that stocks and bonds play in unregulated corporations.

Bonds exist because the less daring among potential investors are willing to invest only if they have to bear very little risk, and the bond is a safe low-risk investment vehicle that tempts these more timid souls to join the ranks of regular investors; bonds promise first priority to payments out of earnings, and first claim to assets, too, in the event of failure. Of course a side effect of making such an offer to bondholders is that the risk in common stock shares will increase. From this one might expect that the better any one firm can tailor its mixture of bonds and stocks to meet the preferences of potential investors, the more effectively it can raise capital, and hence the lower its overall cost of capital will be. In small ways this expectation is sound, particularly when disequilibrium situations can be uncovered by the firm or when stocks and bonds are subject to different tax treatments, but we now know that, with the capital market in equilibrium under simple assumptions (admittedly limiting assumptions such as the absence of taxes), it would be wrong; the particular *mixture* of debt and equity instruments that any one firm issues can be shown to have no effect on the value of that firm. Thirty years ago this claim by Franco Modigliani and Merton Miller threw financial theorists and practitioners into an uproar, sparking a controversy that has since been settled on a theoretical level but that still simmers over the interpretation of empirical results.[27] The Modigliani–Miller conclusion can be sketched in one long sentence: *If we lived in a no-tax world in which it cost nothing beyond the prices involved to make transactions and neither firms nor individuals would ever fail, and if the level expected on average for a firm's earnings before interest payments and the probability distribution of such earnings were known entirely on the basis of its commercial prospects, then the expected level and probability distribution of a firm's earnings alone would determine its value, and nothing the firm did by way of adjusting its capital structure could affect that value.*

The logic behind this Modigliani and Miller claim depends on having no bankruptcy,[28] so firms and individuals can borrow currently at the same rate of interest. Then, if the firm had no debt, its shareholders could borrow money at the going interest rate to finance some of their share purchases and thereby be in the same financial position as if the firm had actually issued debt. Or if the firm already had a large amount of debt in its capital structure, any shareholder who preferred less could lend money at interest, to reach a position as creditor and shareholder, the same as if the firm had less debt in its capital structure. By substituting debt capital for equity, or vice versa, the firm then cannot change its value because if it did investors would immediately want a trade (arbitrage) between personal debt and corporate debt, and their action would eliminate the change in value. Even though the debt of unregulated firms may be issued with a promise to pay interest in nominal terms, which can differ from current interest rates later, the market nevertheless evaluates debt values at current rates and the arbitrage will take place in current terms. The reason current terms are controlling is that equilibrium outcomes in unregulated competitive markets are determined by new entrants whose opportunity costs are based on *current* interest rates and *current* profit rates. Lower (or higher) historical interest rates are an advantage (or a disadvantage) to shareholders of already existing firms, but because the current interest rate motivates entry decisions, it influences the return to shareholders, who also borrow or lend at the current rate in adjusting their portfolios.

The capital market valuation mechanism cannot be counted on to operate in the same way for regulated firms as for unregulated firms. Under *Hope* guidelines there is no role for new entry, which, in relation to demand, determines overall returns in unregulated markets. Moreover, only

---

27 See Modigliani and Miller (1958). There are many possible ways that changes in policies can affect bondholders relative to shareholders. For analysis of these relations, see Jensen and Mechling (1976) and Sherman (1977). On the empirical controversy, see Modigliani and Miller (1966).

28 Bankruptcy is analyzed in Stiglitz (1969).

the return to the equity portion of capital is based on current conditions. Consequently, the historical cost of debt, and the importance of debt in the capital structure of the regulated firm, can influence the overall allowed rate of return. Because current debt cannot be interchanged with the historical debt that influences allowed return, no arbitrage process can offset this effect of capital structure on allowed rate of return. Even though profits taxes, transaction costs, and the possibility of bankruptcy may alter the Modigliani–Miller valuation process,[29] the fact remains that regulation according to *Hope* guidelines may interfere in a more basic way with that process.

Rather than new entrants' current opportunity cost of debt, which would influence returns in unregulated industries, *Hope* guidelines let the *historical* interest rate on bonds influence a regulated firm's cost of capital and, ultimately, its output price. Under this *Hope* procedure, shareholders no longer gain or lose by offsetting risks borne by bondholders, and with historical debt costs influencing prices it is possible that consumers instead will bear risks of price-level or interest-rate change. Moreover, where regulators tie returns to the original cost of assets, shareholders as well as bondholders may experience nominal returns in the face of any unanticipated price-level change, because original-cost valuation of a rate base tends to fix returns to equity in original period dollars. Just such nominal returns for equity have been observed in regulated firms during recent periods of high rates of inflation.[30] So regulated firms may have special preferences among financial instruments, depending on circumstances (Scott 1987; Sherman 1977; Taggart 1981, 1985). In essence, the *Hope* guidelines for setting a return to equity capital can destroy the financial comparability between regulated and unregulated firms on which the guidelines supposedly rest.

Now it is conceivable that investors' valuations reflecting comparable risks can be observed from the shares of other regulated firms, or from a regulated firm's own shares. But stringent conditions are required for obtaining investors' judgments about regulated firms independently of regulators' actions, and the conditions are not apt to be satisfied. In particular, the regulatory process itself is such that it takes time to reach decisions. Sudden cost increases in fuel and other inputs prompt rate requests but

---

[29] The consequences of relaxing strong assumptions are shown in Baumol and Malkiel (1967).

[30] Michael Keran (1976) has found empirically that with respect to dividend yields equity shares in regulated firms behave much like bonds when the rate of inflation is high. This result can be traced to the reliance of most regulatory commissions on the original-cost valuation of assets, which effectively makes stockholder returns more like nominal returns. For more on the cost of capital, see Kolbe, Read, and Hall (1985). For effects of inflation, see Cross (1982) and Lebowitz, Lee, and Linhart (1976).

the delays between requests and regulatory actions can be so great that more problems, calling perhaps for more rate requests, may arise before the first request is settled. Such delays in adjustment interfere with the valuation process, and because of the way the *Hope* guidelines mix historical accounting measures with current measures there is no clear way to undo the consequences. Carleton (1974) has demonstrated that when there is no prompt response to changed conditions, the underlying values will be affected so that the ordinary market valuation process is irreparably distorted. This means that, by observing other regulated firms, it is very hard, if not impossible, to apply properly the comparable earnings standard,[31] because observed capital costs for regulated firms will reflect effects of regulation rather than investor judgments alone.

It is seldom possible to observe a regulated firm's own equity cost as a basis for determining comparable earnings. A major difficulty arises when a public utility is regulated by more than one commission, a common situation because the service areas of utilities do not always stop at state boundaries. The utility has only one cost of equity capital, but its profitability and thus its cost of capital will be affected by decisions of, say, two regulatory commissions. Neither commission can easily trace the consequence of its own rulings or observe investors' judgments independently of regulatory effects because other regulators also influence the firm's profitability. Related problems arise in the regulation of only a portion of a firm's activities. Market returns for the firm will then reflect investors' judgments about activities beyond those being regulated, to confound the determination of capital cost for the regulated activity.

That the *Hope* guidelines lack a sound basis for estimating the very rate of return they sanction is important beyond the obvious practical difficulty this causes. That practical difficulty gives regulators much discretion, when almost any decision they reach will be feasible because the monopoly public utility they regulate will usually be able to earn far more than they allow. In the worst cases, this discretion opens the way for corruption. Even in the best cases, it makes investors wonder not merely about inherent business risk, the risk of the business itself, but rather about *what regulators will decide,* allowing the firm's return for equity capital to possess uncertainties introduced by the regulatory process itself.

The valuation of corporate securities is a complicated function that financial markets perform. Rate-of-return regulation according to *Hope*

---

31 Immediate adjustment in rates to maintain an allowed rate of return is possible, but it leaves consumers as risk bearers while treating shareholders essentially as bondholders. For an experiment with this policy, see New Mexico Public Service Commission Decision and Order in Case no. 1196, *Cost of Service Index for the Public Service Company of New Mexico,* April 22, 1975.

guidelines can intrude on the ordinary market valuation process, and it is important to understand the nature of this intrusion so the effects of present regulation can be understood. Alternative rules may be created for establishing rates of return, but their effect on the valuation process will need study if a sound choice of rule is to be made. Closely related to the way profit is valued in financial markets is the question of who bears the risks of its creation. To the extent that present procedures adjust prices to ensure a rate of return for investors, they may shift large portions of this risk to consumers. Not only may that be undesirable on the face of things, it can also weaken investors' motivation to oversee management performance and as a result reduce efficiency within the firm.

Even if rate-of-return regulation according to the comparable earnings standard could somehow be employed perfectly and continuously, it might fail for lack of incentive. All possible gains from improved efficiency essentially would have to be given up, so the firm's incentive to improve would be sapped; the *Hope* guidelines contain no great profit reward for efficiency, no incentive to elicit extra effort. Whether the firm would undertake research and development, for example, might depend on whether necessary resources would be counted in the cost and in the rate base, and how helpful to the firm the results might be. In part because of delays between price changes, all incentive is not eliminated in regulated firms. But the incentives that remain in firms regulated according to *Hope* guidelines do not serve the efficiency goal faithfully.

7.4   The regulatory agencies

Every one of the 50 states in the United States now has a regulatory commission to regulate within its state borders. Some commissions regulate only public utilities, whereas in other states they regulate insurance, transportation, or other activities. The commissions are quasi-judicial in form and render decisions after receiving evidence through hearings. Parties can appeal their decisions and if not satisfied have recourse to the regular court system. As we have noted, crucial principles of rate-of-return regulation were fashioned in Supreme Court decisions.

We have seen how rate-of-return regulation according to *Hope* guidelines leaves considerable scope for discretion by regulatory agencies, and it is reasonable to ask how that discretion is used. Joskow (1972) set out to determine the influence of economic factors in decisions by the New York Public Service Commission in the 1960s. He found that the commission tended not to grant the full amounts requested by firms; they made relatively higher awards when expert testimony supported the firm's request and lower awards when intervenors opposed them. Joskow (1973) also studied the factors causing a public utility in New York to approach its regulatory agency with a proposal for new rates. Declining earned rate of return, especially in relation to other returns being allowed by the regulatory commission, and weakening financial position raised the likelihood that a regulated firm would request higher rates.

In a more general study of patterns and changes in public utility regulation, Joskow (1974) contrasted the 1960s, when costs of supplying electricity either fell or remained constant, with the 1970s, when costs rose, owing in large part to the rise in the price of oil. Joskow counted 5 rate cases before commissions in 1968, for example, whereas in 1970 the number was 31 and in 1972 it was 53. More recently public utilities have complicated regulation by diversifying into other activities (Trebing 1985).

Political influences on rate decisions have long been suspected but efforts to explain rate decisions consistently on this basis have not been successful.[32] The political explanations often see lower prices going to consumer groups that are more numerous and therefore can be expected to exercise more power at the polls. But political influence can be held by commercial or industrial customers, in which case they may be favored with lower rates. Such customers sometimes have alternative sources, such as their own generators, which enable them to bargain for lower rates. Regulation may also be used to achieve specific income redistribution goals of politicians. It is natural to expect these political arguments to vary with the importance of politics in the regulatory process, as indicated, for example, by whether regulatory commissioners are elected by the public.

Regulatory commission performance must have some influence on outcomes, because major Wall Street advisory services seem to spend as much time evaluating state commissions as they do analyzing the circumstances of individual public utilities. Analysts systematically consider not only the rate of return a commission tends to allow, but such other factors as the time it takes to process rate cases, how construction work in process and other accounting matters are handled, whether automatic input-price adjustment clauses are allowed, and whether the basis for a decision is a recently completed "test" year or a hypothetical future period in which anticipated input price changes are taken into account.[33] The ratings given commissions correlate well with bond ratings and stock values of the utilities that they regulate, and the ratings also have been explained empirically by political variables (e.g., elected commissions tend to have less

---

[32] For a review of some of these efforts, see R. A. Posner (1974). Leading examples are S. Peltzman (1975), G. J. Stigler (1971), and R. A. Posner (1971).

[33] For an example of such an evaluation, with a rating of each commission on a scale of one to five, see Merrill, Lynch, Pierce, Fenner and Smith (1980). A more general description of these evaluations is available in Navarro (1981).

favorable ratings than appointed commissions) and competence measures (e.g., higher salaries tend to be earned at commissions with more favorable ratings).[34] Gegax and Tschirhart (1984) found that firms in more favorable regulatory climates were less apt to reduce capital expenditures by joint plant ownership through power pools. Thus state regulatory commissions have scope to create different environments for the firms they regulate, and apparently they use it.

For electricity, the dividing line between state and federal regulatory responsibilities has been drawn crudely between retailing to consumers (state regulation) and wholesaling to other utilities (federal regulation). Of course, whether transactions are at the retail or wholesale level can be determined to a degree by public utility decisions about organizational form. To this degree, a public utility can decide whether to be regulated by the state or the federal government. If regulation is seen to be more lenient at the state level, utilities will tend to organize so their sales are at the retail level. If federal regulation is seen by utilities to be more lenient, where permitted they may organize as holding companies and make wholesale transactions to subsidiaries, which the Federal Energy Regulation Commission will regulate. On balance, the FERC appears to have been more lenient, particularly when allowing questionable assets to receive any return at all.

The debate over how to value assets to determine profit allowances has received far more attention than a fundamentally more important question, which is whether to allow any return at all. If putting assets in place was a mistake, they presumably should receive no return. This question has arisen in more rate cases recently, for example where nuclear power plants have been abandoned or have had serious accidents that made them unproductive. It is difficult to answer the question in the absence of free entry and exit, which produce the competitive market test for investment success. State regulatory commissions sometimes have denied returns on certain assets, and they have long required that assets be "used and useful" in order to receive a return. They have also imposed a prudency test on investment decisions, and insisted in some cases that assets be completed and be productive before receiving any return, rather than doing so in a stage of construction. When power plant construction projects have been canceled by utilities, some state commissions have not allowed any amortization of their costs. And some state commissions also have reduced in some way the rate base eligible to receive a return, when they

---

[34] See Navarro (1980) and Dublin and Navarro (1982). Hagerman and Ratchford (1978) did not find a significant effect on allowed rate of return traceable to whether commissioners were elected or the salary level, when economic variables (e.g., the interest rate and debt–equity ratio) were also included.

have concluded that the utility has built excessive, or unneeded capacity. In these latter decisions especially, state commissions have attempted to produce results somewhat like a competitive market, where excessive capacity in relation to demand – whatever the reason it was built – will not earn a normal return. When there is excess capacity in competitive markets, the shareholders, who oversee management, suffer rather than consumers.

Although many state commissions have struggled to deal with the important question of whether assets are genuinely needed and should receive a return, the FERC essentially has not pursued the question. FERC responsibility has been limited to wholesale electricity transactions, which traditionally have accounted for a relatively small part of any one electric utility's sales. Perhaps that explains the FERC's reluctance to deny returns to utility assets. An evaluation of investment soundness requires attention to an entire organizational unit and the demand that it is responsible for supplying, a scope of responsibility that can be defined well only for the entire enterprise.

Will a public utility ever build unneeded capacity? We know that incentives within the regulated firm received little attention when rate-of-return regulation was being developed. In recent years state commissions have devoted more attention to the effects of their decisions and policies on efficiency incentives within regulated public utilities, but unwanted effects remain difficult to avoid. The bias toward capital could result in more capacity than needed, and the lack of competition may result in higher costs. But one of the hardest actions for a regulatory commission to take is to deny a normal return on assets of a public utility when they are not needed to meet its maximum expected demand or are far more costly than sound management would allow. A competitive market can ruthlessly punish firms and their shareholders in such a situation. If a return is allowed on the excessive assets in a regulated industry, it will cause prices to be higher and thereby shift risk of a decline in demand or accountability for management failure over to consumers instead of placing them on shareholders. Where there is cause, a decision to disallow return on excessive capital will maintain incentives for sound management in the long run, but such decisions are still seldom made.

7.5 Economic consequences of rate-of-return regulation

Many questions remain about the effectiveness of rate-of-return regulation, particularly on big issues. Within the narrow task of controlling a monopoly's behavior through control over its rate of return, there also are questions to be raised. In addition to the risk allocation problems we have described, it has been claimed that rate-of-return regulation (1) biases the firm's choice among productive inputs, (2) fails to control monopolistic reliance on price discrimination, and (3) does not encourage technological change. We briefly describe these problems here, beginning with the Averch and Johnson (1962) input bias that favors capital use. The second problem, monopolistic pricing such as price discrimination, is less well known and may cause the levels of a public utility's outputs to be inefficiently chosen. The third problem is the most difficult to treat precisely, and it will be discussed only briefly.

Input inefficiency

Although we can question the strength of its profit-seeking motivation, suppose for now that the monopoly firm whose rate of return on assets is limited according to *Hope* guidelines faithfully pursues profit for its shareholders. If regulators can react immediately to all changes while maintaining an allowed rate of return, then in choosing inputs to produce any particular level of output the firm's incentives will be distorted. If the regulated firm is allowed to earn a rate of return greater than the competitive cost of capital but below the monopoly return, it will want to expand its capital beyond the monopoly level. This incentive by itself is desirable, since it will lead to more output. But in hiring inputs other than capital the regulated firm remains monopolistic. Indeed, it becomes schizophrenic in deciding capital use differently from the use of other inputs and it succumbs to what is now well known as the Averch–Johnson effect:[35] To produce any given output, it uses more capital relative to other inputs than is most efficient.

The simplest way to view the incentive for capital use of the rate-of-return regulated firm is to realize that whereas an unregulated firm has one main aim, the rate-of-return regulated firm has two. The unregulated monopolist seeks to earn high profit; the rate-of-return regulated monopolist seeks not only to earn high profit but also to be allowed to keep it. And since the regulated monopolist's profit is limited to some fraction of

---

[35] For the classic analysis, see Averch and Johnson (1962). A review is available in Sherman (1985). For elaboration of the split personality that comes to a firm's input decisions, see Sherman (1972b). More general dynamic formulations of the commission's review process tends to moderate the bias toward capital, and in some conditions to imply efficient outcomes if the allowed return exactly equals the cost of capital. In particular, see Bawa and Sibley (1980), Lipman (1985), and Sibley (1985). There is still a bias if the allowed return is above the cost of capital, and accommodating more realism by considering stochastic demand seems to make the potential bias even greater. For the latter point, see Crew and Kleindorfer (1979b), pp. 140–3.

its assets, the amount of profit it is *allowed* to earn can be increased as more assets are employed in its production process. Imposing rate-of-return regulation on the monopolist may therefore bring greater output as its asset base is expanded from the original monopoly position, but such regulation also invites the use of more capital than is efficient when judged in relation to other inputs. A lower and lower allowed rate of return makes this input distortion more and more serious. Indeed, at the extreme where the equity rate of return almost satisfies the comparable earnings standard, there can be more inefficiency at the margin through distortion of input choice than social gain from a lower price.[36]

One situation brings out the potential perversity of incentives in the rate-of-return regulated firm especially well. Suppose that as regulation is introduced a single-product monopolist is forced away from its unregulated monopoly position and soon would have to enter an inelastic portion of its demand curve, because as price falls and output expands quantity responds less to any given percentage change in price. The regulated firm would want to avoid an inelastic region of its demand curve just as an unregulated monopolist would,[37] for as it expands output where demand is inelastic its total revenue declines while its total cost increases. The regulated monopoly has a simple way to avoid reducing its profit by expanding output; it merely wastes capital instead (if it can get away with it) and thereby raises the amount of profit it is *allowed* to earn. Regulatory commissions try to prevent such capital waste, of course, but the incentive to waste can come directly from rate-of-return regulation.

Rate-of-return regulation can even invite conspiracy between regulated firms and their suppliers to set high capital equipment prices. After electrical equipment producers were convicted of price fixing in 1962, Westfield (1965) demonstrated convincingly "that it can be in the interest of a regulated private power generating company to pay a higher rather than a lower price for the plant and equipment it purchases." Increased equipment costs could be passed through to the consumer in the form of higher prices and at the same time could increase the amount of profit the company was *allowed* to earn by increasing its asset rate base; under rate-of-

---

36 This trade-off between the gain from expanded output and the loss from input inefficiency is treated in Comanor (1970), Sheshinski (1971), and Sherman (1974).

37 When the own-price elasticity of demand is less than one in absolute value (i.e., demand is inelastic), marginal revenue is negative. When demand is inelastic a cut in price of, say, 5 percent will bring an increase in quantity of less than 5 percent, so the marginal effect is to *lower* total revenue (i.e., marginal revenue is negative). But since marginal cost is always positive, a profit-maximizing firm trying to have marginal cost equal marginal revenue will want to operate where marginal revenue is positive; it will never want to operate where demand is inelastic.

return regulation the capital side of the firm is essentially subject to cost-plus regulation.

These are the obvious problems. Apart from such extreme examples, the bias toward capital in selecting production methods can add more moderately, but still unnecessarily, to costs. Technology offers a great range of methods to accomplish almost any production task today, and as long as more profit can be justified under rate-of-return regulation by using more of just one input, capital, quite subtle alterations of technological decisions might occur (Smith 1974). Of course, many factors influence technical decisions in a public utility, and the capital bias from rate-of-return regulation is not apt to be the dominant one. The importance and form of any bias also will vary with circumstances; for instance, recent episodes of harsh regulation might occasionally have sent allowed return below the cost of capital and conceivably induced a bias *against* capital relative to other inputs.[38]

In practice, regulatory commissions do not render immediate decisions. Rate cases can drag on for months, and a firm may even wish to propose new rates before a pending rate case is concluded. When during extensive intervals no price change is possible, the efficiency incentives of the firm will be improved. For example, its use of excessive capital will not lead immediately to a greater profit allowance, and indeed the only way it can act to improve profit immediately is to operate efficiently. As a rate case approaches, however, the incentive to use more capital will be manifested again, as long as the allowed return exceeds the cost of capital, because a regulatory decision is then in the offing.

Empirical tests based on years of normal operating conditions (after the Great Electrical Equipment Conspiracy but before the 1970s oil embargo) have indicated there was a bias toward capital inputs.[39] These studies, all based on the electric utility industry, have tested a strong form of the Averch–Johnson hypothesis by focusing on new base-load electric plants to see whether any bias toward capital could be detected within them. A weaker hypothesis would allow for capital biases in the mixture of different kinds of plants, or even in the utilization of capacity, but the best studies have sought a bias only *within* particular plants because more precise methods can be applied there. The finding of a bias in studies so narrowly confined is strong evidence that rate-of-return regulation reduces input efficiency.

---

[38] For discussion of broader considerations that weaken the bias toward capital, see Joskow (1974) and Giordano (1983).

[39] Empirical evidence supporting a bias toward capital intensity is presented in Spann (1974), Courville (1974), and Petersen (1975a). Some empirical tests have failed to confirm the Averch–Johnson bias. For a review of all previous evidence and a well-constructed test that confirms the Averch–Johnson hypothesis, see Jones (1983).

Output inefficiency

When a monopoly produces only one product for which demand is every-where elastic, and if the profit motive is still assumed, rate-of-return regu-lation can push the monopoly almost to an ideal price and output solution. The only problem comes from input inefficiency, the Averch–Johnson bi-as toward capital we just discussed. However, when a regulated firm sells more than one product – and examination of their price structures will show that all public utilities really sell more than one product – there is a question of whether it will choose efficient *relative* prices, that is, whether its mixture of outputs will be chosen efficiently. In choosing prices, the multiproduct public utility that is regulated according to *Hope* guidelines actually will rely on demand elasticities just as an unregulated monopoly would, and rate-of-return regulation does nothing to thwart this monopo-listic behavior. Rate-of-return regulation introduces an Averch and John-son capital bias through rate structures, too, causing the firm to favor with lower rates those products that will contribute most to the capital rate base. Thus two factors influence the firm's mixture of output – de-mand elasticities in a monopolistic way plus a bias toward capital-inten-sive products – and these two factors distort the outputs of the firm away from an efficient combination.

A special form of the bias toward capital use in pricing can be seen in the failure of regulated firms, until pressured recently by state and fed-eral agencies and allowed only low rates of return, to offer lower prices for services at off-peak times.[40] Sound economics calls for higher prices during peak demand periods than at off-peak times, because only users at the peak demand press upon available capacity and call for its expansion, and so they should be the ones to pay for it; at off-peak times capacity is abundant relative to demand and so consumers do not have to be turned away by a high price. However, rate-of-return regulated firms lack incen-tive to employ this sound pricing principle. They would rather lower price for capital-intensive peak demand in order to justify more capital assets, and charge a high price at off-peak times to realize profit that greater capital will justify.[41] Moreover, long intervals between rate cases will not moderate this pricing tendency. Probably because the practice of rate-of-return regulation is widespread here, the United States lags far behind

---

[40] An early demonstration of the peak and off-peak pricing problem caused by rate-of-return regulation was provided by Wellisz (1963). See also Bailey (1972), Crew and Klein-dorfer (1979b), Primeaux and Nelson (1980), and Eckel (1983).

[41] Demand elasticities at peak and off-peak times conceivably can offset this tendency. See Bailey and White (1974). The existence of diverse technology, such as base-load, inter-mediate, and peaking plants in electricity, also can complicate the simple case treated in the text. See Turvey (1968), Wenders (1976), and Crew and Kleindorfer (1976).

other countries in the use of peak-load pricing.[42] This perverse reluctance to lower off-peak prices is not something to be blamed on any unduly selfish utility president; it is directly motivated under rate-of-return regulation.

Technological change

The process of technological change is a complicated one, imperfectly understood even without rate-of-return regulation. We have assumed that technology is known well and is unchanging, but of course it changes, and firms using technology may devote resources in an effort to alter it. A monopoly may even have greater reason to use resources in this way, because by being alone in its market it can be assured of enjoying the benefits. A competitive firm must rely on patents to protect its rights, and is more likely to waste resources in its effort, since one of its competitors may advance technology ahead of it. On the other hand, a monopoly can do very well without innovating and may even prefer to let existing equipment wear out before introducing new methods, whereas change can be forced on competitors.[43]

Sweeney (1981) examined the speed at which a regulated monopoly might innovate. His analysis applies to a firm that has prices set periodically by a regulator, under simple procedures in which the regulator bases price on cost. The firm will not wish to lower its cost to the maximum extent possible in one period, because, although it will profit by doing so, a large welfare gain will go to consumers as well. If the firm can introduce the the change gradually instead, so costs fall to some extent in each period, slightly lower prices based on those costs will be instituted each time, allowing greater quantity to be sold. As a result of such successive reductions more profit can be accumulated by the firm. Figure 7.1 shows as a shaded area the profit to be made by immediate innovation. If instead the firm can lower cost to P_1 while price is P_0 it will profit by $(P_0 - P_1)Q_0$. The price will be set at P_1 but the firm then can lower cost to P_2 and profit by $(P_1 - P_2)Q_1$, and so forth. As a result of proceeding in this way, it can realize more of the area to the right of the shaded area. This assumes, of course, that the periods are not very long, or the discount rate for valuing future profits is low.

Bailey (1974) observed that a lag, such as that central to Sweeney's (1981) model, is crucial to the incentive for innovation. If regulators respond

---

[42] For examples of peak-load pricing in Europe, see Mitchell et al. (1978).
[43] For a discussion of technological change under regulation see Bailey (1974), Berg and Tschirhart (in press), Sappington (1982, 1983), Smith (1974), Sweeney (1981), and Westfield (1971).

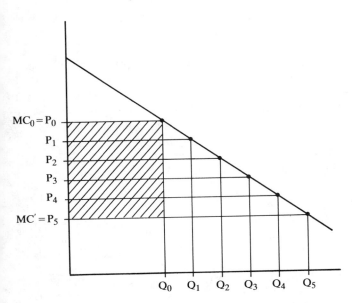

Figure 7.1. The advantage of slow innovation.

immediately to technological changes, price will fall as the new technology is introduced and no benefit will be realized by the firm. Bailey showed that longer regulatory lag could enhance the incentive to reduce costs through innovation, although of course it raised the benefit to firms of innovating by delaying the resultant benefit to consumers. A similar analysis applies to patent life, which also allows greater benefit to an innovator as the patent lasts longer.

Smith (1974) argued that rate-of-return regulation in electric utilities could affect whether innovations would tend to augment capital or other inputs. Further work by Okuguchi (1975) and Magat (1976) still leaves this question unresolved theoretically, and empirical studies have not settled it either. The urge to innovate tends to be reduced by rate-of-return regulation, however. As long as the firm's own costs are important determinants of prices, incentives will not be ideal (Shleifer 1985).

7.6   Summary

Through the gradual resolution of legally defined issues over the past century an institution for regulating public utilities has evolved. That institution was not carefully designed for specific aims but rather involved compromise between vested interests, and its shortcomings can be seen now with hindsight. It does not accord with economic valuation processes, for instance, and in practice it leaves wide scope for discretion in the hands of regulators. Uncertainty about how such discretion will be used is a source of risk, and besides causing inefficient resource allocation, the discretion even has the potential for corruption. Jurisdictional boundaries between state and federal regulators complicate the scene, and may even influence the way firms choose to organize. Even if regulators pursue faithfully an aim of economic efficiency, they may be thwarted by side effects of the institution they control. Two major side effects, input inefficiency and output inefficiency, are treated in turn in the next two chapters.

Questions

7.1. Explain the main features of the decision of the U.S. Supreme Court in *Federal Power Commission v. Hope Natural Gas Co.* Also describe difficulties that a regulatory commission might have in following the guidelines of that decision.

7.2. How is responsibility for the regulatory task divided between state and federal government? Describe problems with this division of responsibility. Try to propose an alternative division of responsibilities or policy that would reduce the problems.

7.3. Explain how rate-of-return regulation might induce a firm to make an inefficient choice of capital relative to other inputs.

7.4. Explain how rate-of-return regulation might induce a multiservice firm to choose prices for its services that are not Ramsey prices.

CHAPTER 8

Input choices under rate-of-return regulation

8.1   Introduction

Even if rate-of-return regulation can be effectively implemented according to guidelines from the *Hope* decision, it may not achieve ideal results, for it can have perverse side effects. The firm has substantial control over the capital input, which serves to determine its allowed profit, so its capital choice may be biased. For instance, if regulators respond immediately with price decisions, the firm may favor capital relative to other inputs if it is allowed a return on capital higher than capital cost. Or if it is allowed a return less than its cost of capital, the firm may try to avoid additional capital use. If there is a long lag before regulators respond, during which prices cannot change, the firm may have more incentive to operate efficiently. But unchanging output prices cause other problems for the firm when input prices change.

Our purpose here is to describe how incentives can induce technical inefficiency in public utility firms when they are regulated by rate-of-return constraint. With immediate responses by regulators, the rate-of-return constraint may cause a public utility to serve society well through its capital choices, but the utility will continue to have the incentives of a monopolist in all its other input decisions. By acting partly as a competitive industry and partly as a monopoly industry, the regulated firm develops a split personality. Such schizophrenia in the regulated firm is the underlying cause of inefficiencies that have been called "regulatory bias" and "overcapitalization." We examine this behavior in the next three sections.

When rate-of-return regulation is considered in more detail, it must be seen not as a continuous mechanism with immediate regulatory response, but rather as a periodic event that requires dynamic analysis. We consider the moderating effect of regulatory decision lags with a dynamic model in Section 8.5. As the allowed rate of return matches the cost of capital more perfectly, the consequences are less perverse in the dynamic model. Another reality that requires explicit consideration is the uncertain nature of demands for services, which we consider in Section 8.6. With uncertain demand, it is more difficult to capture the workings of regulatory institutions, because results are sensitive to the choice of model. On the whole, it seems more difficult to obtain efficient outcomes when uncertainty is present. In Section 8.7 uncertain input prices are shown to increase financial risk when regulatory decision lags exist. Such risk may be relieved, although not perfectly, by automatic adjustment clauses that permit output price responses to input price changes. Empirical study of electrical utilities has yielded some evidence to support inefficiency in the choice of inputs, as noted in Section 8.8, although the effect of the observed inefficiency on cost may be quite small (Jones 1983). Section 8.9 contains a summary.

8.2   Schizophrenia in input choice

We begin by analyzing a model in which the regulator establishes a rate of return, which is then applied to the firm's capital base to determine allowed profit. Such profit is combined with costs to determine allowed total revenue and hence prices. The regulator is assumed also to act immediately to set prices in response to any change. Since this whole procedure is so well defined, the firm can capture the regulator's behavior simply and reliably, and act to maximize profit in the light of that known behavior. This approach to the problem emphasizes the distortions that can be induced by rate-of-return regulation. How they might be lessened when regulators do not act immediately and as a result output prices remain fixed for long periods is taken up after the possible biases are described in this simpler model.

Without any loss in generality, it will simplify our discussion if we think of all inputs other than capital as simply one input, which we shall refer to as labor. To demonstrate that the regulated firm chooses labor as a monopolist and capital more as a welfare maximizer, we want to contrast marginal conditions at three different solutions: (1) welfare maximizing, (2) rate-of-return regulated monopoly, and (3) unregulated monopoly. We take consumers' surplus as a measure of consumer welfare, even though it is only a partial equilibrium measure. Of course, it ignores effects on income distribution by assuming that any dollar benefit is as desirable to society, regardless of who receives it.

Net social welfare will be represented by total revenue plus consumers' surplus less total cost. We assume that optimum conditions of production and exchange are satisfied elsewhere in the economy and that there is no externality. To simplify our welfare measure still further, we shall assume that (i) demand is elastic (inelastic demand is considered in Section 8.3), (ii) production quantity is a linear homogeneous function of inputs, and

(iii) input prices are constant and there are no inframarginal rents.[1] These assumptions let us pose a revenue-maximization problem subject to a constraint that revenue minus cost equal some budgeted sum B. With elastic demand, the revenue-maximizing, single-product firm will want to expand output and mix inputs efficiently until bounded by the profit constraint. If we limit the firm to a competitive return, r, then, with constant returns and constant input prices, total revenue less total cost will have to equal B, and net social benefit will equal the sum of consumers' surplus and producers' surplus. If the budgeted sum, B, is zero, the solution will maximize welfare, and if B is not zero the solution will maximize welfare subject to the constraint that B is earned.

It is easy to obtain a monopolistic solution from the regulated firm model simply by setting the allowed rate of return, s, equal to or greater than the monopoly level, m, so the constraint is not effective. But if s is set equal to the competitive rate of return, r, strictly speaking there is no unique solution to the profit-maximizing problem as it was originally posed for the regulated firm by Averch and Johnson (1962, hereafter, AJ). However, there is a limiting solution that is approached as s approaches r.[2] We can find this limiting solution for the firm regulated at $s = r$ without mathematical difficulty by formulating the regulated firm's problem as Westfield (1965)[3] did to maximize the total net revenue product of capital, a term Westfield adapted from Joan Robinson (1933). Indeed, in posing Westfield's problem with the assumption made above, we can obtain all the solution conditions we wish to contrast.

Now let us set out the problem that will enable us to contrast these different solution conditions. Total net revenue product of capital is revenue less optimal noncapital (here, labor) expenses, and it can be substituted for profit in the AJ problem's objective function simply by omitting an rK

1 Without elastic demand the firm would not reach the optimal output (see Sherman 1972b, Takayama 1969, and Westfield 1965) and with elastic demand and decreasing returns to scale the firm might produce too much (see Kafoglis 1969). For an explanation of the consumers' surplus measure of welfare in the constant average cost case, see Williamson (1966) and Chapter 2 above.
2 Averch and Johnson gave little attention to this $s = r$ case, but they did indicate that in their model it had multiple solutions (1962, p. 1055). The solution we obtain here is the solution a rate-base asset value maximizer would pursue, subject to the rate-of-return constraint, and the regulated profit maximizer would behave the same way until $s = r$. When $s = r$, many solutions will produce the same profit, but only one still maximizes the rate base. Since the profit maximizer approaches that one solution, we take it as a useful limiting case with which to compare other solutions. This approach to comparing solutions was presented in Sherman (1972b).
3 Although different in form, Wellisz's analysis avoided indeterminacy at his equivalent of $s = r$, also by not duplicating the objective function in the constraint. See Wellisz (1963, p. 42).

term (Averch and Johnson 1962, p. 1052). The AJ firm maximized profit, $R - wL - rK$, whereas the Westfield firm maximized the net revenue product of capital, $R - wL$, where R is revenue, w is the wage rate, L is labor, and K is capital value.[4] Given an active profit constraint, $R - wL - sK = B$, either of these objectives will yield the same L and K solution values, and their objective function values will differ by the amount of the rK term. Revenue is the product of quantity, Q, and price, p. Quantity and price are related by the inverse demand function, $p = p(Q)$, and the quantity produced depends on labor and capital, $Q = Q(L, K)$. Maximizing total revenue would simply maximize R. Both the net revenue product of capital objective and the total revenue objective can therefore be represented in the function, $R - \delta wL$, with the particular objective depending on whether $\delta = 0$ or $\delta = 1$. The constraint $R - wL - sK = B$ also could be attached to this composite objective. The resulting Lagrangian problem that will embody all of the problems and solutions we wish to contrast here is thus

$$F(L, K, \lambda) = R - \delta wL - \lambda(R - wL - sK - B), \tag{1}$$

where the variable, λ, is the Lagrange multiplier.

To comply with assumptions (i), (ii), and (iii) above, we consider only cases with constant cost and constant r, s, and w values, and in which $R_Q(\partial R/\partial Q = R_Q)$ at the consumers' surplus-maximizing solution will be positive because demand must be elastic. If $\delta = 0$, $s = r$, and $B = 0$, (1) will be a constrained revenue maximization problem and it will give a welfare maximizing solution. If $\delta = 1$ and $s = r$, (1) becomes Westfield's problem of maximizing the total net revenue product of capital as a regulated firm subject to a competitive rate-of-return constraint. Finally, if $\delta = 1$ and $s \geq m$, (1) becomes an ordinary monopolist's problem.

Assuming that the constraint is always effective,[5] we obtain as first-order conditions for a maximum of problem (1),

$$R_L = \frac{\delta - \lambda}{1 - \lambda} w, \tag{2}$$

$$R_K = \frac{-\lambda}{1 - \lambda} s, \tag{3}$$

$$R - wL - sK = B. \tag{4}$$

Notationally, $\partial R/\partial L = R_L$ and $\partial R/\partial K = R_K$. Specific forms of these conditions for our three problems are gathered together in Table 8.1. That

---

[4] To simplify formulation of the problem, the price of capital equipment is set equal to 1 and depreciation is ignored. See Averch and Johnson (1962).

[5] The constraint will be effective for s values between r and m, and it is simpler to pose the problem this way than to use the more general inequality constraint as Averch and Johnson did. See Takayama (1969).

Table 8.1. *Input efficiency conditions for elastic demand solutions to problem* (1)

	Welfare-maximizing solution		Regulated firm (limiting solution)		Monopoly solution	
δ	0		1		1	
s	r		r		m	
Labor condition	$R_L = \dfrac{-\lambda}{1-\lambda}w$	(5)	$R_L = w$	(9)	$R_L = w$	(13)
Capital condition	$R_K = \dfrac{-\lambda}{1-\lambda}r$	(6)	$R_K = \dfrac{-\lambda}{1-\lambda}r$	(10)	$R_K = r$	(14)
Rate of return	$R - wL - rK = 0$	(7)	$R - wL - rK = 0$	(11)	$R - wL - mK = 0$	(15)
Efficiency condition	$\dfrac{R_K}{R_L} = \dfrac{r}{w}$	(8)	$\dfrac{R_K}{R_L} = \dfrac{-\lambda}{1-\lambda}\dfrac{r}{w}$	(12)	$\dfrac{R_K}{R_L} = \dfrac{r}{w}$	(16)

R_K must equal r at the monopoly solution (14) is demonstrated by West-field (1965, pp. 431–2), and the other conditions require only simple substitutions of the indicated values for δ, s, and B in (2), (3), and (4). The contrasting conditions in Table 8.1 are the results that we have been seeking.

Comparison with welfare-maximization conditions (5) and (6), and with conditions (13) and (14) for the monopoly, show the rate-of-return regulated firm to have a split personality; it follows a monopolist's rule in choosing its labor input ((9) is the same[6] as (13)) and it follows a welfare-maximizing rule in choosing its capital input ((10) is the same as (6)). Labor will always be less attractive as δ is larger, so the rate-of-return regulated firm will use less labor than the welfare-maximizing firm. Indeed, the regulatory constraint really regulates only part of the firm, the capital part, and in doing so it induces the use of two types of decision rule, which we call schizophrenia.

Technical efficiency within the firm calls for $-\partial L/\partial K = R_K/R_L = r/w$; the ratio of the maginal products of inputs must equal the ratio of their prices. This condition is satisfied by both the welfare-maximizing firm and the monopolist. But dividing both sides of (9) by both sides of (10) yields (12), which shows that the rate-of-return regulated firm does not use its inputs efficiently. It joins too little labor with the capital that it employs,

6 The values of the variables will not be the same; only the form of the decision rules taken from necessary first-order marginal conditions will be the same. Of course, the decisions are still made simultaneously. We use the word *schizophrenia* merely to highlight use by the firm of two different types of decision rule.

making $R_K/R_L < r/w$ as long as $-\lambda/(1-\lambda) < 1$. This result is the regulatory bias first shown by AJ, but here it can be traced more obviously to monopolistic behavior in the choice of noncapital inputs.

The Lagrange multiplier in this problem will lie in a range different from that in the AJ problem, and to avoid confusion let us pause to note the differences.[7] Observe that $\lambda = R_K/(R_K - s)$. For the case of $\delta = 1$ and $B = 0$, which creates a problem analogous to the AJ problem, consider what happens to λ as s is lowered from a high initial level. As soon as the constraint is binding (because s is below the unregulated monopoly rate of return, m), λ will have a large negative value. As s is set still lower, λ will become more positive (smaller in absolute value), and $-\lambda/(1-\lambda)$ will become a smaller fraction. Comparing (12) with the efficient condition in (8) or (16), we can see that this will tend to make the bias in input choice more serious as s approaches r. Since the unregulated monopoly has no bias in its input choices, it should not be surprising that the bias grows stronger as we force the firm farther from a monopoly solution toward the extreme where $s = r$.

For convenience, we have relied on a constant average cost assumption in making our comparisons in Table 8.1. If average cost were to decrease with output, then the regulatory commission might no longer attempt to obtain a true price-equals-marginal-cost optimum, since revenues then could not cover costs. Instead, by applying the rate-of-return constraint, the commission would try to avoid a deficit and price at average cost. Indeed, this price-equals-average-cost solution is a compromise that avoids cross-subsidization and thus favors distributional equity over allocative efficiency. It accounts in part for the widespread use in the United States of the independent privately owned and publicly regulated utilities.[8] Our comparisons in Table 8.1 could still serve. The revenue-maximizing firm would use inputs efficiently and would maximize consumers' surplus subject to the constraint that prevents a deficit, roughly as proposed in Boiteux's (1956) classic solution. Besides leading to efficiency in the choice of inputs, the price-equals-average-cost solution would avoid income distribution problems by ensuring that users of the service would also pay for it. Against such a compromise welfare benchmark, the rate-of-return regulated firm still would appear schizophrenic. It would make capital choices by a decision rule comparable to a welfare-maximizing firm that

---

[7] The value of λ was important in the AJ proof. For the AJ problem, λ would lie in the range: $0 < \lambda < 1$. See Averch and Johnson (1962, p. 1056) and also Takayama (1969, p. 258).

[8] Implications of this explicitly second-best solution were first set out by Boiteux (1956). See also Drèze (1964, pp. 24–34), Baumol and Bradford (1970), Mohring (1970), and Guesnerie (1980).

is constrained to break even, but would make labor choices according to a monopolist's decision rule.

Greater difficulties for our comparison will arise if average cost increases with output. As Kafoglis (1969) has shown, the revenue-maximizing firm under increasing cost and subject only to a rate-of-return constraint will produce beyond the welfare-maximizing level. The comparisons in Table 8.1 would have no meaning for this case. But rate-of-return regulation would be difficult to justify under increasing cost conditions anyway. If input prices were not constant, this result and the result noted previously for decreasing average cost might not hold (see Shepherd 1971). Demand at the welfare-maximizing point must also be price elastic or the constrained revenue-maximizing firm will not reach it. The firm would stop instead at a point of unit elasticity where total revenue reaches a maximum.

8.3 Gold plating

The most serious departures from economic efficiency arise from the monopolistic urges that remain in a rate-of-return regulated firm and make it want to escape an inelastic region of its demand curve. Then the regulated firm may prefer to pay higher rather than lower prices for capital, or may install capital that has a marginal product of zero. This possibility was analyzed masterfully by Fred Westfield in 1965, but because his analysis is not widely known there is some confusion about the matter even today. The confusion is due to faulty arguments seeming to show that the firm modeled this way would seldom want to use nonproductive capital. Although these arguments are not technically wrong, they are logically wrong, because they impose conditions that would not hold if the firm were behaving naturally in the situation that is of interest. We first illustrate the perverse behavior brought about by inelastic demand and then show how denials of its existence are wrong.

Table 8.1 comparisons cannot deal with inelastic demand because the welfare benchmark there was derived on the assumption that demand is elastic. We noted above that the regulated firm follows the monopoly rule (equation (9)) in choosing its labor input. As long as w is positive on the right-hand side of (9) in Table 8.1, then R_L on the left must also be positive, and R_L is the product of marginal revenue times the marginal product of labor. Since we expect the marginal product of labor R_L to be positive, we know the marginal revenue must always be positive. This implication of the monopolistic necessary condition (9) simply manifests a well-known characteristic of the monopoly – that is, it operates only where marginal revenue is positive, or *where demand is elastic*. The right-hand side of the capital condition in (10) can be negative, however, for $0 < \lambda < 1$ is feasible in this problem.[9] Since R_K on the left side of (10) contains marginal revenue times the marginal product of capital and we already know marginal revenue is positive, this means that the marginal product of capital may be negative. Of course, if the option of using unproductive capital with zero marginal product is available, that will be used in place of (negatively) productive capital.

Westfield established these results by noting that the firm would try to expand capital, but no matter how much capital was employed *some* variable input would be required. That is why its marginal product would be positive, making marginal revenue positive in a condition like (9). He reached his conclusion, that capital of negative marginal product might be used, while assuming that the regulatory commission imposed no additional rules to supplement the rate-of-return ceiling. Rather than employ capital having negative marginal product, Westfield's firm would want to conspire with suppliers to set capital prices higher; that was equivalent to using capital of zero marginal product, and was preferred to using capital of negative marginal product.[10] Realizing that positive marginal revenue was equivalent to elastic demand, Westfield also pointed out that a regulatory commission "can never with rate of return regulation *alone* succeed in forcing a utility to price and produce on an inelastic portion of the demand curve – an important argument against a regulatory scheme that has as an aim the simulation of competitive markets."[11]

If demand were inelastic at the welfare maximum, we do not even know whether *further* reductions in the allowed rate of return, s, would increase

---

[9] For the solution of the rate-of-return constraint problem in Table 8.1, $\lambda = R_K/(R_K - r)$, and $R_K < r$ is possible when regulation is effective so λ can be negative, but λ may lie between 0 and 1 when $R_K < 0$ because $\partial Q/\partial K < 0$.

[10] Here briefly is a way to visualize the problem that arises when demand is inelastic in the efficient-solution range. Consider a two-input pattern of production isoquants, convex to the origin as they usually are assumed. Since any output must be sold at a unique market-clearing price, a three-dimensional revenue surface could be obtained by thinking of these two input dimensions as a floor and raising every isoquant some distance in a third dimension, that distance representing the amount of revenue each isoquant quantity would yield. The revenue surface would rise with inputs, L and K, until a maximum revenue was obtained along the isoquant representing unit elasticity. All points corresponding to any one isoquant obviously must represent the same amount of revenue, so the surface will be smooth and regular. The cost function will be a plane as long as input prices are constant. The rate-of-return constraint will be another plane, which coincides with the cost plane where capital is zero and rises above the cost plane by an amount proportional to capital if the allowed return exceeds the cost of capital. A solution must be in (or below) the constraint plane but, to clear the market, it must also be in the revenue surface that we have described – even where capital has negative marginal product if need be – to remain near the top part of the revenue surface as far in the capital direction as required. With the most capital in use, the greatest possible allowed profit can be obtained.

[11] Westfield (1965, p. 439), italics in the original.

a regulated firm's output.[12] Opportunities to determine the sign of dQ/ds empirically are slight, but let us briefly examine some evidence. Differentiating the production function, $Q = Q(K, L)$, with respect to s gives

$$\frac{dQ}{ds} = Q_K \frac{\partial K}{\partial s} + Q_L \frac{\partial L}{\partial s}. \tag{17}$$

We know that $\partial K/\partial s < 0$ (see Takayama 1969; Westfield 1965); lowering the allowed rate of return will cause more capital to be used. And for a CES production function homogeneous of degree one plus linear demand, we also know that

$$\frac{\partial L}{\partial s} \gtreqless 0 \quad \text{as} \quad \sigma \gtreqless \frac{\eta - 1}{2}, \tag{18}$$

where η is the absolute value of price elasticity of demand and σ is the elasticity of input substitution.[13] The value of σ has been estimated at about $\frac{1}{2}$ in many manufacturing industries (Nerlove 1967), and even closer to zero in electricity (Dhrymes and Kurz 1964). Whether regulated or not, the monopoly firm will want to operate where $\eta > 1$, and if $\eta = 2$ or more we might expect $\partial L/\partial s < 0$ in (18). Assuming $Q_K > 0$ and $Q_L > 0$ in (17) would then make $dQ/ds < 0$, and reducing the allowed rate of return would increase output. On the other hand, it is possible to have $\partial L/\partial s > 0$ in (18), since some estimates of η for regulated industries such as electricity (Fisher and Kaysen 1962; Cargill and Meyer 1971; Taylor 1975) have been quite low and input substitutability conceivably could make σ greater than $\frac{1}{2}$. With $\partial L/\partial s > 0$ we can still have $dQ/ds < 0$ in (17), as long as $Q_K > 0$, $Q_L > 0$, and $Q_K \partial K/\partial s$ is bigger in absolute value than $Q_L \partial L/\partial s$. But the regulated firm has reason to accept $Q_K < 0$ rather than operate where demand is inelastic, and then either a large absolute value of $Q_K \partial K/\partial s$ or $\partial L/\partial s > 0$ could make $dQ/ds > 0$ in (17). Thus, lowering further the allowed rate of return could conceivably reduce output.

So-called used and useful requirements are imposed by regulatory commissions as criteria for including items in the capital rate base, to prevent firms from counting nonproductive capital. When effectively enforced,

---

12 Sheshinski (1971) argued that regulation can always improve welfare, starting from a monopoly solution where demand is elastic. As the efficient position is approached, however, the input inefficiency loss may come to outweigh consumer surplus gains, as Comanor (1970) originally showed. Lowering the allowed return, from some equilibrium position closer to the cost of capital, may cause the firm to act perversely, to avoid operating where demand is inelastic.

13 See Ferguson (1969, pp. 148–9). Strictly speaking, we need $\partial L/\partial \rho$ at the left-hand side of (15), where $\rho(s)$ is an imputed cost of capital under the constraint. But we expect that $d\rho/ds > 0$ in $(\partial L/\partial \rho)(d\rho/ds) = \partial L/\partial s$, and with continuity the sign of $\partial L/\partial \rho$ will be the same as the sign of $\partial L/\partial s$.

such provisions can prevent some of the most perverse consequences that follow when regulated firms try to avoid inelastic demand. To see the effect of such regulatory control, one could add to the Averch and Johnson regulated firm's Lagrangian problem an additional constraint that $Q_K \geq 0$, a condition AJ satisfied merely by assumption. Then, rather than (1), the firm's problem would be

$$G(L, K, \lambda, \gamma) = R - wL - rK - \lambda(R - wL - sK) - \gamma(Q_K). \qquad (19)$$

In addition to the constraints, necessary conditions for a maximum are

$$R_L = w - \frac{\gamma}{1-\lambda} Q_{KL} \qquad (20)$$

and

$$R_K = r - \frac{\lambda}{1-\lambda}(s-r) + \frac{\gamma}{1-\lambda} Q_{KK}, \qquad (21)$$

where

$$Q_K \left\{ {\geq \atop =} \right\} 0 \quad \text{if} \quad \gamma \left\{ {= \atop <} \right\} 0.$$

Since one can expect $Q_{KL} > 0$ and $Q_{KK} < 0$, when effective the added constraint will urge more use of labor and less use of capital. But even when this used and useful constraint is effective, an efficient solution obviously cannot be expected because when the constraint is effective $Q_K = 0$.

Averch and Johnson simply assumed positive marginal products for all inputs, apparently not realizing the perverse possibility that Westfield would later show. In giving a clear geometric exposition of Averch and Johnson's model, Zajac (1970) apparently proves that the firm generally will not waste capital (pp. 124–5), but the marginal products of all inputs must be positive for this proof, and we have just seen that the marginal product of capital would not be positive if demand at the intended solution were inelastic. Elizabeth Bailey (1973) also discovered that the regulated firm would want to operate in the elastic region of its revenue curve, but went on to prove nevertheless that the firm would not waste capital as long as its marginal product of capital was positive. Of course, Westfield showed that the incentive to waste capital only arises when the marginal product of capital would otherwise *not* be positive.

Because of certain limitations, which will become clear as we proceed, the Averch and Johnson model alone is not a reliable source of implications about rate-of-return regulation, so this matter may seem unimportant. Nevertheless, these misleading arguments should be corrected. They have given some the impression that the rate-of-return regulated firm has no incentive to waste capital (see Das 1980). In fact, Westfield's analysis of the Averch and Johnson type of model shows clearly how the regulated firm can waste capital to avoid inelastic demand, and his explanation of why public utilities paid high prices for capital equipment in the great electrical equipment conspiracy is persuasive. The firm may prefer to pay higher prices for capital or use capital that has zero marginal product. This possible behavior is so perverse that it should not be played down because of the failure to understand it in a simple model.

8.4   Other goals and profit constraints

Input biases have been shown in profit-seeking monopoly firms subject to rate-of-return regulation, but the question remains whether such biases would arise in a firm pursuing a different goal.[14] To the extent that regulation weakens the incentive of owners to oversee managers, there may be scope for pursuing other goals in regulated firms, and their implications for efficiency are therefore of interest. We shall again construct a composite static problem to examine this question for profit, revenue, or output goals. We include profit-per-unit and profit-as-a-percentage-of-cost constraints to show that they do not elicit input biases. This is certainly not an exhaustive list of possible goals or constraints.[15]

The composite objective to be maximized is

$$\alpha R + (1-\alpha)Q(K, L) - \alpha\delta(wL + rK), \tag{22}$$

where $Q(K, L)$ is output and α is an added parameter. Obviously, with $\alpha = 1$ and $\delta = 1$, the objective in (22) reduces to profit; with $\alpha = 1$ and $\delta = 0$, it reduces to revenue; and with $\alpha = \delta = 0$, it becomes output. We are already familiar with the rate-of-return constraint,

$$R - wL - sK = 0. \tag{23}$$

Alternatively, we can constrain profit to be some percent, g, of total cost, by appending the following constraint to the objective in (22):

$$R - (1+g)(wL + rK) = 0. \tag{24}$$

Finally, we shall consider a constraint that allows only a specified profit, f, per unit of output:

$$R - wL - rK - fQ = 0. \tag{25}$$

First-order conditions for maximizing (22) with respect to labor and capital without constraint would be

---

14 Input biases under alternative goals and constraints were examined by Bailey and Malone (1970).
15 Examples of others may be found in Awh and Primeaux (1985), Crew and Kleindorfer (1979a), or Williamson (1967).

Table 8.2. *Input efficiency conditions under alternative goals and constraints*

	Profit		Revenue		Output	
α	1		1		0	
δ	1		0		0	
Rate-of-return constraint	$\dfrac{r}{w} - \dfrac{\lambda(s-r)}{(1-\lambda)w}$	(28)	$\dfrac{s}{w}$	(30)	$\dfrac{s}{w}$	(32)
Profit per unit or percentage of cost constraint	$\dfrac{r}{w}$	(29)	$\dfrac{r}{w}$	(31)	$\dfrac{r}{w}$	(33)

$$\alpha R_L + (1-\alpha)Q_L - \alpha\delta w = 0 \tag{26}$$

and

$$\alpha R_K + (1-\alpha)Q_K - \alpha\delta r = 0. \tag{27}$$

These conditions can be interpreted for any particular goal by assigning appropriate values to α and δ. By adding to (22) one of the three constraints noted above – rate of return (23), percentage of cost (24), or per unit of output (25) – an appropriate Lagrangian can be formed and conditions can be obtained for maximizing any of the goals, subject to any of the constraints.

We noted in Section 8.2 that technical efficiency within the firm requires $-\partial L/\partial K = R_K/R_L = r/w$. The efficiency conditions for solutions that combine different goals and profit constraints are summarized in Table 8.2, which shows the value of $-\partial L/\partial K = R_K/R_L$ for each combination of goal and constraint. Notice that only the rate-of-return constraint causes input inefficiencies, since for all goals under both of the other constraints the ratio of marginal products equals the input price ratio, r/w. Of course, many other constraints, such as a profit allowance per unit of labor, would result in some form of input bias; and because a profit allowance will typically be geared to the capital in use, it is difficult to avoid linking profit to capital.

Even though there is a technical input bias when revenue or output is pursued under a rate-of-return constraint, it is in the opposite direction from the profit case, and we shall speculate that it also is smaller. Notice that for the rate-of-return constraint the ratio of marginal products is set equal to s/w when revenue or output is the goal. Since

$$\frac{s}{w} = \frac{r}{w} + \frac{s-r}{w},$$

this is easily compared with the value under the profit goal of

$$\frac{r}{w} - \left(\frac{\lambda}{1-\lambda}\right)\frac{s-r}{w}.$$

When revenue or output is the goal, marginal products will be set *higher* than the ratio of prices of capital and labor, for there is then an addition to r/w (assuming $s > r$) rather than a reduction. This change in direction of bias makes intuitive sense because the generation of profit interferes with the achievement of a revenue or output objective, and using less of the input that requires profit will further either of those objectives.

Empirical estimates of λ for rate-of-return regulated firms have usually exceeded one-half, and have been closer to 0.7 or 0.8.[16] Such values would make the departure from an efficient input ratio under the profit goal, which is $-(\lambda/(1-\lambda))(s-r)/w$, greater than under the other goals, $(s-r)/w$, because it makes $\lambda/(1-\lambda) > 1$. Thus the input bias might be smaller under alternative goals, but it would still be present and in the opposite direction from the bias under the profit goal.

8.5 Dynamic elements

Thus far, rate-of-return regulation has been examined essentially under static conditions, and under the assumption that prices can be continuously and instantaneously adjusted to satisfy regulators' policies. In practice, long delays occur between a request for price change and the time it might go into effect. On one hand, this delay, which is called "regulatory lag," is a good thing, for continuous adjustment of prices to maintain a particular rate of return could rob the firm of all incentive to be efficient.[17] Fixing output prices for a period of time improves incentive because it enables owners of the regulated firm to benefit from any efficiency gains that lower costs and improve profit, at least until prices are changed. To deal with dynamic elements, however, even in a preliminary way, calls for some changes in the model.

The reason we omitted capital expense, rK, from the profit portion of (1) in Section 8.2 is that, when it is included, in the case of continuous regulation and $s = r$, there is no unique solution to the firm's problem. We would have been unable to look at the interesting benchmark case when $s = r$ without the device we used, which yielded a unique solution. The solution thus obtained for $s = r$ is the one that the firm would approach as s approached r if rK were still in the objective function. In a dynamic

---

16 See Jones (1983).
17 An early proposal for improving efficiency by deliberate use of regulatory lag was made by Baumol (1968). An analysis of the effect of regulatory lag was provided by Bailey and Coleman (1971).

formulation of the problem, this device of omitting rK will not be necessary in order to obtain a solution for $s = r$. A unique solution can more easily be obtained because the full regulatory solution is not enforced all the time. Variables to be solved in the continuous regulation problem are constant during intervals of time in the dynamic formulation. Because actual rate-of-return regulation includes intervals between rate hearings in which variables such as price are unchanged, the dynamic formulation is more like real-world circumstances.

A simple model with some dynamic properties may be obtained by dating variables with subscripts t, after inserting capital cost into the firm's profit expression. For instance, with prices that were set in period $t-1$ remaining in force in period t, the firm would seek to maximize the Lagrangian

$$G(L_t, K_t, \lambda_t) = R_t - wL_t - rK_t - \lambda_t(R_t - wL_t - sK_t)$$
$$- \mu_t[Q_t(p_{t-1}) - Q_t(L_t, K)], \tag{34}$$

where $R_t = p_{t-1}Q_t(p_{t-1})$, and $Q_t(p_{t-1})$ is the demand function. The problem in (34) emphasizes that Q_t is determined by a previously set price, p_{t-1}, by including $Q_t(p_{t-1})$ in the revenue term and then imposing the constraint $Q_t(p_{t-1}) = Q_t(L_t, K_t)$, to ensure that output matches the resulting quantity demanded.

To solve (34) one obtains, in addition to the constraints, the necessary conditions

$$Q_L = \frac{(1-\lambda_t)w}{\mu_t}$$

and

$$Q_K = \frac{r-s\lambda_t}{\mu_t},$$

which yield the technical efficiency measure

$$\frac{Q_K}{Q_L} = \frac{r}{w} - \frac{\lambda_t(s-r)}{(1-\lambda_t)w}. \tag{35}$$

Although the condition in (35) reflects a departure from the efficient outcome for $s \neq r$, just as originally was shown by AJ, the result differs in that a solution can now be obtained for the case of $s = r$ and the solution is efficient. The reason a solution can now be obtained is that output, Q, is determined by last period's price. So instead of an infinite number of L_t, K_t pairs that will deliver a rate of return of $s = r$ at different prices in the AJ model, the firm is now confined to mixtures that will produce a particular Q. There may be two such outputs that will cause $s = r$, and if we assume the one with greater capital will be chosen then we have a determinate solution.[18] Moreover, if p_{t-1} were chosen perfectly, so efficient performance just enables the firm to earn $s = r$, then there should be a unique solution.

These results are difficult to show analytically, because Lagrange multipliers are not defined at the efficient point. And this is true now even if rK is omitted from the firm's objective function. There is either an abundance of solutions (two solutions if p_{t-1} would allow excess profit at an efficient input mixture) or redundancy of constraints (if p_{t-1} allows only $s = r$ at an efficient input mixture). As s approaches r, it is no longer possible to show that the input bias generally worsens, and indeed it is now possible that the input bias will become less serious.

A problem of this sort has been elaborated more fully and solved using optimal control theory. The possibility of review by a regulatory authority (to change p_{t-1}) was also treated as a random variable (Klevorick 1973), and such review has been made more likely as profit was greater (Bawa and Sibley 1980). Although these models yielded an AJ type bias toward capital for $s > r$, the bias tended to be less serious as s approached r. There was also a bias away from capital at $s < r$ and no bias at $s = r$.

The main point to be made here is that when the firm operates according to given last period prices it will be motivated to operate more efficiently. As a rate case approaches, however, the firm's decisions can affect regulators' actions along the lines represented by the immediate action model of Sections 8.2, 8.3, and 8.4. So then the incentive to distort decisions, say, to use excessive capital when $s > r$, can arise.

8.6   Demand uncertainty

The presence of uncertainty concerning future demand, input costs, or other matters, greatly complicates the task of regulation. It complicates the task, first by making prediction difficult, and with lags even sound regulatory decisions may turn out to be ill suited to actual circumstances. Second, uncertainty makes the causes of apparently good or bad performance by a public utility difficult to uncover. As an example on the latter point, with demand uncertainty a public utility's high cost and low capacity utilization might be defended as necessary to ensure reliably high-quality service, even if demand is unexpectedly great, when it actually is due to overly optimistic demand forecasts. Demand uncertainty is also more difficult to deal with when prices cannot be altered for long periods of time.

---

[18] Strictly speaking, there is indeterminacy because if a solution exists the isoreturn circle satisfying $s = r$ can cut the isoquant satisfying $Q_t = Q_t(p_{t-1})$ in two places. In a fuller model there can be input bias (Lipman 1985; Sibley 1985).

Rate-of-return regulation under uncertainty has been modeled in different ways, and in some cases results have been found directly opposite to the AJ bias. Peles and Stein (1976) assumed that whenever the actual return exceeded the allowed return, s, a regulatory authority would immediately intervene to lower the price. This representation of the regulatory process essentially truncated the distribution of returns at the level, s, so the firm could earn less than s but not more. Perrakis (1976a, b) adopted a similar formulation with a return distribution whose truncation, as he emphasized, resulted in the firm's earning on average less than the allowed return, s. This is an awkward result that may fit actual experience, but probably not generally. Since the actual return will be less than the allowed return, s, it is possible when s is close to the cost of capital, r, for the actual realizable return to be less than r. Of course, the occurrence of an "anti-AJ" bias away from capital then would not be surprising, since the effective allowed return could actually lie below the cost of capital.

Just how to incorporate uncertainty had to be chosen in these models, and typically it was through an error term in demand, either an additive or a multiplicative error. Capital was chosen *ex ante,* and then the variable input (and sometimes even price) was chosen after demand for the period was known. Peles and Stein showed that the form of error, additive or multiplicative, would influence whether an AJ conclusion was reached. Perrakis (1976a) also showed that the AJ results did not generalize to the case of stochastic demand and regulation when modeled this way. Rau (1979) revealed some inconsistencies in the multiplicative error case, so contrasts of the alternative specifications of uncertainty are difficult to make.

If regulation is modeled so that the authority looks at expected return and does not truncate the return distribution, uncertainty is not important and AJ results can be obtained. Tschirhart (1980) modeled the regulatory situation this way, however, and obtained some departures from AJ implications, owing mainly to risk aversion of decision makers. The capital asset pricing model has been applied to the regulatory setting by Marshall, Yawitz, and Greenberg (1981). Their primary aim was to determine optimal policies, rather than to evaluate existing regulation by rate-of-return constraint, but they did find that nonoptimal values of capital resulted from the constraint. They showed that the appropriate rate of return to allow when taking risk properly into account depends on capital (and also price), so it cannot be chosen correctly without substituting an optimal level of capital for the firm's chosen level. The regulators' decisions reflecting risk and return are thus endogenous to the valuation process.

Das (1980) proved that the Averch and Johnson bias toward capital would still arise under rate-of-return regulation with stochastic demand. The distortion could even be worse under uncertainty. As pointed out by Crew and Kleindorfer (1979b, pp. 140–3), greater capacity tends to add to service reliability by making supply more likely to be adequate to meet realized demand. To the extent that service reliability is unregulated, the firm might set its capacity high for the purpose of maximizing profit and might use service reliability as an excuse. In the extreme case of inelastic demand noted in Section 8.3, for instance, it might be profitable for the firm to provide extensive excess capacity, and yet it is difficult for the regulator to determine how much of that capacity is really excessive. Any capital might conceivably be used if demand is sufficiently high, and the possibility of use, even if remote, may keep the capital from being classified as wasteful.

Let us illustrate the input bias in a model that contains stochastic demand. Here quantity, through capital and labor decisions, and also price will be set before demand is known and they will not be altered after it is revealed. The demand function is $q = h(P, u)$, where u is a random term. Define M so that $h(p, M) = f(K, L)$, where f is the production function and K and L are capital and labor inputs. Then profit can be expressed as

$$\pi_1 = P \cdot h(p, u) - wL - rK, \quad \text{for } \alpha \le u \le M,$$

$$\pi_2 = P \cdot f(K, L) - wL - rK, \quad \text{for } M \le u \le \beta.$$

Following Das (1980), we define utility of profit, $U(\cdot)$, and express the expected utility of profit goal as

$$\text{Max } H(P, K, L) = \int_\alpha^M U(\pi_1)\phi(u)\, du + U(\pi_2)\int_M^\beta \phi(u)\, du$$

subject to the regulatory constraint

$$P \cdot f(K, L) - wL \le sK.$$

The main conditions for a maximum are

$$P \cdot f_K \cdot U'(\pi_2) \int_M^\beta \phi(u)\, du - r \cdot E[U'(\pi)] + \lambda(s - P \cdot f_K) = 0, \tag{36}$$

$$P \cdot f_L \cdot U'(\pi_2) \int_M^\beta \phi(u)\, du - w \cdot E[U'(\pi)] + \lambda(w - P \cdot f_L) = 0, \tag{37}$$

$$\int_\alpha^M U'(\pi_1)(h + P \cdot h_P)\phi(u)\, du + U'(\pi_2) \cdot f \int_M^\beta \phi(u)\, du + \lambda f = 0, \tag{38}$$

plus the constraint. By rearranging (37) we find that

$$\frac{P \cdot f_L}{w} \left[U'(\pi_2) \int_M^\beta \phi(u) \, du - \lambda \right] = E[U'(\pi)] - \lambda. \tag{39}$$

Das (1980) proved that the right-hand side of (39) is positive:

$$E[U'(\pi)] - \lambda > 0.$$

Since p, w, and f_L are all positive, we must therefore have on the left-hand side of (39)

$$U'(\pi_2) \int_M^\beta \phi(u) \, du - \lambda > 0. \tag{40}$$

But (39) implies from (37) that

$$\frac{1}{f} \int_\alpha^M U'(\pi_1)(h + P \cdot h_P)\phi(u) \, du < 0. \tag{41}$$

All the left-hand-side terms of (41) are surely positive except $h + P \cdot h_P$, so that term must be negative. The term, $h + P \cdot h_P$, when divided by the negative term, h_P, equals marginal revenue. We thus have to conclude that marginal revenue will always be positive. So once again we find that rate-of-return regulation cannot force the firm to operate where demand is inelastic.

Under uncertainty it is also possible for capital to be wasted. To see this, replace the capital variable, K, with $K + K^*$, where K^* is defined as capital having zero marginal product. By solving the maximization problem, one can test whether $K^* > 0$, which would indicate capital waste. On introducing $K + K^*$ the same necessary conditions are obtained, but in addition there is $\partial H/\partial K^* = 0$. If $K^* > 0$, then from this new necessary condition $r \cdot E[U'(\pi)] - \lambda s = 0$. On substituting this condition into (36), and recalling that $U'(\pi) \int_H^\beta \phi(u) \, du - \lambda > 0$ from (39), it is possible to infer that $f_K = 0$. If K^* is used, it must be no less productive than K, and $K^* > 0$ may appear in a solution as long as $f_K = 0$. Thus capital that has zero marginal product may be used under uncertainty, just as Westfield (1965) showed under certainty.

8.7   Input price uncertainty and automatic adjustment clauses

When output prices are kept fixed without continuous adjustment, so that the dynamic problem of Section 8.5 arises, and in addition if input prices are uncertain, then added risk is created for the firm. Changes in input prices cannot be reflected in output prices, so profit will be affected. This form of risk does not arise to such a degree in unregulated markets, because the costs of all firms are affected by input price changes so market prices also respond. Delays in regulated output price changes combined with input price fluctuations create risks unique to regulated public utilities.

One means of lessening the added risk for the firm due to regulatory lag is the automatic adjustment clause. An automatic adjustment clause is a set of rules for adjusting output prices in response to input price changes. Their purpose is to prevent the firm's profit from being considerably altered by the input price change, and to do that through an output price adjustment that does not require a formal rate hearing. Such adjustment clauses are especially common for the fuel input in regulated electric utilities. However, they do not always ensure an efficient outcome (Baron and De Bondt 1979, 1981). The harshest criticism of them is that they usurp regulatory commission responsibility and allow cost inefficiencies to be translated into higher prices for consumers to pay.

The design of an automatic adjustment clause is not a simple task, and such clauses will almost certainly have some undesirable consequences (Schmidt 1981). For example, electric utility fuel adjustment clauses are of two main types: fixed-heat-rate and variable-heat-rate, the latter being more common.[19] Variable-heat-rate clauses allow the utility to use its adjusted fuel mixture as a basis for changing output price as fuel prices change, whereas fixed-heat-rate clauses adhere to a predetermined fuel mixture. The variable clause thus allows the firm more scope for altering output price through its fuel mix decisions. It may even invite perverse responses such as using *more* of the input when its price has risen, because that will allow a greater rise in output price. Scott (1979) showed that variable-heat-rate clauses produce a bias toward fuel use and lower the variance of profit. Scott also pointed out that the incentive of a manager to search for lower-priced fuel is weakened by a fuel adjustment clause, and he found evidence of higher fuel prices being paid by firms operating under fuel adjustment clauses.

Baron and De Bondt (1981) have provided a general analysis of fuel adjustment clauses in a principal–agent framework, where the inability of the regulator (principal) to observe the firm's (agent's) range of possible actions can lead to inefficiency. They find adverse effects for choice of technology as well as for fuel type chosen and fuel price actually paid, and propose guidelines for moderating firm incentives and sharing risks. Two-part prices can be useful for this purpose, by affecting the incentive for marginal effort within firms.

8.8   Empirical evidence

At least eight major studies have empirically examined whether there is AJ bias in input choices of electric utilities. Studies by Spann (1974), Baron

---

19 See Salomon Brothers (1973). The role of fuel adjustment clauses in gas and electricity price increases is traced in a congressional study (U.S. Senate 1977).

and Taggart (1977), and Pescatrice and Trapani (1980) relied on data from entire regulated firms, and thus were exposed to problems of aggregating vastly different technologies and different asset vintages and price-level valuations. Studies by Courville (1974) and Boyles (1976) focused on a single type of plant but assumed a homogeneous production function, despite estimates by Belinfante (1969) and Christensen and Green (1976) suggesting that the production function for electricity is not homogeneous (or even homothetic). Only a strong form of the AJ hypothesis can be tested within a single type of plant, for there is much greater scope for the bias to be realized in choosing a mixture of plants of different capital intensity than within one specific production technique. But production function estimation cannot be undertaken as effectively over a range of plant types to test that weaker, and more general, form of the AJ hypothesis.

The production function studies have found effects on capital intensity due to the type of fuel used (more capital is needed for a plant to burn coal than oil) and the construction requirements due to climate, but only Graham (1976) and Jones (1983) controlled for such effects. Graham pointed out that geographic patterns in the tightness of regulation, combined with this omission, would tend wrongly to confirm the AJ hypothesis. Simultaneous equations bias probably was present in the Graham study, and also in Baron and Taggart, Courville, and Spann; that problem was avoided by Petersen (1975a) only by making an untenable assumption that output was fixed exogenously. All used current or recent input prices except Jones, who relied also on forecasts and trends of input prices that would be considered by those building new facilities.

Most of these studies found support for the AJ hypothesis, at least as to the direction of its effect. Boyles did not, but he used data from the period of the great electrical conspiracy. Graham also did not, but his results were almost significant. Baron and Taggart (1977) found an undercapitalization bias, but they used an unusual model that would be difficult to estimate reliably. Jones, who attempted explicitly to overcome the shortcomings of previous studies, found strong support for a bias toward capital within the sample he studied of new base-load generating facilities, although the effect of the bias on cost was not large.

There are other sources of evidence about the capital bias. One is the rare use of peak-load pricing in the United States, relative to European countries where it is common and rate-of-return regulation is not used (Mitchell, Manning, and Acton 1978). Peak-load pricing has been shown to conserve capacity and lower capital needs in France (Balasko 1976). Gegax and Tschirhart (1984) also found that privately owned, rate-of-return regulated private firms were less willing than publicly owned firms to own capacity jointly through power pools, presumably because it would reduce the capital base used to justify profit. Moreover, the regulated firms that would participate tended to be operating in hostile regulatory climates where returns might not exceed the cost of capital, so adding to the rate base would not be profitable.

8.9   Summary

Rate-of-return regulation began as a means of determining, by reference to the amount of capital used, an appropriate profit for the firm to earn. But since the firm can choose the amount of capital it uses, linking profit to capital introduces a perverse incentive. If the allowed return exceeds the cost of capital (but is less than an unregulated monopoly could earn) and regulatory decisions are immediate, the firm will want to use more than an efficient amount of capital; if the allowed return is lower than the cost of capital then it will want to use less. This distortion in input choices arises because decisions regarding other inputs are made according to a monopolistic decision rule. Capital is expanded to raise output toward the socially optimal level, but relative to all other inputs it is used inefficiently. This tendency to use more capital relative to other inputs is potentially important because even under ideal conditions capital tends to be enormous in regulated industries.

Extreme forms of capital input distortion are possible. Like a monopolist, the rate-of-return regulated firm wishes to operate only where demand is elastic, where marginal revenue is positive. If the social optimum occurs in an inelastic region of demand, the profit-seeking rate-of-return regulated firm will not want to operate there. The firm is motivated to waste capital or pay high prices for capital in an effort to justify a higher price in the elastic region of demand instead. This motivation to avoid the inelastic region of demand exists also when demand is uncertain; then the firm can use its obligation to be prepared for extremely high (if unlikely) demand as an excuse for using excessive capital.[20]

Dynamic properties of rate-of-return regulation can serve to reduce the perverse incentive that it fosters. Usually there are long intervals between rate cases, and even after a rate change is proposed a lengthy period called "regulatory lag" passes before a decision on the proposal can have effect. During these intervals no change in price is possible. Since losses will not be restored and profits will not be confiscated during that period, the firm has incentive to operate efficiently. It is only with respect to the use of the record at the time of the next rate case that the firm is motivated to behave strategically. To incur more costs in an effort to win a rate increase – for

---

20 To the extent quality of service is related to capital intensity, quality will also be (inefficiently) high (Spence 1975).

example, from purchasing excessive capital – requires a current sacrifice in funds. So the firm will not do it unless later gains justify it.

Long intervals with constant output prices will expose the firm to input price fluctuations as a source of risk. Because fuel prices are known to fluctuate, many regulatory commissions have adopted automatic fuel price adjustment clauses that allow changes in the prices of fuel to affect output price according to preset formulas. These arrangements can cause the firm to favor fuel as an input and can weaken the firm's incentive to search for the lowest priced fuel. But they also moderate the added risk that rigid output prices otherwise would cause.

Thus the institution of rate-of-return regulation, which was originally conceived only to determine a profit allowance, is not well designed as a genuine instrument of social regulation. Its procedures cannot reliably motivate the firm to operate where demand is inelastic, so a social optimum in that region of demand may not even be pursued. However, the dynamic properties of the process invite some efficiency incentive, and the generally good intentions of regulated firms and regulatory agencies may prevent grossly perverse outcomes that the institutional mechanism itself could elicit.

Questions

Here we shall pursue one continuing problem and give answers along the way. Try to work out each question before reading the answer. This problem is something like an instructive puzzle, and is quite difficult to solve.

It is obvious from a comparison of the regulated firm's marginal conditions for labor and capital (see Table 8.1) that, when regulated by rate-of-return constraint, the firm continues to choose labor according to a monopolist's decision rule while it uses more capital than a monopolist would. In order to alter this schizophrenic tendency in its input choices, consider a subsidy that would invite the firm to expand its use of noncapital inputs, which will be represented as labor. This subsidy proposal is not likely to be adopted, but thinking about it can help you understand the effects of rate-of-return regulation.

Derive necessary conditions for a solution under a scheme that taxes capital at T per dollar of capital, K, to pay for a subsidy (at S per dollar of labor, in amount L at wage w) to labor, which is assumed to be the only other input. Assume that demand is everywhere elastic, and that the allowed return, s, exceeds the cost of capital, r. Assume that the regulatory commission does *not* impose on one firm the requirement that labor subsidy (SwL) equal capital tax (TK); but that the commission chooses S and T with that aim in mind. (Finding operational necessary conditions to this problem is difficult and will require some cleverness.)

8.1. Solve for T and S. Can you obtain solution values in terms only of known parameters?

8.2. If the commission errs in setting T and S, so $SwL \neq TK$, who bears the consequences?

8.3. Can a tax on capital be used instead of a subsidy to all other inputs?

8.4. Can the tax and subsidy scheme induce the firm to operate where demand is inelastic?

Answers

8.1. Let S be the subsidy per dollar of labor expense and let T be the tax per dollar of capital value. Remember that demand is elastic, and that $s > r$. The firm would attempt to maximize

$$\Pi = R - (1 - S)wL - (r + T)K.$$

If the regulatory agency also constrains the firm to rate of return, s, but ignores payment of the tax and subsidy, the firm must satisfy

$$R - wL - sK \leq 0.$$

Thus, the firm subject to the tax and subsidy as well as the rate-of-return constraint would seek to maximize the Lagrangian function

$$H(L, K, \lambda) = R - (1 - S)wL - (r + t)K - \lambda(R - wL - sK). \tag{Q1}$$

The necessary conditions for a maximum of (Q1) are

$$R_L = \frac{(1 - \lambda - S)w}{(1 - \lambda)}, \tag{Q2}$$

$$R_K = \frac{r + T - \lambda s}{(1 - \lambda)}, \tag{Q3}$$

and

$$R - wL - sK = 0. \tag{Q4}$$

Now suppose that S and T values are chosen to break even on tax and subsidy payments by satisfying

$$SwL - TK = 0. \tag{Q5}$$

A trick to obtaining an operational solution is to adopt the modest aim of making

$$|\partial L/\partial K| = s/w, \tag{Q6}$$

rather than $|\partial L/\partial K| = r/w$. Using (Q2), (Q3), (Q5), and (Q6), values of S and T then can be obtained that do not contain the unknown λ. They will take the form

$$S = \frac{(s - r)K}{(wL + sK)} \tag{Q7}$$

and

$$T = \frac{(s - r)sL}{(wL + sK)}. \tag{Q8}$$

These values are not ideal because they achieve an efficiency level of $\partial L/\partial K = s/w > r/w$. (This is precisely the input bias that will be obtained under total revenue or output goals shown in Section 8.4.) The tax and subsidy scheme embodied in (Q7) and (Q8) essentially converts rate-of-return regulation to "cost-plus" regulation, or to regulation that allows profit as a percentage of revenue.

It is possible to implement the subsidy and the tax rates defined by equations (Q7) and (Q8). The unknown λ does not appear in either expression, and each is a product of $(s-r)$ and some fraction involving the firm's costs. The regulatory agency would have to estimate an allowed rate of return s separate from the cost of capital r, and in present-day adversary proceedings that estimation would be difficult; but it is not impossible. The authority does not have to observe the marginal rate of technical substitution. Moreover, the size of S relative to T is very well defined; S is to T as K is to wL. So the crucial relative magnitude of the subsidy and the tax rates can be determined reliably.

To illustrate the tax and subsidy scheme, suppose the capital rate-base of a firm is three times its annual revenues, that annual revenues typically are divided so that 30 percent go to capital and 70 percent to other inputs, and that the allowed rate of return is 1 percent above the cost of capital so $s-r=0.01$. Substituting such values into equations (Q7) and (Q8) will yield $S=0.03$ and $T=0.007$. If regulatory authorities anticipate a reduction in capital relative to other inputs in response to introduction of the tax and subsidy plan, they initially can set a slightly lower value of S and a slightly higher T, being guided by the modifications they expect the firm to make in K and in wL as they in turn affect S and T in equations (Q7) and (Q8). Once the transition is accomplished to the tax and subsidy policy, the values can be chosen more easily because further responses in K and wL will be small.

8.2.   If the regulatory commission errs, so that tax and subsidy proceeds are not equal, the effect of the error will be borne by the firm or firms in the commission's jurisdiction. (It is possible to design schemes so the commission, or the public, bears this risk. See Sherman 1976.) Specific S and T parameters would have to be assigned ahead of time and any imbalance between what actually is due to, or owing from, a firm would have to be paid. For if a firm knew that its own tax and subsidy payments automatically would balance, it could ignore the tax and subsidy altogether. (That is why the constraint, $SwL-TK=0$, is not used in problem (Q1).) Even the knowledge that its payments would be made to balance over time might undercut the incentive effects of the tax-subsidy scheme. Where possible, the same values of S and T should apply to a group of firms so any one firm would not expect that its own tax and subsidy payments would automatically be equal.

8.3.   The subsidy to labor, and not the tax on capital, is crucial for leading the firm to increase the marginal rate of technical substitution between inputs, $|\partial L/\partial K|$. It really is the allowed rate of return s that determines the profit-maximizing solution for the regulated firm, rather than capital cost r or $r+T$, and the tax rate T simply affects profitability at the solution. To see this, set $S=0$ in equation (Q1) and consider the necessary conditions with a tax but no subsidy. Equations (Q2) and (Q4) could be solved for L and

K, and they involve s but not r or T. For given s and r, any change in T in equation (Q3) will affect only the value of the Lagrange multiplier λ; it will not change the solution values of L and K.

8.4. The tax and subsidy scheme cannot reliably move the firm to an efficient point in the inelastic region of demand. Tilting the total cost surface, which is what the tax and subsidy scheme will accomplish, can create two local constrained profit maxima, one that is capital intensive and one that is not capital intensive. Recall the total revenue surface described in footnote 10, with labor and capital inputs determining isoquants that were converted to isorevenue levels. Descending into the "valley" of that total revenue hill where demand is inelastic will not be as profitable as operating inefficiently, but close to the top ridge of the revenue hill where demand is unit elastic. There the rate of return constraint will meet the revenue hill at a point farthest above the cost plane. We have already noted how the tax and subsidy can convert rate-of-return regulation to "cost-plus" or "percentage-of-revenue" regulation, and in those cases the incentive of the firm to raise cost rather than move into an inelastic demand region is well known.

CHAPTER 9

Pricing under rate-of-return regulation

9.1 Introduction

Rate-of-return regulation of a profit-seeking firm not only invites an inefficient choice of inputs to produce any given level of output, it may also cause output levels to be chosen inefficiently. Much attention has been accorded the technical input distortion discussed in Chapter 8. We focus in this chapter on the second distortion, the inefficient output levels resulting from nonoptimal relative prices for multiple outputs. Our approach is to see whether firms will adopt second-best welfare-maximizing prices when seeking profit or other goals while subject to profit regulation. We shall find that pricing efficiency is not reliably motivated in firms regulated under *Hope* guidelines.

An early analysis of rate-of-return regulation by Wellisz (1963) stressed the resulting economic inefficiency in pricing, specifically between peak and off-peak prices. Averch and Johnson (1962) also described a pricing distortion that rate-of-return regulation might induce in a multiproduct firm. Bailey (1973) extended Wellisz's peak-load pricing analysis and asked whether input distortions beyond those due to inefficient pricing would arise and whether inefficient pricing between peak and off-peak periods would result if firms sought to maximize output instead of profit. Waverman (1975) has since confirmed that, along with peak and off-peak pricing distortions, the Averch and Johnson (1962) type of bias between capital and other inputs would also result. Needy (1975) provided a systematic description of output distortions in the profit-maximizing, rate-of-return regulated firm. Pricing distortions due to both monopolistic reliance on demand elasticities and bias toward capital were set out in Bailey and White (1974), Eckel (1983), Sherman and Visscher (1979, 1982a), and Srinagesh (1986). But the general failure of rate-of-return regulation to deal with monopolistic urges to discriminate in price is still not fully appreciated.

In Section 9.2 assumptions are made to simplify the welfare-maximizing problem as a standard for later comparisons. Pricing solutions are defined that are quasi-efficient in that they maximize a welfare objective subject to alternative profit constraints, and then solutions under the profit goal are obtained for comparison under the same constraints. The inefficiencies in pricing rules of profit-seeking regulated firms are illustrated in Section 9.3. Peak-load and nonuniform prices are treated in Sections 9.4 and 9.5. Dynamic elements are introduced in Section 9.6. Empirical evidence on pricing is considered in Section 9.7. Section 9.8 contains a summary.

9.2 Capital bias and monopolistic elements in pricing

To focus as directly as possible on pricing incentives, we assume a technology with constant marginal productivity for each of two input categories: capital and all other inputs. This technology invites the use of inputs in fixed proportions, and rules out the Averch–Johnson input bias as long as demands are always price elastic, which we shall assume.[1] Of course, none of these assumptions has general practical relevance, but they are not extreme and all are helpful in allowing analysis of pricing inefficiencies because they prevent input inefficiencies from intruding.

Consider the enterprise that seeks to maximize welfare when constrained to a certain profit level. Solving that imaginary enterprise's pricing problem yielded second-best pricing rules in Chapter 5. We simplify them here with the constant marginal productivity assumption, and we also elaborate them to include several other forms of profit constraint that invite different biases.[2] Given these forms of the profit constraint, we find a second-best welfare-maximizing price for each case.

Let consumer welfare be represented simply by the consumer surplus from quantities of goods or services, Q_i's, as $S = S(Q_1, ..., Q_n)$. We assume that cross-price elasticities of demand are zero here in order to keep solutions simple, and because no surprising results arise from nonzero cross-elasticities. Our representation of welfare accepts the current income distribution; it implicitly weights each consumer in the social welfare function according to the inverse of that consumer's marginal utility of income, so a dollar of additional benefit has the same impact on social welfare whoever receives it. Social welfare will be consumer surplus, S, plus total profit, Π, or equivalently consumer surplus, S, plus total revenue, R, less total cost, C. One consequence of assuming this consumer surplus representation of welfare is that $\partial(CS + TR)/\partial Q_i = p_i$. We add a

---

[1] In trying to avoid an inelastic region of the demand curve, we know from Chapter 8 that a profit-regulated firm can be very wasteful, and, with the fixed proportions, technology capital waste need never cause a negative marginal product of capital. See Westfield (1965), Needy (1975), and Sherman (1972b). The input bias is small with a rate-of-return constraint if the allowed rate of return is close to the cost of capital and the firm's goal is maximum sales or output. See Bailey and Malone (1970) and also Crew and Kleindorfer (1979a).

[2] The arbitrary profit limit yields a solution with the least distortion. Since any reasonable constraint might be defended as most workable or feasible in creating a second-best outcome, we examine several.

constraint on profit and seek to obtain a second-best optimum.[3] Society thus faces the Lagrangian

$$G(Q_1, \ldots, Q_n, \lambda_0) = CS + TR - TC + \lambda_0(\Pi - \bar{\Pi}), \tag{1}$$

where $\Pi = R(Q_1, \ldots, Q_n) - TC(Q_1, \ldots, Q_n)$ is profit, $\bar{\Pi}$ is the fixed profit limit, and λ_0 is the Lagrange multiplier.

Differentiating (1) with respect to Q_i and setting the result equal to zero yields

$$\partial G/\partial Q_i = p_i - TC_{Q_i} + \lambda_0(p_i + Q_i \,\partial p_i/\partial Q_i - TC_{Q_i}) = 0$$
$$\text{for } i = 1, \ldots, n. \tag{2}$$

Letting $C_{Q_i} = MC_i$, we obtain from (2) the implicit pricing rules,

$$(p_i - MC_i)/p_i = \lambda_0/(1 + \lambda_0)\eta_i \quad \text{for } i = 1, \ldots, n, \tag{3}$$

where, for the ith product or service, we have price elasticity of demand defined as

$$\eta_i = -(\partial Q_i/\partial p_i)(p_i/Q_i). \tag{4}$$

The second-best optimum price can also be represented as

$$p_i = MC_i/(1 - (1/\eta_i)\lambda_0/(1 + \lambda_0)) \quad \text{for } i = 1, \ldots, n. \tag{5}$$

Observe that (3) (or (5)) is a monopolistic pricing rule modified so that elasticities are overstated.[4] For if $\lambda_0/(1 + \lambda_0)$ were replaced by 1, (3) would be the well-known pricing rule of an unconstrained, profit-maximizing monopolist. The value of λ_0 is such that for every i,

$$\lambda_0 = (p_i - MC_i)/(MC_i - MR_i), \tag{6}$$

where $MR_i = p_i + Q_i \,\partial p_i/\partial Q_i$ is marginal revenue. Since we can expect the solution value of Q_i to exceed the monopoly output level, standard assumptions about cost and demand make $MC_i > MR_i$. We shall also confine attention to cases where $p_i > MC_i$, either because of scale economies or a positive $\bar{\Pi}$ in the profit constraint (but $\bar{\Pi}$ is less than the monopoly profit level). Thus, although we present here no solution value of λ_0, we know from these relations that $\lambda_0 > 0$, which means $\lambda_0/(1 + \lambda_0) < 1$, and so the right-hand side of (3) will be reduced from what it would be for a

---

[3] Without any profit constraint, of course, the optimal price will equal marginal cost in each case. This is clear from equation (3) below, which requires $p_i = MC_i$ if the Lagrange multiplier is zero because the constraint is not binding.

[4] Recall that Boiteux (1956) first demonstrated how in a welfare-maximizing enterprise all elasticities of demand are to be overstated by a constant that is chosen so the budget constraint is just satisfied. See Section 5.2 (and Baumol and Bradford 1970) for a review of literature related to the problem.

monopolist. Essentially, the profit-constrained, welfare-maximizing enterprise overstates demand elasticity by the same constant, $(1+\lambda_0)/\lambda_0$, for every i.

The same form for the pricing rule will follow when the profit limit is cast in other terms, such as a rate of return on capital or a percentage of revenue. So that we may identify effects of constraints on input use, let $TC = wV + rK$, where K is capital measured in numeraire terms and r is the cost of capital, V represents all other inputs with w as their index price, and $V = \Sigma Q_i V_{Q_i}$ and $K = \Sigma Q_i K_{Q_i}$.[5] Now suppose that profit is constrained in any of these additional ways:

1. *Rate of return on capital:*
   $TR - wV - sK = 0$,
   where s is the rate of return on capital allowed as profit.
2. *Profit as a percentage of total cost:*
   $TR - TC(1+g) = 0$,
   where g is the percentage of cost allowed as profit.
3. *Profit per unit of output:*
   $TR - TC - \Sigma_{i=1}^{n} Q_i h_i = 0$,
   where h_i is the profit allowed per unit of the ith product sold.

The socially optimal prices corresponding to these various forms of profit constraint can be obtained as they were in (5) above. They are:

1. *Rate of return on capital:*
   $p_i = [MC_i + (s-r)K_{Q_i}/(1+\lambda_1)]/[1 - \lambda_1/(1+\lambda_1)\eta_i]$,
   for $i = 1, \ldots, n$.
2. *Profit as a percentage of total cost:*
   $p_i = MC_i(1 + \lambda_2 g/(1+\lambda_2))/[1 - \lambda_2/(1+\lambda_2)\eta_i]$,
   for $i = 1, \ldots, n$.
3. *Profit per unit of output:*
   $p_i = [MC_i + h_i\lambda_3/(1-\lambda_3)]/[1 - \lambda_3/(1-\lambda_3)\eta_i]$,
   for $i = 1, \ldots, n$.

All of these problems and solutions share the same general features. The objective is always $CS + \Pi$ where $\Pi = TR - TC$. The constraint is always of the form $TR - TC - F$, where F is an added term that may contain TR or Q or TC, or some portion of TR or TC, and the solution price for the ith product always can be put in the form

[5] We assume V_{Q_i} and K_{Q_i} are constant. This assumption is not necessary here, but it greatly simplifies the analysis by making it unnecessary to maximize with respect to V and K; solution values of V and K can be determined easily from solution Q_i's when V_{Q_i} and K_{Q_i} are constant. In addition, this technology avoids input bias in producing any given output when demand is price elastic.

Table 9.1. *Summary of welfare-maximizing prices where*
$p_i = (\alpha MC_i + \gamma)/(1 - \beta/\eta_i)$

Constraint	α	γ	β
Fixed profit limit	1	0	$\dfrac{\lambda_0}{1+\lambda_0}$
Rate of return on capital	1	$\dfrac{\lambda_1(s-r)K_{Q_i}}{1+\lambda_1}$	$\dfrac{\lambda_1}{1+\lambda_1}$
Profit as a percentage of total cost	$\dfrac{1+\lambda_2(1+g)}{1+\lambda_2}$	0	$\dfrac{\lambda_2}{1+\lambda_2}$
Profit per unit of output	1	$\dfrac{\lambda_3 h_i}{1+\lambda_3}$	$\dfrac{\lambda_3}{1+\lambda_3}$

$$p_i = (\alpha MC_i + \gamma)/(1 - \beta/\eta_i). \tag{7}$$

The values of p_i that maximize welfare under the various constraints are summarized in Table 9.1 according to values of the parameters α, γ, and β of the form given in (7). Marginal cost may be modified in some way though α and/or γ, because the various constraints invite departures from ideal efficiency. When profit is constrained to some percentage of revenue, marginal cost is not distorted, but elasticity is adjusted in a different way. In general, however, through β the price is set as if demand is more elastic than it really is, as the simplest welfare-maximizing rule (equation (3)) required.

When $\lambda > 0$,[6] the α and γ terms in Table 9.1 that differ from 1 and 0 bring slight overstatements of marginal cost. Notice in particular that with return on capital constrained, the γ term adds more to marginal cost, thus raising price, as the marginal capital requirement K_{Q_i}, is greater. There is a bias here *against* capital, because by increasing the profit allowance its use tends to reduce welfare.[7] Constraining profit to be some percentage of total cost, or some amount per unit output, also brings a price farther above marginal cost to discourage high-cost products or high outputs

---

[6] We have already shown that with $p_i > MC_i$, λ_0 always should be greater than zero, and similar arguments apply to Lagrange multipliers in the other cases. For λ_1 through λ_4 the numerator has the same form as λ_0's numerator. The denominators differ from λ_0's by an extra term but that term only helps to ensure that the denominator is positive, so λ_1 to λ_4 will be positive just as λ_0 was. Let us also note that in all these cases $\lambda < 1$ as long as $MC_i - MR_i > p_i - MC_i$. This latter inequality should be met at the solution under a constraint that is well chosen to promote welfare, for it will tend to be satisfied when price is closer to the welfare optimum than to the monopoly level.

[7] See Section 8.4.

Table 9.2. *Summary of constrained profit-maximizing prices where* $p_i = (\alpha MC_i + \gamma)/(1 - \beta/\eta_i)$

Constraint	α	γ	β
Rate of return on capital	1	$\dfrac{-\lambda_1(s-r)K_{Q_i}}{1-\lambda_1}$	1
Profit as a percentage of total cost	$\dfrac{1-\lambda_2(1+g)}{1-\lambda_2}$	0	1
Profit per unit of output	1	$\dfrac{-\lambda_3 h_i}{1-\lambda_3}$	1

when they are the basis for profit requirements that reduce welfare. In all cases, β is simply $\lambda/(1+\lambda)$, a constant that serves to overstate elasticity and thus reduce its influence from the level of monopolistic markups over marginal costs.[8]

Although it defines a desirable outcome, consumer welfare is not a goal that can be given direct operational meaning. We turn, then, to consider another goal, the profit of the multiproduct enterprise, which we presume exists in public utilities. As soon as the abstract welfare goal is replaced by the profit objective, the firm's tendency to overstate elasticity vanishes, and with it goes the tendency to approach efficient price structures. Rather than overstate demand elasticities to reduce markups over costs in setting prices, the profit-regulated firm turns out to be influenced by the full demand elasticities, just as a monopolist is. And this influence may produce inefficient price structures whenever goods or services with different elasticities can be distinguished by the rate-of-return regulated firm.

It is a simple matter to delete consumer surplus from the Lagrangian (1), leaving profit alone as the objective, and to append one of the constraints on profit already discussed. Of course, it makes no sense to maximize profit while holding profit at the fixed level, $\bar{\Pi}$, so more interesting problems will include the rate-of-return, percentage-of-cost, or profit-per-unit constraint. The profit-maximizing pricing rule that results for each good under each constraint is given in Table 9.2. It is possible to show that all λ's lie between 0 and 1, which ensures that every combination of α and γ in a pricing rule will serve to understate marginal cost. Since β

---

[8] If profit is set at some percentage of total revenue, no distortion of marginal cost is introduced ($\alpha = 1$ and $\gamma = 0$), but the β term that alters the influence of demand elasticity on price is modified by the element $[1 - f(1 - \eta_i)]$, which raises β where elasticity is greater. It thereby works to reduce revenue, and with it the profit requirement that lessens welfare.

always equals one, the cost understatement is the *only* means of lowering price; no overstatement of demand elasticity harnesses the monopolist's discriminating tendency now.

Information about the range of values for λ's allows us to interpret the pricing rules of Table 9.2 to see how marginal costs are understated. With profit as objective and $0 < \lambda < 1$, α and γ will always lower marginal costs for the purpose of pricing, because $0 < \alpha < 1$ and $\gamma < 0$. With the rate-of-return constraint, the understatement of marginal cost is greater where marginal capital need, K_{Q_i}, is greater. With the profit-per-unit-of-output constraint, the understatement varies with the allowed unit profit, h_i. With the profit-as-a-percentage-of-total-cost constraint, there is a percentage understatement in marginal cost that depends on the profit percentage, g. If the price elasticities of demand for the firm's various products or services differ, the profit-seeking firm regulated by any of the profit constraints shown (including the rate-of-return constraint) may cross-subsidize through its understatement of marginal costs. Where η_i is higher, $1 - 1/\eta_i$ will approach one, so the understatement of marginal cost may dominate, leading to a price below *true* marginal cost. But where η_i is lower, the markup above even understated marginal cost might produce a generous profit contribution over *true* marginal cost. Although constrained in the amount of profit it can earn, the firm will follow the monopolistic practice of earning more profit where demand is less elastic. These cross-subsidization incentives arise from the influence of demand elasticity under all goals in Table 9.2.

9.3   Illustrations of pricing bias

To illustrate the pricing practices implied by the results in Table 9.2, let us consider simple examples involving two goods, one example stressing the effect of a capital bias on price and the other the effect of demand elasticity. We shall assume these demands and costs are independent of one another and that consumption of neither good affects other activities importantly. So that we can see the effect of capital on prices, we assume in Figure 9.1 that demands for two goods, Q_1 in panel (a) and Q_2 in panel (b), are similar but that the costs differ; the marginal capital required to produce a unit of the first product, k_1, is greater than the capital, k_2, required to produce one unit of the second product. The (constant) marginal cost is also higher for the first product. These differences make the allowed profit increase more with output of the first product, as comparison of allowed profits shown in the lower sections of the two panels reveals. The firm regulated only by an overall constraint on total profit can

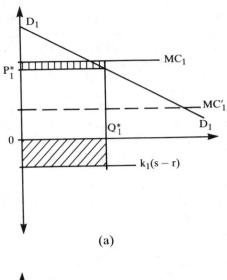

(a)

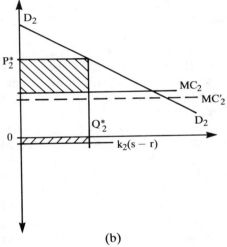

(b)

Figure 9.1. How capital affects price.

be expected to take full advantage of this effect on allowed profit of producing Q_1. It does so in Figure 9.1 by choosing a large Q_1^*, even causing a loss, and using the handsome profit allowance thereby created to justify high profit earned on Q_2 at the price P_2^*.

Since it brings a profit benefit, the allowed profit from producing any good might reasonably be viewed by the rate-of-return regulated firm as a reduction in that good's marginal cost. In any case, the pricing rule in Table 9.2 for the rate-of-return regulated profit-seeking firm is $p_i = [MC_i - \lambda_1(s-r)K_{Q_i}/(1-\lambda_1)]/(1-1/\eta_i)$, where $\lambda_1(s-r)K_{Q_i}/(1-\lambda_1)$ is clearly a reduction in marginal cost (see Callen, Mathewson, and Mohring 1976). In Figure 9.1, implicit marginal costs are represented as MC_1' and MC_2' and in keeping with the greater marginal capital need of Q_1, MC_1' embodies a greater reduction from MC_1 than MC_2' does from MC_2. In terms of marginal costs adjusted thus, the firm maximizes profit as shown in Figure 9.1, essentially by subsidizing Q_1 and making a high profit on Q_2.

Now to see the effects of demand elasticity, assume that the two products have the same marginal cost and marginal capital requirements but differ in demand elasticities. In Figure 9.2, $MC_1 = MC_2$ and $k_1 = k_2$, but the demand for Q_1 in panel (a) is less elastic than the demand for Q_2 in panel (b). The lower shaded areas of both panels indicate that one unit of each product adds the same amount to allowed profit. More profit can be earned from less elastic demand $D_1 D_1$ than from $D_2 D_2$, however, and the regulated firm will take advantage of that fact. The rate-of-return regulated firm's solution prices can be seen as profit-maximizing ones where marginal revenue equals implicit marginal cost, $MC_1' = MC_2'$, which is lower than true marginal cost because of the rate-of-return constraint. Notice that in Figure 9.2 the firm sets a very profitable price P_1^* on Q_1 and uses the output of Q_2 mainly to generate allowed profit in order that profit from Q_1 can be retained. Indeed, in the Figure 9.2 example a loss is sustained on Q_2 in order that more profit from the sale of Q_1 can be retained.

We know immediately that solutions reached in Figures 9.1 and 9.2 cannot maximize welfare, because in each case one price is below marginal cost. A price below marginal cost might conceivably add to welfare when some external benefit can be claimed or when one such subsidized product stands in a strong complementary relationship to another.[9] Here such interrelations have been ruled out by assumption. Without any such justification, a price below marginal cost causes inefficiency by attracting to the industry resources that would be valued more by consumers in other uses (at least at their marginal costs); in addition, a financial loss results from pricing one product below marginal cost, which requires that the price of the other product be even farther above its marginal cost, thus causing a greater welfare loss there. We have shown by our examples that a rate-of-return regulated firm can adopt nonoptimal price structures, either because of differences in capital intensities of the two goods

---

[9] See, e.g., Mohring (1970).

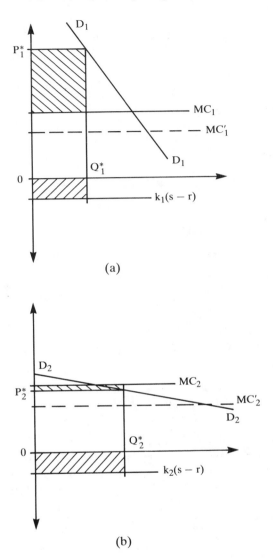

Figure 9.2. How demand elasticity affects price.

(and the argument easily extends to a greater number) or because of differences in the price elasticities of their demands.

It is obvious from Table 9.2 that the profit-per-unit-of-output constraint will also cause a term to be subtracted from marginal cost, in this case

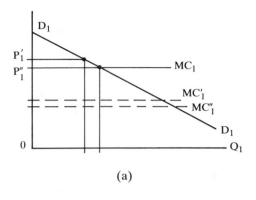

(a)

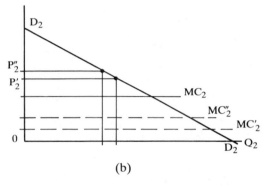

(b)

Figure 9.3. Absolute and percentage reductions in marginal cost.

$\lambda_3 h_i/(1-\lambda_3)$, in the pricing rule. Thus the example just completed could be repeated for the profit-per-unit constraint with identical results except that the weights h_i will now control allowed profit for each good. If the allowed profit per unit is the same for every good, the amount subtracted from marginal cost in pricing every good will be the same. In the case of the percentage-of-total-cost profit constraint, marginal cost is multiplied by the fraction $[1-\lambda_2(1+g)]/(1-\lambda_2)$ in the pricing rule. In this case, the magnitude of marginal cost can influence the degree of understatement across products, because the understatement is no longer independent of marginal cost. In all cases an understated marginal cost still is used, with the full monopolistic effect of demand elasticity on prices.

The difference between an absolute understatement of marginal cost (through $-\gamma$ for the rate-of-return or profit-per-unit constraints) and a percentage reduction of marginal cost (through α for the percentage-of-cost constraint) is shown in Figure 9.3. The demand and marginal cost conditions are exactly the same as in Figure 9.1, demand being similar for the two goods, but marginal cost is higher for Q_1 in panel (a) than for Q_2 in panel (b). If we take the simplest case, where allowed profit-per-unit is the same for every good ($h_1 = h_2$), the same absolute amount will be subtracted from each marginal cost to obtain MC_1' and MC_2'. Prices P_1' and P_2' would then be chosen by the firms. Comparable results would follow for the rate-of-return constraint with marginal capital requirements identical for the two goods ($K_{Q_1} = K_{Q_2}$). If a profit-as-percentage-of-cost constraint is applied, in contrast, the same *percentage* understatement will be made in MC_1 and MC_2, through α, resulting in MC_1'' and MC_2''. Prices P_1'' and P_2'' would then be chosen.

9.4 Peak-load pricing and quality

A special form of the capital bias in pricing can be seen in the failure of rate-of-return regulated firms, until pressured recently by state and federal agencies in the United States to offer lower prices during off-peak periods when capital equipment is no constraint on output. Only peak-demand users press upon available capacity and call for its expansion, so ideally they should be the ones that pay for it. If capacity is abundant relative to demand at off-peak times, consumers do not have to be turned away by a high price. Rate-of-return regulated firms lack incentive to employ this very sound pricing principle, however, whenever the allowed return exceeds the cost of capital. They would rather lower the price for capital-intensive peak demand in order to justify more capital assets, and charge a monopoly price at off-peak times to realize profit that greater capital will justify.[10]

A bias in peak-load pricing can be illustrated through reinterpretation of Figure 9.1. Imagine that $k_1(s - r)$ for the regulated firm depicted in Figure 9.1a is large, because marginal usage requires capital expansion, whereas $k_2(s - r)$ is zero in Figure 9.1b because service 2 is provided at the off-peak time, when service can be expanded without more capacity. Then the regulated firm's peak price P_1 might be even lower than shown in Figure 9.1, and the off-peak price P_2 even higher. Perhaps because of rate-of-return regulation, the United States is far behind other countries in the application of peak-load pricing.[11]

---

10 Demand elasticities at peak and off-peak times conceivably can offset this tendency. See Bailey and White (1974). The existence of diverse technology, such as base-load, intermediate, and peaking plants in electricity, also can complicate the simple case treated in the text. See Turvey (1968, pp. 28–31), Wenders (1976), and Crew and Kleindorfer (1979b, pp. 170–3).

11 For examples of peak-load pricing in Europe, see Mitchell et al. (1978). All such pricing is not ideal (Slater and Yarrow 1983). Another application can be seen in Mitchell (1978). Complications when a durable good is involved are analyzed by Mills (1976).

Although a capital bias favors lower peak prices as long as the allowed return exceeds the cost of capital, demand elasticities still play a role that may support or offset that effect (Bailey and White 1974; Sherman 1980b). If the situation in Figure 9.2 were modified – for example, so that capital was required for Q_1 as shown in panel (a) and profit of $k_1(s-r)$ was allowed, but no capital was needed and no profit allowed for Q_2 in panel (b) – then price p_2^* would be raised to the profit maximum and p_1^* would be lowered until profit there just equaled $k_1(s-r)$. Here the elasticities actually would tend to encourage a higher peak price while the capital bias works the other way. Had the peak demand (D_1D_1) been less elastic than off-peak demand (D_2D_2), that would tend to raise off-peak price and lower peak price, just as the capital bias would.

In industries such as telecommunications or gas or electricity, customer classes are a common basis for differences in rate structures. Residential, commercial and industrial customers are charged different rates. Costs may differ in serving these types of customers, but the classes could also serve other purposes, as Eckel (1983, 1985) has demonstrated. In particular, if systematic peak and off-peak demand patterns exist by customer class, pricing by class could allow a crude approximation to peak-load pricing. On the other hand, pricing by class could also be a means of taking advantage of demand elasticity differences, even in a monopolistic way. Some classes also are created for social purposes, such as "lifeline" rates in electricity to allow at least modest consumption for anyone (Scott 1981).

The larger capacity that results when peak-load prices do not exceed off-peak prices may be interpreted as higher-quality service, since peak users are able to receive service at their most preferred times. But this higher quality comes at the expense of off-peak users, who pay substantially more than the marginal cost of service they receive. More generally, Spence (1975) has shown that if greater quality is associated with greater capital intensity, rate-of-return regulation may be expected to elicit higher quality (see also Schmalensee 1970). By the same token, if quality depends on labor intensity, the rate-of-return regulated firm may skimp on quality.

How easily a service can be defined also will influence its quality. Electricity seems well defined, but the uniformity of wattage and freedom from breakdowns in service may vary. Telephone service may involve few or many "busy" signals. Or there may be prompt or slow responses to requests for installation of service. It is possible for physical capacity to be adequate to meet peak demands while labor is not adequate or well supervised, and then the possible benefit of a high level of peak service will not be realized.

9.5   Nonuniform pricing

Two-part pricing

Consider technologies that require capital not only to increase output but also to connect additional consumers.[12] Suppose that a monopoly sets one price, p_n, for the right to purchase units and a marginal price, p_Q, per unit. Allowing the number of consumers to be variable while imposing a charge for consuming even one unit, like a fixed entrance or connection fee, leads to a very complex monopoly problem, which Oi (1971) has demonstrated.[13] But if consumers differ only by their incomes, and the income distribution is convenient, there will be a market demand function for units of the monopolist's output $Q = Q(p_n, p_Q, I)$, and a market patronage function for the number of the monopolist's customers $n = n(p_n, p_Q, I)$, where I represents other prices and the general income level that are unchanged by decisions in this regulated market. This is the demand model we developed for the two-part pricing problem in Section 4.5 and extended to consider second-best prices in Chapter 5. The Q and n functions having the properties $Q_{p_n} < 0$, $Q_{p_Q} < 0$, $n_{p_n} < 0$, and $n_{p_Q} < 0$ (Q and n are complementary) are implied if all consumers have identical tastes with diminishing marginal rates of substitution and differ only in their incomes, Q never being inferior, and if we can approximate n with a differentiable function for convenience. In a particular case, of course, the functions could be different and solutions could be very difficult to find and compare.

Suppose that there is a population of N consumers who have the same utility function, $U = U(g, q)$ for an amount, q, of the monopolist's good and an amount, g, of a composite of all other goods, but they differ by incomes. The consumers' incomes y are distributed according to the relative density function $f(y)$, with cumulative distribution function $F(y)$; with $\underline{y}$ the lowest in income and $\bar{y}$ the highest income, $F(\underline{y}) = 0$ and $F(\bar{y}) = 1$. We assume other prices are constant and replace I in demand functions by income y. The demand for an individual having income y will then be $q = q(p_n, p_Q, y)$. Individuals whose incomes are below some minimum level, y_m, will not pay the fee p_n to consume $q > 0$ at price p_Q, and for

---

12 The book value of capital used by privately owned U.S. electric utilities in the transmission of electricity, which can be expected to depend partly on the number of customers, exceeds the book value used in generating electricity. Of course, marginal capital requirements might vary considerably according to circumstances. For book values of capital by function, see Office of Accounting and Finance, Federal Power Commission, *Statistics of Privately Owned Electric Utilities in the United States, 1974 – Classes A and B Companies* (Washington, D.C.: Government Printing Office, 1974), especially Table 17.

13 If consumers are identical, even to having the same incomes, perfect price discrimination is possible in the form of a fixed charge that takes each consumer's surplus and an efficient marginal price. Bailey and White (1974) treated this case in a peak-load context.

them $q = 0$. All the income of a person with $y < y_m$ will be spent on another (or all other) consumption good, g, which has a price of 1, so expenditure on g will be y and utility will be $U(y, 0)$. The "cutoff" income y_m obviously depends on p_n and p_q, and we assume $\underline{y} < y_m < \bar{y}$. Under these conditions, the total patronage and market demand functions can be calculated as

$$n(p_n, p_Q) = \int_{y_m}^{\bar{y}} f(y) \, dy \tag{8}$$

and

$$Q(p_n, p_Q) = \int_{y_m}^{\bar{y}} q(p_n, p_Q, y) f(y) \, dy, \tag{9}$$

which have the properties assumed above.

Let K_n units of capital plus L_n units of labor be required to add (connect) another consumer and let K_Q units of capital plus L_Q units of labor be required to produce a marginal unit of Q. By assuming that L_Q, L_n, K_Q, and K_n are constant, we avoid the Averch and Johnson input bias in order to focus attention on pricing effects. With the cost of capital and the cost of labor both constant at r and w, profit for the firm is

$$\Pi = (p_n - rK_n - wL_n)n(p_n, p_Q) + (p_Q - rK_Q - wL_Q)Q(p_n, p_Q). \tag{10}$$

To represent welfare for those who consume Q, it is convenient to use the indirect utility function, $V(p_n, p_q, y)$, obtained by maximizing direct utility subject to the individual's budget constraint. Let $\mu(y)$ be the marginal utility of income for the individual with income y. Total consumer welfare can be represented as

$$\int_{y_m}^{\bar{y}} V(p_n, p_Q, y) w(y) f(y) \, dy, \tag{11}$$

where $w(y)$ is the social weight given an individual having income y. If the consumer welfare function in (11) has welfare weights equal to the reciprocals of the marginal utilities of income for all y's then $w(y)\partial V/\partial p_n$ equals -1 and $w(y)\partial V/\partial p_Q$ equals $-q$. We know that welfare weights have this property implicitly when the current income distribution is accepted in a well-functioning competitive economy,[14] or whenever income distribution can be ignored so income is valued the same by society regardless of who receives it. We make this assumption about welfare weights formally in

$$w(y) = 1/\mu(y). \tag{12}$$

---

[14] See Section 2.4 and also Negishi (1960). Notice that we are not maximizing with respect to incomes, and must accept them as given.

Four solutions will now be described, one for each of the following four goals: (1) to maximize welfare, (2) to maximize welfare subject to a budget constraint, (3) to maximize profit subject to regulatory rate-of-return constraint, and (4) to maximize monopoly profit. If social welfare is defined as the sum of consumer welfare given above in (11), plus profit given in (10), or

$$W = C + \pi, \tag{13}$$

then we know from Section 4.5 that ideal prices are

$$p_n = rK_n + wL_n \tag{14}$$

and

$$p_Q = rK_Q + wL_Q. \tag{15}$$

Thus, the ideal price structure has the declining block property, but only to the point where prices conform to marginal costs.

The objective of maximizing social welfare subject to the constraint that profit equal some fixed amount, B, was pursued for two-part prices in Section 5.5. There, with increasing returns to scale, pursuing welfare allowed pricing for maximum efficiency subject to the constraint, say, that there be no deficit. Even with the constant returns to scale in both n and Q assumed here, there can be a second-best problem if a positive profit is required from the enterprise, or if some additional fixed cost must be covered. The Lagrangian formed to maximize welfare subject to a profit constraint is

$$L(p_n, p_q, \lambda) = C + \pi + \lambda(\pi - B). \tag{16}$$

Following the same steps as in Chapter 5, we can obtain from necessary conditions for a maximum of (16) the pricing rules

$$\frac{p_n - rK_n - wL_n}{p_n} = \frac{-\lambda}{1+\lambda} \cdot \frac{\xi_{QQ} - \xi_{nQ}}{\xi_{nn}\xi_{QQ} - \xi_{Qn}\xi_{nQ}} = \frac{-\lambda E_n}{1+\lambda} \tag{17}$$

and

$$\frac{p_Q - rK_Q - wL_Q}{p_Q} = \frac{-\lambda}{1+\lambda} \cdot \frac{\xi_{nn} - \xi_{Qn}}{\xi_{nn}\xi_{QQ} - \xi_{Qn}\xi_{nQ}} = \frac{-\lambda E_Q}{1+\lambda}, \tag{18}$$

where $\xi_{nQ} = (\partial n/\partial p_Q)p_Q/n$, and other elasticities are defined similarly. These equations are solved for p_n and p_Q and restated in Table 9.3. We shall interpret these rules and the E_n and E_Q terms after we derive regulated and unregulated monopoly pricing rules for comparison.[15]

---

[15] For more general derivation of second-best welfare-maximizing two-part tariffs, see Ng and Weisser (1974) and Schmalensee (1981). The optimal single tariff for each firm in the same circumstances is due to Boiteux (1956).

Table 9.3. *Rate structures under alternative goals and constraints*

Tariff	Maximizing welfare	Maximizing welfare with budget constraint	Maximizing profit with rate-of-return constraint	Maximizing profit with no constraint
p_n	$rK_n + wL_n$ (14)	$\dfrac{rK_n + wL_n}{1-(\lambda/(1-\lambda))E_n}$ (17')	$\dfrac{\gamma K_n + wL_n}{1-E_n}$ (25)	$\dfrac{rK_n + wL_n}{1-E_n}$ (27)
p_Q	$rK_Q + wL_Q$ (15)	$\dfrac{rK_Q + wL_Q}{1-(\lambda/(1-\lambda))E_Q}$ (18')	$\dfrac{\gamma K_Q + wL_Q}{1-E_Q}$ (26)	$\dfrac{rK_Q + wL_Q}{1-E_Q}$ (28)

The rate-of-return regulated firm seeks to maximize profit

$$\pi = (p_n - rK_n - wL_n)n + (p_Q - rK_Q - wL_Q)Q \tag{19}$$

subject to the constraint

$$(p_n - sK_n - wL_n)n + (p_Q - sK_Q - wL_Q)Q \leq 0, \tag{20}$$

where again s is the allowed rate of return and we assume $s > r$. The Lagrangian that represents the firm's constrained maximization problem is

$$G = (1 - \phi)[(p_n - rK_n - wL_n)n + (p_Q - rK_Q - wL_Q)Q]$$
$$+ \phi(s - r)[K_n n + K_Q Q]. \tag{21}$$

In addition to the constraint, a maximum requires that derivatives of G with respect to p_n and p_Q equal zero:

$$(p_n - \gamma K_n - wL_n)\frac{\partial n}{\partial p_n} + n + (p_Q - \gamma K_Q - wL_Q)\frac{\partial Q}{\partial p_n} = 0 \tag{22}$$

and

$$(p_n - \gamma K_n - wL_n)\frac{\partial n}{\partial p_Q} + (p_Q - \gamma K_Q - wL_Q)\frac{\partial Q}{\partial p_Q} + Q = 0, \tag{23}$$

where

$$\gamma = r - \frac{\phi(s - r)}{1 - \phi} \tag{24}$$

is the shadow cost of capital. It can readily be shown that $0 < \phi < 1$, and since we assume $s > r$, it must be true that $\gamma < r$.[16] This means that the firm sets prices using an understated marginal cost, what Callen, Mathewson, and Mohring (1976) called pseudo-marginal cost. The necessary conditions yield

$$\frac{p_n - \gamma K_n - wL_n}{p_n}\xi_{nn} + \frac{p_Q - \gamma K_Q - wL_Q}{p_Q}\xi_{Qn}\frac{p_Q Q}{p_n n} = -1$$

and

$$\frac{p_n - \gamma K_n - wL_n}{p_n}\xi_{nQ}\frac{p_n n}{p_Q Q} + \frac{p_Q - \gamma K_Q - wL_Q}{p_Q}\xi_{QQ} = -1.$$

Solving simultaneously gives the pricing rules (25) and (26) in Table 9.3.

An unregulated monopolist will maximize (21) without the constraint, or with $\phi = 0$. It is easy to solve this simpler problem to obtain pricing rules (27) and (28) in Table 9.3.

---

[16] We assume that $\gamma > 0$ throughout. From (22) we have $\gamma = r - \phi(s - r)/(1 - \phi)$. As s goes from the monopoly return toward r, ϕ goes from 0 toward 1. The net effect is to make the implicit cost of capital, γ, lower as s is set closer to r.

Now let us interpret the pricing rules in Table 9.3. Maximizing welfare makes no use of demand elasticities, as (14) and (15) simply call for each price to equal marginal cost. The constrained welfare-maximizing rules in (17) and (18) are like the unregulated profit-maximizing monopoly rules (27) and (28) except that, as with Ramsey pricing generally, elasticities influence prices fractionally in constrained welfare-maximizing price rules (17) and (18), just enough to raise money for the budget constraint. Notice that the regulated monopolist's rules in (25) and (26) make full use of demand elasticities, just like the unregulated monopolist's pricing rules in (27) and (28). The regulated and unregulated monopolists differ only in that the regulated monopolist substitutes $\gamma < r$ for r, and thereby understates the marginal cost of capital and thus the marginal cost of output, using this lower pseudo-marginal cost in setting its prices. The rate-of-return regulated monopolist clearly does not choose the welfare-maximizing rate structure of (14) and (15) or the constrained welfare-maximizing rate structure of (17) and (18). Indeed, the regulated firm relies no less than an unregulated monopolist on demand elasticity in setting its prices, while reducing prices to meet the rate-of-return constraint simply by understating the capital portions of marginal costs.

Although these pricing rules in Table 9.3 are less precise than ones tailored to the two-part pricing circumstances, as shown in Chapter 5, they do afford simple interpretation. Note that

$$E_n = \frac{\xi_{QQ} - \xi_{nQ}}{\xi_{nn}\xi_{QQ} - \xi_{Qn}\xi_{nQ}}$$

and

$$E_Q = \frac{\xi_{nn} - \xi_{Qn}}{\xi_{nn}\xi_{QQ} - \xi_{Qn}\xi_{nQ}}$$

have the same denominator, which will be positive as long as own price elasticities of demand exceed cross-elasticities, a condition we should expect to be satisfied. Although it is not possible to determine a priori the relative magnitudes of E_n and E_Q, characteristics of industries that are regulated will tend to make $|E_n| > |E_Q|$.[17] These industries usually supply important services people do not wish to do without, like water and electricity. Any such service would have a low (in absolute value) elasticity of demand in the access fee, p_n. Moreover, since so many consume at

---

[17] Ordinarily, both terms in the numerators will be negative, and we can reasonably expect $|\xi_{QQ}| > |\xi_{Qn}p_Q Q/p_n n|$ so $E_n > 0$, and $|\xi_{nn}| > |\xi_{nQ}p_n n/p_Q Q|$ so $E_Q > 0$. However, since n and Q are complementary, it is possible for $|\xi_{nn}| < |\xi_{nQ}p_n n/p_Q Q|$, making $E_Q < 0$. The monopolist in that case would set output price p_Q below true marginal cost, and the regulated monopolist would set p_Q below *understated* marginal cost. It is conceivable that instead $E_n < 0$, which could motivate the special incentives that used to be offered to builders of all-electric homes by electric utilities.

least *some* quantity of the service, changes in p_n are apt to have small effects on Q because they are essentially income effects. These characteristics suggest that $|\xi_{nn}|$ and $|\xi_{Qn}|$ are both very small,[18] which helps to make $\xi_{Qn} - \xi_{nn} < \xi_{nQ} - \xi_{QQ}$ and thus $|E_n| > |E_Q|$. This inequality would, of course, tend to make the fixed fee, p_n, be set farther above marginal cost than the usage fee, p_Q (by the markup, $1/(1 - E_n)$, being larger than $1/(1 - E_Q)$), so that the declining block character of the rate structure would be exaggerated. Marginal capital intensities could also cause a difference in the relation of p_n and p_Q to their true marginal costs, and if marginal output is more capital intensive than marginal consumer connections, so $K_Q/L_Q > K_n/L_n$, then γK_Q would cause a greater understatement of the marginal cost of Q than γK_n would cause for n. As a result, the declining-block property of the rate structure would again tend to be exaggerated.

Of course, it is possible for equity concerns to alter the welfare-maximizing price benchmarks that we have used.[19] In particular, social welfare weights may be larger than the reciprocals of marginal utilities of incomes as incomes are lower. Then the assumption in (12) would no longer hold, and from arguments in Chapter 6 we should expect the ideal p_Q to be larger and the fixed (regressive) fee, p_n, to be smaller. This tendency could be found in the solution chosen by a rate-of-return regulated firm if connecting new customers is more capital intensive than adding output, or if elasticity effects are such that $E_Q > E_n$. But whether regulation could meet welfare aims would depend on technology and demand elasticities, which are beyond the control of the regulatory authority and therefore cannot generally be achieved through policy actions. Moreover, just the opposite tendencies can typically be expected from technology and demand elasticities.

Quantity-dependent pricing

The effect of rate-of-return regulation on the choice of a continuous quantity-dependent price schedule has been shown by Srinagesh (1986). He first obtained a monopoly solution with marginal revenue equaling marginal cost, as we observed in Chapter 5. With no income effect present, the marginal price at the largest quantity will equal marginal cost. Under rate-of-return regulation with $s > r$, marginal cost is understated, as

---

[18] We assume that all demands are elastic, to avoid perverse behavior that the regulated firm might undertake (even with fixed coefficients in production) in an effort to avoid operating where demand is inelastic. That rate-of-return regulated monopolies want to operate where demand is elastic, like unregulated monopolies, was first shown by Westfield (1965) and discussed in Chapter 8.

[19] See Section 6.3.

pseudo-marginal cost, because the implicit price of capital is lower than its true opportunity cost. As a result, the price schedule is everywhere lower under regulation than it would be for an unregulated monopoly. Since the marginal price would equal marginal cost at the largest quantity without regulation, that price and prices at nearby large quantities under regulation will be lower than true marginal cost. So if continuous nonuniform prices are used, as long as capital is a part of marginal cost, rate-of-return regulation will cause a marginal price to lie below marginal cost.

The form of the continuous quantity-dependent price schedule may be more or less steeply sloped than a monopoly schedule or a welfare-maximizing schedule. It depends on the properties of marginal revenue, which may vary with price reductions by different amounts at each q. Since marginal prices at *all* quantities are reduced, by virtue of the pseudo-marginal cost being lower, y_m must be lower than with monopoly, and some who would not consume from a monopoly become consumers. The change from a monopoly price at any q will be greater if $\partial MR/\partial P$ is small, so if $\partial(\partial MR/\partial P)/\partial q$ is positive, the price schedule will come closer to a uniform schedule with regulation. If there is a general pattern the other way, so $\partial(\partial MR/\partial P)/\partial q < 0$, the price schedule will have greater quantity discounts under regulation than under monopoly.

The Srinagesh model does not have a separate cost for connecting consumers, which was easy to examine in the previous section with a two-part price. Had such a cost been included, it would tend to raise the price of the first unit consumed. Such an entry fee could differ from the one a monopoly would use, as would the remaining price structure, depending on the degree of capital intensity in serving customers or in producing units. Only if all capital was used to connect consumers and none was used to produce output, however, would there be no incentive for a marginal price under regulation to lie below true marginal cost.

9.6   Dynamic elements

We saw in Section 8.5 that operating with unchanging prices for an extended period of time could improve technical efficiency in the firm. Whether prices can be changed or not does not alter the essentially monopolistic pricing incentives of the firm, however, so regulatory lag will not reduce output inefficiency. At the same time, acting as if quantities are fixed can improve pricing incentives, and we shall examine this possibility.

If quantities are held at fixed values, the variables left in the firm's control may be chosen by the firm not perversely, to influence its profit allowance, but constructively, to improve efficiency. As we saw in Chapter 3, Vogelsang and Finsinger (1979) have demonstrated for a simple setting, in which allowed profit is set without reference to capital, that efficiency can be served by firms choosing prices. Their simple scheme needs remarkably little information, merely accounting data from the firm, and contains an iterative adjustment process that allows the firm to make price changes and retain resulting profit during the interval of a lag period, but then lose excess profit at the end of the period. When the profit gain is taken away, only the consumer welfare gain remains, in the form of ideal relative prices among multiple products.

In adjusting its prices during any one period by the Vogelsang and Finsinger scheme, the firm must always comply with a constraint that *new* prices times *old* quantities not exceed the product of *old* prices times the *old* quantities. The authors prove that adherence to old quantities, which essentially allows the firm discretion only for incremental changes, has the surprising effect that profit-seeking and welfare-maximizing incentives will lead to the same relative prices. But the quantities for which allowed profit is calculated must be from some previous period rather than the current one. As Sappington (1980) has stressed, to be foolproof the scheme requires that management of the firm look no further than the current period when seeking maximum profit. That is, the effect of current outputs on allowed profit *next* period is to be ignored.

As an example, suppose that the actual quantities from a past test period are to be used in all allowed profit calculations in a rate hearing, rather than forecasted quantities at proposed rates, for some future test period. Future test periods are more commonly used during periods of high inflation, because they can reflect anticipated input price changes, but here we propose to use past quantities instead. As we just noted, one possible drawback in using output quantities from some previous test period is that the firm, in anticipation of their later use, might select those quantities in part to make later allowed profit greater. The firm might maintain currently nonoptimal outputs because of the gain it anticipates in a later period when its target revenues depend on those outputs. If the interval between output price decisions is long enough, however, this incentive of the firm will be muted, because to achieve later benefits the firm will have to forgo current profit. As the firm focuses more on gaining profit currently, past outputs will be regarded as exogenous.[20]

---

[20] Suppose that the firm does not merely accept past outputs, but influences them by having designed its current prices in the past with a view to their future influence on target revenue. In the unlikely event that the firm can take such a long-term view, a main alternative scheme would be to construct a reference mixture of outputs for the firm from industry data. Although this clearly would prevent influence by the firm on the outputs that determine its allowed profit, the fact that one firm may face demand patterns quite different from others in the industry can make construction of such output quantities very difficult. Then using the firm's own outputs from a test period in the past may still be preferable.

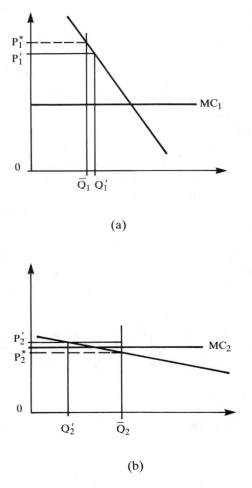

(a)

(b)

Figure 9.4. Inducing welfare improving prices.

The effect of having exogenous outputs as a basis for target revenue can be briefly illustrated. Recall that Figure 9.2 shows a pricing solution for the regulated firm selling two products that have the same constant marginal cost and capital requirement but different demand elasticities. The constant marginal capital requirement makes rate-of-return regulation equivalent to profit-per-unit-of-output regulation, so that allowed profit varies with currently chosen outputs, just as Figure 9.2 indicates. Note that prices are inefficient under the profit-per-unit regulation (one price is below marginal cost). Figure 9.4 reproduces the demands and marginal costs from Figure 9.2, and also shows the quantities chosen by the firm. In Figure 9.4 those quantities are labeled $\bar{Q}_1$ and $\bar{Q}_2$; they will be taken as the last period's outputs to be used currently as the basis for allowed profit. In choosing prices to maximize its current profit, now the regulated firm determines its allowed profit not from current outputs, as in Figure 9.2, but from the unchanging $\bar{Q}_1$ and $\bar{Q}_2$, while current outputs at the chosen prices determine actual profit. Consider a small rise in P_2 to P_2' just above MC_2, and an equal decline in P_1 to P_1'. Since $\bar{Q}_2$ is greater than $\bar{Q}_1$ the increase in allowed profit from raising P_2 is bound to be larger than the reduction from lowering P_1, that is, $(P_2 - P_2^*)\bar{Q}_2 > (P_1^* - P_1)\bar{Q}_1$, since $P_2 - P_2^* = P_1^* - P_1$ and $\bar{Q}_2 > \bar{Q}_1$. With these changes, profit from product 2 obviously will increase since it was negative before. Profit on product 1 will decline slightly, but, with allowed profit greater, the profit on both products at the new prices can be better than it would be if the old prices had been maintained. If actual profit is not as great as allowed profit, both prices can be raised until it is, and if allowed profit is exceeded, both prices can be lowered until equality is reached. Besides raising profit, this change in P_1 *relative* to P_2 is obviously in a direction that improves welfare, since it is away from the cross-subsidization present in Figure 9.2. Indeed, repeated application of this regulatory adjustment procedure can lead the one-period profit-seeking firm to approach second-best, or Ramsey, prices.

Two qualifications about this pricing solution should be noted. First, if the firm's costs do not match the level expected, perhaps because of an input price change, results will not be ideal. Automatic adjustment clauses afford only an imperfect way to deal with this problem. The second point is that, when we refer to efficient prices, we include second-best, or Ramsey, prices discussed in Chapter 5 and presented in (5) above, prices that may depart from marginal costs but in a manner that will minimize consequent welfare losses. Iterative adjustment has been proven to approach these second-best prices when allowed profit is based on last-period quantities and current prices that the firm chooses in order to maximize current profit.[21]

9.7   Empirical evidence

Public utility rate structures have repeatedly been seen as being somehow inefficient. Possible explanations have included, among other things, political influences (Jackson 1969; Littlechild and Rousseau 1975; Peltzman 1971; Stigler 1971; Stigler and Friedland 1962) and income distribution

---

[21] The main idea is from the Vogelsang and Finsinger (1979) proposal. See also Sherman (1980a), Finsinger and Vogelsang (1981, 1982), and experimental tests such as Harrison and McKee (1985) and Cox and Isaac (1987).

aims (Jones 1985; Posner 1971). Stigler and Friedland (1962) expected regulators to reduce domestic relative to industrial electricity rates, on the ground that more votes lie with domestic users, but they found no significant effect. Jackson (1969) hypothesized that instead large industrial users, as an effective special interest group, would win favored rates, and he found some support for that position. In part because of inconsistencies from tests of their implications, these political theories have been notably unsuccessful in explaining rate structures (Posner 1974), and yet price discrimination has been shown empirically (Eckel 1983, 1987; Primeaux and Nelson 1980; Naughton 1986).

Primeaux and Nelson (1980) estimated the ratio of price to marginal cost for electricity rates, and from differences observed in that ratio across customer classes they concluded that price discrimination was present. Eckel (1983) examined the pricing incentives of rate-of-return regulated firms and showed how they were motivated to choose other than welfare-maximizing price structures. In electric utility cost and elasticity data she also found evidence that actual electricity prices were more like those motivated under profit-maximization than welfare maximization. Sringesh (1986) cited regulated telephone rate structures as being consistent with the implication that continuous nonuniform prices will lie below marginal cost for users of large quantities.

There has been a sharp contrast in peak versus off-peak pricing between the United States and other Western countries for many years. That rate-of-return regulated firms would resist using peak-load pricing was emphasized in an early paper by Wellisz (1963). In other countries, peak-load pricing is well developed in telephone, electricity, and other public utility industries (see, e.g., Balasko 1976; Mitchell et al. 1978). But in the United States peak-load pricing was seldom used until governmental pressure was brought in support of it in telephone and electricity industries in the 1970s. Since rate-of-return regulation would tend to be biased against higher prices at peak times, its widespread use in the United States may help to explain why peak-load pricing is so rare.

9.8   Summary

Rate-of-return regulation was not designed specifically to elicit efficient prices, and it does not do so. The incentives within the firm invite it to act as if marginal capital costs are lower than they really are. This effect on capital cost draws the firm into lower prices and larger outputs than an unregulated monopoly would offer. The price reductions are distributed among goods and services in relation to their marginal capital needs, however, not as second-best pricing would dictate. A firm seeking to maximize

welfare while also meeting a budget constraint should price as if all demand elasticities are proportionately larger than they are, until the budget constraint is just satisfied. But the rate-of-return regulated firm responds to elasticities in their original form after it favors marginal capital
costs. It reduces marginal cost based on capital use to a pseudo-marginal
cost level, and then the rate-of-return regulated firm is motivated to use
demand elasticities in setting its prices just as an unregulated monopolist
would. As a consequence, the firm's relative prices will usually be distorted
from efficient relationships and cross-subsidization is even possible.

Peak-load service usually presses on capacity limits, so that marginally
it is more capital intensive than off-peak service. And since capital is favored under rate-of-return-regulation incentives, higher peak-load prices
may not be pursued by rate-of-return regulated firms. A comparison of
pricing across nations shows that peak-load pricing is used much less in
the United States than in many other countries, perhaps because of rate-
of-return regulation. The same incentive to favor capital may distort two-
part prices, possibly tending to favor quantity discounts more heavily.
And quantity-dependent prices are apt to have their last segment for largest
users offered at a price below marginal cost. Evidence suggests that public utilities in the United States discriminate in price more as profit maximizers than as welfare maximizers. Some incentive schemes may avoid
inefficient pricing, but regulatory lag alone will not prevent it. Dynamic
schemes that allow prices in the future to be chosen subject to a constraint
based on previous quantities might induce the firm to approach Ramsey
prices. More attention to pricing incentives is needed to overcome the un-
intended perverse incentives that arise under rate-of-return regulation.

Questions

9.1. Suppose that a rate-of-return regulated public utility offers two services,
Q_1 and Q_2, with demands

$$P_1 = 15 - 0.025Q_1,$$
$$P_2 = 10 - 0.025Q_2.$$

The cost of producing Q_1 is $5 per unit. Service Q_2 requires capital and Q_1
does not. To produce a unit of Q_2 requires $100 in capital. Suppose that the
allowed rate of return is 7 percent and the cost of capital is 5 percent.
(a) Find Ramsey prices on the assumption that total revenue must equal
total cost.
(b) Find prices for the profit-maximizing public utility subject to rate-of-
return constraint.
(c) Explain any difference between answers in (a) and (b).
(d) Is your answer to (b) sustainable?

9.2. Construct a single-product firm problem that calls for an efficient, welfare-maximizing, price where demand is inelastic. Prove that a rate-of-return constraint will not force the enterprise to a solution where demand is inelastic.

CHAPTER 10

The budget-constrained public enterprise

10.1 Introduction

The budget-constrained, government-owned public enterprise is a common form of organization for producing public services in many countries. At the federal government level in the United States, examples of public enterprises are the U.S. Postal Service, the Corporation for Public Broadcasting, the Tennessee Valley Authority operating recreation areas and a huge hydroelectric dam, the Federal Deposit Insurance Corporation, and the St. Lawrence Seaway Corporation, among others. Mixed ownership arrangements include Amtrak, COMSAT, ConRail, and even the National Academy of Sciences. At state and local government levels public enterprises number in the thousands.[1] The magnitude of a public enterprise is often considerable, too; for instance, the U.S. Postal Service alone spends more than $30 billion a year. Public enterprises provide electricity and telephone as well as postal services in many European countries. In other parts of the world, government-owned enterprises can be found in agriculture, health, manufacturing, and other areas. Thus it is important to understand their behavior.

A large literature now combines knowledge from politics and economics to predict the consequences of providing goods or services through public or private enterprise.[2] Direct implications of these theories are difficult to test, however, because they depend on unknowns like the political importance and cost of organizing all the affected groups. Moreover, the theories adduce too many possible explanations for events. Indeed, on a number of points the accumulating evidence cannot distinguish among

---

[1] See Walsh (1978) for an estimate of how widely used public enterprises are and for a history of their origins in the United States. Canadian mixtures of government and private ownership are described in Boardman et al. (1983). Pricing principles for such enterprises are briefly reviewed by Webb (1976) and management is discussed by Aharoni (1986).

[2] See Peltzman (1976) and the literature review by De Alessi (1974). This work also treats the question of when government regulation will be sought by private parties. See especially Stigler (1971), Posner (1971), Peltzman (1976), and Borcherding (1981). Effects of partial government ownership on market value are examined in Eckel and Vermaelen (1986).

hypotheses, and sharper hypotheses are needed if effects are to be successfully identified.[3]

As Chapter 3 indicated, in the absence of competition, firms are not easily induced to pursue economic welfare. Under rate-of-return regulation, a privately owned firm presumably has a goal of maximizing profit while meeting constraints imposed by regulation or other influences. In the last three chapters we examined problems in channeling that profit motive into pursuit of economic welfare. Although private ownership creates a goal, our institutions have not manipulated the profit motivation so that it serves welfare ends perfectly. With public ownership, we have a different problem. Since profit in the private sense is no longer a goal, we are not sure what sort of motivation takes its place.

What goal can be assumed for the managers of a public enterprise? If the enterprise is subject to a budget constraint that limits profit to a specified amount (or limits a publicly subsidized loss), a profit goal has little meaning. Consumer welfare might be pursued as a goal, and of course a normative theory that prescribes prices in relation to costs is well developed for that goal.[4] Yet we know consumer welfare is difficult to measure and even if it is measurable management would not strive to maximize welfare without any incentive, which in this case could not easily be given operational form. Instead, managers might indulge their own preferences, seeking a large organization, high salaries, or other aims, depending in part on the constraints imposed on them. The budget constraint itself, which requires a fixed difference between revenue and cost, does not seem very restrictive, especially if the management is free to propose prices for enterprise products or services. So it might be well to examine the implications of a general managerial goal.

We shall see that several possible goals of the firm yield essentially the same pricing rule, and it is not a desirable rule. One goal that can yield some of the strongest consequences of managerial discretion is that of expenditure, or budget, maximization. The budget-maximizing aim was articulated for bureaucracies by Niskanen (1971, pp. 36–42), and a goal like it was used to represent managerial discretion by Crew and Kleindorfer (1979a) in their study of regulated firms. Budget maximizing is only a crude and unsubtle goal for government enterprises, as Lindsay (1976) has pointed out, but it yields sharp pricing implications. Revenue maxi-

---

[3] Some clearly political influences have been observed, such as the pricing under a state regulatory commission that benefits state residents relative to nonresidents (see Littlechild and Rousseau 1975), or that the rich benefit from telephone and postal pricing in Great Britain (see Waverman 1977). But much evidence is ambiguous or conflicting, as Posner (1974) has demonstrated.

[4] This theory was described in Part II.

mization has been claimed as a goal for large private enterprises by Baumol (1967). The expenditure or revenue goal usefully subsumes many possible goals of managers, however, because either one of these goals fosters control over resources, and that could serve many other goals. Expenditure maximization is consistent with revenue maximization when a budget constraint is imposed, since maximizing one then maximizes the other. Total output is another possible goal. These goals are well defined, so they can yield clear implications for pricing in a multiproduct enterprise.

It is useful to consider real-world public enterprises and their problems. They are created by political institutions and each can be quite different from any other. We briefly discuss the U.S. Postal Service and the development of London Regional Transport. The U.S. Postal Service appears to have come only slowly toward optimal pricing in its almost 20-year history. Transportation organization in London has seen much turmoil and a variety of pricing policies over the past half century.

In Section 10.2 we derive budget-maximizing, revenue-maximizing, and output-maximizing pricing rules and contrast them with welfare-maximizing and profit-maximizing (monopoly) pricing. In Section 10.3 we consider the effects on pricing of granting monopoly rights to public enterprises in the form of entry protection. In Section 10.4 the behavior of a large public enterprise, the U.S. Postal Service, is examined to assess its conformance with these pricing implications. In Section 10.5 we describe urban transportation pricing problems and trace development of London Regional Transport. Section 10.6 summarizes results.

10.2 Pricing rules to maximize the budget

For a point of reference, consider a hypothetical budget-constrained public enterprise seeking to choose its outputs $Q_1, \ldots, Q_n$ in order to maximize welfare, which we shall assume to be the sum of consumer surplus and producer surplus represented by $W(Q_1, \ldots, Q_n)$.[5] With prices $p_1, \ldots, p_n$, cost represented by the convex function $E(Q_1, \ldots, Q_n)$, and with the allowed budget deficit equal to D, the enterprise will maximize the Lagrangian

$$\pounds(Q_1, \ldots, Q_n, \mu) = W(Q_1, \ldots, Q_n) + \mu \left[D + \sum_{i=1}^{n} p_i Q_i - E(Q_1, \ldots, Q_n) \right]. \quad (1)$$

Maximizing with respect to the Q_i's will yield the well-known Ramsey pricing rule,

---

5 We assume that income elasticity of demand is zero and so consumer surplus is well defined. The income elasticity of demand should be small for most public services that do not absorb a large fraction of private expenditures.

$$\frac{p_i - \partial E/\partial Q_i}{p_i} = \frac{\mu}{1+\mu}\frac{1}{\eta_i} \quad \text{for} \quad i = 1, \ldots, n, \tag{2}$$

where $\eta_i = -(\partial Q_i/dp_i)p_i/Q_i$, own-price elasticity of demand for the ith service; cross-elasticities are assumed to be zero. We know from the form of the Lagrangian (1) that $\mu > 0$, so $0 < \mu/(1+\mu) < 1$, which means that demand elasticities are overstated at the welfare optimum.

The budget-constrained public enterprise seeking to maximize expenditure faces the Lagrangian problem

$$l(Q_1, \ldots, Q_n, \lambda) = E(Q_1, \ldots, Q_n) + \lambda\left[D + \sum_{i=1}^{n} p_i Q_i - E(Q_i, \ldots, Q_n)\right], \tag{3}$$

where D is the deficit allowed to the firm and revenue is assumed concave in the Q_i's. Still assuming that demands for the n services are independent of each other,[6] necessary conditions are

$$\frac{\partial l}{\partial Q_i} = \frac{\partial E}{\partial Q_i} + \lambda\left[p_i + Q_i\frac{\partial p_i}{\partial Q_i} - \frac{\partial E}{\partial Q_i}\right] = 0, \quad i = 1, \ldots, n. \tag{4}$$

When rearranged, these conditions yield the implicit pricing rule,

$$\frac{p_i - ((\lambda-1)/\lambda)(\partial E/\partial Q_i)}{p_i} = \frac{1}{\eta_i} \quad \text{for} \quad i = 1, \ldots, n. \tag{5}$$

The solution also calls for $\lambda \geq 0$. Indeed, with $\partial E/\partial Q_i = MC_i$ as marginal cost and $p_i + \partial_i p_i/\partial Q_i$ as marginal revenue, it is evident from (4) that $\lambda = MC_i/(MC_i - MR_i)$. We can therefore expect $\lambda > 1$ as long as demand is elastic so $MR_i > 0$ and the firm operates beyond the monopoly output (which it should do to expand expenditures) so $MC_i > MR_i$.[7] And with $\lambda > 1$ it follows that $(\lambda-1)/\lambda < 1$. Thus the pricing rule in (5) calls for the expenditure-maximizing, budget-constrained public enterprise to understate marginal cost for each of its services by the same fraction, $(\lambda-1)/\lambda < 1$.[8]

---

6 Interdependencies among products or services complicate the analysis by bringing cross-elasticities into the solution, and are not of major interest here. Indeed, we are interested to learn whether cross-subsidization might arise without nonzero cross-elasticities as a cause. See Mohring (1970) for an analysis of the effects of cross-elasticities in a welfare-maximizing model, and George (1973), Sherman and George (1979), and Scott (1986) for discussion of their importance in U.S. Postal Service pricing.

7 Marginal cost must exceed marginal revenue at outputs beyond the profit maximum, from second-order conditions for that maximum. The budget-constrained expenditure-maximizing firm will try to avoid entering an inelastic region of demand, because revenue, and hence cost, would be lower there.

8 This possibility was developed in Sherman (1980b, 1983b). Note that, with $\lambda > 1$, sufficient conditions for a maximum of (1) will be satisfied. Consider the two-good case and let the constraint be represented by F. The expanded bordered Hessian, which must be positive for a maximum, then has the value $H = -l_{Q_1 Q_1}(F_{Q_2})^2 - l_{Q_2 Q_2}(F_{Q_1})^2 + 2l_{Q_1 Q_2}F_{Q_1}F_{Q_2}$. We have $F_{Q_1} < 0$ and $F_{Q_2} < 0$ from the argument in the text that $MC > 0$. As long as the second derivative of revenue is negative, $\lambda > 1$ ensures $l_{Q_1 Q_1} < 0$ and $l_{Q_2 Q_2} < 0$. Although

If the goal (3) had been to maximize total revenue rather than expenditure, while the constraint remained the same, the resulting pricing rule would be essentially the same as the one in (5). The Lagrange multiplier term that serves to understate marginal costs would have a slightly altered form, but its effect would be exactly the same.[9] Intuitively, the budget constraint makes these two problems the same because when it is effective it forces an exact correspondence between revenue and cost. To maximize one is then to maximize the other.

To aid in the interpretation of (5), let us contrast it with the unconstrained profit-maximizing solution and the welfare-maximizing solution under the budget constraint. Maximizing the unconstrained profit objective, $\Sigma p_i Q_i - E$, will yield the familiar monopoly pricing rule,

$$\frac{p_i - \partial E/\partial Q_i}{p_i} = \frac{1}{\eta_i}. \tag{6}$$

We already have in (2) the welfare-maximizing pricing rule. Contrasts among these three solutions will be clearer if we solve explicitly for prices p_i^E under constrained expenditure maximization, p_i^M under monopolistic profit maximization, and p_i^W under constrained welfare maximization. Also let $(\lambda - 1)/\lambda = \alpha_1 < 1$ and $(1 + \mu)/\mu = \alpha_2 > 1$. Solving (5), (6), and (2) we then have

$$p_i^E = \frac{\alpha_1 \partial E/\partial Q_i}{1 - 1/\eta_i}, \tag{7}$$

$$p_i^M = \frac{\partial E/\partial Q_i}{1 - 1/\eta_i}, \tag{8}$$

and

$$p_i^W = \frac{\partial E/\partial Q_i}{1 - 1/\alpha_2 \eta_i}. \tag{9}$$

In comparing (9) with (8), one observes directly the well-known result that the budget-constrained, welfare-maximizing firm actually adopts a monopolist's pricing rule except for systematically overstating all demand elasticities by the simple multiple, α_2. Similarly, comparing (7) with (8) shows that the budget-constrained, expenditure-maximizing public enter-

---

$l_{Q_1 Q_2} < 0$, we can expect $l_{Q_1 Q_2} < l_{Q_1 Q_1}$ and $l_{Q_1 Q_2} < l_{Q_2 Q_2}$; thus $H > 0$ for a maximum with two goods. Conditions for extreme points in problems such as this are set out in Arrow and Enthoven (1961).

9 Replacing $E(Q_1, ..., Q_n)$ by $\Sigma p_i Q_i$ as the goal in (3), with λ' as Lagrange multiplier, yields as necessary condition $(1 + \lambda')(p_i + Q_i(\partial p_i/\partial Q_i)) - \lambda' \partial E/\partial Q_i = 0$, and

$$[p_i - (\lambda'/(1 - \lambda'))(\partial E/\partial Q_i)]/p_i = 1/\eta_i.$$

This rule will be seen as the same as (5) when it is realized that $\lambda = MC_i/(MC_i - MR_i)$ whereas $\lambda' = MR_i/(MC_i - MR_i)$.

prise also uses a modified monopoly pricing rule, but instead of overstating demand elasticity, it understates marginal cost for every i by the same fraction, α_1. Since it does not act as if its elasticities were greater than they really are, the expenditure-maximizing public enterprise following the pricing rule in (7) will rely more on the monopoly power implicit in less elastic demand. Rather than have prices depart optimally from the true marginal costs and rely just enough on demand elasticities to meet the budget constraint, as the welfare rule in (9) calls for, the expenditure-maximizing public enterprise systematically understates marginal costs for all its services. And the revenue-maximizing enterprise will price in the same way.

Suppose that the budget-constrained public enterprise attempts to maximize a weighted sum of its total output, where the weight given to output i is α_{3i}. Its problem then is to maximize

$$
G(Q_1, \ldots, Q_n, \psi) = \sum_{i=1}^{n} \alpha_{3i} Q_i + \psi \left[D + \sum_{i=1}^{n} p_i Q_i - E(Q_1, \ldots, Q_n) \right], \tag{10}
$$

and necessary conditions for a solution will yield the pricing rule

$$
\frac{p_i - (\partial E/\partial Q_i - \alpha_{3i}/\psi)}{p_i} = \frac{1}{\eta_i}, \tag{11}
$$

or with p_i^O representing the constrained output-maximizing price,

$$
p_i^O = \frac{\partial E/\partial Q_i - \alpha_{3i}/\psi}{1 - 1/\eta_i}. \tag{12}
$$

Once again, demand elasticity is not overstated, whereas it would be to maximize welfare. Marginal cost is understated, but now by an amount to be subtracted from each marginal cost rather than by a multiplicative constant.

The main difference between the behavior to be expected under an expenditure or revenue goal on the one hand and the output goal on the other is in responses to inelastic demand. Rather than operate where demand is inelastic, the revenue- or expenditure-maximizing firm will want to depart from the efficient expenditure function $E(Q_1, \ldots, Q_n)$ to raise costs, whereas the output-maximizing firm still has incentive to be efficient. Raising costs obviously can make expenditures higher and justify higher prices which, with inelastic demand, would also yield higher revenue. We shall not explore this most perverse possibility, and merely assume that, if it occurs, a fixed cost of waste can be added to the expenditure function and we shall be left with the same marginal conditions. The fact that wasteful costs might be incurred is of course important.

An example will illustrate these pricing rules. Consider an enterprise serving two demands, $Q_1 = p_1^{-2}$ and $Q_2 = p_2^{-5}$, with constant marginal cost (equal to average cost) at simply \$1 per unit. In these monetary units it is easy to show that the unconstrained profit maximum calls for $p_1^M = \$2$ and $p_2^M = \$1.25$. If a break-even constraint is imposed, we know the welfare optimum will require $p_1^W = \$1$ and $p_2^W = \$1$. When similarly constrained to break even, however, a budget-maximizing firm will choose $p_1^E = \$1.42$ and $p_2^E = 89¢$. At this solution, total revenue, and hence total expenditure, will be larger at \$2.32, compared with \$2.00 at the welfare optimum and 90¢ at the unconstrained profit maximum. Notice that cost and unweighted output are the same in this simple example, which means that the output-maximizing solution is the same as the budget-maximizing solution. The budget- or revenue- or output-maximizing solution involves cross-subsidization because the service with more elastic demand, Q_2, obviously will be priced below its marginal cost of \$1, whereas the service with less elastic demand, Q_1, will be priced to make a contribution above its marginal cost. Indeed, α_1 for equation (7) is equal to 0.71 in this example so it is as if marginal cost is seen at only 71 percent of its true value, and profit is then maximized on the basis of this artificially low marginal cost.

10.3   Entry protection and pricing discretion

From Chapter 3 we know that a firm protected from entry has greater discretion in choosing its prices. If the expenditure function $E(Q_1, \ldots, Q_n)$ has the properties of decreasing ray average cost and economies of scope, Baumol et al. (1977) have shown that adopting the Ramsey prices given in (2) may prevent entry, even when it is allowed. When those convenient properties for $E(Q_1, \ldots, Q_n)$ are lacking, however, a grant of monopoly protection may be needed to prevent socially inefficient entry into some or all of the public enterprises' markets (Faulhaber 1975). If entry is prevented by law in any market, demand elasticity there may appear lower, and even a welfare-maximizing enterprise will set a higher price in that market. A budget-maximizing firm will set a still higher price, because the enterprise will make full use of indicated demand elasticities rather than overstate them. Even though the resulting prices are not sustainable, they may persist because entry is barred.

To illustrate, suppose that entry is forbidden in market 1 and so demand elasticity is altered from η_1 to $\eta_1 \beta_1$, where $0 < \beta_1 < 1$. Then if the Ramsey pricing formula (9) is applied to market 1, the reduced demand elasticity will cause a rise in p_1, and the greater contribution that results will allow reductions in other prices and make entry into those markets even more difficult. Thus, by affecting observed demand, the denial of entry may prevent genuine application of Ramsey pricing even if the enterprise seeks to promote welfare, because only $\eta_1 \beta_1$ can be observed. With entry limited, the constrained expenditure-maximizing firm may follow the pricing rule

$$p_i^E = \frac{\alpha_1 \, \partial W / \partial Q_i}{1 - 1/\eta_i \beta_i}, \tag{7'}$$

where $0 < \beta_i < 1$ in markets protected from entry, which is perverse compared with $\alpha_2 > 1$ in (9). Indeed, lower demand elasticities that result from barring new entry could bring prices in some markets far above marginal costs. Since under the budget-maximizing goal all marginal costs are understated by $\alpha_1 < 1$, other prices that are set close to understated marginal cost may actually lie below true marginal cost, thereby resulting in cross-subsidization, as found in the example in Section 10.2. Such cross-subsidization can follow only if marginal costs and elasticities of demand across products differ substantially, as they are apt to do when one or a few of the demand elasticities are reduced (in absolute value) by statutory entry barriers.

When entry to any of its markets is limited, the public enterprise also has more scope to pursue goals other than welfare. But it is not easy to distinguish which goal the enterprise is pursuing by observing the pricing rule it employs. Revenue maximization and budget maximization are indistinguishable, as we have noted. If the enterprise maximizes output, it will follow the slightly different pricing rule in (12). Cost and output weights must differ to bring about price differences for the output goal, however, unless there is inelastic demand which the revenue- or expenditure-maximizing enterprise would raise prices (and costs) to avoid.

Under terms of the 1970 Postal Reorganization Act, the U.S. Postal Service was converted from a bureaucracy as a government department into a public enterprise. The Postal Service was to realize revenues each year just $920 million below total costs[10] and that amount of subsidy was to be made up by Congress through a continuing appropriation. A uniform price has long been required for all first-class letter mail to "bind the nation together," even though delivery in dense urban areas costs less than delivery in sparsely populated rural areas. The uniform price creates

---

[10] 84 Stat. 719 (August 12, 1970). The $920 million was to be reduced gradually from 1979 to 1984 to half that level, where it would remain. This sum excludes so-called phasing appropriations that subsidize classes bearing sharp price increases under the act, to ease the transition from old policies. The act also was amended to allow greater one-time deficits by the Postal Reorganization Act Amendments of 1976, 90 Stat. 1303 (September 10, 1976).

opportunities for entry into letter delivery in the urban areas, because delivery costs there tend to be lower, so to achieve the goal of a uniform price, entry into letter mail services has been forbidden since 1845 by the Private Express Statutes. The Postal Reorganization Act placed some new constraints on fees for postal services, like requiring that fees cover marginal costs in order to avoid cross-subsidization. Postal fees must be approved by a Postal Rate Commission, which holds hearings on proposals, and by the Governors of the Postal Service, but the initiative for proposing fees lies primarily with the Postal Service. In this situation, with the letter mail entry barrier, we should examine whether any evidence for output- or revenue- or budget-maximizing behavior can be found in the way that the Postal Service has priced its services.

10.4   The example of the U.S. Postal Service

After its formation in 1970, the U.S. Postal Service was repeatedly accused of understating its marginal costs to circumvent rules intended to prevent cross-subsidization among mail classes. The first postal rate case decided by the fledgling Postal Rate Commission (Docket R71–1) accepted as correct the Postal Service's imputations of costs to the various mail classes, but when the decision was appealed, the District of Columbia Court of Appeals described the Postal Service's cost estimates as inadequate.[11] Of the roughly ten billion dollars of annual cost incurred by the Postal Service at that time, slightly less than half had been traced in any way to the classes of mail that might have caused it; the remainder was classified as fixed or institutional, unrelated to mail volume. The Postal Service justified the resulting low marginal costs by claiming great economies of scale, a claim that the court found unsubstantiated.[12]

Available empirical evidence, although incomplete because of limitations in data, has failed to support the Postal Service claim that because of great scale economies added mail volume requires little increase in cost. An early study of labor productivity by Fred Dziadek (1959) actually found decreasing returns across 42 post offices for 1954 and 1958, and an early study of average operating costs by Morton Baratz (1962) found no tendency for such costs to decrease with output. A later cross-sectional study of labor productivity by Edmund Mantell (1974) was equivocal on the

[11] *Association of American Publishers, Inc. v. Governors, U.S. Postal Service*, 485 F. 2nd 768, D.C. Cir. 1973, especially pp. 777–8.
[12] Complaints about U.S. Postal Service pricing are set out in Chief Administrative Law Judge's Initial Decision, Postal Rate Commission Docket R74–1, May 28, 1975, Vol. 1, especially pp. 12–13. See also *Association of American Publishers, Inc. v. Governors, U.S. Postal Service*, 485 F. 2nd 768, D.C. Cir. 1973 and *National Association of Greeting Card Publishers v. U.S. Postal Service*, D.C. Cir., December 28, 1976.

question of economies of scale but, if anything, it would indicate constant or decreasing returns rather than increasing returns. In a cross-sectional study of post offices, Leonard Merewitz (1971) found economies of scale for small offices (up to 1,400 employees) but diseconomies for large ones, and the net effect of mixing post offices of different sizes would not be large-scale economies for the entire postal system. Studies of total postal costs were handicapped before 1961 because data on capital input costs were unavailable. When Rodney Stevenson (1973) studied costs over time after 1961 for the entire postal system, however, he found no economies of scale. Even in its own statistical study[13] the Post Office Department had found no evidence of economies of scale.

By examining the costs that might be saved by eliminating each mail class separately, George Wattles (1963) made an estimate of incremental costs, to evaluate what now would be called economies of scope.[14] The economies he found were much more modest than claimed by the Postal Service. Economies of scope arise whenever one organization can provide multiple services at lower cost than if separate organizations provide them. Incremental cost, the added cost to an organization of providing a particular service while the levels and variety of its other services are held constant, will be lower for that organization if it experiences economies of scope. No full-fledged analysis of postal costs has yet settled the question of whether economies of scope exist in the U.S. Postal Service, although techniques described by Fuss (1980) exist for carrying out such an analysis. Until that work is properly carred out, true postal costs cannot reliably be known.

Accounting methods that the Postal Service inherited from the Post Office Department were biased toward making economies of scale and economies of scope appear greater than they really were, and marginal costs therefore lower. First, the Postal Service for some time imputed only short-run costs to the classes of mail, and by being classified as fixed costs, many long-run costs of capacity were simply excluded from the costs attributable to only one mail class.[15] Second, as long as a particular

---

[13] See Bureau of Finance and Administration, Post Office Department, *Summary Report of Cost System Task Force on Incremental Costs* (Washington, D.C.), May 1970.

[14] See Panzar and Willig (1977b) for a description of economies of scope, and Baumol et al. (1977) for a demonstration of their importance to pricing. For the influence of economies of scope on firm organization, or lack thereof, see Teece (1980).

[15] Stevenson (1973, 1976) charged the Postal Service with having excess capacity relative to demands, and pointed out how the provision of excess capacity will tend to make the observed marginal cost lower than the optimal level. The Chief Administrative Law Judge found in Initial Decision on Postal Rate and Fee Increases, U.S. Postal Rate Commission Docket R74–1 (May 28, 1975) that many costs were classified as fixed, or institutional, costs even though they could have been traced to classes of mail; see vol. I, pp. 8, 9. See also Miller and Sherman (1980).

cost was traceable to two or more classes of mail it was not attributed to any class. That is how the cost of the billion-dollar bulk mail system, which is devoted almost exclusively to third- and fourth-class mail, was not attributed to those classes by the Postal Service when it was first introduced, but was classified instead as an institutional cost. Third, to be attributed to a class of mail, a cost had literally to vary in direct proportion to the volume of mail in that class. Such costs as mail sacks and stamps were not attributed to mail classes because they did not move perfectly proportionately to mail volumes, even though the movements were almost proportional and the logical connection of the cost to the class of mail was inescapable.

With strong criticism from appeals courts, the Postal Rate Commission brought pressure on the Postal Service to trace its costs more fully to the classes of mail that cause them. In 1976 the Postal Rate Commission insisted (Postal Rate Commission Docket R76–1) that 60 percent of total cost be attributed to the classes of mail. And in 1977 (Postal Rate Commission Docket R77–1) the portion of total cost traced to mail classes went slightly above 70 percent. More recently, however, that trend was reversed, and no great increase in the attribution of costs to mail classes has occurred. A Commission on Postal Service, which was formed under terms of the Postal Reorganization Act Amendments of 1976[16] and could be described as sympathetic to the Postal Service,[17] even recommended new legislation that would limit to 60 percent the proportion of cost attributed to classes of mail.[18] Limiting how much cost can be imputed to mail services is certainly a bizarre purpose for legislation. Yet bills introduced in Congress afterward (notably H.R. 7700 and S. 3229) contained that provision. If enacted, such legislation actually could have helped the Postal Service maintain high expenditures, by keeping estimates of marginal costs below the true marginal costs.

The Postal Service practices that serve to understate marginal costs generally affect all mail service costs as if by a percentage reduction, and they thus appear to be consistent with the pricing formula for budget or revenue maximization. However, the omission of bulk mail system costs would primarily have reduced marginal costs of third- and fourth-class

---

[16] 90 Stat. 1303 (September 10, 1976).

[17] The commission had seven members, plus the postmaster general and chairman of the Postal Rate Commission ex officio. Two of the seven chosen members were also to be Postal Service employees. As it turned out, two others were affiliated with magazines that tended to favor old Post Office Department pricing. Many of the consultants that were selected had argued Postal Service positions before. For example, the main analysis of postal rate-setting practices was supervised by the Postal Service's former assistant postmaster general for rates and classification.

[18] *Report of the Commission on Postal Service* (Washington, D.C.), April 18, 1977.

mail, and might be seen as serving a goal of output maximization, with heavy weights applied to those classes of mail. Thus it is not possible to distinguish among possible goals of the enterprise. But the evidence is consistent with pursuit of a set of goals different from welfare, and suggests that the budget constraint alone is not sufficient to control behavior of the public enterprise.

10.5   A complex problem: urban transit

Vehicle transportation in urban areas raises special problems of coordination, especially when a variety of public and private transport means coexist. A public enterprise might be well suited to handle the task of providing public transportation in such circumstances. That at least was the argument of Herbert Morrison (1933), who, as Minister of Transport for England in 1929, proposed the unification of buses, tramways, and the underground in London. Organizing such an entity from separate privately owned and local publicly owned enterprises was complicated enough, and a change of governments in 1931 almost doomed the effort to failure. After much negotiation, a single enterprise was formed, under the London Passenger Transport Act of 1933 (Barker and Robbins 1974). To appreciate only the pricing task of such an enterprise, we shall first examine the problem of urban traffic congestion.[19]

Consider an economy in which each of n consumers ($i = 1, ..., n$) derives satisfaction from traveling by two different modes, private automobile passenger miles (t_a^i) and public bus passenger miles (t_b^i), and also from consuming units of a composite commodity (g^i). Utility functions are quasi-concave, continuous, and twice differentiable:

$$U^i = U^i(t_a^i, t_b^i, g^i), \quad i = 1, ..., n. \tag{13}$$

Average input quantities required to produce units t_a and t_b are represented by composite variables (including fuel, tires, and vehicle) r_a and r_b, with average input requirements interdependent:

$$r_a = r_a(t_a, t_b), \tag{14}$$

$$r_b = r_b(t_a, t_b). \tag{15}$$

Average inputs r_a and r_b are each (continuous and twice differentiable) increasing functions of both t_a and t_b during periods of congestion. The input resource, r, can be transformed from (into) composite commodity,

---

[19] The model presented here is from Sherman (1971, 1972a). It has origins in the classical Pigou (1920) roads problem, made well known by Knight (1924), which has been analyzed carefully by Buchanan (1956) and Mills (1981). The problem was examined from a second-best standpoint by Levy-Lambert (1968) and Marchand (1968).

g, according to the convex (continuous and twice differentiable) transformation surface:

$$f(g, r) = 0. \tag{16}$$

The price of r in terms of g will be denoted by π.

Notice that the two transit modes are imperfect substitutes, so each mode appears in utility functions (13) and leads to a separate demand function (cf. Levy-Lambert 1968; Marchand 1968). Transit input requirements are also interdependent, as represented in (14) and (15); travel by one mode can add to congestion in both modes. A greater marginal congestion effect from auto passenger miles seems reasonable because of the well-known greater requirements of auto passengers for "passenger car units," common-denominator determinants of road congestion. A bus requires roughly three passenger car units but actually carries well over three times as many passengers as a passenger car.[20] The congestion effects due to a marginal auto passenger mile are represented by $\partial r_a / \partial t_a$ and $\partial r_b / \partial t_a$, and the effects due to a marginal passenger bus mile are $\partial r_a / \partial t_b$ and $\partial r_b / \partial t_b$. A greater contribution to congestion by auto passenger miles will thus be specified in the following assumption:

$$\frac{\partial r_a}{\partial t_a} > \frac{\partial r_a}{\partial t_b} \quad \text{and} \quad \frac{\partial r_b}{\partial t_a} > \frac{\partial r_b}{\partial t_b}. \tag{17}$$

We shall find convenient the additional assumption

$$\frac{\partial r_a / \partial t_b}{\partial r_a / \partial t_a} = \frac{\partial r_b / \partial t_b}{\partial r_b / \partial t_a}, \tag{18}$$

which requires the same *relative* marginal contribution from each mode in congestion of either mode. This equality is plausible as long as passenger car units are crucial determinants of congestion.[21]

With prices P_a and P_b per unit of t_a and t_b, g as numeraire, and y^i as the ith consumer's income, budget constraints are

$$g^i + P_a t_a^i + P_b t_b^i = y^i, \quad i = 1, \dots, n. \tag{19}$$

Maximization of (13) subject to (19) for each i requires

$$\frac{\partial U^i}{\partial g^i} = \lambda^i, \quad i = 1, \dots, n, \tag{20}$$

---

[20] See Road Research Laboratory (1965, pp. 200–201).
[21] Evidence from rural roads (Road Research Laboratory 1965, p. 115) can be interpreted (Walters 1968, p. 176) to support $\partial r_a / \partial t_a > \partial r_b / \partial t_a$ and also $\partial r_a / \partial t_b > \partial r_b / \partial t_b$. These relations do not imply equality in (18) but they are at least consistent with it. A relation close to (18) is implicit in the successful use of passenger car units for both rural and urban traffic capacity studies (Road Research Laboratory 1965, p. 200).

$$\frac{\partial U^i}{\partial t_a^i} = \lambda^i P_a, \quad i = 1, \ldots, n, \tag{21}$$

$$\frac{\partial U^i}{\partial t_b^i} = \lambda^i P_b, \quad i = 1, \ldots, n, \tag{22}$$

where λ^i is the ith consumer's marginal utility of income. These conditions, including (5), yield demand functions

$$g^i = g^i(P_a, P_b, y^i), \quad i = 1, \ldots, n, \tag{23}$$

$$t_a^i = t_a^i(P_a, P_b, y^i), \quad i = 1, \ldots, n, \tag{24}$$

$$t_b^i = t_b^i(P_a, P_b, y^i), \quad i = 1, \ldots, n. \tag{25}$$

By substituting these solution values into (1), we derive indirect utility functions,

$$U^i = V^i(P_a, P_b, y^i),$$

as in Section 2.2.

We shall now examine possible responses of this economy to a price per auto passenger mile that equals average cost rather than marginal cost.[22] Extreme bottleneck situations in which average cost curves "bend backward" (take on negative slopes) will not be considered. Nor is consideration given to road construction finance, or to allocation problems that can arise from differences among transit modes in the fixed and per mile expenditure patterns that they may require (Sherman 1967a, b).

A second-best rush-hour transit fare

Let us consider a second-best welfare-maximization problem, given interdependent sources of congestion and imperfect substitutability of modes. To avoid interfering with off-peak optimality, we shall not levy any taxes on inputs, as we did in Section 4.6, even though doing so might help to control rush-hour congestion. Instead we shall adjust the bus fare for rush-hour travel, in an effort to reduce inefficiency from the nonoptimal auto price that we cannot alter. Auto travelers take into account only the average cost and not the marginal cost of auto passenger miles, so that

$$P_a = \pi r_a. \tag{26}$$

In setting the urban bus fare, P_b, given (26), we are concerned with an optimal departure from the average cost of t_b. Thus, we seek an optimal p in the expression

[22] For efficiency, we would of course prefer full pricing of road use, wherever feasible.

$$P_b = \pi r_b + p. \tag{27}$$

We emphasize conditions that make the optimal bus fare less than the average cost of service ($p < 0$), because that calls for subsidization of the public transit service. That the optimal public transit fare should lie below average cost is a stronger implication than that the fare lie below marginal cost, since with congestion average cost is below marginal cost.

The input commodity, r, may include consumers' time as well as gas, tires, and the like. In that case the prices, P_a and P_b, must for consistency reflect the value of consumers' time as well. Then to preserve single prices, an assumption of equal valuation of time by all consumers is forced upon us. Although a price below average cost still indicates a loss for the transit agency, the exact amount of the loss, in an accounting sense, is not available.[23]

Using arbitrary weights, β^i, we form a linear combination of indirect utility functions that we wish to maximize subject to constraints:

$$\max_{p, P_a, P_b, t_a, t_b, r, g, y^i} \sum_{i=1}^{n} \beta^i V^i(P_a, P_b, y^i) \tag{28}$$

subject to

$$\pi r_a = P_a \quad (\mu_a), \tag{29}$$

$$\pi r_b + p = P_b \quad (\mu_b), \tag{30}$$

$$\sum t_a^i = t_a \quad (\tau_a), \tag{31}$$

$$\sum t_b^i = t_b \quad (\tau_b), \tag{32}$$

$$t_a r_a + t_b r_b = r \quad (\gamma), \tag{33}$$

$$\sum g^i = g \quad (\chi), \tag{34}$$

$$f(g, r) = 0 \quad (\phi), \tag{35}$$

where Greek letters at the right are Lagrange multipliers associated with the constraints. In addition to constraints (29) through (35), first-order conditions for a maximum of (28) are

$$\mu_b = 0, \tag{36}$$

[23] It would be possible to express a public transit loss solely in marketable variables by defining r without including consumer time, a definition that would be reasonable for the analysis carried out here because the other inputs also tend to behave as postulated for r_a and r_b functions (see Walters 1961). But the analysis would then require some awkward assumptions about the consumer's opportunity to substitute his own time for commodity q. Time could also be treated separately, but only by complicating the analysis considerably.

$$\sum \beta^i \frac{\partial V^i}{\partial P_a} + \mu_a - \tau_a \sum \frac{\partial t_a^i}{\partial P_a} - \tau_b \sum \frac{\partial t_b^i}{\partial P_a} - \chi \sum \frac{\partial g^i}{\partial P_a} = 0, \tag{37}$$

$$\sum \beta^i \frac{\partial V^i}{\partial P_a} + \mu_b - \tau_a \sum \frac{\partial t_a^i}{\partial P_b} - \tau_b \sum \frac{\partial t_b^i}{\partial P_b} - \chi \sum \frac{\partial g^i}{\partial P_b} = 0, \tag{38}$$

$$-\mu_a \pi \frac{\partial r_a}{\partial t_a} - \mu_b \pi \frac{\partial r_b}{\partial t_a} + \tau_a - \gamma\left(r_a + t_a \frac{\partial r_a}{\partial t_a} + \tau_b \frac{\partial r_b}{\partial t_a}\right) = 0, \tag{39}$$

$$-\mu_a \pi \frac{\partial r_a}{\partial t_b} - \mu_b \pi \frac{\partial r_b}{\partial t_b} + \tau_b - \gamma\left(r_b - \tau_b \frac{\partial r_b}{\partial t_b} + t_a \frac{\partial r_a}{\partial t_b}\right) = 0, \tag{40}$$

$$\chi - \phi \frac{\partial f}{\partial g} = 0, \tag{41}$$

$$\gamma - \phi \frac{\partial f}{\partial r} = 0, \tag{42}$$

$$\sum \beta^i \frac{\partial V^i}{\partial y^i} - \tau_a \sum \frac{\partial t_a^i}{\partial y^i} - \tau_b \sum \frac{\partial t_b^i}{\partial y^i} - \chi \sum \frac{\partial g^i}{\partial y^i} = 0. \tag{43}$$

These conditions can be used to obtain an optimal value of p.[24] From properties of the indirect utility function (see in particular (17) and (20) in Section 2.2), we can replace the partial derivatives of indirect utility $\partial V^i/\partial P_a = \lambda^i t_a^i$ and $\partial V^i/\partial P_b = \lambda^i t_b^i$ in (37) and (38), and $\partial V^i/\partial y^i = \lambda^i$ in (30). The resultant $\beta^i \lambda^i$'s in (37) and (38) can then be replaced by their values in (43). Next define $S_{t_a P_a} = \sum_{i=1}^{n}((\partial t_a^i/\partial P_a) + t_a^i(\partial t_a^i/\partial y^i))$ as the Slutsky effect on demand for auto passenger miles of a compensated change in their price, and similarly for $S_{t_b P_a}$, $S_{t_a P_b}$, and $S_{t_b P_b}$. For simplicity, we drop t and P from the subscripts whenever a and b are also distinguished, always keeping the t subscript to the left (e.g., $S_{t_a P_b} = S_{ab}$). We can then use the fact that[25]

$$P_a S_{aa} + P_b S_{ba} + S_{g P_a} = P_a S_{ab} + P_b S_{bb} + S_{g P_b} = 0 \tag{44}$$

to convert equations (37) and (38) into the form:

$$\left(\frac{\tau_a}{\chi} - P_a\right) S_{aa} + \left(\frac{\tau_b}{\chi} - P_b\right) S_{ba} = \frac{\mu_a}{\chi}, \tag{45}$$

$$\left(\frac{\tau_a}{\chi} - P_a\right) S_{ab} + \left(\frac{\tau_b}{\chi} - P_b\right) S_{bb} = 0. \tag{46}$$

Relations (45) and (46) can be solved, in turn, for

$$\frac{\tau_a}{\chi} - P_a = \frac{\mu_a}{\chi} \frac{S_{bb}}{D} \tag{47}$$

[24] The steps are analogous to those followed in Section 4.6, but must take added complications into account here.
[25] See Samuelson (1947, p. 105, n. 11).

and

$$\frac{\tau_b}{\chi} - P_b = \frac{\mu_a}{\chi} \frac{S_{ab}}{D}, \tag{48}$$

where $D = S_{aa} S_{bb} - (S_{ab})^2$. Conditions (41) and (42) imply that in equilibrium

$$\gamma = \chi \left(\frac{-dg}{df} \right). \tag{49}$$

Substituting this relation into (39) and (40), we have

$$\frac{\tau_a}{\chi} = \frac{\mu_a}{\chi} \pi \frac{\partial r_a}{\partial t_a} + \left(\frac{-dg}{dr} \right) \left(r_a + t_a \frac{\partial r_a}{\partial t_a} + t_b \frac{\partial r_b}{\partial t_a} \right), \tag{50}$$

$$\frac{\tau_b}{\chi} = \frac{\mu_a}{\chi} \pi \frac{\partial r_a}{\partial t_b} + \left(\frac{-dg}{dr} \right) \left(r_b + t_b \frac{\partial r_b}{\partial t_b} + t_a \frac{\partial r_a}{\partial t_b} \right). \tag{51}$$

Now by substituting (50) and (51) together with (26) and (27) into (47) and (48), and eliminating μ_a/χ, we can finally obtain the optimal value of p, p^*:

$$p^* = \frac{D\pi (\partial r_a/\partial t_b) + S_{ab}}{D\pi (\partial r_b/\partial t_a) - S_{bb}} \left[\pi r_a - \left(\frac{-dg}{dr} \right) \left(r_a + t_a \frac{\partial r_a}{\partial t_a} + t_b \frac{\partial r_b}{\partial t_a} \right) \right]$$

$$- \left[\pi r_b - \left(\frac{-dg}{dr} \right) \left(r_b + \tau_b \frac{\partial r_b}{\partial t_b} + t_a \frac{\partial r_a}{\partial t_b} \right) \right]. \tag{52}$$

Since there is no tax on inputs and we assume competition in other markets, we can here assume equality between the marginal rate of transformation and the price ratio for g and r:

$$- \frac{dg}{dr} = \pi. \tag{53}$$

With this equality, and setting $(D\pi(\partial r_a/\partial t_b) + S_{ab})/(D\pi(\partial r_a/\partial t_a) - S_{bb}) = E$, (52) reduces to

$$p^* = \pi \left[t_a \left(\frac{\partial r_a}{\partial t_b} - \frac{\partial r_a}{\partial t_a} E \right) + t_b \left(\frac{\partial r_b}{\partial t_b} - \frac{\partial r_b}{\partial t_a} E \right) \right]. \tag{54}$$

Now we are in a position to ask what conditions call for a subsidy, with $p^* < 0$. We first define cost elasticities,

$$\xi_{jk} = \frac{\partial r_j}{\partial t_k} \cdot \frac{t_k}{r_j}, \quad j = a, b; \ k = a, b,$$

and compensated demand elasticities,

$$\eta_{jk} = S_{jk} \frac{P_k}{t_j}, \quad j = a, b; \ k = a, b.$$

If we substitute for E in (54) and multiply through by the denominator of E, which is positive, then with assumption (18) all terms involving D in the result will vanish. And the sign of p^* will be negative if

$$\left(\frac{\partial r_a}{\partial t_b}t_a + \frac{\partial r_b}{\partial t_b}t_b\right)(-S_{bb}) < \left(\frac{\partial r_a}{\partial t_a}t_a + \frac{\partial r_b}{\partial t_a}t_b\right)(S_{ab}).$$

Dividing both sides by $(-S_{bb})(t_a\,\partial r_a/\partial t_a + t_b\,\partial r_b/\partial t_a)$ and using (18) to simplify the left-hand side of the inequality yields

$$\frac{\partial r_a/\partial t_b}{\partial r_a/\partial t_a} = \frac{\partial r_b/\partial t_b}{\partial r_b/\partial t_a} < \left(\frac{S_{ab}}{-S_{bb}}\right).$$

Multiplying through by t_b/t_a and converting the result into elasticity terms, we obtain

$$\frac{\xi_{ab}}{\xi_{aa}} = \frac{\xi_{bb}}{\xi_{ba}} < \left(\frac{\eta_{ab}}{-\eta_{bb}}\right). \tag{55}$$

Thus, for $p^* < 0$, a compensated increase in P_b must cause a greater relative increase in both r_a and r_b through the effect on t_a than decrease through the effect on t_b. It must be noted that whether condition (55) is satisfied depends on values at the solution. But since it can be expressed in cost and demand elasticities, and is an inequality, (55) might hold over a relevant range of prices, and should therefore be a useful starting point for examining the appropriateness of subsidization.

The economic policy interpretation of this result for peak periods with no input tax is reasonably straightforward. The price of public transit should be set lower, as the cost elasticities are relatively higher for auto passenger miles. And as a decrease in the price of public transit elicits a greater response from auto travelers, the price should be set lower, even to the point of requiring a subsidy, for a lower fare can then reduce overall congestion. This suggests that perfect substitutability of t_a and t_b would definitely make p^* negative and imply a subsidy, a result that is easily shown. If we take only one of the left-hand terms in (55), since they are equal, and replace elasticities by their definitions, we have

$$\frac{(\partial r_b/\partial t_b)(t_b/r_b)}{(\partial r_b/\partial t_a)(t_a/r_b)} < \frac{S_{ab}P_b/t_a}{(-S_{bb})P_b/t_b}.$$

With perfect substitution, this inequality reduces to

$$\frac{\partial r_b/\partial t_b}{\partial r_b/\partial t_a} < 1, \tag{56}$$

a condition that will always be satisfied by assumption (17). With interdependence, the sign of p^* thus depends entirely on the relative contributions of the modes to total congestion when the modes are perfect substitutes, and depends also on the degree of substitutability when that is imperfect.

Input taxes and second-best off-peak transit fares

One way to deal with a second-best price below average cost is to attach a balanced budget constraint to the second-best (now third-best?) problem, in a manner we examined in Chapter 5. But this is not the only way. As Marchand (1968) indicated and as we saw in Section 4.6, a tax on inputs together with an optimal p can eliminate completely the transit misallocation. But because many transit service inputs need not be purchased at the time they are used, an inputs tax cannot effectively be varied by time of day, so an inputs tax that is optimal at rush hour will cause misallocation at off-peak times. If we can find an optimal combination of transit fare and input tax to deal with the rush-hour problem, however, we can then determine an optimal (second-best) transit fare in off-peak hours that will minimize off-peak misallocation due to the (still effective) inputs tax. In cities where most travel occurs during rush hours, this policy could offer genuine allocative advantages.

Finding an optimal fare *and* inputs tax is actually easier than finding the fare alone. To accommodate an inputs tax, we depart from (53) and let the solution price ratio, π, exceed the marginal rate of transformation, as in Section 4.6. Now maximize (28) subject to constraints (29) through (35) also with respect to π. We can carry through the same solution steps as above ((44) to (52)), but as a result of differentiating with respect to π, $\mu_a = \mu_b = 0$, making the first-order conditions simple enough to yield values of P_a and P_b directly. From these values, using (29) and (30), we can obtain solution values π' and p':[26]

$$\pi' = \left(\frac{-dg}{dr}\right)\left(1 + \frac{t_a}{r_a} \cdot \frac{\partial r_a}{\partial t_a} + \frac{t_b}{r_a} \cdot \frac{\partial r_b}{\partial t_a}\right), \tag{57}$$

$$p' = \left(\frac{-dg}{dr}\right)\left[t_a\left(\frac{\partial r_a}{\partial t_b} - \frac{r_b}{r_a}\frac{\partial r_a}{\partial t_a}\right) + t_b\left(\frac{\partial r_b}{\partial t_b} - \frac{r_b}{r_a}\frac{\partial r_b}{\partial t_a}\right)\right]. \tag{58}$$

With assumption (18), by simply rearranging terms in parentheses in (58) and multiplying by t_b/t_a to convert to cost elasticities, we can obtain the condition for a negative p':

[26] The values of π' and p' given in (44) and (45) will yield P_a' and P_b' that equal the marginal social costs of t_a and t_b, and thus eliminate the misallocation due to (13). The number of travelers is assumed large enough to justify simple expectation functions, so adjustments are parametric and externalities are separable for each decision maker. If all auto and bus travelers made up only two decision units, the (reciprocal) externalities would be nonseparable and success could not be claimed for this tax-subsidy policy. See Davis and Whinston (1962) and also Diamond (1973).

$$\frac{\xi_{ab}}{\xi_{aa}} = \frac{\xi_{bb}}{\xi_{ba}} < \frac{\pi' r_b t_b}{\pi' r_a t_a}. \tag{59}$$

The right-hand term in (59) is a ratio of total expenditures on inputs in public transit compared to auto transit. Condition (59) indicates that with an optimal inputs tax a lower price is optimal for public transit, even to the point of causing a loss, as the expenditure for auto travel is relatively smaller, which of course makes more of the burden of the inputs tax (from π') fall on public transit passengers. A greater excess of cost elasticity with respect to t_a over that with respect to t_b will permit the expenditure for auto travel to be larger and still have the optimal p' negative.

With the inputs tax, a loss for the transit agency at its optimum price no longer implies that a net subsidy is needed, since the transit agency loss can be offset by proceeds from the inputs tax. Indeed, by forming an expression for the net proceeds from both inputs tax and transit fare, $(\pi' - (-dg/dr))r + p't_b$, and substituting from (57) and (58), it is easy to show that net proceeds (before transfers) will not be negative. Moreover, even the net proceeds from public transit alone, *ignoring the tax payments of auto travelers,* will be positive (these proceeds are $t_b(t_a\, \partial r_a/\partial t_b + t_b\, \partial r_b/\partial t_b)(-dg/dr)$). Thus, although the transit agency may show a deficit, the deficit will not exceed the value of inputs taxes that are simultaneously being imposed on the agency.

Now let us consider a second-best fare for the off-peak hours, given an input tax that makes $\pi'' > -dg/dr$ part of an optimal rush-hour solution but holds at off-peak times as well. We assume that at off-peak times there is no congestion, and we can specify an off-peak second-best problem by modifying (14) and (15), and every equation in which their derivatives appear, to reflect

$$\frac{\partial r_a}{\partial t_a} = \frac{\partial r_a}{\partial t_b} = \frac{\partial r_b}{\partial t_a} = \frac{\partial r_b}{\partial t_b} = 0.$$

Tracing through the solution steps ((44) to (52)) again for this simpler problem, we can readily find an optimal off-peak value of p, p'':

$$p'' = -\left[\pi'' - \left(-\frac{dg}{dr}\right)\right]\left[r_b - r_a \frac{S_{ab}}{(-S_{bb})}\right]. \tag{60}$$

The value of p'' will be negative for any $\pi'' > (-dg/dr)$ if the extreme right-hand expression in parentheses in (60) is positive. Dividing through that expression by r_a and multiplying by t_b/t_a to convert to compensated demand elasticities, we can obtain the condition:

$$\frac{\eta_{ab}}{(-\eta_{bb})} < \frac{\pi'' r_b t_b}{\pi'' r_a t_a}. \tag{61}$$

Thus in the presence of an inputs tax that is ideal only at peaks, the off-peak public transit price should be lower, even to the point of causing a loss, as the expenditure for auto travel is relatively smaller, making more of the burden of the inputs tax (from π'') fall on public transit passengers. As the elasticity of compensated demand in response to changes in P_b is greater (in absolute value) for t_b compared to t_a, the expenditure for auto travel can be larger and still the optimal p'' will be negative. Again, any apparent subsidy to the transit agency will not be a net subsidy, for it will be offset by proceeds from the inputs tax much as it was in the rush-hour inputs tax case above.[27]

Public enterprise for transportation

Four years of planning and negotiation led to the creation in 1933 of the London Passenger Transport Board, a public agency charged with coordinating into one movable force a total of 92 separate public and private transport services in the London area (Barker and Robbins 1974). Transport services under the board were to raise revenues sufficient to cover their costs, with a revenue pool arrangement among separate units and a committee to ensure their cooperation. Capital was raised on favorable terms with government guarantees, and facilities were expanded and improved, including electrification of railways, until World War II limited what could be done.

The development of London transportation organizations shows both the problems and possibilities in tackling coherently the general problems of urban transit coordination described above. World War II saw cost increases in London unmatched by fare increases, and after the war greater government control of the struggling units was seen as inevitable. There were problems of changing technology, with trolley buses that had looked so promising in the 1930s becoming less effective than the simple bus. After coming to power in 1945, the Labor Party nationalized London Transport and the railways, and since that time political forces have influenced policies.

After control over transport in London was given to local government in 1970, a break-even policy was adopted, with the intention that revenues would cover costs. But a national aim of controlling prices limited fare increases, and in the 1970s necessary local subsidies ranged from 20 percent to almost 40 percent of working expenditures (Bös 1986). From 1981 to

---

[27] Net off-peak (tax-subsidy) proceeds from the transit agency will be
$$[\pi'' - (-dg/dr)](r_a t_b)\eta_{ab}/(-\eta_{ab}),$$
which is positive for any positive inputs tax.

1983 fares were substantially reduced, increased, and then reduced again, as a Labor government in London disputed with the Conservative national government. Finally in 1984 control of London bus and underground service was returned to the national government under London Regional Transport with two subsidiaries, London Bus Ltd. and London Underground Ltd. London Regional Transport is to develop fare structures and other policies to bring maximum use of the services provided. The scheme adopted had sufficient flexibility to allow subsidization with local funds, if that was seen as desirable. Indeed, the deregulation of bus services, which has been permitted in parts of England and could complicate subsidization, was not allowed – at least for the time being – in London. Fares tended to cover only about three-fourths of total costs, although that was higher than in many other European cities at the same time.

If there were not inputs taxes in London, empirical analysis combines with the theory above to suggest that peak bus fares should be subsidized, and with inputs taxes in existence both peak and off-peak fares would seem to warrant subsidization for second-best optimality (Sherman 1967a). A case has been made also for subsidizing underground travel in order to relieve road congestion (Levy-Lambert 1968). The widespread policy of subsidizing public transport in Europe probably accounts for the higher quality of transportation in European cities relative to American cities. Possible effects of strong actions are hinted also by restrictions that have occurred at various times. For example, when the Suez Canal was closed in 1956 motor fuel became scarce in England and was rationed. With the resulting decline in automobile traffic, bus performance was judged to improve by more than 90 percent, and London's economic life was successfully sustained with much reduced auto traffic (Barker and Robbins 1974).

Yet developing the institutions that will implement with efficiency such policies of subsidization remains difficult (Pucher, Markstedt, and Hirschman 1983). Desirable policies may emerge as an almost accidental result of political conflict, although they can be influenced by careful analyses. Entry limitations may be needed, which complicates controlling enterprise performance. And it is difficult to find truly comparable situations elsewhere to use as a basis for evaluating performances. The real coordination task itself is far more complicated than our discussion can indicate, and any institution facing it will have to contend with political as well as economic forces.

10.6   Summary

A public enterprise typically is constrained by its budget to have only a certain difference (perhaps zero) between total revenue and total cost.

Without more extensive limits on its behavior, such an enterprise may seek to maximize its total expenditures, as a bureaucracy has been claimed to do, or its revenue, as large private firms have been accused of doing. Unlike the welfare-maximizing enterprise, which follows a monopoly-like pricing rule but overstates demand elasticities to form Ramsey prices, the expenditure- or revenue-maximizing public enterprise will follow a monopoly-like pricing rule and understate its marginal costs by a constant percentage. An output-maximizing public enterprise also will understate its marginal costs, but by a uniform amount. A public enterprise pursuing any of these goals may draw more heavily on its monopoly power when setting prices than a welfare-maximizing enterprise would. Statutory entry barriers magnify this perverse effect by enhancing the monopoly power of the enterprise.

Urban transportation involves more complex pricing to control congestion externalities. If an automobile passenger contributes more to congestion than a bus passenger, then a case may be made for subsidizing bus and even subway transport to relieve road congestion. But it is difficult to win political agreement for such policies. If entry is restricted, it is also difficult to create efficiency incentives in institutions. Of course some entry is almost inevitable, in the form of private vehicles.

Since its chartering in 1970 as a public corporation (after operating many years as a bureaucracy), the U.S. Postal Service seems to have behaved as a cost or revenue maximizer. It has repeatedly been accused of understating the marginal costs of individual mail services and has admitted they are higher only when prodded by the Postal Rate Commission. The Postal Service and its predecessor the Post Office Department have been accused of cross-subsidization, which can easily result from the pricing rules implied by expenditure, revenue, or output maximization. London Transport faces a more complex pricing problem, in that greater subsidization may be desirable, and output maximization may be a more defensible goal. Political influence has dominated pricing policies to the point of preventing consistency, but it may lead to adoption of the subsidization policy.

Questions

10.1. Suppose that a public enterprise offers two telegraph services, one (Q_1) with short messages and quick delivery and the other (Q_2) with longer messages but less rapid delivery. Demand is given by

$$P_1 = 15 - 0.025Q_1,$$
$$P_2 = 10 - 0.025Q_2,$$

and total cost (TC) of production is given by

$$TC = 1250 + 5Q_1 + 5Q_2.$$

(a) Find Ramsey prices on the assumption that the public enterprise must have total revenue equal to total cost.

(b) Suppose that the public enterprise attempted to maximize total cost rather than welfare, while subject to the constraint that total revenue must equal total cost. Determine P_1 and P_2, and interpret any changes from Ramsey prices found in part (a) (give a rationale for any specific changes brought by changing from the welfare goal served by Ramsey prices to the maximum total cost goal).

(c) If free entry is allowed into both services, are Ramsey prices from part (a) sustainable? Are prices found in part (b) sustainable?

PART IV

Conclusion

CHAPTER 11

Conclusion

11.1 Introduction

The welfare goal that competitive markets serve can be set out also as an objective for regulation to achieve when competition cannot function well. We have focused attention on expressing such ideal outcomes, taking economic efficiency as our dominant goal. Chapter 2 presented ways to represent economic welfare and Part II was devoted to the study of prices that would make such welfare as large as possible. But Chapter 3 brought out difficulties inducing the pursuit of welfare through regulation, and Part III showed that real-world regulatory institutions are not really designed to pursue that aim. Indeed, the contrast between Parts II and III reveals how far institutions are from idealized conceptions.

We now want to consider what might be done to improve regulatory performance, especially where monopoly power exists because entry is prevented. In Section 11.2 we briefly review ways to persuade present organizations to pursue welfare aims. Since these organizations and their regulation were influenced by contending parties understandably promoting their own interests, it is not surprising that they are not ideal. Without the forces of competition, it can be difficult to induce welfare aims in a firm or industry. But that is not the only problem. Regulatory institutions have grown out of conflict among different consumers and between consumers and enterprise owners or managers. Political and judicial institutions have played an important role in their formation, and outcomes have represented compromises between opposing positions. In Section 11.3 we acknowledge the difficulty of reconciling contending interests. Conflict among vested interests is likely to remain a serious problem as long as it is resolved by political means, but opportunity for improvement does exist. Section 11.4 provides a summary.

11.2 Institutional design

How to organize the provision of public services, such as electricity, water, gas, transportation, or telecommunications, particularly when they require enormous investments and can be produced at lowest cost by one

283

organization rather than by competing sellers, is a question faced by all societies. In some countries a government department provides many of them, with expenses budgeted out of general revenues and with proceeds from sales being deposited in the government's treasury. In other times or places a public enterprise is the organization of choice, a unit separated from government in that it can use its own revenues to meet its expenses, but solely or substantially owned by government and also subject to governmental oversight. Elsewhere, and especially in the United States, privately owned corporations provide public services. State regulatory agencies have been concerned primarily with determining a rate of profit for such private firms. Mixed public and private enterprises may also be found, sometimes operating in many respects like a private firm but with a large fraction of shares owned by government. Needless to say, the degree to which market forces are relied on in the economy will have some bearing on this choice, along with a country's history regarding control over the means of production.

Regardless of the form of organization chosen, it is safe to say that its regulation will not be ideal. Rate-of-return regulation of private firms possesses systematic biases in input and output choices; and incentives for the control of costs, including the introduction of new technologies, may be quite weak. Public enterprises function in a variety of political circumstances but are seldom greatly restrained, so a range of outcomes from them is possible. Even less is known about the performance of government departments.

Some excellent performances stand out. Thirty years ago the French public enterprise, Electricité de France, applied theories of welfare pricing like those described in Chapters 4 and 5 and also contributed importantly to their development. The U.S. Postal Service record reviewed in Chapter 10 is not so favorable. Some uneconomic practices there can be traced to the predecessor Post Office Department, which reflected political preferences related to congressional influence that nearly two decades of operation as a public enterprise has not entirely overcome. The regulation of public utilities is so widespread, being practiced in all 50 states, that one might hope the institution would be effective. But its features suggest the paraphrase of an old maxim: "You can lead a public utility to a rate hearing but you can't make it pursue welfare." Still, knowledge about incentives is steadily increasing, and improvements over existing institutions should be possible.

Free entry makes many parties eligible to provide services, and thus to test an existing producer. When entry is barred, that outside challenge is lost, and the single producer may face only some form of administrative oversight, which we can call a regulator, rather than competitors who force it to serve society well. Long-distance telephone service and airline, truck, and bus transportation have recently been opened to the force of free entry. There is no equally effective substitute for the remarkable process by which competition converts profit-seeking behavior to desirable social ends. Competition will not always function satisfactorily, however, so an alternative arrangement may have to be chosen involving statutory monopoly with an extramarket regulator, who of course has a monopoly position over regulation. Between the firm and the regulator a variety of incentive problems can develop.

Even with entry barred, information about a regulated monopoly's performance possibilities may be obtained from producers operating elsewhere. Breaking our national telephone company into seven regional companies, for example, improves prospects for obtaining such information to compare performances. If other firms produce the same product under similar conditions elsewhere, such "yardstick" information can be used about costs, qualities, and other performance aspects to induce one firm to put forth optimum effort (Shleifer 1985). Although conditions elsewhere may never be exactly the same, efforts to account for differences and use performance achievements of others are extremely desirable (Yarrow 1985), and they were used with positive effect under airline regulation by the Civil Aeronautics Board. Contemporaneous performance of others will reflect available technology and going input prices, so it offers the performance reference point closest to a competitive market. It can be considered the best standard next to that resulting from free entry.

Little explicit attention was given to consumer welfare in the design of current institutions. Drawing from proposals of Loeb and Magat (1979), Vogelsang and Finsinger (1979), and Finsinger and Vogelsang (1981, 1982), it would be possible to induce incentives for welfare pricing, and institutional design may be made more effective by experimental study (e.g., Harrison and McKee 1985; Cox and Isaac 1987). On the cost-control side, greater focus on axiomatic costs might improve control over enterprises. Gains might follow from incentive sharing arrangements, which are founded on an understanding of the fundamental principal–agent problem. Improvements are possible simply by holding principal and agent to an announced plan. This "pretend-but-perform" idea (Sertel 1982; Koray and Sertel in press) captures some of the reality in the principal–agent relation by focusing on and even limiting what the parties actually can communicate to one another. Combining bidding for the right to serve as agent with detailed contractual features might also add to the effectiveness of regulation (Laffont and Tirole 1987; McAfee and McMillan 1987a; Riordan and Sappington 1987).

Much remains to be done in designing incentives into regulatory institutions when entry is unavailable as a check on firm performance. New and more detailed rules need to be drawn to specify incentives. Here we have only sketched the form of the problem and the nature of some approaches (see, e.g., Joskow and Schmalensee 1986). As we saw in Part III, existing institutions were not designed with efficiency incentives in mind, and indeed the very idea of bonus payments and risk sharing arrangements is still foreign to regulatory institutions. Yet the need for incentives, especially to serve welfare in the absence of free entry, is now obvious. Existing public enterprise and public utility institutions were derived from those used in private markets, but they do not pursue economic welfare without the free entry of private markets.

To avoid giving the wrong impression, it should be said that many public utilities perform admirably in their situations. But examples such as Electricité de France, which adopted more fully a welfare goal, suggest that some institutions may be better designed. The issue is whether institutions of regulation are designed so their effort achieves the most customer benefit, not whether the institutions are conscientious or public spirited. Given the institutions that we have chosen, we probably are fortunate that they have performed as well as they have.

11.3   Conflicting interests in regulation

The recent trend in the United States has been to reduce the government's regulatory role, through a movement called "deregulation." Cross-subsidization in airlines and telecommunications had created disadvantaged customers of these services who effectively opposed the old policies. New potential providers of services also complained of unreasonable barriers preventing them from providing services. Federal legislation ended fare and entry regulation of airlines by the Civil Aeronautics Board, which was phased out of existence. In addition, a celebrated court case broke up American Telephone and Telegraph into seven local service monopolies and allowed competition in long-distance service. Much greater attention to cost exists now that the reorganization of these industries has brought competing providers of services.

Familiarity with the effects on prices of sugar import quotas, which benefited domestic producers for many years, or even recent "voluntary restraints" on Japanese automobile manufacturers, shows that government intervention does not always improve overall welfare. When new rules can be drawn through political acts, new rents can be created, and interest groups will form to seek them (Buchanan, Tollison, and Tullock 1980). Those with more knowledge and influence will usually benefit, but a large number of more diffuse and unorganized citizens will lose. So government action cannot automatically be assumed to be beneficial, perhaps even if both regulated firms and regulators favor it.

Regulation in the United States has passed beyond the earliest stages of intervention that confirmed governmental authority and established a role for courts. The scope of public utility rate cases continues to be broad, however, and to invite lengthy debate over issues, sometimes without sound economic justification. Adoption of narrower rules, at least for certain aspects of the regulation, could reduce uncertainty caused by regulatory discretion and could also reduce inappropriate political influence. Essentially, this requires that regulatory agencies commit their policies to the form of rules, in order to create for regulated firms a more predictable environment. The rules would give incentives for desirable behavior, perhaps along the lines sketched in Chapter 3, so the firm would not depend as much on regulator judgments, which are hard to predict. This step might appear as a reduction in regulator authority, and so be resisted by regulators. It would limit the opportunity of regulators to change their minds, and to apply their judgments with the latest information available. But it could also bring predictability and planned incentives into monopoly regulation now seriously lacking them.

A debate has taken place for half a century over the conduct of monetary policy, where clearer rules were advocated in place of the discretion of authorities. However sound a decision might be at the time it is taken, uncertainty about it before then can reduce its effectiveness (Simons 1936). That debate about rules versus discretion is not entirely settled, but the advocates for rules have clearly established the advantages of their position. In monopoly regulation, clear rules would serve an even more transparent aim of giving new incentives to enterprises. Incentives now serve investor interests but do not systematically serve consumers in the way missing elements like free entry would require. Interests of parties like investors and consumers are so obvious under monopoly regulation that rules might be challenged, perhaps in court. That is where clearer understanding of regulatory principles and incentive effects is valuable. It can help to produce sound rules and make their enforcement more predictable.

The creation of new institutions affords a good time to narrow the scope of negotiation by agreeing on rules, although the task of creating new institutions is itself so great that ideal regulatory arrangements may not immediately be created. Under England's recent privatization of British Telecom, for instance, price guidelines call for overall price increases that allow for the rate of inflation, less a targeted percentage for improvement in productivity. As a regulatory device, this provides no real guidance for rate structure and leaves the question of how to determine the percentage departure of price changes from inflation up in the air. Still, the slender rule offers efficiency incentive, since it does not base a firm's prices on its own costs, and it is of a type that can induce welfare pricing (Vogelsang 1988). Presumptions about how it operates may develop, however, perhaps favoring the special interests involved, and the presumptions may be legitimated. Then change to better arrangements will be difficult because wealth positions will be predicated on the existing practices (Tullock 1975).

When those involved already have positions to protect, it is hard to avoid compromise between their interests, even though compromise on disputed issues may not yield the most efficient results. The history leading to rate-of-return regulation reflects fully this battle of vested interests. It was resolved sensibly; seeming comparability to market processes was attempted in compromise form to determine investor returns. But real issues of regulation, such as, "What should be the enterprise aim and how can it be induced?" were not treated. The compromises between legal arguments did not yield an effective institution for the general public welfare purpose that reasonably ought to be pursued.

Once interests are well established, change is difficult. But as in airlines and telecommunications, when parties see flaws in current procedures they may be willing to accept change, particularly when authorities are devoted to improving regulation. Some gains can be made merely from consistent behavior of the parties, as in "pretend-but-perform" proposals. Improvements almost certainly will require rules that create better incentives for enterprises to serve consumers and that specify in greater detail how regulation will function. The range of circumstances, on the one hand, and the range of possibilities, on the other, are great. New arrangements are being tried in many jurisdictions. Out of such experiments we should seek improved institutions of monopoly regulation.

11.4   Summary

Welfare economics affords a way to represent how pricing and other policies will benefit a large population of consumers, and provides a standard for regulatory performance. Actual policies involving statutory monopolies do not always allow the most consumer benefit, largely because free entry to force consumer benefit is missing. Outcomes can reflect some monopoly tendencies, or even distortions from efficiency that regulation itself may induce. Such results should not be surprising because existing regulatory institutions were not designed to promote welfare. They grew instead out of conflicts that were often settled in court through compromise between contending parties. Better design of regulatory institutions is possible, if based in part on the knowledge reviewed here. Of course, it is difficult to make changes in institutions unless affected parties ap-prove, but much change has occurred recently in response to regulatory problems.

New rules are needed in monopoly regulation, rules that create incentives for firms to pursue welfare. Such rules should narrow and replace regulator discretion, which now adds to uncertainty without motivating firms positively. Innovations are attempted from time to time in public utility regulation, often with cooperation of all parties. Because rate-of-return regulation of public utilities developed out of court cases, judicial process continues to be the main avenue for change. Some principle may become the subject of court review, as it did in the *Hope* case, and open the possibility for general change. The same is true of many public enterprises, such as the U.S. Postal Service, where regulation has also been influenced by the courts. But regulatory agencies need to take initiatives for change to occur, even though some desirable initiatives may seem to reduce their power and be unappealing to them for that reason. Still, institutional changes of many kinds are being attempted at present, and we should hope for more improvements in the future.

References

Adams, W. J. and J. Yellen (1976), "Commodity Bundling and the Burden of Monopoly," *Quarterly Journal of Economics,* 90: 475–98.

Aharoni, Y. (1986), *The Evolution and Management of State-Owned Enterprises,* Cambridge, Mass.: Ballinger.

Alkan, A. and M. R. Sertel (in press), "The Pretend-but-Perform Mechanism in Sharecropping," *European Journal of Political Economy.*

Allais, M. (1968), "Vilfredo Pareto," *International Encyclopedia of the Social Sciences,* vol. 11, New York: Macmillan and Free Press.

Anderson, D. D. (1980), "State Regulation of Electric Utilities," in J. Q. Wilson, ed., *The Politics of Regulation,* New York: Basic Books.

(1981), *Regulatory Politics and Electric Utilities,* Boston, Mass.: Auburn House.

Arrow, K. J. (1963), *Social Choice and Individual Values,* 2d. ed., New York: John Wiley and Sons.

(1970), *Essays in the Theory of Risk Bearing,* Amsterdam: North-Holland.

(1985), "The Economics of Agency," in J. W. Pratt and R. J. Zeckhauser, eds., *Principals and Agents,* Cambridge, Mass.: Harvard Business.

Arrow, K. J. and A. C. Enthoven (1961), "Quasi-Concave Programming," *Econometrica,* 29: 779–800.

Arrow, K. J. and R. C. Lind (1970), "Uncertainty and the Evaluation of Public Investment Decisions," *American Economic Review,* 60: 364–78.

Auerbach, A. J. and A. J. Pellechio (1978), "The Two-Part Tariff and Voluntary Market Participation," *Quarterly Journal of Economics,* 92: 571–87.

Aumann, R. J. and L. S. Shapley (1974), *Values of Non-Atomic Games,* Princeton, N.J.: Princeton University Press.

Averch, H. and L. L. Johnson (1962), "Behavior of the Firm under Regulatory Constraint," *American Economic Review,* 52: 1053–69.

Awh, R. Y. and W. J. Primeaux, Jr. (1985), "Managerial Discretion and Expense Preference Behavior," *Review of Economics and Statistics,* 67: 224–31.

Bailey, E. E. (1972), "Peak-Load Pricing under Regulatory Constraint," *Journal of Political Economy,* 80: 662–79.

(1973), *Economic Theory of Regulatory Constraint,* Lexington, Mass.: D. C. Heath.

(1974), "Innovation and Regulation," *Journal of Public Economics,* 3: 285–95.

Bailey, E. E. and R. D. Coleman (1971), "The Effect of Lagged Regulation in an Averch–Johnson Model," *Bell Journal of Economics,* 2: 278–92.

Bailey, E. E. and J. Malone (1970), "Resource Allocation and the Regulated Firm," *Bell Journal of Economics,* 1: 129–42.

291

Bailey, E. E. and L. J. White (1974), "Reversals in Peak and Off-Peak Prices," *Bell Journal of Economics,* 5: 75–92.

Balasko, Y. (1976), "A Contribution to the History of the Green Tariff," in H. M. Trebing, ed., *New Dimensions in Public Utility Pricing,* East Lansing: Michigan State University Press.

Baratz, M. S. (1962), *The Economics of the Postal Service,* Washington, D. C.: Public Affairs Press.

Barker, T. C. and M. Robbins (1974), *A History of London Transport,* London: Allen and Unwin.

Baron, D. P. and D. Besanko (1984), "Regulation, Asymmetric Information, and Auditing," *Rand Journal of Economics,* 15: 447–70.

(1987), "Commitment and Fairness in a Dynamic Regulatory Relationship," *Review of Economic Studies,* 54: 413–36.

Baron, D. P. and R. R. De Bondt (1979), "Fuel Adjustment Mechanisms and Economic Efficiency," *Journal of Industrial Economics,* 27: 243–69.

(1981), "On the Design of Regulatory Price Adjustment Mechanisms," *Journal of Economic Theory,* 24: 70–94.

Baron, D. P. and R. B. Myerson (1982), "Regulating a Monopolist with Unknown Costs," *Econometrica,* 50: 911–30.

Barron, D. P. and R. A. Taggart (1977), "A Model of Regulation under Uncertainty and a Test of Regulatory Bias," *The Journal of Economics,* 8: 151–67.

Barton, D. M. and E. O. Olsen (1983), "The Benefits and Costs of Public Housing in New York City," *Journal of Public Economics,* 20: 299–332.

Barzel, Y. (1974), "A Theory of Rationing by Waiting," *Journal of Law and Economics,* 17: 73–95.

Bauer, J. (1925), *Effective Regulation of Public Utilities,* New York: Macmillan.

Baumol, W. J. (1967), *Business Behavior, Value and Growth,* New York: Harcourt, Brace and World.

(1968), "Reasonable Rules for Rate Regulation: Plausible Policies for an Imperfect World," in A. Phillips and O. E. Williamson, eds., *Prices: Issues in Theory, Practice, and Public Policy,* Philadelphia: University of Pennsylvania Press.

(1977), "On the Proper Cost Tests for Natural Monopoly in a Multiproduct Industry," *American Economic Review,* 67: 809–22.

Baumol, W. J., E. E. Bailey, and R. D. Willig (1977), "Weak Invisible Hand Theorems on the Sustainability of Prices in a Multiproduct Natural Monopoly," *American Economic Review,* 67: 350–65.

Baumol, W. J. and D. F. Bradford (1970), "Optimal Departures from Marginal Cost Pricing," *American Economic Review,* 60: 265–83.

Baumol, W. J. and B. G. Malkiel (1967), "The Firm's Optimal Debt Equity Combination and the Cost of Capital," *Quarterly Journal of Economics,* 81: 547–78.

Baumol, W. J., J. Panzar, and R. D. Willig (1982), *Contestable Markets and the Theory of Industry Structure,* New York: Harcourt Brace Jovanovich.

Baumol, W. J. and R. D. Willig (1981), "Fixed Costs, Sunk Costs, Entry Barriers, and Sustainability of Monopoly," *Quarterly Journal of Economics,* 95: 405–31.

Bawa, V. S. and D. S. Sibley (1980), "Dynamic Behavior of a Firm Subject to Stochastic Regulatory Review," *International Economic Review,* 21: 627–42.

Belinfante, A. E. E. (1969), "Technical Change in the Steam Electric Power Generation Industry," Ph.D. diss., University of California, Berkeley.

Berg, S. V. and J. Tschirhart (in press), *Natural Monopoly Regulation: Principles and Practice,* New York: Cambridge University Press.

Bergson, A. (1972), "Optimal Pricing for a Public Enterprise," *Quarterly Journal of Economics,* 86: 519–44.

Besanko, D., S. Donnenfeld, and L. J. White (1987), "Monopoly and Quality Distortion," *Quarterly Journal of Economics,* 102: 743–67.

Billera, L. J. and D. C. Heath (1982), "Allocation of Shared Costs: A Set of Axioms Yielding a Unique Procedure," *Mathematics of Operations Research,* 7: 32–9.

Billera, L. J., D. C. Heath, and J. Raanan (1978), "Internal Telephone Billing Rates – A Novel Application of Non-atomic Game Theory," *Operations Research,* 26: 956–65.

Blinder, Alan S. (1982), "On Making the Tradeoff between Equality and Efficiency Operational," in G. R. Feiwel, ed., *Samuelson and Neoclassical Economics,* The Hague: Kluwer-Nijhoff.

(1987), *Hard Heads, Soft Hearts,* Boston, Mass.: Addison-Wesley.

Boadway, R. W. (1974), "The Welfare Foundations of Cost–Benefit Analysis," *Economic Journal,* 84: 926–39.

Boardman, A., C. C. Eckel, M. Linde, and A. Vining (1983), "An Overview of Mixed Enterprises in Canada," *Business Quarterly,* 48: 101–6.

Boiteux, M. (1956), "Sur la Gestion des Monopoles Publics astrients a l'Équilibre Budgétaire," *Econometrica,* 24: 22–40.

(1960), "La Tarification des Demands en Pointe: Applications de la Théorie de la Vente au Coût Marginal," *Revue Générale de l'Électricité,* 58: pp. 321–40, translated as "Peak-Load Pricing," *Journal of Business,* 33: 157–79.

Borch, K. (1962), "Equilibrium in a Reinsurance Market," *Econometrica,* 30: 424–44.

Borcherding, T. E. (1981), "Toward a Positive Theory of Public Sector Supply Arrangements," in R. Prichard, ed., *Public Enterprise in Canada,* Toronto: Butterworth.

Bös, D. (1986), *Public Enterprise Economics,* Amsterdam: North-Holland.

Bös, D. and G. Tillman (1983), "Cost-Axiomatic Regulatory Pricing," *Journal of Public Economics,* 22: 243–56.

(1984), "Cost Axiomatic Versus Welfare-Maximizing Marginal Cost Pricing," in Marchand, Pestieau and Tulkens, eds., *The Performance of Public Enterprises,* Amsterdam: North-Holland.

Boyles, W. J. (1976), "An Empirical Examination of the Averch–Johnson Effect," *Economic Inquiry,* 14: 25–35.

Braeutigam, R. R. (1979), "Optimal Pricing with Intermodal Competition," *American Economic Review,* 69: 38–49.

(1980), "An Analysis of Fully Distributed Cost Pricing in Regulated Industries," *Bell Journal of Economics,* 11: 182–96.

Brock, G. W. (1981), *The Telecommunications Industry,* Cambridge, Mass.: Harvard University Press.

Brown, G., Jr. and M. Bruce Johnson (1969), "Public Utility Pricing and Output under Risk," *American Economic Review,* 59: 119–28.

Brown, S. J. and D. S. Sibley (1986), *The Theory of Public Utility Pricing,* New York: Cambridge University Press.

Browning, E. K. (1987), "On the Marginal Welfare Cost of Taxation," *American Economic Review,* 77: 11–13.

Buchanan, J. M. (1951), "Knut Wicksell on Marginal Cost Pricing," *Southern Economic Journal,* 17: 173–8.

(1953), "The Theory of Monopolistic Quantity Discounts," *Review of Economic Studies,* 20: 199–208.

(1956), "Private Ownership and Common Usage: The Road Case Reexamined," *Southern Economic Journal,* 22: 305–15.

(1962), "Politics, Policy, and the Pigovian Margins," *Economica,* 29: 17–28.

(1966), "Peak Loads and Efficient Prices: Comment," *Quarterly Journal of Economics,* 80: 463–71.

(1968), "A Public Choice Approach to Public Utility Pricing," *Public Choice,* 2: 1–17.

Buchanan, J. M. and W. C. Stubblebine (1962), "Externality," *Economica,* 29: 371–84.

Buchanan, J. M. and G. Tullock (1966), *The Calculus of Consent,* Ann Arbor: University of Michigan Press.

Buchanan, J. M., R. D. Tollison, and G. Tullock (1980), *Toward a Theory of the Rent-Seeking Society,* College Station, Texas: Texas A&M.

Burstein, M. L. (1960), "The Economics of Tie-In Sales," *Review of Economics and Statistics,* 42: 68–73.

Callen, J., G. F. Mathewson, and H. Mohring (1976), "The Benefits and Costs of Rate-of-Return Regulation," *American Economic Review,* 66: 290–7.

Cargill, T. F. and R. A. Meyer (1971), "Estimating the Demand for Electricity by Time of Day," *Applied Economics,* 4: 233–46.

Caritat, M. J. A. N. (the Marquis de Condorcet) (1785), *Essai sur l'Application de l'Analyse à la Probabilité des Décisions Rendues à la Pluralité des Voix,* Paris (reprinted in 1973 by Chelsea Press, New York).

Carleton, W. T. (1974), "Rate of Return, Rate Base and Regulatory Lag under Conditions of Changing Capital Costs," *Land Economics,* 50: 172–84.

Carlton, D. W. (1977), "Peak-Load Pricing with Stochastic Demand," *American Economic Review,* 67: 1006–10.

Chadwick, Sir Edwin (1859), "Results of Different Principles of Legislation and Administration in Europe: of Competition for the Field, as Compared with the Competition Within the Field of Service," *Journal of the Royal Statistical Society,* 22: 381–420.

Chiang, A. C. (1974), *Fundamental Methods of Mathematical Economics,* 3d ed., New York: McGraw-Hill.

Christensen, L. R. and W. H. Green (1976), "Economies of Scale in U.S. Electric Power Generation," *Journal of Political Economy,* 84: 655–76.

Coase, R. H. (1946), "The Marginal Cost Controversy," *Economica,* 13: 169–82.

(1960), "The Problem of Social Cost," *Journal of Law and Economics,* 3: 1–44.

(1972), "Durability and Monopoly," *Journal of Law and Economics,* 15: 143–9.

Cohen, M. (1979), "Efficiency and Competition in the Electric-Power Industry," *Yale Law Journal,* 88: 1511–49.

Cole, L. P. (1981), "A Note on Fully Distributed Cost Prices," *Bell Journal of Economics,* 12: 329–34.

Comanor, W. (1970), "Should Natural Monopolies be Regulated," *Stanford Law Review,* 22: 510–18.

Corlett, W. J. and D. C. Hague (1953–4), "Complementarity and the Excess Burden of Taxation," *Review of Economic Studies,* 21: 21–30.

Coursey, D., R. M. Isaac, and V. L. Smith (1984), "Natural Monopoly and Contested Markets: Some Experimental Results," *Journal of Law and Economics,* 27: 91–113.

Coursey, D., R. M. Isaac, M. Luke, and V. L. Smith (1984), "Market Contestability in the Presence of Sunk (Entry) Costs," *Rand Journal of Economics,* 15: 69–95.

Courville, L. (1974), "Regulation and Efficiency in the Electric Utility Industry," *Bell Journal of Economics,* 5: 53–74.

Cox, J. C. and R. M. Isaac (1987), "Mechanisms for Incentive Regulation: Theory and Experiment," *Rand Journal of Economics,* 18: 348–59.

Crandall, R. W. (1968), "Vertical Integration and the Market for Repair Parts in the U.S. Automobile Industry," *Journal of Industrial Economics,* 16: 212–34.

Crew, Michael A. (1968), "Peak Load Pricing and Optimal Capacity: Comment," *American Economic Review,* 53: 168–70.

Crew, Michael A. and Paul R. Kleindorfer (1976), "Peak Load Pricing with a Diverse Technology," *Bell Journal of Economics,* 7: 207–31.

(1978), "Reliability and Public Utility Pricing," *American Economic Review,* 68: 31–40.

(1979a), "Managerial Discretion and Public Utility Regulation," *Southern Economic Journal,* 45: 696–709.

(1979b), *Public Utility Economics,* New York: St. Martins.

(1986), *The Economics of Public Utility Regulation,* Cambridge, Mass.: MIT Press.

Cross, J. G. (1970), "Incentive Pricing and Utility Regulation," *Quarterly Journal of Economics,* 84: 236–53.

Cross, S. M. (1982), *Economic Decisions under Inflation: The Impact of Accounting Measurement Errors,* Greenwich, Conn.: JAI Press.

Cummings, F. J. and W. E. Ruhter (1979), "The *Northern Pacific* Case," *Journal of Law and Economics,* 22: 329–50.

296   References

Currie, J. M., J. A. Murphy, and A. Schmitz (1971), "The Concept of Economic Surplus and Its Use in Economic Analysis," *Economic Journal,* 81: 741–90.

Das, S. P. (1980), "On the Effect of Rate of Return Regulation under Uncertainty," *American Economic Review,* 70: 456–60.

Davis, O. A. and A. B. Whinston (1962), "Externalities, Welfare and the Theory of Games," *Journal of Political Economy,* 70: 241–62.

(1965), "Welfare Economics and the Theory of Second Best," *Review of Economic Studies,* 32: 1–14.

De Alessi, L. (1974), "An Economic Analysis of Government Ownership and Regulation," *Public Choice,* 19: 526–38.

Demsetz, H. (1968), "Why Regulate Utilities?" *Journal of Law and Economics,* 11: 55–65.

Dhrymes, P. J. and M. Kurz (1964), "Technology and Scale in Electricity Generation," *Econometrica,* 32: 287–315.

Diamond, Peter A. (1973), "Consumption Externalities and Imperfect Corrective Pricing," *Bell Journal of Economics,* 4: 526–38.

Drèze, J. (1964), "Some Postwar Contributions of French Economists," *American Economic Review,* 54: 1–64.

Dublin, J. A. and P. Navarro (1982), "Regulatory Climate and the Cost of Capital," in M. A. Crew, ed., *Regulatory Reform and Public Utilities,* Lexington, Mass.: D. C. Heath.

Dupuit, J. (1844), "De la Mesure de l'Utilité des Travaux Publics," *Annales des Ponts et Chausees* 8, reprinted with comments by Mario di Bernardi and Luigi Einaudiun, "De l'Utilité et de sa Mesure," *La Riforma Soziale,* Turin (1932), and in English in K. J. Arrow and T. Scitovsky, eds. (1969), *Readings in Welfare Economics,* Homewood, Ill.: Irwin.

Dziadek, F. (1959), "The Productivity of the U.S. Postal Service: An Intertemporal and Cross-sectional Study of Post Office Labor Productivity," Ph.D. diss., Johns Hopkins University, Baltimore, Md.

Eckel, C. C. (1983), "Customer Class Pricing by Electric Utilities," Ph.D. diss., University of Virginia.

(1985), "A General Theory of Customer Class Pricing," *Economics Letters,* 17: 285–9.

(1987), "Customer Class Price Discrimination by Electric Utilities," *Journal of Economics and Business,* 39: 19–33.

Eckel, C. C. and T. Vermallen (1986), "The Effects of Partial Government Ownership on Stock Prices," *Journal of Law and Economics,* 29: 381–404.

Ehrlich, I. and R. A. Posner (1974), "An Economic Analysis of Legal Rule Making," *Journal of Legal Studies,* 3: 257–86.

Ekelund, R. B., Jr. and R. S. Higgins (1982), "Capital Fixity, Innovations, and Long Term Contracting: An Intertemporal Theory of Regulation," *American Economic Review,* 72: 32–46.

Faulhaber, G. R. (1975), "Cross Subsidization: Pricing in Public Enterprises," *American Economic Review,* 65: 966–77.

Faulhaber, G. R. and S. B. Levinson (1981), "Subsidy-Free Prices and Anonymous Equity," *American Economic Review,* 71: 1083–91.

Feldman, A. M. (1980), *Welfare Economics and Social Choice Theory,* Boston, Mass.: Martinus Nijhoff.

Feldstein, M. S. (1972a), "Distributional Equity and the Optimal Structure of Public Prices," *American Economic Review,* 62: 32–6.

(1972b), "Equity and Efficiency in Public Pricing," *Quarterly Journal of Economics,* 86: 175–87.

Ferguson, C. E. (1969), *The Neoclassical Theory of Production and Distribution,* Cambridge: Cambridge University Press.

Finsinger, J. and I. Vogelsang (1981), "Alternative Institutional Frameworks for Price Incentive Mechanisms," *Kyklos,* 34, no. 3: 388–404.

(1982), "Performance Indices for Public Enterprises," in L. P. Jones, ed., *Public Enterprise in Less Developed Countries,* Cambridge: Cambridge University Press.

Fisher, F. M. and C. Kaysen (1962), *A Study in Econometrics: The Demand for Electricity in the United States,* Amsterdam: North-Holland.

Fuss, M. A. (1980), "Cost Allocation: How Can the Costs of Postal Service be Determined?" in R. Sherman, ed., *Perspectives on Postal Service Issues,* Washington, D.C.: American Enterprise Institute.

Gabor, A. (1955), "A Note on Block Tariffs," *Review of Economic Studies,* 23: 32–41.

Gegax, D. and J. Tschirhart (1984), "An Analysis of Interfirm Cooperation: Theory and Evidence from Electric Power Pools," *Southern Economic Journal,* 50: 1077–97.

George, A. (1973), "Second-Best Pricing in the Postal Service," Ph.D. diss., University of Virginia.

Giordano, J. N. (1983), "The Changing Impact of Regulation on the U.S. Electric Utility Industry," *Eastern Economic Journal,* 9: 91–101.

Goldberg, V. (1976), "Regulation and Administered Contracts," *Bell Journal of Economics,* 7: 426–48.

Goldman, M. (1987), *Gorbachev's Challenge,* New York: Norton.

Goldman, M. B., H. E. Leland, and D. S. Sibley (1984), "Optimal Nonuniform Pricing," *Review of Economic Studies,* 51: 305–19.

Graham, D. R. (1976), "A Test of the Averch–Johnson Model of Regulation using Electricity Utility Data," Ph.D. diss., University of California, Los Angeles.

Gravelle, H. S. E. (1982), "Incentives, Efficiency and Control in Public Firms," *Zeitschrift fur Nationalokonomie,* 42: Supp. 2, 79–104.

Guesnerie, R. (1980), "Second-Best Pricing Rules in the Boiteux Tradition," *Journal of Public Economics,* 13: 51–80.

Gul, F., H. Sonnenschein, and R. Wilson (1986), "Foundations of Dynamic Monopoly and the Coase Conjecture," *Journal of Economic Theory,* 39: 155–90.

Hadley, G. (1964), *Nonlinear and Dynamic Programming,* Boston: Addison-Wesley.

Hagerman, R. L. and B. T. Ratchford (1978), "Some Determinants of Allowed Rates of Return on Equity to Electric Utilities," *Bell Journal of Economics,* 9: 46–55.

Harberger, A. C. (1984), "Basic Needs versus Distributional Weights in Cost-Benefit Analysis," *Economic Development and Cultural Change,* 32: 455–74.

Harris, M. and A. Raviv (1978), "Some Results on Incentive Contracts," *American Economic Review,* 68: 20–30.

(1981), "A Theory of Monopoly Prices with Uncertain Demand," *American Economic Review,* 71: 347–65.

Harrison, G. W. and M. McKee (1985), "Monopoly Behavior, Decentralized Regulation, and Contestable Markets: An Experimental Evaluation," *Rand Journal of Economics,* 16: 51–69.

Hausman, W. J. and J. L. Neufeld (1984), "Time-of-Day Pricing in the U.S. Electric Power Industry at the Turn of the Century," *Rand Journal of Economics,* 15: 116–26.

Henderson, A. (1947), "The Pricing of Public Utility Undertakings," *Manchester School,* 15: 223–50.

Hicks, J. R. (1939), "Foundations of Welfare Economics," *Economic Journal,* 49: 696–712.

(1940), "The Valuation of Social Income," *Economica,* 7: 105–24.

(1941), "The Rehabilitation of Consumer's Surplus," *Review of Economic Studies,* 8: 103–16.

(1943), "The Four Consumers' Surpluses," *Review of Economic Studies,* 11: 31–41.

Holmström, B. (1979), "Moral Hazard and Observability," *Bell Journal of Economics,* 10: 74–91.

Holt, C. A., Jr. (1979), "Uncertainty and the Bidding for Incentive Contracts," *American Economic Review,* 69: 697–705.

Holt, C. A., Jr. and R. Sherman (1982), "Waiting-Line Auctions," *Journal of Political Economy,* 90: 280–94.

Hotelling, H. (1938), "The General Welfare in Relation to Problems of Taxation and of Railway and Utility Rates," *Econometrica,* 6: 242–69.

Houthakker, H. S. (1951), "Electricity Tariffs in Theory and Practice," *Economic Journal,* 61: 1–25.

Huneke, W. F. (1983), *The Heavy Hand: Government and the Union Pacific, 1862–1898,* New York: Garland.

Jackson, R. (1969), "Regulation and Electric Utility Rate Levels," *Land Economics,* 45: 372–6.

Jensen, M. and W. H. Mechling (1976), "Theory of the Firm: Managerial Behavior, Agency Costs and Ownership Structure," *Journal of Financial Economics,* 3: 305–60.

Johnson, B. (1984), "Regulation of the Intercity Bus Industry: A Comparison of the Public Interest Theory and the Economic Theory of Regulation," Ph.D. diss., University of Virginia.

References

Jones, F. (1983), *Input Biases under Rate-of-Return Regulation*, New York: Garland Press.

Jones, L. P. (1985), "Public Enterprise for Whom?: Perverse Distributional Consequences of Public Operational Decisions," *Economic Development and Cultural Change*, 33: 333–47.

Jordan, W. A. (1972), "Producer Protection, Prior Market Structure and the Effects of Government Regulation," *Journal of Law and Economics*, 15: 151–76.

Joskow, P. L. (1972), "The Determination of the Allowed Rate of Return in a Formal Regulatory Hearing," *Bell Journal of Economics*, 3: 632–44.

(1973), "Pricing Decisions of Regulated Firms: A Behavioral Approach," *Bell Journal of Economics*, 4: 118–40.

(1974), "Inflation and Environmental Concern: Structural Changes in the Process of Public Utility Regulation," *Journal of Law and Economics*, 17: 291–327.

(1976), "Contributions to the Theory of Marginal Cost Pricing," *Bell Journal of Economics*, 7: 197–206.

Joskow, P. L. and R. Schmalensee (1983), *Markets for Power*, Cambridge, Mass.: MIT Press.

(1986), "Incentive Regulation for Electric Utilities," *Yale Journal on Regulation*, 4: 1–49.

Kafoglis, M. (1969), "Output of the Restrained Firm," *American Economic Review*, 59: 583–9.

Kahn, A. E. (1970), *The Economics of Regulation: Vol. I*, New York: Wiley.

(1971), *The Economics of Regulation: Vol. II*, New York: Wiley.

(1987), "The Future of Local Telephone Service: Technology and Public Policy," Fishman-Davidson Center Discussion Paper no. 22, Wharton School, University of Pennsylvania.

Kaldor, N. (1939), "Welfare Propositions of Economics and Interpersonal Comparisons of Utility," *Economic Journal*, 49: 549–52.

Kamien, M. I. and N. L. Schwartz (1981), *Dynamic Optimization*, New York: North Holland.

Katz, M. L. (1983), "Nonuniform Pricing, Output, and Welfare Under Monopoly," *Review of Economic Studies*, 50: 37–56.

(1984), "Nonuniform Pricing with Observable Numbers of Purchases," *Review of Economic Studies*, 51: 461–70.

Kay, J. A., C. Mayer, and D. J. Thompson, eds. (1986), *Privatisation and Regulation – The UK Experience*, Oxford: Clarendon.

Kay, J. A. and D. J. Thompson (1986), "Privatization: A Policy in Search of a Rationale," *Economic Journal*, 96: 18–32.

Keran, M. W. (1976), "Inflation, Regulation and Utility Stock Prices," *Bell Journal of Economics*, 7: 268–74.

Klevorick, A. K. (1973), "The Behavior of the Firm Subject to Stochastic Regulatory Review," *Bell Journal of Economics*, 4: 57–88.

Knight, F. H. (1924), "Some Fallacies in the Interpretation of Social Cost," *Quarterly Journal of Economics*, 38: 582–606.

Kolbe, A. L., J. A. Read, Jr., and G. R. Hall (1985), *The Cost of Capital: Estimating the Rate of Return for Public Utilities,* Cambridge, Mass.: MIT Press.

Kolko, G. (1963), *The Triumph of Conservatism 1900–1916,* New York: Free Press of Glencoe.

Koray, S. and M. Sertel (in press), "Regulating a Duopoly by a Pretend-but-Perform Mechanism," *European Journal of Political Economy.*

Laffont, J-J. and J. Tirole (1986), "Using Cost Observations to Regulate Firms," *Journal of Political Economy,* 94: 614–41.

(1987), "Auctioning Incentive Contracts," *Journal of Political Economy,* 95: 921–37.

Lebowitz, J. L., C. O. Lee, and P. B. Linhart (1976), "Some Effects of Inflation on a Firm with Original Cost Depreciation," *Bell Journal of Economics,* 7: 463–77.

Leibenstein, H. (1966), "Allocative Efficiency versus X-efficiency," *American Economic Review,* 56: 392–415.

Leland, H. E. and R. A. Meyer (1976), "Monopoly Pricing Structures with Imperfect Information," *Bell Journal of Economics,* 7: 449–62.

Lereah, D. (1983), "Information Problems and Regulation in Insurance Markets," Ph.D. diss., University of Virginia.

Lerner, A. (1970), "On Optimal Taxes with an Untaxable Sector," *American Economic Review,* 60: 284–94.

Leventhal, H. (1965), "Vitality of the Comparable Earnings Standard for Regulation of Utilities in a Growth Economy," *Yale Law Journal,* 74: 989–1018.

Levine, M. (1987), "Airline Competition in Deregulated Markets: Theory, Firm Strategy, and Public Policy," *Yale Journal of Regulation,* 4: 393–494.

Levy-Lambert, H. (1968), "Tarification des Services à Qualité Variable-Application aux Péages de Circulation," *Econometrica,* 36: 564–74.

Lindsay, C. M. (1976), "A Theory of Government Enterprise," *Journal of Political Economy,* 84: 1061–77.

Lipman, B. L. (1985), "Dynamic Behavior of a Firm Subject to Stochastic Regulatory Review: A Comment," *International Economic Review,* 26: 511–15.

Lipsey, R. G. and K. Lancaster (1956), "The General Theory of Second Best," *Review of Economic Studies,* 24: 11–32.

Littlechild, S. C. and J. J. Rousseau (1975), "Pricing Policy of a U.S. Telephone Company," *Journal of Public Economics,* 4: 35–6.

Loeb, M. and W. A. Magat (1979), "A Decentralized Method for Utility Regulation," *Journal of Law and Economics,* 22: 399–404.

Machina, M. J. (1987), "Choice under Uncertainty: Problems Solved and Unsolved," *Economic Perspectives,* 1: 121–54.

Magat, W. A. (1976), "Regulation and the Rate and Direction of Induced Technological Change," *Bell Journal of Economics,* 7: 478–96.

Maloney, M. T., R. E. McCormick, and R. D. Tollison (1984), "Economic Regulation, Competitive Governments, and Specialized Resources," *Journal of Law and Economics,* 27: 329–38.

Mantell, E. H. (1974), "Factors Affecting Labor Productivity in Post Offices," *Journal of the American Statistical Association:* 303–9.

Marchand, M. G. (1968), "A Note on Optimal Tolls in an Imperfect Environment," *Econometrica,* 36: 575–81.

—— (1973), "The Economic Principles of Telephone Rates under a Budget Constraint," *Review of Economic Studies,* 40: 507–15.

Marshall, A. (1920), *Principles of Economics,* 8th ed., London: Macmillan.

Marshall, W. J., J. B. Yawitz, and E. Greenberg (1981), "Optimal Regulation under Uncertainty," *Journal of Finance,* 36: 909–21.

Maskin, E. and J. Riley (1984), "Monopoly with Incomplete Information," *Rand Journal of Economics,* 15: 171–96.

Masten, S. E. and K. J. Crocker (1985), "Efficient Adaptation in Take-or-Pay Contracts: Take-or-Pay Provisions for Natural Gas," *American Economic Review,* 75: 1083–93.

McAfee, R. P. and J. McMillan (1987a), "Competition for Agency Contracts," *Rand Journal of Economics,* 18: 296–307.

—— (1987b), "Auctions and Bidding," *Journal of Economic Literature,* 25: 699–738.

McCormick, R. E., W. F. Shughart, and R. D. Tollison (1984), "The Disinterest in Deregulation," *American Economic Review,* 74: 1075–9.

McKean, R. N. and J. H. Moore (1972), "Uncertainty and the Evaluation of Public Investment Decisions: Comment," *American Economic Review,* 62: 165–7.

Merewitz, L. (1971), "Costs and Returns to Scale in U.S. Post Offices," *Journal of the American Statistical Association:* 504–9.

Merrill, Lynch, Pierce, Fenner and Smith, Inc. (1980), *Utility Research: Recent Regulatory Decisions and Trends,* New York: Securities Research Division.

Meyer, R. A. (1975), "Monopoly Pricing and Capacity Choice under Uncertainty," *American Economic Review,* 65: 326–37.

Miller, J. C. and R. Sherman (1980), "Has the Postal Reorganization Act Been Fair to Mailers?" in R. Sherman, ed., *Perspectives on Postal Service Issues,* Washington, D.C.: American Enterprise Institute.

Mills, D. E. (1981), "Ownership Arrangements and Congestion-Prone Facilities," *American Economic Review,* 71: 493–502.

—— (1984), "Demand Fluctuations and Endogenous Firm Flexibility," *Journal of Industrial Economics,* 33: 55–71.

—— (1986), "Flexibility and Firm Diversity with Demand Fluctuations," *International Journal of Industrial Organization,* 4: 203–15.

Mills, D. E. and L. Schumann (1985), "Industry Structure with Fluctuating Demand," *American Economic Review,* 75: 758–67.

Mills, E. S. (1959), "Uncertainty and Price Theory," *Quarterly Journal of Economics,* 73: 116–30.

Mills, G. (1976), "Public Utility Pricing for Joint Demand Involving a Durable Good," *Bell Journal of Economics,* 7: 299–307.

Ministry of Transport (1964), *Road Pricing: The Economic and Technical Possibilities,* London: Her Majesty's Stationery Office.

Mirman, L. J., D. Samet, and Y. Tauman (1983), "An Axiomatic Approach to the Allocation of a Fixed Cost through Prices," *Bell Journal of Economics,* 14: 139–51.

Mirman, L. J. and D. S. Sibley (1980), "Optimal Nonlinear Prices for Multiproduct Monopolies," *Bell Journal of Economics,* 11: 659–70.

Mirman, L. J. and Y. Tauman (1982), "Demand Compatible, Equitable Cost Sharing Prices," *Mathematics of Operations Research,* 7: 40–56.

Mirman, L. J., Y. Tauman, and I. Zang (1985a), "Supportability, Sustainability, and Subsidy-Free Prices," *Rand Journal of Economics,* 16: 114–26.

(1985b), "Monopoly and Sustainable Prices as a Nash Equilibrium in Contestable Markets," in G. R. Feiwel, ed., *Issues in Contemporary Microeconomics and Welfare,* London: Macmillan.

(1986), "Ramsey Prices, Average Cost Prices and Price Sustainability," *International Journal of Industrial Organization,* 4: 123–40.

Mitchell, B. M. (1978), "Optimal Pricing of Local Telephone Service," *American Economic Review,* 68: 517–37.

Mitchell, B. M., W. G. Manning, and J. P. Acton (1978), *Peak-Load Pricing: European Lessons for U.S. Energy Policy,* Cambridge, Mass.: Ballinger.

Modigliani, F. and M. Miller (1958), "The Cost of Capital, Corporation Finance, and the Theory of Investment," *American Economic Review,* 48: 261–97.

(1966), "Some Estimates of the Cost of Capital to the Electric Utility Industry, 1954–57," *American Economic Review,* 56: 331–66.

Mohring, H. (1970), "The Peak Load Problem with Increasing Returns and Pricing Constraints," *American Economic Review,* 60: 693–705.

(1971), "Alternative Welfare Gain and Loss Measures," *Western Economic Journal,* 9: 349–68.

Mohring, H., J. Schroeter, and P. Wiboonchutikula (1987), "The Values of Waiting Time, Travel Time, and a Seat on a Bus," *Rand Journal of Economics,* 18: 40–56.

Montgomery, R. (1931), "Judicial Fair Return and the Price Level," *Southwestern Social Science Quarterly,* 12: 221–53.

Morrison, H. (1933), *Socialization and Transport,* London: Constable.

Mueller, D. C. (1980), *Public Choice,* New York: Cambridge University Press.

Mussa, M. and S. Rosen (1978), "Monopoly and Product Quality," *Journal of Economic Theory,* 18: 301–17.

Myerson, R. (1983), "Mechanism Design by an Informed Principal," *Econometrica,* 51: 1767–97.

Naughton, M. C. (1986), "The Efficiency and Equity Consequences of Two-Part Tariffs in Electricity Pricing," *Review of Economics and Statistics,* 68: 406–14.

Navarro, P. (1980), "Public Utility Commission Regulation: Performance, Determinants, and Energy Policy Impacts," Harvard University Energy and Environmental Policy Center Discussion Paper E-80-05.

(1981), "Electric Utility Regulation and National Energy Policy," *Regulation,* 5: 20–27.

Needy, C. W. (1975), *Regulation-Induced Distortions*, Lexington, Mass.: D. C. Heath.

Negishi, T. (1960), "Welfare Economics and Existence of an Equilibrium for a Competitive Economy," *Metroeconomica*, 12: 92–7.

Nerlove, M. (1967), "Recent Empirical Studies of the CES and Related Production Functions," in *The Theory and Empirical Analysis of Production*, Princeton, N.J.: Princeton University Press.

Ng, Y. K. (1980), *Welfare Economics*, New York: John Wiley & Sons.

Ng, Y. K. and M. Weisser (1974), "Optimal Pricing with a Budget Constraint – The Case of the Two-part Tariff," *Review of Economic Studies*, 61: 337–45.

Nichols, D. A., E. Smolensky, and T. N. Tideman (1971), "Discrimination by Waiting Time in Merit Goods," *American Economic Review*, 61: 312–23.

Niskanen, W. A., Jr. (1971), *Bureaucracy and Representative Government*, Chicago, Ill.: Aldine-Atherton.

Oi, W. Y. (1971), "A Disneyland Dilemma: Two-Part Tariffs for a Mickey Mouse Monopoly," *Quarterly Journal of Economics*, 85: 77–96.

Okuguchi, O. (1975), "The Implications of Regulation for Induced Technical Change: Comment," *Bell Journal of Economics*, 6: 103–5.

Owen, B. M. and R. Braeutigam (1978), *The Regulation Game: Strategic Use of the Administrative Process*, Cambridge, Mass.: Ballinger.

Panzar, J. C. and R. D. Willig (1977a), "Free Entry and the Sustainability of Natural Monopoly," *Bell Journal of Economics*, 8: 1–22.

(1977b), "Economies of Scale and Economies of Scope in Multi-Output Production," *Quarterly Journal of Economics*, 91: 481–93.

Peles, Y. C. and J. L. Stein (1976), "The Effect of Rate of Return Regulation is Highly Sensitive to the Nature of Uncertainty," *American Economic Review*, 66: 278–89.

Peltzman, S. (1971), "Pricing in Public Enterprise: Electric Utilities in the United States," *Journal of Law and Economics*, 14: 109–47.

(1976), "Toward a More General Theory of Regulation," *Journal of Law and Economics*, 19: 211–40.

Perrakis, S. (1976a), "On the Regulated Price-Setting Monopoly Firm with a Random Demand Curve," *American Economic Review*, 66: 410–16.

(1976b), "Rate of Return Regulation of a Monopoly Firm with Random Demand," *International Economic Review*, 17: 149–62.

Pescatrice, D. R. and J. M. Trapani (1980), "The Performance and Objectives of Public and Private Utilities Operating in the U.S.," *Journal of Public Economics*, 13: 259–76.

Petersen, H. (1975a), "An Empirical Test of Regulatory Effects," *Bell Journal of Economics*, 6: 11–26.

(1975b), "The Effect of Regulation on Production Costs and Output Prices in the Private Electric Utility Industry," Stanford University Growth Center Memo 151, Sept.

Phillips, O. R. and R. C. Battalio (1983), "Two-Part Tariffs and Monopoly Profits When Visits Are Variable," *Bell Journal of Economics*, 14: 601–14.

Picard, P. (1987), "On the Design of Incentive Schemes under Moral Hazard and Adverse Selection," *Journal of Public Economics,* 33: 305-31.

Pigou, A. C. (1920), *The Economics of Welfare,* London: Macmillan.

Plott, C. R. and M. E. Levine (1978), "A Model of Agenda Influence on Committee Decisions," *American Economic Review,* 68: 146-60.

Pomerantz, L. S. and J. E. Suelflow (1977), *Allowance for Funds Used during Construction,* East Lansing, Mich.: Michigan State University Press.

Posner, R. A. (1969), "Natural Monopoly and Its Regulation," *Stanford Law Review,* 21: 548-643.

(1971), "Taxation by Regulation," *Bell Journal of Economics,* 2: 22-50.

(1974), "Theories of Economic Regulation," *Bell Journal of Regulation,* 5: 335-58.

(1975), "The Social Costs of Monopoly and Regulation," *Journal of Political Economy,* 83: 807-27.

Pratt, J. W. (1964), "Risk Aversion in the Small and the Large," *Econometrica,* 32: 122-36.

Primeaux, W. J. (1978), "Rate-Base Methods and Realized Rates of Return," *Economic Inquiry,* 16: 95-107.

(1986), *Direct Electric Utility Competition: The Natural Monopoly Myth,* New York: Praeger.

Primeaux, W. J. and R. A. Nelson (1980), "An Examination of Price Discrimination and Internal Subsidization by Electric Utilities," *Southern Economic Journal,* 47: 84-99.

Pucher, J., A. Markstedt, and I. Hirschman (1983), "Impacts of Subsidies on the Costs of Urban Public Transport," *Journal of Transport Economics and Policy,* 17: 155-76.

Ramsey, F. (1927), "A Contribution to the Theory of Taxation," *Economic Journal,* 37: 47-61.

Rau, N. (1979), "On Regulation and Uncertainty: Comment," *American Economic Review,* 69: 190-4.

Rees, R., (1968), "Second Best Rules of Public Enterprise Pricing," *Economica,* 35: 260-73.

(1985), "The Theory of Principal and Agent, Parts I and II," *Bulletin of Economic Research,* 37: 3-26, 75-95.

Rhoads, S. E. (1985), *The Economist's View of the World,* New York: Cambridge University Press.

Riordan, M. H. and D. E. M. Sappington (1987), "Awarding Monopoly Franchises," *American Economic Review,* 77: 375-87.

Road Research Laboratory (1965), *Research on Road Traffic,* London: Her Majesty's Stationery Office.

Roberts, K. W. S. (1979), "Welfare Considerations of Nonlinear Pricing," *Economic Journal,* 89: 66-83.

Robinson, J. (1933), *Economics of Imperfect Competition,* London: Macmillan.

Robson, W. A. (1960), *Nationalized Industry and Public Ownership,* London: Allen and Unwin.

Sadka, E. (1978), "On the Optimal Taxation of Consumption Externalities," *Quarterly Journal of Economics,* 92: 165–74.

Salomon Brothers (1973), "Fuel Mix Data and Fuel Adjustment Clause Survey," July, New York.

Samet, D. and Y. Tauman (1982), "The Determination of Marginal Cost Prices under a Set of Axioms," *Econometrica,* 50: 895–909.

Samuelson, P. A. (1947), *Foundations of Economic Analysis,* Cambridge, Mass.: Harvard University Press.

Sandmo, A. (1976), "Optimal Taxation," *Journal of Public Economics,* 6: 37–54.

Sappington, D. (1980), "Strategic Firm Behavior under a Dynamic Regulatory Adjustment Process," *Bell Journal of Economics,* 11: 360–72.

  (1982), "Optimal Regulation of Research and Development under Imperfect Information," *Bell Journal of Economics,* 13: 354–68.

  (1983), "Optimal Regulation of a Multiproduct Monopoly with Unknown Technological Capabilities," *Bell Journal of Economics,* 14: 453–63.

  (1986), "Commitment to Regulatory Bureaucracy," *Information Economics and Policy,* 2: 243–57.

Schmalensee, R. (1970), "Regulation and the Durability of Goods," *Bell Journal of Economics,* 1: 54–64.

  (1979), *The Control of Natural Monopolies,* Lexington, Mass.: D. C. Heath.

  (1981), "Monopolistic Two-Part Pricing Arrangements," *Bell Journal of Economics,* 12: 445–66.

Schmalensee, R. and B. W. Golub (1984), "Estimating Effective Concentration in Deregulated Wholesale Electricity Markets," *Bell Journal of Economics,* 15: 12–26.

Schmidt, M. (1981), *Automatic Adjustment Clauses: Theory and Applications,* East Lansing: Michigan State University Press.

Schulz, W. (1980), "Pre-conditions for Franchise Bidding in the Electricity Sector in West Germany," in B. M. Mitchell and P. R. Kleindorfer, eds., *Regulated Industries and Public Enterprise,* Lexington, Mass.: D. C. Heath.

Scitovsky, T. (1941), "A Note on Welfare Propositions in Economics," *Review of Economic Studies,* 8: 77–88.

Scott, F. A., Jr. (1979), "An Economic Analysis of Fuel Adjustment Clauses," Ph.D. diss., University of Virginia.

  (1981), "Estimating Recipient Benefits and Waste from Lifetime Electricity Rates," *Land Economics,* 57: 536–43.

  (1986), "Assessing U.S.A. Postal Rate Making: An Application of Ramsey Prices," *Journal of Industrial Economics,* 34: 279–90.

Scott, L. O. (1987), "A Role for Preferred Stock in the Capital Structure of a Public Utility," University of Illinois working paper.

Seagraves, J. (1984), "Regulating Utilities with Efficiency Incentives," *Public Utilities Fortnightly,* 114: 18–23.

Sertel, M. R. (1982), *Workers and Incentives,* Amsterdam: North-Holland.

Shavell, S. (1979), "Risk Sharing and Incentives in the Principal and Agent Relationship," *Bell Journal of Economics,* 10: 55–73.

Shepherd, A. R. (1971), "Output of the Restrained Firm: Comment," *American Economic Review,* 61: 237-9.

Shepherd, W. G. (1984), "'Contestability' vs. Competition," *American Economic Review,* 74: 572-87.

Sherman, R. (1967a), "Club Subscriptions for Public Transport," *Journal of Transport Economics and Policy,* 1: 1-6.

(1967b), "A Private Ownership Bias in Transit Choice," *American Economic Review,* 57: 1211-17.

(1970), "The Design of Public Utility Institutions," *Land Economics,* 24: 51-8.

(1971), "Congestion Interdependence and Urban Transit Fares," *Econometrica,* 39: 565-76.

(1972a), "Subsidies to Relieve Urban Transit Congestion," *Journal of Transport Economics and Policy,* 6: 1-10.

(1972b), "The Rate-of-Return Regulated Public Utility Firm is Schizophrenic," *Applied Economics,* 4: 23-32.

(1974), *The Economics of Industry,* Boston, Mass.: Little, Brown.

(1977), "*Ex Ante* Rates of Return for Regulated Utilities," *Land Economics,* 53: 172-84.

(1980a), "Hope Against *Hope,*" in M. A. Crew, ed., *Issues in Public Utility Economics and Regulation,* Lexington, Mass.: D. C. Heath.

(1980b), "Pricing Policies of the U.S. Postal Service," in B. M. Mitchell and P. R. Kleindorfer, eds., *Regulated Industries and Public Enterprise,* Lexington, Mass.: D. C. Heath.

(1983a), "Is Public Utility Regulation Beyond *Hope?*" in A. L. Danielson and D. R. Kamerschen, eds., *Current Issues in Public Utility Economics: Essays in Honor of J. C. Bonbright,* Lexington, Mass.: D. C. Heath.

(1983b), "Pricing Behavior of the Budget-Constrained Public Enterprise," *Journal of Economic Behavior and Organization,* 4: 381-93.

(1985), "The Averch and Johnson Analysis of Public Utility Regulation Twenty Years Later," *Review of Industrial Organization,* 2: 1-15.

Sherman, R. and A. George (1979), "Second-Best Pricing for the U.S. Postal Service," *Southern Economic Journal,* 45: 685-95.

Sherman, R. and Michael Visscher (1978), "Second-Best Pricing with Stochastic Demand," *American Economic Review,* 68: 41-53.

(1979), "Rate-of-Return Regulation and Price Structure," in M. A. Crew, ed., *Problems in Public Utility Economics and Regulation,* Lexington, Mass.: D. C. Heath.

(1982a), "Rate-of-Return Regulation and Two-Part Tariffs," *Quarterly Journal of Economics,* 97: 27-42.

(1982b), "Nonprice Rationing and Monopoly Price Structure When Demand is Stochastic," *Bell Journal of Economics,* 13: 254-62.

Sheshinski, E. (1971), "Welfare Aspects of a Regulatory Constraint: Note," *American Economic Review,* 61: 175-8.

Shleifer, A. (1985), "A Theory of Yardstick Competition," *Rand Journal of Economics,* 16: 319-27.

Sibley, D. S. (1985), "Reply to Lipman and Further Results," *International Economic Review,* 26: 517–20.

Silberberg, E. (1978), *The Structure of Economics: A Mathematical Analysis,* New York: McGraw-Hill.

Simons, H. C. (1936), "Rules versus Authorities in Monetary Policy," *Journal of Political Economy,* 44: 1–30.

Slater, M. D. E. and G. K. Yarrow (1983), "Distortions in Electricity Pricing in the U.K.," *Oxford Bulletin of Economics and Statistics,* 45: 317–38.

Slutsky, E. (1915), "Sulla Teoria del Bilancio del Consumatore," *Giornale degli Economisti,* 51: 19–23.

Smith, V. K. (1974), "The Implications of Regulation for Induced Technological Change," *Bell Journal of Economics,* 5: 623–32.

Sorenson, J., J. Tschirhart, and A. Whinston (1976), "A Game Theoretic Approach to Peak-Load Pricing," *Bell Journal of Economics,* 7: 497–520.

(1978), "A Theory of Pricing under Decreasing Costs," *American Economic Review,* 68: 614–25.

Spann, R. M. (1974), "Rate of Return Regulation and Efficiency in Production: An Efficiency Test of the Averch–Johnson Thesis," *Bell Journal of Economics,* 5: 38–52.

Spence, M. (1975), "Monopoly, Quality, and Regulation," *Bell Journal of Economics,* 6: 417–29.

(1977), "Nonlinear Prices and Welfare," *Journal of Public Economics,* 8: 1–18.

(1980), "Multi-Product Quantity-Dependent Prices and Profitability Constraints," *Review of Economic Studies,* 47: 821–41.

Srinagesh, P. (1986), "Nonlinear Prices and the Regulated Firm," *Quarterly Journal of Economics,* 101: 51–68.

Steinberg, R. (1987), "Voluntary Donations and Public Expenditures in a Federalist System," *American Economic Review,* 77: 24–36.

Steiner, Peter O. (1957), "Peak Loads and Efficient Pricing," *Quarterly Journal of Economics,* 71: 585–610.

Stevenson, R. E. (1973), "Postal Pricing Problems and Production Functions," Ph.D. diss., Michigan State University.

(1976), "The Pricing of Postal Services," in H. Trebing, ed., *New Dimensions in Public Utility Pricing,* East Lansing: Michigan State University Press.

Stigler, G. J. (1939), "Production and Distribution in the Short Run," *Journal of Political Economy,* 47: 305–27.

(1971), "The Theory of Economic Regulation," *Bell Journal of Economics,* 2: 3–21.

Stigler, G. J. and C. Friedland (1962), "What Can Regulators Regulate?: The Case of Electricity," *Journal of Law and Economics,* 5: 1–16.

Stiglitz, J. (1969), "A Re-Examination of the Modigliani–Miller Theorem," *American Economic Review,* 59: 784–93.

(1974), "Risk Sharing and Incentives in Sharecropping," *Review of Economic Studies,* 61: 219–56.

Stokey, N. L. (1981), "Rational Expectations and Durable Goods Pricing," *Bell Journal of Economics,* 12: 112–28.

Sweeney, G. (1981), "Adoption of Cost-Saving Innovations by a Regulated Firm," *American Economic Review,* 71: 437–47.

Taggart, R. A., Jr. (1981), "Rate-of-Return Regulation and Utility Capital Structure Decisions," *Journal of Finance,* 36: 383–93.

  (1985), "Effects of Regulation on Utility Financing: Theory and Evidence," *Journal of Industrial Economics,* 33: 257–76.

Takayama, A. (1969), "Behavior of the Firm under Regulatory Constraint," *American Economic Review,* 59: 255–60.

Taylor, L. D. (1975), "The Demand for Electricity: A Survey," *Bell Journal of Economics,* 6: 77–110.

Teece, D. J. (1980), "Economies of Scope and the Scope of the Enterprise," *Journal of Economic Behavior and Organization,* 1: 223–47.

Thompson, H. E. and L. W. Thatcher (1973), "Required Rate of Return for Equity Capital under Conditions of Growth and Consideration of Regulatory Lag," *Land Economics,* 49: 148–62.

Trebing, H. M. (1985), "The Impact of Diversification in Economic Regulation," *Journal of Economic Issues,* 19: 463–74.

Tschirhart, J. (1978), "Stochastic Demand, Monopoly Pricing and Ramsey Rules," Research Paper 272, Institute for Policy Research, University of Wyoming.

  (1980), "On Public Utility Pricing under Stochastic Demand," *Scottish Journal of Political Economy,* 27: 216–34.

Tschirhart, J. and F. Jen (1979), "Behavior of the Monopoly Offering Interruptible Service," *Bell Journal of Economics,* 10: 244–58.

Tullock, G. (1967), "The Welfare Costs of Tariffs, Monopolies, and Theft," *Western Economics Journal,* 5: 224–32.

  (1975), "The Transitional Gains Trap," *Bell Journal of Economics,* 6: 671–8.

Turvey, R. (1968), *Optimal Pricing and Investment in Electricity Supply,* London: Allen and Unwin.

U.S. Senate (1977), "Electricity and Gas Utility Rate and Fuel Adjustment Clause Increases, 1976," by Congressional Research Service for Subcommittees on Intergovernmental Relations and Reports, Accounting and Management, Government Printing Office, Washington.

Veljanovski, C. (1987), *Selling the State,* London: Weidenfeld and Nicolson.

Vickers, J. and G. Yarrow (1985), *Privatisation and the Natural Monopolies,* London: Public Policy Centre.

Vickery, W. S. (1948), "Some Objections to Marginal-Cost Pricing," *Journal of Political Economy,* 56: 218–38.

  (1955), "Some Implications of Marginal-Cost Pricing for Public Utilities," *American Economic Review,* 45: 605–20.

Visscher, M. (1973), "Welfare-Maximizing Price and Output with Stochastic Demand: Comment," *American Economic Review,* 63: 224–9.

Vogelsang, I. (1988), "Price Cap Regulation of Telecommunications Services: A Long-Run Approach," Rand Corporation Note N-2704-MF, Santa Monica, Calif.

Vogelsang, I. and J. Finsinger (1979), "A Regulatory Adjustment Process for Optimal Pricing by Multiproduct Monopoly Firms," *Bell Journal of Economics,* 10: 157–71.

von Weizsäcker, C. C. (1980), *Barriers to Entry: A Theoretical Treatment,* New York: Springer-Verlag.

(1985), "Free Entry into Telecommunications?" *Information Economics and Policy,* 1: 231–42.

Walsh, A. H. (1978), *The Public's Business,* Cambridge, Mass.: MIT Press.

Walters, A. A. (1961), "The Theory and Measurement of Private and Social Cost of Highway Congestion," *Econometrica,* 29: 676–99.

(1968), *The Economics of Road User Charges,* Baltimore, Md.: Johns Hopkins University Press.

Warren, G. F. and F. A. Pearson (1933), *Prices,* New York: John Wiley & Sons.

Waterson, M. (1988), *Regulation of the Firm and Natural Monopoly,* Oxford: Basil Blackwell.

Wattles, G. M. (1963), "The Rates and Costs of the United States Postal Service," *Journal of Law and Economics,* 16: 89–118.

Waverman, L. (1975), "Peak-Load Pricing under Regulatory Constraint: A Proof of Inefficiency," *Journal of Political Economy,* 83: 645–54.

(1977), "The Pricing of Telephone Services in Great Britain: Quasi-Optimality Considered," *Industrial Organization Review,* 5: 1–10.

Webb, M. G. (1976), *Pricing Policies for Public Enterprises,* London: Macmillan.

Weitzman, M. L. (1977), "Is the Price System or Rationing More Effective in Getting a Commodity to Those Who Need It Most?" *Bell Journal of Economics,* 8: 517–24.

(1980), "The 'Ratchet Principle' and Performance Incentives," *Bell Journal of Economics,* 11: 302–8.

Wellisz, S. H. (1963), "Regulation of Natural Gas Pipeline Companies: An Economic Analysis," *Journal of Political Economy,* 55: 30–43.

Wenders, J. T. (1976), "Peak Load Pricing in the Electric Utility Industry," *Bell Journal of Economics,* 7: 232–41.

Westfield, F. (1965), "Regulation and Conspiracy," *American Economic Review,* 55: 424–43.

(1971), "Innovation and Monopoly Regulation," in W. M. Capron, ed., *Technological Change in Related Industries,* Washington, D.C.: Brookings.

White, L. J. (1972), "Quality Variation When Prices are Regulated," *Bell Journal of Economics,* 3: 425–36.

Williamson, O. E. (1966), "Peak-Load Pricing and Optimal Capacity under Indivisibility Constraints," *American Economic Review,* 56: 810–27.

(1967), *The Economics of Discretionary Behavior,* Chicago: Markham.

(1975), *Markets and Hierarchies: Analysis and Antitrust Implications,* New York: Free Press.

(1976), "Franchise Bidding for Natural Monopolies – In General and with Respect to CATV," *Bell Journal of Economics,* 7: 73–104.

Willig, R. D. (1976), "Consumer Surplus without Apology," *American Economic Review,* 66: 589–97.

(1978), "Pareto-Superior Nonlinear Outlay Schedules," *Bell Journal of Economics,* 9: 56–69.

(1979a), *Welfare Analysis of Policies Affecting Prices and Products,* New York: Garland.

(1979b), "Customer Equity and Local Measured Service," in Joseph A. Baude, et al., eds., *Perspectives in Local Measured Service,* Kansas City: Rocky Mountain Telephone Co.

Wood, W. C. (1981), *Nuclear Liability, Nuclear Safety and Economic Efficiency,* Greenwich, CT: JAI Press.

Yarrow, G. K. (1985), "Strategic Issues of Industrial Policy," *Oxford Review of Economic Policy,* 1: 95–109.

Yoshitake, K. (1973), *An Introduction to Public Enterprise in Japan,* London: Sage.

Zajac, E. E. (1970), "A Geometric Treatment of Averch–Johnson's Behavior of the Firm Model," *American Economic Review,* 60: 117–25.

Index

DATE DUE